Other Colours

OTHER COLOURS

ESSAYS AND A STORY

Orhan Pamuk

Translated from the Turkish by
Maureen Freely

faber and faber

First published in the UK in 2007
by Faber and Faber Limited
3 Queen Square London WC1N 3AU
Published in the United States by Alfred A. Knopf, a division of Random House, Inc.,
New York

Printed in England by
Mackays of Chatham plc, Chatham, Kent

Originally published in Turkey as *Öteki Renkler: Seçme Yazılar ve Bir Hikâye* by İletişim,
Istanbul, in 1999. Copyright © 1999 by İletişim Yayıncılık A. Ş.

The following pieces originally appeared in *The New Yorker*: "Frankfurter," "My Father's
Suitcase," "My First Passport," "The View," and "What I Know About Dogs."

Grateful acknowledgment is made to Ángel Gurría-Quintana for permission to reprint
his interview with Orhan Pamuk from *The Paris Review* (Fall/Winter 2005, Issue 175),
copyright © 2005 by Ángel Gurría-Quintana. Reprinted by permission
of Ángel Gurría-Quintana.

The author's Nobel Prize Address appears here as "My Father's Suitcase."
Copyright © 2006 by The Nobel Foundation.

ART CREDITS: 285 (Şirin looking at the portrait of Khusraw): © British Library Board.
All Rights Reserved; 286 (Khusraw sees Şirin bathing): courtesy of the Topkapı Palace
Library; 291 (waiting groom with horse in wooded grove): courtesy of the Freer
Gallery of Art, Smithsonian Institution, Washington, D.C.; 315 (Sultan Mehmet II):
Gentile Bellini, Layard Bequest 1916 © The National Gallery, London; 317 (seated
Turkish scribe or artist), 1479/80 (pen & ink, gouache & gilt on paper) by Gentile
Bellini (c. 1429–1507) (attr. to) © Isabella Stewart Gardner Museum,
Boston, MA, USA/The Bridgeman Art Library; 322 (three men and a donkey):
courtesy of the Topkapı Palace Library; 324 (a demon carries off a man):
courtesy of the Topkapı Palace Library

A CIP record for this book
is available from the British Library

ISBN 978-0-571-23686-2

2 4 6 8 10 9 7 5 3 1

BOOKS AND READING

Contents

PREFACE

This is a book made of ideas, images, and fragments of life that have still not found their way into one of my novels. I have put them together here in a continuous narrative. Sometimes it surprises me that I have not been able to fit into my fiction all the thoughts I've deemed worth exploring: life's odd moments, the little everyday scenes I've wanted to share with others, and the words that issue from me with power and joy when there is an occasion of enchantment. Some fragments are autobiographical; some I wrote very fast; others were left to one side when my attention was elsewhere. I return to them in much the same way that I return to old photographs, and—though I rarely reread my novels—I enjoy rereading these essays. What I most like are the moments when they rise above the occasion, when they do more than just meet the requirements of the magazines and newspapers that commissioned them, saying more about my interests, my enthusiasms, than I intended at the time. To describe such epiphanies, such curious moments when truth is somehow illuminated, Virginia Woolf once used the term "moments of being."

Between 1996 and 1999 I wrote weekly sketches for *Öküz* (*Ox*), a magazine devoted to politics and humor, and I illustrated them as I saw fit. These were short lyrical essays written in one sitting, and I very much enjoyed talking about my daughter and my friends, exploring objects and the world with fresh eyes, and seeing the world in words. Over time, I have come to see the work of literature less as narrating the world than "seeing the world with words." From the moment he begins to use words like colors in a painting, a writer can begin to see how wondrous and surprising the world is, and he breaks the bones of language to find his own voice. For this he needs paper, a pen, and the optimism of a child looking at the world for the first time.

I gathered up these pieces to form a totally new book with an autobiographical center. I discarded many fragments and shortened others, taking only excerpts from my hundreds of articles and journals and assigning quite a few essays to strange locations that seemed to fit the arc of that story. For example, the three speeches that have been published as a separate volume in Turkish and many other languages under the title *My Father's Suitcase* (containing the Nobel lecture of the same name, as well as "In Kars and Frankfurt," the speech I gave to mark the German Peace Prize, and "The Implied Author," the speech I gave at the Puterbaugh Conference) appear here in separate sections to reflect the same autobiographical story.

This edition of *Other Colors* was built from the same skeleton as the book of the same name first published in Istanbul in 1999, but the earlier book took the form of a collection, while this book is shaped as a sequence of autobiographical fragments, moments, and thoughts. To talk about Istanbul, or to discuss my favorite books, authors, and paintings, has for me always been an excuse to talk about life. My New York pieces date from 1986, when I was visiting the city for the first time, and I wrote them to record the first impressions of a foreigner, with Turkish readers in mind. "To Look out the Window," the story at the end of the book, is so autobiographical that the hero's name might well have been Orhan. But the older brother in the story is, like the older brothers in all my stories, evil and tyrannical, bearing no relation to my real older brother, Şevket Pamuk, the eminent economic historian. When I was putting together this book, I noticed with consternation that I had a special interest in and predisposition toward natural disasters (the earthquake) and social disasters (politics), and so I left out quite a few of my darker political writings. I have always believed there to be a greedy and almost implacable graphomaniac inside me—a creature who can never write enough, who is forever setting life in words—and that to make him happy I need to keep writing. But when I was putting this book together, I discovered that the graphomaniac would be much happier, and less pained by his writing illness, if he worked with an editor who gave his writings a center, a frame, and a meaning. I would like the sensitive reader to pay as much attention to my creative editing as to the effort I put into the writing itself.

I am hardly alone in being a great admirer of the German writer-philosopher Walter Benjamin. But to anger one friend who is too much in awe of him (she's an academic, of course), I sometimes ask, "What is so great about this writer? He managed to finish only a few books, and if he's famous, it's not for the work he finished but the work he never managed to complete." My friend replies that Benjamin's oeuvre is, like life itself, boundless and therefore fragmentary, and this was why so many literary critics tried so hard to give the pieces meaning, just as they did with life. And every time I smile and say, "One day I'll write a book that's made only from fragments too." This is that book, set inside a frame to suggest a center that I have tried to hide: I hope that readers will enjoy imagining that center into being.

LIVING AND WORRYING

CHAPTER ONE

The Implied Author

I have been writing for thirty years. I have been reciting these words for some time now. I've been reciting them for so long, in fact, that they have ceased to be true, for now I am entering into my thirty-first year as a writer. I do still like saying that I've been writing novels for thirty years—though this is a bit of an exaggeration. From time to time, I do other sorts of writing: essays, criticism, reflections on Istanbul or politics, and speeches. But my true vocation, the thing that binds me to life, is writing novels. There are plenty of brilliant writers who've been writing much longer than I, who've been writing for half a century without paying the matter much attention. There are also the great writers to whom I return again and again, Tolstoy, Dostoyevsky, and Thomas Mann, whose careers spanned more than fifty years. . . . So why do I make so much of my thirtieth anniversary as a writer? I do so because I wish to talk about writing, and most particularly novel writing, as a habit.

In order to be happy I must have my daily dose of literature. In this I am no different from the patient who must take a spoon of medicine each day. When I learned, as a child, that diabetics needed an injection every day, I felt bad for them as anyone might; I may even have thought of them as half dead. My dependence on literature must make me half dead in the same way. Especially when I was a young writer, I sensed that others saw me as cut off from the real world and so doomed to be "half dead." Or perhaps the right term is "half a ghost." I have sometimes even entertained the thought that I was fully dead and trying to breathe life back into my corpse with literature. For me, literature is a medicine. Like the medicine that others take by spoon or injection, my daily dose of literature—my daily fix, if you will—must meet certain standards.

First, the medicine must be good. Its goodness is what tells me how true and potent it is. To read a dense, deep passage in a novel, to enter into that world and believe it to be true—nothing makes me happier, nothing more surely binds me to life. I also prefer that the writer be dead, because then there is no little cloud of jealousy to darken my admiration. The older I get, the more convinced I am that the best books are by dead writers. Even if they are not yet dead, to sense their presence is to sense a ghost. This is why, when we see great writers in the street, we treat them like ghosts, not quite believing our eyes as we marvel from a distance. A few brave souls approach the ghosts for autographs. Sometimes I remind myself that these writers will die soon and, once they are dead, the books that are their legacy will occupy an even more cherished place in our hearts. Though of course this is not always the case.

If my daily dose of literature is something I myself am writing, it's all very different. Because for those who share my affliction, the best cure of all, and the greatest source of happiness, is to write a good half page every day. For thirty years I've spent an average of ten hours a day alone in a room, sitting at my desk. If you count only the work that is good enough to be published, my daily average is a good deal less than half a page. Most of what I write does not meet my own standards of quality control. These, I put to you, are two great sources of misery.

But please don't misunderstand me: A writer who is as dependent on literature as I am can never be so superficial as to find happiness in the beauty of the books he has already written, nor can he congratulate himself on their number or what these books achieved. Literature does not allow such a writer to pretend to save the world; rather, it gives him a chance to save the day. And all days are difficult. Days are especially difficult when you don't do any writing. When you cannot do any writing. The point is to find enough hope to get through the day, and, if the book or the page you are reading is good, to find joy in it, and happiness, if only for a day.

Let me explain what I feel on a day when I've not written well, am unable to lose myself in a book. First, the world changes before my eyes; it becomes unbearable, abominable. Those who know me can see it happening, for I myself come to resemble the world I see around me. For example, my daughter can tell I have not written well that day from the abject hopelessness on my face in the evening. I would like to be able to hide this from her, but I cannot. During these dark moments, I feel as if there is no line between life and death. I don't want to speak to anyone— just as well, since no one seeing me in this state has any desire to speak

to me either. A mild version of this despair descends on me every afternoon, between one and three, but I have learned how to treat it with reading and writing: If I act promptly, I can spare myself a full retreat into
death-in-life.

If I've had to go a long stretch without my paper-and-ink cure, be it
due to travel, an unpaid gas bill, military service (as was once the case),
political affairs (as has been the case more recently), or any number of
other obstacles, I can feel misery setting inside me like cement. My body
has difficulty moving, my joints get stiff, my head turns to stone, my per-
spiration even seems to smell differently. This misery is likely to grow,
for life is full of things that conspire to keep a person from literature. I
might be sitting in a crowded political meeting, or chatting with my
classmates in a school corridor, or eating a holiday meal with my relatives, struggling to converse with a well-meaning person of unlike mind,
or occupied with whatever is on the TV screen; I can be at an important
business meeting or making an ordinary purchase, making my way to the
notary or having my picture taken for a visa—when suddenly my eyelids
grow heavy and, though it is the middle of the day, I fall asleep. When I
am far from home, and so unable to return to my room to spend time
alone, my only consolation is a nap in the middle of the day.

So yes, the real hunger here is not for literature but for a room where
I can be alone with my thoughts. In such a room I can invent beautiful
dreams about those same crowded places—those family gatherings,
school reunions, festive dinners, and all the people who attend them. I
enrich the crowded holiday meals with imagined details and make the
people themselves more amusing. In dreams, of course, everything and
everyone is interesting, captivating, and real. I make the new world from
the stuff of the known world. Here we come to the heart of the matter. To
write well, I must first be bored to distraction; to be bored to distraction,
I must enter into life. It is when I am bombarded with noise, sitting in an
office full of ringing phones, surrounded by friends and loved ones on a
sunny seashore or at a rainy funeral—in other words, at the very moment
when I begin to sense the heart of the scene unfolding around me—that I
will suddenly feel as if I'm no longer really there but watching from the
sidelines. I'll begin to daydream. If I'm feeling pessimistic, I think only
about how bored I am. Either way, a voice inside urges me to go back to
the room and sit down at the table.

I have no idea how most people answer such voices, but my manner
of response turns people like me into writers. My guess is that it turns us
more typically into writers of prose and of fiction than of verse. Here,

then, is a bit more insight into the properties of the medicine I must make sure to take every day. We can see now that its active ingredients are boredom, real life, and the life of the imagination.

The pleasure I take in this confession and the fear I feel speaking honestly about myself—together they lead me to a serious and important insight I would now like to share with you. I would like to propose a simple theory that begins from the idea that writing is a solace, even a remedy, at least for novelists like me: We choose our subjects, and shape our novels, to suit our daily daydream requirements. A novel is inspired by ideas, passions, furies, and desires—this we all know. To please our lovers, to belittle our enemies, to extol something we adore, to delight in speaking authoritatively about something of which we know nothing, to take pleasure in times lost and remembered, to dream of making love or reading or engaging with politics, to indulge in one's particular worries, one's personal habits—these and any number of other obscure or even nonsensical desires are what shape us, in ways both clear and mysterious. . . . These same desires inspire the daydreams to which we give voice. We may not understand where they come from or what, if anything, our daydreams may signify, but when we sit down to write it is our daydreams that breathe life into us, as wind from an unknown place stirs an aeolian harp. One might even say that we surrender to this mysterious wind like a captain who has no idea where he's bound.

At the same time, in one part of our minds, we can pinpoint our location on the map exactly, just as we can remember the point toward which we are traveling. Even at those times when I surrender unconditionally to the wind, I am able—at least according to some other writers I know and admire—to retain my general sense of direction. Before I set out I will have made plans: divided the story I wish to tell into sections, determined which ports my ship will visit and what loads it will carry and drop off along the way, estimated the time of my journey, and charted its course. But if the wind, having blown in from unknown quarters and filled my sails, decides to change the direction of my story, I will not resist. For what the ship most ardently seeks is the feeling of wholeness and perfection in plying its way under full sail. It is as if I am looking for that special place and time in which everything flows into everything else, everything is linked, and everything is aware, as it were, of everything else. All at once, the wind will die down and I will find myself becalmed in a place where nothing moves. Yet I'll sense that there are things in these calm and misty waters that will, if I am patient, move the novel forward.

What I most long for is the sort of spiritual inspiration I described in my novel *Snow*. It is not dissimilar to the sort of inspiration Coleridge describes in "Kubla Khan." I long for inspiration to come to me (as poems did to Coleridge—and to Ka, *Snow*'s hero) in a dramatic way, preferably already formed as scenes and situations that might sit well in a novel. If I wait patiently and attentively, my wish comes true. To write a novel is to be open to these desires, winds, and inspirations, and also to the dark recesses of our minds and their moments of mist and stillness.

For what is a novel but a story that fills its sails with these winds, that answers and builds upon inspirations that blow in from unknown quarters, and seizes upon all the daydreams we've invented for our diversion, bringing them together into a meaningful whole. Above all else, a novel is a vessel that carries inside it a dream world we wish to keep, forever alive and forever ready. Novels are held together by the little pieces of daydreams that help us, from the moment we enter them, forget the tedious world we long to escape. The more we write, the richer these dreams become and the broader, more detailed, more complete seems that second world inside the vessel. We come to know this world through writing, and the better we know it, the easier it is to carry it around in our heads. If I am in the middle of a novel and writing well, I enter easily into its dreams. For novels are new worlds into which we move happily through reading or even more fully by writing: A novelist shapes his works in such a way as to most easily carry the dreams he wishes to elaborate. Just as these works offer happiness to the attentive reader, so, too, do they offer the writer a solid and sound new world in which to lose himself and seek happiness at any hour of the day. If I feel able to create even a tiny part of such a miraculous world, I feel content the moment I reach my desk, with my pen and paper. In no time at all I can leave behind the familiar boring world of every day for this other, bigger place and wander freely; most of the time I have no desire to return to real life or to reach the end of the novel. This feeling is, I think, related to the response I am happiest to hear when I tell readers that I am writing a new novel: "Please make your novel really long!" I am proud to boast that I hear this a thousand times more often than the publisher's perennial entreaty: "Make it short!"

How is it that a habit drawing on a single person's joys and pleasures can produce a work that interests so many others? Readers of *My Name Is Red* like to recall Shekure's remarks to the effect that trying to explain everything is a sort of idiocy. My own sympathies in this scene are not with Orhan, my little hero and namesake, but with the mother, who is gently poking fun at him. If, however, you will permit me to commit another idiocy and act like Orhan, I'd like to try to explain why dreams that work as medicine for the writer can serve the reader the same way: Because if I am entirely inside the novel and writing well—if I have distanced myself from the ringing phone, from all the troubles and demands and tedium of everyday life—the rules by which my free-floating heaven operates recall the games I played as a child. It is as if everything has become simpler, as if I am in a world where I can see into every house, car, ship, and building because they are all made of glass; they have begun to reveal to me their secrets. My job is to divine the rules and listen: to watch with pleasure the goings-on in each interior, to step into cars and buses with my heroes and travel about Istanbul, visiting places that have come to bore me, seeing them with new eyes and, in so doing, transforming them; my job is to have fun, be irresponsible, because while I'm amusing myself (as we like to tell children) I might just learn something.

An imaginative novelist's greatest virtue is his ability to forget the world in the way a child does, to be irresponsible and delight in it, to play around with the rules of the known world—but at the same time to see past his freewheeling flights of fancy to the deep responsibility of later allowing readers to lose themselves in the story. A novelist might spend the whole day playing, but at the same time he carries the deepest conviction of being more serious than others. This is because he can look directly into the center of things the way that only children can. Having found the courage to set rules for the games we once played freely, he senses that his readers will also allow themselves to be drawn into the same rules, the same languages, the same sentences, and therefore the story. To write well is to allow the reader to say, "I was going to say the same thing myself, but I couldn't allow myself to be that childish."

This world I explore and create and enlarge, making up the rules as I go, waiting for my sails to fill with a wind from an unknown quarter, and poring over my map—it is born of childlike innocence that is at times closed to me. This happens to all writers. A moment arrives when I get stuck, or I will go back to the point in the novel where I've left off sometime before and find I am unable to pick it up again. Such afflictions are commonplace, though I may suffer from them less than other writers—if I can't pick up where I left off, I can always turn instead to another gap in the novel. Because I've studied my map very carefully, I can begin writing in another section; I needn't work in the order of reading. Not that this is so important. But last autumn, while I was grappling with various political matters and running into a similar problem of getting stuck, I felt as if I'd discovered something that also bears on novel writing. Let me try to explain.

The case that was opened against me, and the political quandaries in which I then found myself, turned me into a far more "political," "serious," and "responsible" person than I wanted to be: a sad state of affairs and an even sadder state of mind—let me say it with a smile. This was why I was unable to enter into that childlike innocence without which no novel is possible, but this was easy to understand; it didn't surprise me. As the events slowly unfolded, I would tell myself that my fast-vanishing spirit of irresponsibility, my childish sense of play and childish sense of humor, would one day return and I would then be able to finish the novel I'd been working on for three years. Nevertheless, I would still get up every morning, long before Istanbul's ten million other inhabitants, and try to enter into the novel that was sitting unfinished in the silence of midnight. I did this because I so longed to get back into my beloved second world, and after exerting myself greatly, I'd begin to pull bits of a novel from my head and see them playing out before me. But these fragments were not from the novel I was writing; they were scenes from an entirely different story. On those tedious, joyless mornings, what passed before my eyes was not the novel on which I'd been working for three years but an ever-growing body of scenes, sentences, characters, and strange details from some other novel. After a while, I began to set down these fragments in a notebook, and I jotted down thoughts I had never before entertained. This other novel would be about the paintings of a deceased contemporary artist. As I conjured up this painter, I found myself thinking just as much about his paintings. After a while, I understood why I'd been unable to recapture the child's spirit of irresponsibility during those tedious days. I could no longer return to childishness, I could return only so far as my childhood, to the days when (as I describe in *Istanbul*) I dreamed of becoming an artist and spent my waking hours doing one painting after another.

Later, when the case against me was dropped, I returned to *The Museum of Innocence,* the novel on which I had already spent three years. Nevertheless, today I am planning the other novel, which came to me scene by scene during those days when, unable to return to pure childishness, I half returned via the passions of my childhood. This experience taught me something important about the mysterious art of writing novels.

I can explain this by taking "the implied reader," a principle put forward by the great literary critic and theorist Wolfgang Iser, and twisting it to my own ends. Iser created a brilliant reader-oriented literary theory. He says that a novel's meaning resides neither in the text nor in the context in which it is read but somewhere between the two. He argues that a novel's meaning emerges only as it is read, and so when he speaks of the implied reader, he is assigning him an indispensable role.

When I was dreaming up the scenes, sentences, and details of another book instead of continuing the novel I was already writing, this theory came to mind, and what it suggested to me by way of corollary was this: For every unwritten but dreamed and planned novel (including, in other words, my own unfinished work) there must be an implied author. So I would be able to finish that book only when I'd again become its implied author. But when I was immersed in political affairs or—as happens so often in the course of normal life—my thoughts were too often interrupted by unpaid gas bills, ringing phones, and family gatherings, I was unable to become the author implied by the book in my dreams. During those long and tedious days of politicking, I could not become the implied author of the book I longed to write. Then those days passed, and I returned to my novel—a love story that takes place between 1975 and the present, among the rich of Istanbul or, as the papers like to call it, "Istanbul society"—and to my former self just as I had so longed to do, and whenever I think how close I am to finishing it, I feel happy too. But having come through this experience, I now understand why, for thirty years, I have devoted all my strength to becoming the implied author of the books I long to write. It is not difficult to dream a book. I do this a lot, just as I spend a great deal of time imagining myself as someone else. The difficult thing is to become your dream book's implied author. Perhaps all the more so in my case because I only want to write big, thick, ambitious novels, and because I write so very slowly.

But let's not complain. Having published seven novels, I can safely say that, even if it takes some effort, I am reliably able to become the author who can write the books of my dreams. Just as I've written books and left them behind, so too have I left behind the ghosts of the writers who could write those books. All seven of these implied authors resemble me, and over the past thirty years they have come to know life and the world as seen from Istanbul, as seen from a window like mine, and because they know this world inside out and are convinced by it, they can describe it with all the seriousness and purposeful abandon of a child at play.

My greatest hope is to be able to write novels for another thirty years and to use this excuse to wrap myself up in other new personas.

CHAPTER TWO

My Father

I came home late that night. They told me my father had died. With the first stab of pain came an image from childhood: my father's thin legs in shorts.

At two in the morning I went to his house to see him for the last time. "He's in the room at the back," they said. I went inside. When I returned to Valikonağı Avenue many hours later, just before dawn, the streets of Nişantaşı were empty and cold, and the dimly lit shop windows I had been passing for fifty years seemed distant and alien.

In the morning, sleepless and as if in a dream, I spoke on the phone, received visitors, and immersed myself in the funeral arrangements; and it was while I was receiving notes, requests, and prayers, settling small disputes, and writing the death announcement that I came to feel I understood why it is that, in all deaths, the rituals become more important than the deceased.

In the evening we went to Edirnekapı Cemetery to prepare the burial. When my elder brother and my cousin went into the cemetery's small administrative building, I found myself alone with the driver in the front seat of the taxi. That was when the driver told me he knew who I was.

"My father died," I told him. Without forethought, and much to my surprise, I began to tell him about my father. I told him that he had been a very good man and, more important, that I had loved him. The sun was about to set. The cemetery was empty and silent. The gray buildings towering over it had lost their everyday bleakness; they radiated a strange light. While I spoke, a cold wind we could not hear set plane trees and cypresses swaying, and this image engraved itself on my memory, like my father's thin legs.

When it became clear that the wait would be much longer still, the driver, who by now had told me that we shared a name, gave me two firm but compassionate slaps on the back and left. What I'd said to him, I said to no one else. But a week later, this thing inside me merged with my memories and my sorrow. If I didn't set it down in words, it would grow and cause me immense pain.

When I'd told the driver, "My father never once scowled at me, never even scolded me, never hit me," I'd been speaking without much thought. I'd omitted to mention his greatest acts of kindness. When I was a child, my father would look with heartfelt admiration at every picture I drew; when I asked his opinion, he would examine every scribbled sentence as if it were a masterpiece; he would laugh uproariously at my most tasteless and insipid jokes. Without the confidence he gave me, it would have been much more difficult to become a writer, to choose this as my profession. His trust in us, and his easy way of convincing my brother and me that we were brilliant and unique, came from a confidence in his own intellect. In his childishly innocent way, he sincerely believed that we were bound to be as brilliant, mature, and quick-witted as he, simply by virtue of being his sons.

He was quick-witted: He could, at a moment's notice, recite a poem by Cenap Şahabettin, take pi to the fifteenth digit, or offer up a brilliantly knowing guess about how a film we were watching together would end. He was not very modest, relishing stories about how clever he was. He enjoyed telling us how, for example, when he was in middle school, still in short pants, his math teacher had called him into a class with the oldest boys in the lycée, and how—after little Gündüz had gone to the blackboard and solved the problem that had stumped these boys three years older than he and the teacher had commended him with a "Well done"—the little boy then turned to the others and said, "So there!" In the face of his example, I found myself caught between envy and a longing to be more like him.

I can speak in the same way about his good looks. Everyone was always saying that I resembled him, except he was formed more handsomely. Like the fortune left to him by his father (my grandfather) that he had never, despite his many business failures, quite managed to exhaust, his good looks allowed a life of fun and ease, so that even in the worst days, he remained naïvely optimistic, afloat on good intentions and an unrivaled, unshakable sense of self-worth. For him, life was not something to be earned but to be enjoyed. The world was not a battlefield but a playing field, a playground, and as he grew older he came to feel slightly annoyed that the fortune, brains, and good looks he had enjoyed so fully in his youth had not magnified his fame or power as much as he might have wished. But, as in all instances, he did not waste time worrying about it. He could shrug off frustration with the same childish ease as he dispensed with any person, problem, or possession that brought him trouble. So even though his life went downhill after he reached thirty, leading to a long succession of disappointments, I never much heard him complain. When he was an old man, he had dinner with a renowned critic who, when next we met, exclaimed with some resentment, "Your father has no complexes whatsoever!"

His Peter Pan optimism delivered him from fury and obsession. Although he had read many books, dreamed of becoming a poet, and had, in his time, translated quite a few of Valéry's poems, I believe he was too comfortable in his skin, and too assured about the future, ever to be gripped by the essential passions of literary creativity. In youth he had a good library, and later he was happy for me to plunder it. But he didn't read the books as I did, voraciously and dizzy with excitement; he read them for pleasure, to divert his thoughts, and mostly he left off reading them midway. Where other fathers might speak in hushed tones of generals and religious leaders, my father would tell me about walking through the streets of Paris and seeing Sartre and Camus (more his kind of writer), and these stories made a big impression on me. Years later, when I met Erdal İnönü (a friend of my father's from childhood and the son of Turkey's second president, who was Atatürk's successor) at a gallery opening, he told me with a smile about a dinner at the presidential residence in Ankara that my father, then twenty, had attended; when Ismet Pasha brought the subject around to literature, my father asked, "Why don't we have any world-famous authors?" Eighteen years after my first novel was published, my father somewhat bashfully gave me a small suitcase. I know very well why finding inside it his journals, poems, notes, and literary writings made me uneasy: It was the record— the evidence—of an inner life. We don't want our fathers to be individuals, we want them to conform to our ideal of them.

I loved it when he took me to films, and I loved listening to him discuss the films we'd seen with others; I loved the jokes he made about the idiotic, the evil, and the soulless, just as I loved hearing him talk about a new kind of fruit, a city he'd visited, the latest news, or the latest book; but most of all I loved it when he caressed me. I loved it when he took me out for a ride, because together, in the car, I felt at least for a while that I wouldn't lose him. When he was driving, we couldn't look each other in the eye so he could speak to me as a friend, touching upon the most difficult and delicate questions. After a time, he'd pause to tell a few jokes, fiddle with the radio, and speak about whatever music reached our ears.

But what I loved most was being close to him, touching him, being at his side. When I was a lycée student, and even in my first years at university, during the deepest depression of my life, I would, in spite of myself, long for him to come to the house and sit down with me and my mother and say a few things to lift our spirits. When I was a small child, I loved to climb onto his lap or lie down next to him, smell his smell, and touch him. I remember how, on Heybeliada, when I was very small, he taught me how to swim: As I was sinking to the bottom, thrashing wildly, he would grab hold of me and I would rejoice, not just because I could breathe again but because I could wrap my arms around him and, not wishing to sink back to the bottom, cry, "Father, don't leave me!"

But he did leave us. He'd go far away, to other countries, other places, corners of the world unknown to us. When he was stretched out on the sofa reading, sometimes his eyes would slip away from the page and his thoughts would wander. That was when I'd know that, inside the man I knew as my father, there was another I could not reach, and guessing that he was daydreaming of another life, I'd grow uneasy. "I feel like a bullet that's been fired for no reason," he'd say sometimes. For some reason this would make me angry. Quite a few other things made me angry. I don't know who was in the right. Perhaps by then I too was longing to escape. But still I loved it when he put on his tape of Brahms's First Symphony, passionately conducting an imaginary orchestra with his imaginary baton. It would annoy me when, after a lifetime of seeking pleasure and running away from trouble, he would lament the fact that self-indulgence offered no meaning beyond itself and seek to blame others. In my twenties, there were times when I said to myself, "Please don't let me turn out like him." There were other times when I was troubled by my failure to be as happy, comfortable, carefree, and handsome as he was.

Much later, when I'd put all that behind me, when anger and jealousy no longer clouded my view of the father who had never scolded me, never tried to break me, I slowly came to see—and to accept—the many and inescapable similarities between us. So that now, when I am grumbling about some idiot or other, or complaining to a waiter, or biting my upper lip, or throwing some books into the corner half read, or kissing my daughter, or taking money out of my pocket, or greeting someone with a lighthearted joke, I catch myself imitating him. This is not because my arms, legs, wrists, or the mole on my back resemble his. It is something that frightens—terrifies—me and reminds me of my child-hood longing to be more like him. Every man's death begins with the death of his father.

CHAPTER THREE

Notes on April 29, 1994

The French weekly Le Nouvel Observateur *asked hundreds of authors to describe their activities on April 29 in whatever corner of the world they happened to be that day. I was in Istanbul.*

TELEPHONE. I disconnected the phone and, as always happens during the hours I spend working—for better or for worse—on my novel, a moment arrived when I imagined that someone was trying to reach me at that very moment to speak to me about something important, a matter of huge consequence, but could not get through. But still I did not reconnect the phone. When I did, much later, I had a few conversations I would immediately forget. A journalist calling from Germany told me he would visit Istanbul and hoped to talk to me about the rise of "fundamentalism" in Turkey and the success of the Islamist Refah Party in the municipal elections. I asked again what television station he worked for, and he rattled off a few letters.

LETTERS, LOGOS, AND BRANDS. Once again I was most struck by the letters in the blue jeans and bank advertisements I came across in newspapers, on television, and on street signs. A friend I met on the street, a university professor, dipped into her bag to give me a list of companies and brand names that I come across every day. Their owners support the Islamist Refah Party, she'd been told; she informed me that quite a few people had decided to stop buying this brand of biscuits and that brand of yogurt and never again to set foot in the shops and restaurants on the list. As always, extreme boredom prompted me to ignore the mirror in the lift in my building and to look instead at the plaque: Wertheim. On a Casio calculator I made a simple computation that will appear at the end of this essay. On the street I came across a 1960 Plymouth, and a 1956 Chevrolet still in service as a taxi.

STREETS AND AVENUES. Although Turkey's currency halved in value overnight two months ago, plunging us into an economic crisis, the streets and avenues were as crowded as ever. As always, I wondered where all these people were going, and this in turn reminded me that literature was a futile profession: I saw women with children gazing into shop windows, lycée students whispering and giggling in huddles, vendors who had spread their wares—black-market foreign cigarettes, Nescafé, Chinese porcelain, old romance novels, and well-thumbed foreign fashion magazines—along the full length of the mosque wall; I saw a man with a three-wheeled cart selling fresh cucumbers and buses packed with people. The men gathered in front of the buffets in the foreign exchange shops were clutching sandwiches or cigarettes or plastic bags stuffed with money as they watched the rise of the dollar on the electronic notice board. A grocery boy was unloading a crate of bottled water, lifting the demijohns onto his back. I caught another glimpse of the madman who had recently arrived in the neighborhood, noticing that he was the only person on the crowded pavement who was not carrying a plastic bag. In his hands was a steering wheel salvaged from a real car; he twisted it to the left and to the right as he made his way through the crowd. At lunchtime, after I had drunk my orange juice and was returning to the small office where I write, I saw an old friend in the crowd coming out of Friday prayers and we had a few laughs.

JOKES, LAUGHTER, AND HAPPINESS. My painter friend and I were laughing about several rich people we knew who were facing ruin after various banks in which they had money had gone under. Why were we laughing? Because it had turned out that they were neither as adroit as they'd assumed nor as intelligent, that's why. In the early evening, a translator friend of mine rang to invite me to come out to drink in the street outside a few *meyhanes* "in protest" against Istanbul's Refah Party mayor, and we had a good laugh too. Because the new mayor had been harassing *meyhanes* and removing the tables they'd set up in the streets, hundreds of intellectuals were planning to take to the streets and drink themselves senseless on the pavements. Once upon a time, politically minded friends took a dim view of drink, but now suddenly it seemed to have been decided that to drink was to engage in a mature political action. When my two-and-a-half-year-old daughter, Rüya, laughed as I was tickling her before bedtime, I laughed too. Perhaps these several laughs were not expressions of happiness, perhaps they were merely appreciation of the sort of silence that a person longs for in a city like Istanbul, with its ceaseless roar.

ISTANBUL'S NOISE. Even when I am paying it the least attention and feeling most lonely, I (along with some ten million others) hear this roar all day long: car horns, grumbling buses, sputtering motors, sounds of construction, children's screams, loudspeakers on vendors' wagons and on minarets, ship horns, police and ambulance sirens, music cassettes playing everywhere, slamming doors, metal shutters crashing to the ground, telephones, doorbells, traffic altercations on street corners, police whistles, school vans. . . . Toward evening, just as the sky was darkening, there was the usual lull, something close to silence; looking out into the garden from the back windows of my office, I saw the swarms of madly chirping swallows flying over the cypresses and mulberry trees. From the table where I was sitting, I could see lamps and television screens glowing in neighboring apartments.

TELEVISION. After supper, I could tell from the synthetic colors flashing in their windows that quite a few people kept changing channels just as I did: a bleached-blond chanteuse singing old Turkish songs, a child eating chocolate, a woman prime minister saying everything was going to turn out fine, a football match on an emerald field, a Turkish pop group, journalists arguing about the Kurdish question, American police cars, a child reading the Koran, a helicopter exploding into flames in midair, a gentleman walking onto the stage and doffing his hat as the audience applauds, the same woman prime minister, a housewife telling an inquiring microphone a thing or two as she hangs up her laundry, an audience applauding the woman who has given the right answer in a general knowledge quiz. . . . At one point I looked out the window and it occurred to me that—except for the travelers on the Bosphorus ships whose lights I could see in the distance—all of Istanbul was watching the same images.

NIGHT. The noise of the city changed, turning into a whisper, a sleepy sigh. At a late hour, as I was walking back to my office, thinking I might be able to write a bit more, I saw a pack of four dogs roaming the empty streets. In a coffeehouse below street level there were still people playing cards and watching television. I saw a family, and it was obvious they were returning from a visit to relatives—the little boy was asleep on his father's shoulder, the mother was pregnant—they passed me in silence and in haste, as if something had frightened them. In the middle of the night, long after I had sat down at my table, the phone rang and gave me a fright.

FEAR, PARANOIA, AND DREAMS. It was the lunatic who called me every night, never saying a word, echoing my silence with his. I disconnected the phone and worked for a long time, but in some corner of my mind there were premonitions of evil, impending disaster: Perhaps, before long, people would begin again to shoot one another in the streets; perhaps we'd see a civil war; perhaps this summer the severe water shortage they'd been predicting in the newspapers would come to pass; perhaps the great earthquake that had been expected for so many years now would flatten the entire city. After midnight, after all the televisions had been turned off and the lamps in the apartments extinguished, a garbage truck clattered past. As always, there was a man who kept eight or ten paces ahead of the truck, emptying the bins that had been left on the street, hastily combing them for useful bottles, metalware, and packs of paper and putting these into his sack. Later still, a junk dealer, his horse cart creaking under the weight of old newspapers and a washing machine, passed down the empty street where I have lived for forty years. I sat down at my table and took out my calculator.

TOTAL. I did a simple calculation, days multiplied by years. If the figure is correct, I have now lived exactly 15,300 days like this. Before I went to sleep, it occurred to me that I would be a very lucky man if I had an equal number of days ahead of me.

CHAPTER FOUR

Spring Afternoons

*Between 1996 and 1998 I wrote short weekly pieces for a small political
humor magazine called* Oküz *(Ox); I illustrated these lyrical exercises with
drawings in keeping with the magazine's mood.*

I don't like spring afternoons: the city's aspect, the way the sun beats
down, the crowds, the shop windows, the heat. I long to flee the heat and
the light. There is a cool draft wafting through the tall doors of certain
stone and concrete apartment buildings. Inside these apartment buildings, it's even cooler and, of course, darker. The darkness and cold of
winter have retreated inside.

If only I could walk into one of those apartments, if only I could go
back into winter. If only there were a key in my pocket, if only I could
open a familiar door, take in the familiar smell of a cool and dark apartment, and slip blithely into the back room, away from the sun and the
oppressive crowds.

If there were a bed in that back room, a bedside table, and on it a pile
of newspapers and books, my favorite magazines for me to leaf through,
and a television. If I could stretch out on that bed fully dressed and
rejoice at being alone with my despair, my misery, my wretched life.
There is no greater happiness than coming face-to-face with your own
squalor and wretchedness. There is no greater happiness than being out
of sight.

Yes, all right, I also wish there were this sort of girl: as tender and soft
as a mother, as smart as a seasoned businesswoman. Because she knows
very well what I need to do, I trust her too.

If she asks me, "What's troubling you?"

If I say, "You already know. It's these spring afternoons."

"You're depressed."

"It's worse than depression. I want to disappear. I don't care if I live or die. Or if the world comes to an end, even. In fact, if it ended right this minute, so much the better. If I have to spend a few years in this cool room, then so be it. I could smoke cigarettes. I could do nothing but smoke cigarettes for years."

But as time passes, I can no longer hear that voice inside me. That is the worst moment. I am alone, abandoned on the busy streets.

I don't know if this happens to other people too, but sometimes on spring afternoons it seems as if the world has become heavier. Everything turns to concrete, dull as concrete, and soaking in my sweat I am astounded at the way others are able to go about their daily lives.

They wander down the street, peering into shop windows, and they peer at me through bus windows, before the bus spews its exhaust fumes into my face. The fumes? They're hot too. I run about in a panic.

I go into a passage. Inside, it is cool and dark and I calm down. The people in here seem less anxious and easier to understand. But still I sense trouble. As I walk to the cinema, I look into the shops.

In the old days they used to use dog meat in sausage sandwiches—in other words, in the sausages. I don't know if this still happens.

According to the papers, they caught the men who had been making soft drinks in the same vats people washed their feet in.

They live here, they see each other, they fall in love, and then they marry these girls who bleach their hair such an ugly shade of blond.

In our pockets, paper money has turned to dough from the humidity.

Here is the sort of American film that would do me wonders right now: A boy and a girl are running away, heading for another country. Loving each other as dearly as they do, they're always arguing, but these arguments only bring them closer together. I should be sitting in one of the seats at the very front. The film should be so clear that I can see the pores on the girl's skin; she and the film and the cars should seem more real than anything here. When they start killing a huge number of people, I should be there to see it.

CHAPTER FIVE

Dead Tired in the Evening

I come home dead tired in the evenings. Looking straight ahead, at the roads and the pavements. Angry about something, hurt, incensed. Though my imagination is still conjuring up beautiful images, even these pass quickly in the film in my head. Time passes. There's nothing. It's already nighttime. Doom and defeat. What's for supper?

The lamp atop the table is lit; next to it sits a bowl of salad and bread, all in the same basket; the tablecloth is checkered. What else? . . . A plate and beans. I imagine the beans, but it's not enough. On the table, the same lamp is still burning. Maybe a bit of yogurt? Maybe a bit of life?

What's on television? No, I'm not watching television; it only makes me angry. I'm very angry. I like meatballs too—so where are the meatballs? All of life is here, around this table.

The angels call me to account.

What did you do today, darling?

All my life . . . I've worked. In the evenings, I've come home. On television—but I'm not watching television. I answered the phone a few times, got angry at a few people; then I worked, wrote. . . . I became a man . . . and also—yes, much obliged—an animal.

What did you do today, darling?

Can't you see? I've got salad in my mouth. My teeth are crumbling in my jaw. My brain is melting from unhappiness and trickling down my throat. Where's the salt, where's the salt, the salt? We're eating our lives away. And a little yogurt too. The brand called Life.

Then I gently reached out my hand, parted the curtains, and in the darkness outside caught sight of the moon. Other worlds are the best consolations. On the moon they were watching television. I finished off with an orange—it was very sweet—and my spirits lifted.

Then I was master of all worlds. You understand what I mean, don't you? I came home in the evening. I came home from all those wars, good, bad, and indifferent; I came home in one piece and walked into a warm house. There was a meal waiting for me, and I filled my stomach; the lights were on; I ate my fruit. I even began to think that everything was going to turn out fine.

Then I pressed the button and watched television. By then, you see, I was feeling just fine.

CHAPTER SIX

Out of Bed, in the Silence of Night

On the table there is an ugly little fish. Its mouth is wide open, it's frowning, and its eyes are wide with pain. It's a little ashtray in the shape of a fish. You flick your ashes into the fish's huge mouth. Maybe the fish is in convulsions because of that cigarette jammed into its mouth so suddenly. Just like that—*pftt!*—the ash fell into the fish's mouth, but this will never happen to the smoker himself, not once in his life. Someone made a porcelain ashtray in the shape of a fish, and the poor fish will be burned by cigarettes for years on end, its mouth opened wide enough so that it's not just dirty ashes it will have to swallow; its mouth is big enough to accommodate butts, matches, and all manner of filth.

Right now the fish is on the table, but a moment ago there was no one in the room. When I walked in, I saw the fish's mouth and I could see that the ashtray creature had been waiting in pain for hours in the silence of night. I don't smoke so I won't touch it, but even now, as I walk silently through the dark apartment in my bare feet, I know that, before long, I'll have forgotten all about this poor fish.

On the carpet is a child's tricycle; its wheels and its saddle are blue, its basket and its front mudguard are red. The mudguard is only there for decoration, of course: The tricycle was made to be ridden slowly by small children indoors and on balconies and other mud-free surfaces. But still this mudguard gives it an aura of fullness and perfection. It is as if it covers the tricycle's imperfections, growing and maturing it; by bringing it closer to the idea of a full-sized archetype of bicycle, the mudguard makes it look more serious. But when I have looked more closely at the tricycle, in this silence where nothing moves, I see at once that what binds me to the tricycle and makes it possible for us to have a relationship is that, like all bicycles and tricycles, it has a handlebar. If I am able to look at the tricycle as if at a living being, a living creation, it's because of the handlebar. The handlebar is the tricycle's head, its brow, its horns. To find the person in the tricycle, I do the same thing I do with people: First I study the face, or the handlebar. This small lazy tricycle has, like all unhappy tricycles, bowed its head; its handlebar is not facing forward but tilted sideways. As with all sad creatures, its hopes are limited. But it seems at least to be at ease with itself inside its plastic shell, and that helps chase away the misery.

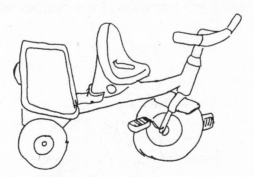

I enter the dark kitchen in silence. The inside of the refrigerator is as bright and crowded as the boulevard of a distant happy city.

I take out a beer. Sitting down at the dining table, I solemnly drink it. There, in the silence of the night, a transparent plastic pepper mill is watching me.

CHAPTER SEVEN

When the Furniture Is Talking, How Can You Sleep?

Some nights when I get out of bed, I cannot understand why the linoleum is like this. Every square has all these lines on it. Why? And every square is different from the others.

Later, it's the same with the furnace pipe. It seems to be writhing of its own volition, as if to say, I'm bored. I want to be a furnace for a while, not a pipe.

The lamp's looking just as strange. If you can't see the lightbulb, you can imagine that the light is emanating from its zinc stem and its satin shade. You know, the way light might radiate from a person's face—something like that. I know this happens to you sometimes too: So, for example, if there were a lightbulb burning inside my skull, somewhere deep inside, between my eyes and my mouth, how beautifully that light would ooze from my pores—you too are capable of such a thought. The light pouring especially from our cheeks and our foreheads: in the evenings, when there is a power cut. . . .

But you never admit to thinking such things.

Neither do I. I don't tell anyone.

That the empty bottles left in front of the door belong neither to the world nor to one another. That doors, in any event, are never fully closed or open and so give cause for hope.

That all night long, until morning, the snail shapes in the armchair cover keep muttering, "We twist and turn but no one notices."

That somewhere nearby, three inches beneath my feet or inside the ceiling, strange larvae are slowly gnawing through iron and concrete, like termites.

That the scissors on the table suddenly spring into action to embark on a long-demanded much-dreamed-of cutting spree, attacking anything that comes before them, but that this bloody drama will last no longer than fifteen minutes.

That the telephone is talking to another telephone, which is why it has fallen silent.

I don't talk about these things to anyone. There was a time when I was troubled, even nervous, about not being able to share these hyper-real images with others; no one talks about such things, and so maybe I'm the only one who sees them. The attendant sense of responsibility is more than just a burden. It prompts one to ask why it is that this great secret of life is revealed only to oneself. Why does that ashtray tell only me of its sadness and defeat? Why am I the confessor of the door latch in its misery? Why am I the only one who thinks that by opening the refrigerator I shall come to a world exactly like the one I knew twenty years ago? Why must I alone listen to the seagulls next to that clock and the little creatures rattling at the base of the walls?

Have you ever looked at the fringe on the carpet? Or the hidden signs in its pattern?

When the world is shimmering with so many signs and curiosities, how can anyone sleep? I try to calm myself by telling myself that people cannot have so little interest in these signs. In a while, when I'm asleep, I too shall become part of a story.

CHAPTER EIGHT

Giving Up Smoking

It has been 272 days since I gave up smoking. I think I'm used to it now. My anxiety has abated, and I no longer feel as if a part of my body has been amputated. No, correction: I have not stopped feeling the lack, I've not stopped feeling as I've been parted from the whole me, it's just that I'm accustomed now to feeling this way; to put it more accurately, I've accepted bitter reality.

I'm never going to smoke again, ever.

I say this and then I still have daydreams in which I'm smoking. If I say these are daydreams so secret, so dreadful, that we hide them even from ourselves . . . do you understand? Anyway, it will be right in the middle of one such daydream, and whatever I am contriving to do at that particular moment, as I watch the film that is my dream slowly approaching its climax, I feel as happy as if I had just lit a cigarette.

So this was the main purpose of cigarettes in my life: to slow the experience of pleasure and pain, desire and defeat, sadness and joy, the present and the future; and between each frame, to find new roads and shortcuts. When these possibilities disappear, a person feels almost naked. Disarmed and helpless.

Once I got into a taxi, the driver was chain-smoking, and the inside of the car was thick with magnificent smoke. I began to breathe it in.

"I beg your pardon," the man said. He was opening the window.

"No," I said, "keep it closed. I've given up smoking."

I can go for a long time without longing for a cigarette, but when I do, the longing comes from deep inside me.

I am reminded then of a forgotten self, a self occluded by medicines, fabrications, and health warnings. I want to be that other man, the Orhan

I once was, the smoking man, who was so much better at fighting the Devil.

The question when I remember my old self is not whether I should at once light up a cigarette. I no longer feel the chemical craving of the early days. I just miss my old self, the way I might miss a dear friend, a face; all I want is to return to the man I once was. I feel as if I've been forced to wear clothes I haven't chosen, as if they have made me into a man I never wished to be. If I smoked, I would again feel the intensity of the night, the terrors of the man I once thought I was.

When I long to return to my old self, I remember that in those days I had vague intimations of immortality. In the old days, time did not flow; at times when I smoked, I'd sometimes feel such happiness, or such intense despair, that I'd think everything would remain unchanged. As I blithely smoked my cigarette, the world stood in place.

Then I began to fear death. That smoking man could drop dead at any moment; the papers were entirely convincing on this point. To stay alive, I had to dismiss the smoker and become someone else. This I succeeded in doing. Now the self I abandoned has joined forces with the Devil to call me back to the days when time never moved and no one died.

His call does not frighten me.

Because, as you can see, writing—if you're happy with it—undoes all sorrows.

CHAPTER NINE

Seagull in the Rain

Concerning the Seagull on the Roof Opposite My Desk

The seagull is standing on the roof, in the rain, as if nothing has happened. It is as if it's not raining at all; the seagull is just standing there, as still as ever. Or else the seagull is a great philosopher, too great to take offense. There it stands. On the roof. It's raining. It's as if that seagull standing there is thinking, I know, I know, it's raining; but there's not much I can do about that. Or: Yes, it's raining, but what importance does that have? Or maybe something like this: By now I've accustomed myself to rain; it doesn't make much of a difference.

I'm not saying they're very tough, these seagulls. I watch them through the window, I watch them when I'm trying to write, when I'm pacing up and down the room; even seagulls can get panicky about things beyond their own lives.

One had babies. Two little gray balls of squeaky clean wool, just a bit frantic and silly. They'd venture across the once-red tiles now whitened by the lime in their own droppings and their mother's, veering left and then right, and then they would stop somewhere and rest. You couldn't really call it rest, though; they just came to a stop. They exist, nothing more. Seagulls, like most humans and most other creatures, spend most of their time doing nothing, just standing there. You could call this a form of waiting. To stand in this world waiting: for the next meal, for death, for sleep. I don't know how they die.

The babies can't stand straight, either. A wind is ruffling their feathers, ruffling their entire bodies. Then they stop again; again they stop. Behind them the city keeps moving; below them the ships, the cars, the trees all aquiver.

The anxious mother I was talking about—from time to time she finds something somewhere and brings it back to her children to eat. There's quite a commotion then: a burst of activity, industry, panic. The maca-roni-like organs of a dead fish—pull, pull, let's see if you can pull that—is parceled out and eaten. After the meal, silence. The seagulls stand on the roof and do nothing. Together we wait. In the sky are leaden clouds.

But still there is something that has escaped my notice. Something that suddenly came to me as I paced in front of the window: A seagull's life is not simple. How many of them there are! Seagulls boding evil, standing on every roof, silently thinking about something of which I know nothing. Thinking treacherous thoughts, I would say.

How did I come to understand this? Once, I noticed they were all gaz-ing at the yellow light of dawn, that faint yellow light. First a wind came, and then a yellow rain. As that yellow rain was slowly falling, all the seagulls turned their backs on me, and as they gabbled among them-selves it was clear that they were waiting for something. Down below, in the city, people were racing for shelter in houses and cars; above, the seagulls were waiting, straight and silent. I thought then that I under-stood them.

Sometimes, the seagulls take flight all together to rise slowly into the air. When they do, their fluttering wings sound like rainfall.

CHAPTER TEN

A Seagull Lies Dying on the Shore

This Is Another Seagull

A seagull lies dying on the shore. Alone. Its beak is resting on the pebbles. Its eyes are sad and sick. The waves beat against the nearby rocks. The wind ruffles feathers that look dead already. Then the seagull's eyes begin to follow me. It's early in the morning; the wind is cool. Above, life goes on; in the sky are other seagulls. The dying seagull is a baby.

Seeing me, the seagull suddenly tries to get up. The legs under its body quiver hopelessly. Its chest pushes forward, but it can't raise its beak from the pebbles. As it struggles, a meaning forms in its eyes. Just then, it falls back onto the pebbles, spreading out now into an attitude of death. The meaning in its eyes is lost among the clouds and the waves. There's no doubt now. The seagull is dying.

I don't know why it's dying. Its feathers are graying and unkempt. All this season, I have, as always, watched a great many baby seagulls growing up, trying to fly. Yesterday, after two brushes with the wind and the waves, one took to the air with great joy, with the cutting, fearless arcs that seagulls trace across the sky when they first master it. This baby, I noticed later, had a broken wing. It seemed as if it was not just its wing but its entire body that was broken.

To die in the coolness of a summer morning, as the other seagulls on your hill sing with joy and anger—that must be hard. But it's as if the seagull is not dying so much as being saved from life. Maybe there were things it felt, things it wanted, but very little came its way, or nothing. What can a seagull think, what can it feel? Around its eyes is a sorrow that calls to mind an old man who is ready for death. To die is to crawl under some sort of quilt, or so it seems. Let it be, let it be so I might go, it seems to say.

Even now, I am glad that I am closer to it than the impudent seagulls wheeling above us. I came to this lonely shore to enter the sea; I'm in a hurry, caught up in my own thoughts, and in my hand is a towel. Now I've stopped to look at the seagull. Silently, respectfully. In the pebbles beneath my bare feet, a whole world. It's not the broken wings that make me feel the seagull's death but its eyes.

Once upon a time, it saw so much, noticed so much; you know this. In the space of one season it has become as tired as an old man, and perhaps it is sorry to be this tired. Slowly it leaves all things behind. I can't be sure, but maybe it is this seagull that the other seagulls in the sky are cawing about. Perhaps the sound of the sea makes death easier.

Later, much later, six hours later, when I returned to the pebble beach, the seagull was dead. It had spread one wing as if to fly, and turned on its side, opening one eye as wide as it could to stare blankly at the sun. There were no other seagulls flying near its hill.

I ran into the cool sea as if nothing had happened.

CHAPTER ELEVEN

To Be Happy

I s it vulgar to be happy? I've often wondered about this. Now I think about it all the time. Even though I have often said that people who are capable of happiness are evil and stupid, from time to time, I think this too: No, to be happy is not rude, and it takes brains.

When I go to the seaside with my four-year-old daughter, Rüya, I become the happiest man in the world. What does the happiest man in the world want most? He wants, of course, to carry on being the happiest man in the world. This is why he knows how important it is to do the same things every time. And that's what we do, always the same things.

1. First I tell her: Today we're going to the seaside, at such and such a time. Then Rüya tries to draw that time nearer. But her concept of time is a bit confused. So for example she'll suddenly come to my side and say, "Isn't it time yet?"

"No."

"Will it be time in five minutes?"

"No, it will be time in two and a half hours."

Five minutes later, she may come back to ask in all innocence, "Daddy, are we going to the seaside now?" Or later, in a voice designed to trick me, Rüya will ask, "So shall we go now?"

2. It seems as if the time will never come, but then it does. Rüya is now in her swimsuit and sitting in her four-wheeled Safa children's wagon. Inside it are towels, more swimsuits, and a silly straw bag that I shift to her lap before I pull the wagon forward in the usual way.

3. As we go down the cobblestone alleyway, Rüya opens her mouth to say Aaaaah. As the cobblestones rattle the wagon, this changes to Aa-aa-aaaah. The stones are making Rüya sing! Hearing it, we both laugh.

4. Down the small and featureless path to the beach. When we leave the wagon next to the steps leading down to the beach, Rüya always says, "Robbers never come here."

5. We quickly spread out our things on the stones, undress, and go knee-deep into the sea. Then I say, "It's calm now, but don't ever go too far. Let me take a swim, and when I come back we can play. Okay?"

"Okay."

6. I set off for a swim, leaving my thoughts behind. When I stop, I look back at the shore to see Rüya, who in her swimsuit now looks like a red stain, and I think how much I love her. I feel like laughing here in the water. She is paddling near the shore.

7. I go back. When I reach the shore we play: (A) kicking; (B) splashing; (C) Daddy squirting water from his mouth; (D) pretending to swim; (E) throwing stones into the sea; (F) conversation with the talking cave; (G) come on, no chickening out, now swim, and all our other favorite games and rituals, and when we've played them all we play them again.

8. "Your lips are purple, you're cold." "No, I'm not." "You're cold, we're getting out." This goes on for some time, and after the arguments are over we get out, and while we dry Rüya and change her swimsuit—

9. Suddenly she springs from my arms and runs naked across the beach, laughing as she goes. As I try to run across the stones in my bare feet, I limp, and this makes naked Rüya laugh all the more. "Look, if I put my shoes on, I can catch you," I say. I do just this, as she screams.

10. On the way back, while I'm pulling Rüya's wagon, we're both tired and happy. We're thinking about life, and about the sea behind us, and we don't say a word.

CHAPTER TWELVE

My Wristwatches

I began to wear my first wristwatch in 1965, when I was twelve. Then, in 1970, I got rid of it; by then it was too old. It wasn't a fancy brand, just an ordinary one. In 1970 I bought an Omega, and I used it until 1983. This, my third watch, is an Omega too. It's not very old; my wife bought it for me at the end of 1983, a few months after *The Silent House* was published.

A watch feels like part of my body. When I write it sits on my desk, and I look at it a little nervously. Before I sit down to write, when I take it off and set it on the table, I feel like someone who has taken off his shirt to play football. Like a boxer preparing for a match—especially if I put my watch on the table after coming in from the street. For me it is a gesture that denotes a preparation for battle. In the same way, when I'm leaving the house—if after working for five or six hours things have gone well, if I've been able to write successfully—I very much like putting my watch back on, so much so that doing it gives me the pleasure of achievement, of work completed. I rise from my table quickly; as soon as I've put my key and my money into my pocket I walk straight out. I don't wait to put on my watch; my watch will be in my hand; it's when I've reached the pavement, when I'm walking down the street, that I put on my watch. For me this is a great pleasure. All these things are merged in my mind with having struggled and prevailed.

I've never caught myself thinking, *How quickly time passed!*

I'll look at the face of the watch and it will seem as if the hour and the minute hands have arrived at the place where they were meant to be, but I don't think of this as an idea or even as a particle of time. This is why I shall never buy a digital watch. Digital watches represent those particles of time as numbers, whereas the face of my watch is a mysterious icon. I love to look at it. The face of time; in some way it conjures up that meta-physical conceit, or something close to it.

My most beautiful watch is the oldest one, the one I'm most used to. I feel attached to my watch as an object. This metaphysical affinity, this sense of enchantment, goes back to my first days of watch-wearing, in middle school. But later it became linked in my mind with school bells, and so it has remained for many years.

I take an optimistic view of time. As a rule, if a chore takes me 12 minutes, I think I can do it in 9. Or if a chore takes 23 minutes, I can do in 17. But even if I can't, I don't get discouraged.

When I go to bed I take off my watch and put it somewhere near me. The first thing I do when I wake up is to reach out and look at it. My watch is like a very close friend. I don't even like changing the straps when they get worn; they carry the scent of my skin.

In the old days I would begin to write around twelve o'clock and work until evening. But my real writing time was between 11 p.m. and 4 a.m. I would go to bed at four.

Until my daughter was born, I would work nights, right through to morning. During these hours when everyone was asleep, my watch face would watch me. Then this routine changed. From 1996, I got into the habit of waking at five and working until seven. Then I would wake up my wife and my daughter, and after eating breakfast with them, I'd take my daughter to school.

CHAPTER THIRTEEN

I'm Not Going to School

I'm not going to school. Because I'm sleepy. I'm cold. No one likes me at school.

I'm not going to school. Because there are two children there. They're bigger than me. They're stronger than me. When I go past them, they stick out their arms and block my way. I'm afraid.

I'm afraid. I'm not going to school. At school, time just stops. Everything gets left outside. Outside the school door.

My room at home, for example. Also my mother, my father, my toys, and the birds on the balcony. When I'm at school and I think about them, I want to cry. I look out the window. In the sky outside, there are clouds.

I'm not going to school. Because I don't like anything there.

The other day I did a picture of a tree. The teacher said, "That's really a tree, well done." I did another one. This one had no leaves either.

Then one of those children came over and made fun of me.

I'm not going to school. When I go to bed at night, and I think about going to school the next day, I feel terrible. I say, "I'm not going to school." They say, "How can you say that? Everyone goes to school."

Everyone? So let everyone go, then. What's going to happen if I stay home? I went yesterday, didn't I? How about if I don't go tomorrow, and then go the day after that?

If only I were at home in my bed. Or in my room. If only I were anywhere but that school.

I'm not going to school, I'm sick. Can't you see? The moment someone says *school* I feel sick, I get a stomachache. I can't even drink that milk.

I'm not going to drink that milk, I'm not going to eat anything, and I'm not going to school either. I'm so upset. No one likes me. There are those two children. They stick out their arms and block my way.

I went to the teacher. The teacher said, "Why are you following me?" I'll tell you something if you promise not to get mad. I'm always following the teacher, and the teacher is always saying, "Don't follow me."

I'm not going to school, ever again. Why? Because I just don't want to go to school, that's why.

When it's recess I don't want to go outside, either. Just when everyone's forgotten me, then it's recess. Then everything gets all mixed up, everyone starts running.

The teacher gives me a nasty look, and she doesn't look too good to start with. I don't want to go to school. There's one child who likes me, he's the only one who looks at me nicely. Don't tell anyone, but I don't like that child either.

I just sit down and stay there. I feel so lonely. Tears run down my cheeks. I don't like school at all.

I don't want to go to school, I say. Then it's morning and they take me to school. I can't even smile, I look straight in front of me, I want to cry. I climb up the hill with a bag on my back that is as big as a soldier's, and I keep my eyes on my little feet as they climb the hill. Everything's so heavy: the bag on my back, the hot milk in my stomach. I want to cry.

I walk into school. The black metal garden gate closes behind me. I cry, "Mommy, look, you left me inside."

Then I go into my classroom and sit down. I want to become one of those clouds outside.

Erasers, notebooks, and pens: Feed them to the hens!

CHAPTER FOURTEEN

Rüya and Us

1. Every morning we go to school together: one eye on the watch, one eye on the bag, the door, the road. In the car, we always do the same things: (A) wave at the dogs in the little park; (B) knock back and forth as the car accelerates around a corner; (C) say, "To the right and down the hill, Mr. Driver!" casting a sidelong glance at each other and laughing; (D) laughing when we say, "To the right and down the hill, Mr. Driver!" because he knows exactly where we're going, as we always take taxis from the same taxi stand; (E) get out of the taxi and walk hand in hand.

2. After I have hung her bag on her shoulder, kissed her, and led her into school, I watch her from behind. I have memorized the way Rüya walks, and I love watching her walk into school. I know she knows I'm watching her. It is as if her knowing I'm watching makes us both feel secure. First there is a world she enters and explores every day, and then there is the world we two share. When I watch her, and she turns around to watch me, we keep our world going. But then she breaks into a run and enters a new life where my eyes cannot go.

3. Let me brag a little: My daughter is intelligent and knows what she likes. She insists without a moment's hesitation that I tell the best stories, and on weekend mornings she lies down next to me and demands her due. Because she knows who she is, she knows what she wants. "It should be a witch again, she should escape from prison but she shouldn't go blind and she shouldn't grow old, and in the end she shouldn't catch the little child." She doesn't want me skipping the parts she likes. She tells me which parts she doesn't like while I'm still telling the story. This is why telling her a story means both writing it and reading it as the child who wrote it.

4. As with all intimate relationships, ours is a power struggle. Who will decide: (A) which channel to watch on television; (B) what time is bedtime; (C) what game will be played or not played, and how this decision, and many other similar decisions, discussions, disputes, tricks, sweet deceptions, bouts of tears, rebukes, sulks, reconciliations, and acts of contrition will be resolved after long political negotiations. All this effort makes us tired and happy, but in the end it accumulates and becomes the history of the relationship, the friendship. You come to an understanding, because you're not going to give up on each other. You think about each other, and when you're parted you remember each other's smell. When she's gone I miss the smell of her hair terribly. When I'm gone, she smells my pajamas.

CHAPTER FIFTEEN

When Rüya Is Sad

D o you know what, darling? When you're this sad, I'm sad too. I feel as if there is this instinct buried somewhere deep inside me— in my body, my soul—well, somewhere: When I see you sad, I get sad. It's as if some computer inside me says, WHEN YOU SEE THAT RÜYA IS SAD YOU GET SAD TOO.

I can get sad for no reason, too, and just as suddenly. I can be in the middle of an ordinary day, tending to the refrigerator or the paper or my mind or my hair. My mind goes off on a tangent: this life . . . but let's stop for a moment. I look at Rüya, and her face is dark and clouded; she's curled up on the divan, just lying there—what's made her so unhappy?— watching the world from the corner of her eye and her father watching her watch the world.

In one hand is a blue rabbit.

On her other hand she is resting her unhappy face.

I walk back to the kitchen, to rummage through the drawers of the refrigerator and my mind. What could it be? I wonder. Does she have a stomachache? Or maybe she is discovering the taste of her melancholy. Let her be, let her be sad, let her lose herself in solitude and her own smell. The first aim of an intelligent person is to achieve unhappiness when everyone around her is happy. So I once thought. I like it when people say Borgesian things: "Indeed, I try whenever possible to be as unhappy as all young people." That's good, but beware, she's not a young person yet; she's a child.

Silence.

I open the refrigerator, pick up a huge bright-red apple, and bite into it as hard as I can. I leave the kitchen. She's still lying there in a ball. I pause to think.

Make an approach. Say, Come, let's play dice, and, Where's the box? Find the box and, as you open it, ask each other, What color are you going to be? I'm green. Okay, then I'll be red. Then throw the dice, count the squares, and make sure she wins. If she starts wanting to win, if she starts enjoying herself, she'll brighten up and say,

I'm winning!

So take the lead then. Win every game.

Sometimes I get fed up, I think, Let me win, even if it's just once; let this girl learn how to lose.

It doesn't work. She throws away the dice. She overturns the game board. She goes off to sulk in the corner.

Why don't I suggest a game of Stay Off the Floor? You can go from the table to the dining chairs, from the dining chairs to armchairs, the divan, the other table, the side of the radiator. You can touch the floor, but if you get caught with your foot on the floor, you're It. But don't try to jump too far.

The best game is Chase. All around the house, around the table, from room to room, around the dining chairs, while the television drones on about the latest paradises, coups, rebellions, and beauty contests, and the dollar, and the stock exchange; and look at us, see how we're chasing each other and paying no attention to you and all your nonsense? As we run about madly, overturning baskets, knocking over lamps, crushing castles of newspaper piles, coupons, and cardboard, starting to sweat, shouting, but without knowing what exactly we're shouting about; we sometimes take off our clothes. If only you knew how fast we can run over chocolate wrappers, coloring books, broken toys, old newspapers, discarded water bottles, slippers, and boxes.

But I couldn't even do this.

I sat in a corner and watched the color of dirt settling quietly over the roar of the city. The television was on, but there was no sound, none at all. One of those seagulls was walking slowly across the roof; I recognized it from its patter. The two of us gazed out the window without speaking for the longest time, I in my chair and Rüya on the divan, and we both—Rüya sadly and I with joy—thought about how beautiful it was.

CHAPTER SIXTEEN

The View

I was going to talk about the world and the things inside it.

Why I began here, I cannot say. It was a hot day, my five-year-old daughter, Rüya, and I were out on Heybeliada, and later we went for a ride in a horse-drawn carriage. I sat facing backward and my daughter sat facing me. She was looking at the road ahead. We rode past gardens full of trees and flowers, low walls, wooden houses, vegetable patches. As the carriage lurched this way and that, I watched my daughter's face, seeking in her expressions some sense of what she saw in the world around her.

Things: objects, trees, and walls; posters, notices, streets, and cats. Asphalt. Heat. Had it ever been this hot?

Then we started up the hill; the horses were straining and the driver cracked his whip. The carriage slowed down. I looked at a house. As the world flowed past us, it was as if my daughter and I saw exactly the same things. One by one we looked at them: a leaf, a rubbish bin, a ball, a horse, a child. But also: the greenness of the leaf, the redness of the rubbish bin, the bounce of the ball, the horse's expression, the child's face. Then each of these things slipped away; we weren't really looking at them anyway; our eyes kept moving. We weren't really looking at any part of this hot afternoon world. It was slipping past us, this flimsy world that seemed to be evaporating before our eyes. It was almost as if we were drifting off ourselves! We see things and we don't. The world is bathed in the color of heat, and in our minds we can see this too.

We passed the forest, but even here it wasn't cool. It seemed to be radiating heat. When the road grew steeper, the horses slowed down again. We listened to the cicadas. The carriage was moving very slowly now, and just as the road seemed about to disappear into the trees, we saw the view.

"*Brrrs,*" said the driver, to stop the horses. "Let them rest," he said.

We looked at the view. We were at the edge of a cliff. Beneath us there were rocks, the sea, and, rising out of the steam, the other islands. What a beautiful blue the sea was, with the sun sparkling on its surface: Everything was where it should be, gleaming and immaculate. Before us was a perfectly formed world. Rüya and I admired it in silence.

The driver lit a cigarette; we could smell the smoke.

Why was it so beautiful, this view of the world? Perhaps because we could see it all. Perhaps because if we fell off the edge we would die. Perhaps because nothing looks bad from a distance. Perhaps because we'd never seen it from this height. So what were we doing here, in this world?

"Is it beautiful?" I asked Rüya. "What makes it beautiful?"

"If we fell off the edge, would we die?"

"Yes, we'd die."

For a moment she gazed fearfully at the cliff. Then she got bored. The cliff, the sea, the rocks: They never changed, never moved. Boring. A dog appeared. "A dog!" we both said. It was wagging its tail and moving. We both turned to admire him, and neither of us looked at the view again.

CHAPTER SEVENTEEN

What I Know About Dogs

This was a mud-colored dog, nothing out of the ordinary. It was wagging its tail. Its eyes were sad. It didn't sniff us the way curious dogs do. It used its mournful eyes to try to get to know us. When it had done so, it stuck its wet nose into the carriage.

Silence. Rüya was scared. She pulled back her legs and looked at me.

"Don't be afraid," I whispered. I shifted from my seat to Rüya's.

The dog drew back too. Together we examined him carefully. A four-legged creature. What must it be like to be a dog? I closed my eyes. As I began to think about what it must be like to be a dog, I tried to recall all the things I knew about dogs.

1. Recently an engineer friend of mine was telling me how he'd sold a Sivas Kangal to some Americans. The dog pictured in the brochure he then showed me was a strong, handsome, upright Kangal, and the caption said, "Hello, I'm a Turkish Kangal. My average height is [this many centimeters], I'm [this number of] years old, I'm this intelligent, and this is my breeding. A while back, a friend of ours went missing, but we followed the scent for four hundred miles until we found its owner. So that's how clever and loyal we are," et cetera.

2. Turkish dogs in comics, and dogs who have been translated into Turkish, say *hav!* But dogs in foreign comic books say *woof!*

That was as much as I could come up with about dogs. I tried, but I could think of nothing more. I must have seen tens of thousands of dogs in my lifetime, but nothing else came to mind. Except, of course, that dogs have pointed teeth and growl.

"Daddy, what are you doing?" Rüya asked. "Don't close your eyes like that, I'm bored."

I opened my eyes. "Driver," I said, "where is this dog from?"

"Where's the dog?" he asked, and I showed him. "Those dogs are heading for the dump just ahead," the driver said.

The dog looked straight in front of him, as if he knew we were talking about him.

"In the winter they go hungry, they suffer, they tear one another apart."

There was a silence. For a long time no one spoke.

"Daddy, I'm bored," said Rüya.

"Driver, let's get going," I said.

When the carriage began to move, Rüya turned her attention to the trees, the sea, and the road and forgot me too. That was when I closed my eyes again and tried one last time to remember what I knew about dogs.

3. Once there was a dog I loved. If a long time had passed since he'd last seen me, this dog would so ecstatically wriggle on his back waiting for me to pet him that he'd wet himself. Then they poisoned him and he died.

4. It's easy to draw a dog.

5. In a neighborhood where a friend of mine lived, there was a dog that barked furiously at any poor passerby, but the rich he let pass without making a sound.

6. The sound of a dog dragging a broken chain along the ground scares me. It must remind me of something traumatic.

7. That dog back there didn't follow us.

I opened my eyes and this was what I thought: People actually remember very little. I'd seen tens of thousands of dogs in this world, and when I'd seen them they'd struck me as beautiful. The world surprises us in the same way. It is here, there, right next to us. Then it fades away; everything turns to nothing.

8. Two years after I wrote this piece and published it in a magazine, I was attacked by a pack of dogs in Maçka Park. They bit me. I had to have five injections at the Rabies Hospital in Sultanahmet.

CHAPTER EIGHTEEN

A Note on Poetic Justice

W hen I was little, a boy the same age as I—his name was Hasan—
hit me just under the eye with a stone from his slingshot. Years
later, when another Hasan asked me why all the Hasans in my novels
were evil, this memory returned to me. In middle school, there was a big
fat bully who used to find any excuse to torment me at recess. Years later,
to make a character less attractive, I had him sweat like this tough fatso;
he was so fat he had only to stand there and these beads of sweat would
form on his hands and his forehead, until he looked like a giant pitcher
that had just come out of the refrigerator.

When I was little and my mother took me shopping, I used to dread
the butchers who worked such long hours in their stinking shops wearing
bloody aprons and wielding their great long knives, and I didn't eat too
many of the chops they cut for us because they were too fatty. In my
books, butchers figure as people who cut up contraband animals and
engage in bloody, shady activities. And the dogs that have followed me
all my life are portrayed as creatures that cause alarm and suspicion in
the heroes to whom I feel close.

A similarly innocent sense of justice has meant that bankers, teachers,
soldiers, and elder brothers are never cast as good people. Nor are barbers, because when I was very little I'd be in tears when taken to the barber, and over time my relations with them continued to be poor. Because
I came to love horses during my childhood summers on Heybeliada, I've
always given very good parts to horses and their carriages. My horse
heroes are sensitive, delicate, forlorn, innocent, and often the victims of
evil. Because my childhood was full of good, well-meaning people who
always smiled at me, there are lots of good people in my books too, but
justice reminds us first and foremost of evil. In the mind of such a reader,

as for a person strolling through an art gallery, there is this faint feeling of justice: What we expect from poets is that they should avenge evil somehow.

As I've been trying to explain, I try to avenge evil single-handedly, and mostly I do this in a most personal way, but in such a way that the reader isn't meant to notice and sees the revenge as beautiful. Because poetic justice reaches its high point at the end of children's books and adventure comics, when the hero punishes the villain, saying, "And this blow is for such and such . . . and *this* blow for . . . ," I invented just such a scene as a novelist: Line by line, I enumerate every heinous act committed by an evil Hasan or a butcher, until the butcher or whoever panics and drops the knife in his hand and is cleaning up the shop, crying, "Please, my brother, I beg you not to treat me harshly; I have a wife and children!"

Revenge breeds revenge. Two years ago, when eight or nine dogs cornered and attacked me in Maçka Park, it seemed as if they had read my books and knew I had exacted poetic justice on them to punish them for roaming, especially in Istanbul, in packs. This, then, is the danger in poetic justice: Taken too far, it might ruin not just your book—your work—but your very life. You might carry out your revenge with elegance, and with no one the wiser, your writing more and more a thing of beauty, but there are always dogs waiting to catch the vengeful poet alone at a corner and sink their teeth into him.

CHAPTER NINETEEN

After the Storm

After the storm, when I went out into the streets in the early morning, I saw that everything had changed. I am not talking about broken and fallen branches or yellow leaves lying in the muddy streets. Something deeper and harder to see had changed, as if in the early light of morning the armies of snails that were now everywhere, the discomfiting smell of the water in the soil, the stale air—all these were signs that something had changed forever.

I stood next to a puddle; I looked into it. At the bottom I saw the soil in the form of soft mud, as if waiting for a sign, an invitation. A little farther along, yellowing grass, broken ferns, green herbs, on the sides of clovers, that looked like drops of water, and, at the base of the cliff to my right, along which I walked with wonder and decisiveness, the slowly swirling seagulls seemed more dangerous and determined than ever before.

Of course all these things—this clarity of perception, this sudden chilling of the air by a wind from nowhere, this sky that the storm has wiped so clean, this new color that all of nature has taken on—they could be fooling me. But as I walked it occurred to me that before the storm the birds and the bugs, the trees and the stones, that old rubbish bin and this tilting electricity pole—everything had lost interest in the world, lost sight of its aims, forgotten what it was here for. Later, after midnight and before the first light of dawn, the storm swooped in to restore the lost meaning, the lost aspirations.

To sense that life is deeper than we think it is, and the world more meaningful, does a person have to wake in the middle of the night to clattering windows, to wind blowing through a gap in the curtains, and the sounds of thunder? Like a sailor who wakes up in a storm and instinctively rushes to his sails, I jumped still half asleep from my bed, closing the open windows one by one and turning off a table lamp that had been left burning, and after doing all this I sat in the kitchen and drank a glass of water as the kitchen's overhead light swayed in the wind howling through the cracks. Suddenly a great gust came that seemed to shake the whole world and there was a power outage. Everything went dark, and the kitchen tiles felt cold under my bare feet.

From where I was sitting, I could look through the window, through the swaying pines and poplars, and see the whiteness of the froth on the ever-larger waves. Between the thunder claps, it seemed as if a bolt of lightning might have struck at sea somewhere nearby. Then, amid the continual flashes of lightning, the racing clouds, and the tips of the swaying branches, land and sky blended into each other. As I stood at the kitchen window looking out at the world, in my hand an empty glass, I felt content.

But in the morning, as I wandered around trying to make sense of what had happened, like an investigator combing the scene of a violent incident, a legendary crime, a world in turmoil, this is what I said to myself: It is in times of violence, times of storms, that we remember we all live in the same world. Later still, as I was looking at broken branches and bicycles that had been thrown from their resting places, this came to my mind too: When a storm hits, we don't just understand that we live in the same world, we begin to feel as if we are all living one and the same life.

A bird, a little sparrow, had fallen into the mud—I don't know why—and was dying. As I was sketching it in curiosity and cold blood, rain began to pelt down on my open notebook and all the other sketches in it.

CHAPTER TWENTY

In This Place Long Ago

One day when I was lost in thought and very tired, I went down that road. I wasn't looking for anything in particular, I had no set destination in mind, I just wanted to reach the end of every road I entered—a man impatient to get home. As I walked and walked, and my mind wandered, I suddenly raised my head and that road was stretching out before me, and there, amid the trees, I saw a roof; I saw the sweet

way the road curved, and the shrubs along the side, and the first fallen leaves of autumn.

I was so taken by what I saw that I stopped in the middle of the road. I looked at the bicycle tracks stretching out before me, the dark shadowy tip of the cypress tree in my path. The trees on my left, the gentle curve of the road, the clear sky, the way it all lined up—how beautiful this place was!

I had warm associations with this road, as if I'd lived here long ago, despite the fact that I was visiting it for the first time. Why did it look so beautiful to me? The view resembled the place I'm always trying to reach. How often I'd thought about this, that sweet curve in the road just ahead of me, the shelter of the trees, the pleasure of standing here and gazing at this view. I'd thought about the view before me so often that it now seemed like a memory, laden with the memories of all the things I'd seen long ago without paying them any mind.

But in one corner of my mind, I knew I was walking down this road for the first time. I did not have any desire to return to this place, nor did I have the inclination or even the appetite to dwell on it too long. My aim was to forget it, the way we all forget the roads along which we have come. My mind would just not settle. I had other things to do.

So even as I marveled at the beauty of the view, I continued on my way. I wanted to forget what I'd seen. But I never have forgotten it, never.

After returning to the noise of the city, plunging once again into the pandemonium of everyday life, that road, that place—which had so enthralled me even as I tried to forget it—came to me as a memory. This time it was a real memory. I'd passed down that road, and its beauty had touched me, but—what a shame—I'd still hurried on. Now the place I'd turned my back on returned to me. It belonged to my memories now, to my own past.

What bound me to it? Its abundant beauty, that's what; the fact of happening upon it without even knowing such a beautiful and wondrous place was there, and then, on seeing it, of opening my eyes, my heart; of this I have no doubt. Perhaps it was *because* I had no doubt that I was frightened by the beauty I saw before me and continued on my way. But the thing on which I turned my back came to me at the following times and in the following shapes:

1. When surrounded by a crowd, eating in company, chattering with friends and acquaintances, I'd take offense at some tiny slight, and

suddenly I'd remember that road stretching out before me, the cypresses and plane trees, that mysterious roof, and those leaves on the ground, and think about them for a long time. It would be very difficult to get that view out of my mind.

2. At night, when I was awoken by thunder and a storm, or while the woman on television told me what the weather would be the next day, I'd suddenly imagine rain falling on that place, and storms raging; I'd hear thunder and imagine that lightning had struck somewhere nearby. When the sky and the earth had blended into each other, when the plane tree that had witnessed my silence shook in the storm, when the storm had restored that pristine view, who knew what beauties one might find? I was wasting my life on such stupid things here, so far away from there.

3. If I'd gone back to that point in the road, back to that place where I'd stopped to look at the view, and just stood there waiting, my life would have taken an entirely different course. How would this have happened? I have no idea. I think I would have begun walking again after a time, but knowing deep inside myself that this road was going to take me to an entirely different place, and once I reached that place I would live an entirely different life.

CHAPTER TWENTY-ONE

The House of the Man
Who Has No One

This is the house of the man who has no one. It sits on the top of a hill, at the end of a long and winding road. The road is the white of lime in some places and in others the green of grass, and when it reaches the top it dwindles away. This is where we stop to catch our breath and be cooled by the wind. If you walk a little farther, you arrive at a point where you can suddenly see the other side of the hill; the wind stops and you are in a hot and sunny place facing south. This part of the road is so far off the beaten track that ants build their nests here; it's impossible to distinguish the road from the open field.

The fig trees. The fragments of perforated bricks. Plastic bottles. Pieces of disintegrating and no longer transparent plastic wrap. Sometimes it's hot, sometimes windy. These things belong to the man who has no one. He must have brought all these things and piled them up here because it's a place no one else visits.

Once upon a time he wasn't a man with no one. When he came here he had his wife with him. She was a good woman, people say; she had friends living nearby, in the houses below. But like the man who would come to have no one, she had no relatives, no one from the city where she was born. Those friends were from some other Black Sea city. If what I'm told is true, the man who has no one once owned property in that city; he was rich, but—they always smiled when they told me this— he was always making trouble with people and so had as much difficulty settling there as he'd had here. No. Before he wasn't like that. One day his wife had to go into the hospital down the hill. He went there too, to the hospital. Then his wife died. All this went on for years; for years his wife was ill. Now all he does is watch television, smoke cigarettes, and

make trouble, and in the summers he works as a waiter in a restaurant on the shore.

It's the television that shocks me—because the sweeping view from his house, from this hill, is stunning, extraordinary. A person could spend years here, gazing at the other hills, at the reflections of the sun on the wind-brushed sea, at the ships moving in on the city from all directions, at the islands, at the ferries traveling to and fro, at the crowds in the neighborhoods below that are too far away to cause harm, at the miniature mosques in the distance and the houses that sink into a faint cloud of mist in the mornings, at the whole city. They stopped building new houses here years ago.

A hearty seagull lets out a long cry. With the wind comes the sound of a radio somewhere below.

Actually, the house is proof that he really did bring some money from the city where he was born. That's what they say. He laid the tiles on the roof in clean and tidy rows. He made the roof of the extension with good-quality tin plate, lining it with stones to keep it in place. The toilet that you can see behind the house as you approach he made from briquettes, the plastic water tank he added later; the chairs, planks and scraps, you can see among the thorns, the shrubs, and the baby pines.

One evening, as we are standing in the wind, looking at the neighborhoods on other city hills, at houses made of the same tiles, bricks, plastics, and stones, the man comes out and gives us a long hard look. In his hands is something I've never seen before: an iron, or perhaps the handle of a small pot. That's when I notice that his house is bound together with a large quantity of wire, pipe, and cable.

He goes inside and disappears.

CHAPTER TWENTY-TWO

Barbers

I n 1826, after the Ottoman army had suffered a string of defeats at the hands of the West and the Janissaries who had traditionally served as its soldiers had resisted attempts to modernize them and bring them up to European standards, the reformist Sultan Mahmud II dispatched his new disciplined army to attack the Janissary headquarters in Istanbul, reducing it to rubble. It was an important moment, not just in the history of Istanbul but in the history of the Ottoman Empire, one that all lycée students in Turkey are taught to view from a Westernizing, modernizing, nationalist perspective and to call "The Propitious Event." What is less well known is that this propitious event, which involved clashes with tens of thousands of Janissaries in the center of the city and wholesale slaughter in its streets and shops, changed the face of Istanbul in ways that can be seen even today.

Certainly there is some truth in the story as told by nationalist modernizing historians. Throughout their 450-year ascendancy, most Janissaries belonged to the same Sufi sect, Bektaşis who were closely linked with the city's shopkeepers. The Janissaries were stationed all over the city and walked the streets armed, performing many of the duties of today's police and gendarmes and owning all variety of shops; their blustering street presence meant they were in a position to mount a strong resistance against the reformist state. Mahmud II sent his armies first to the coffeehouses and barbershops, most of whose owners belonged to the Janissary fraternity; having secured a military victory, he (like so many other sultans wishing to quell rebellions in the street, most notably Murad IV, who is said still to wander the city streets in disguise by night) went on to shut those coffeehouses and barbershops down. Here we might draw a parallel with something else I've seen often in my own lifetime: the modern Republic's predilection for shutting down newspapers. For until very recently, each coffeehouse and barbershop in the city served (like the *dolmuşes,* the shared taxis, of my childhood) as places where news, legends, and rampant rumors, outright lies, and tales of wrath and resistance were fabricated and enriched to undermine the pronouncements of religious leaders and the state, thus paving the way for rumors of plots against them, while in the neighborhoods surrounding mosques, churches, and markets, and in the villages along the Bosphorus, each served also as a local newspaper.

In those days Istanbul boasted many humor magazines, of which *Vulture* was the most distinguished; because their embroideries of news and enlargements of urban myths offered the fullest expression of this spirit of resistance, they were available in all barbershops of my childhood. Today, there is always a television blaring, drowning out older channels of communication and so greatly reducing the power of gossip and resistance in the city's coffeehouses and barbershops; it should not come as a surprise that, with the advent of television, the golden age of Istanbul's humor magazines, which once enjoyed a combined circulation close to a million, also came to an end. (Years later, when I went to a barbershop in New York and saw that the men waiting to be served were given not a humor magazine but a copy of *Playboy,* I was not terribly surprised.) As for *Vulture,* the magazine without which no barbershop was complete in the days of my childhood, it later emerged that its owner, Yusuf Ziya Ortaç, received secret assistance from a private fund controlled by Prime Minister Adnan Menderes and the ruling Democrat Party, but this sort of thing dates back to the 1870s, when Sultan Abdülhamit undertook to control the opposition by buying up its publications—a tradition that in a subtler way continues to this day.

When I was a boy waiting my turn at the barbershop, flipping through the pages of *Vulture,* stopping now and again to study locally drawn caricatures of citizens aghast at the prices of things, enjoying jokes about bosses and their secretaries, stories by the popular humorist Aziz Nesin, and cartoons lifted from Western magazines, my ears were always alert to the conversations around me. Of course the topic discussed at the greatest length was football and the football pools. Some, like Toto, the head barber, would, as he moved among the three customers in the three chairs, offer up his thoughts on boxing or the horses, which he played from time to time. His barbershop, which bore the fanciful name Venus, was at the end of the passageway across the street from our house in Nişantaşı. Toto was a tired and sulky man with white hair, and the other of the two older owners was irritable and bald, while the third owner was in his forties and sported a thin Douglas Fairbanks mustache. I remember he was less interested in chatting with his customers about high prices, new shops in the neighborhood, singers and stars of the day, or domestic politics than he was in discussing international affairs and the state of the world. What most impressed me was how, when a customer arrived who was particularly eminent, learned, expert, powerful, or upper class, this barber and the others would start with humble questions beginning with *We of course have no idea . . . ,* and once they had drawn him out they would quickly move the conversation square into the man's field of knowledge and power. If they got an answer like *It costs this many liras* or *Those cargo ships are bigger than a football field,* or if they were told that a famous politician had a shocking weakness or had committed an act of cowardice, they would either mutter something like *chk-chk-chk* or *chirp-chirp-chirp,* like so many little birds, or the razor that had been gliding so smoothly and close would stop for a moment while barber and customer eyed each other in the mirror and an interesting silence would ensue.

If, after trying to open a conversation with questions like *So, what's happening?* or *How are things?* or *May I offer you tea?* the customer remained grim and silent, they would jabber among themselves. In these conversations, one played the man always down on his luck, the second the butt of every joke, and the third ever the cunning one; the way they used to needle one another in these conversations (as in "Mehmet outwitted Toto once again this week") reminded me of the sparring I'd hear on the radio between Karagöz, the hero of traditional shadow theater, and his sharp-tongued wife, Hacivat. Once, after a customer had had his shave, taken off his apron, allowed the boy to comb his hair, given out his tips, and left the shop, the Fairbanks mustache–sporting owner, who had shown him such courtesy and deference only moments earlier, began to curse this man's mother and his wife: This was how I discovered that the adult world was populated by duplicitous types whose anger was deeper than anything I had known in my child's world. At the barbershops of my childhood, they used scissors, huge clippers they would angrily toss away when they didn't cut well, combs, cotton balls to keep hair out of the ears, cologne, powder, and, for the grown-ups, cutthroat razors, shaving cream, shaving combs, and white aprons. Today, apart from a handful of electric appliances—like the hair dryer—the tools have not changed much, and this must remind us that though Istanbul writers have never recorded their traditions, these barbers (who have been using the same tools for centuries, gossiping as they work) must have been speaking in the same way for just as long.

We can see in miniatures of the age that the cutthroat razor was in use in the seventeenth century. When passing before Sultan Ahmet, representatives of the barbers' guild, wishing to prove their fine talents, had a barber suspended upside down from the roof of the exhibition carriage as he gave his customer a perfect shave. In those days, the head of the man to be shaved would rest against the barber's knee; this custom paved the way for a classic love story in which a man contrived to have all his hair, his beard, his mustache, and his every whisker and bristle removed, just to be near a beautiful barber's apprentice. We see the same motif in the folk tale about Kerem and Aslı, in which the lover has teeth pulled just to be close to a beautiful dentist, a reminder that barbers and dentists were both seen as possessing expert knowledge and somewhat overlapping expertise. Barbers also performed circumcisions and other small surgical procedures, some in their coffeehouses and others in separate establishments: This gave them a central importance in Istanbul society. But when I was a child, what frightened me about barbers was that they could pull words from our mouths as skillfully as dentists extract teeth and disseminate them as fast as any newspaper.

This is why, when I was sitting in the Venus barbershop reading *Vulture* and heard a voice say, "Come along now, young master," I would be as tense as if I had been invited to take my place in a dentist's chair. It was not just because the trimmer sometimes pulled the hairs on my neck or the point of the scissors dug into me (my visits to the barbershop always seemed to involve pain); I was afraid because I thought I might let some family secret slip. I had an uncle who'd gone to America and never returned. After they had passed a white cloth over my head and fastened it as one might about a man headed for the gallows, the first question they would ask was, "When is your uncle coming back from America?" I didn't know. "How many years has he been gone?"

"He's been gone soooooo long," another would answer. "He'll never come back, no, never. Did he ever do his military service?" There would follow a silence. I would stare in front of me, as ashamed as if I had been the one who'd "fled" the country before his military service, and I'd remember my grandmother crying as she read my uncle's ever more infrequent letters in ever more broken Turkish. But my real fear was that the barbers might extract from me yet other secrets that my family had succeeded in hiding and that I had no wish to remember.

Was it because I'd foreseen these perils, and because I felt from the moment I walked in that I would soon be sweating as profusely as I might today, sitting opposite a journalist with an interest in my private life, that on my very first visit to the barber I burst into tears? For my next few haircuts, and on days when I was ill, Toto, the owner with the white hair and the joyless face, would pack the tools of his trade into a bag and come to the house to cut my hair. He'd spread a newspaper on the table, place a stool on top, and sit me on it so I was at the same height as his scissors. This gloomy man who held himself apart from his loquacious friends remained silent here too, and because I enjoyed this interlude as little as he did, it wasn't long before I returned to the barbershop for my haircuts. That was when I understood that a barber who shaves you in silence, without drawing a word from your mouth or sharing any neighborhood or political gossip, and cursing no one, is not a barber at all.

CHAPTER TWENTY-THREE

Fires and Ruins

Before I was born, my grandparents lived in a great stone mansion that they shared with my uncles, my father and mother, and the rest of our large family; it was later rented by a private primary school, and then it was torn down. My own primary school was in another great mansion, until it burned down. When I was in middle school, we played football in the garden of yet a third old mansion; this too succumbed to fire and was later demolished, like so many shops and buildings from my childhood.

The history of Istanbul is the history of fires and ruins. From the middle of the sixteenth century, when the building of wooden houses first became popular, through the first quarter of the twentieth century—for more than 350 years, then—what has shaped the city and opened up its avenues and streets (leaving aside the construction of the big mosques) have been its fires. The site of a house fire was a subject of much discussion during my childhood and carried a whiff of bad luck. Because first floors were made of stone and brick, there would remain a few walls that had been burned but not destroyed, the first-floor stairs (of which the marble steps would have been ruined or stolen), tiles, broken glass, and vases; amid this debris little fig trees would sprout up and children would play there.

I wasn't old enough to have witnessed the burning and destruction of entire neighborhoods; what I witnessed were the fires that destroyed the last wooden mansions. Most of them happened under mysterious circumstances, in the middle of the night. Until the fire brigade arrived, all the children and young people in the neighborhood would gather in the garden of the empty house where they once played and whisper to one another as they watched the raging flames.

"They burned the beautiful mansion down," my uncle would say later, at home.

In those days it was against the law to knock down your old home to make room for the new apartment building that would show the world how rich and modern you were. But people would move out, and once the mansion had become uninhabitable due to neglect, rotting wood, and age you could get permission to tear it down. Some would try to speed up the process by pulling out tiles to let in the rain and the snow. A faster, bolder option was to burn it down one night when no one was looking. It was said for a time that these fires were set by the gardeners left in charge. It was also said that, before they burned down, the houses had been sold to contractors whose own men set them afire.

They were the objects of contempt in our family, these rich people who burned down houses in which three generations had once lived together, houses that were full of memories, destroyed in the middle of the night as if by common criminals. Appalled and affronted as they were, my family too had been coldhearted enough to sell the three-story art deco mansion in which my father, my uncles, and my grandmother had once lived and eventually to build a very ugly apartment house in its place. Later, to convince me that he had not been a party to this plan and had never "really" wanted that beautiful old house to be torn down, my father often talked of our return from Ankara, where we'd moved because of his work; when we'd come back and he'd seen the old house crumble under the sledgehammers, he'd stood before the garden door and wept.

As in so many old Istanbul families who owned these mansions, the "move to the apartment" provoked many disputes to which I was a witness. In principle, no one wanted to see those old houses destroyed. But no one could stop the squabbling, the feuding, or the deep-seated rivalries that led so many families to take their property disputes to court, in the end tearing down the disputed mansion and building in its place a new and ugly apartment building that no one liked from the outset. Later on, they would all speak mournfully of the old mansion destroyed, but of course they harbored the unspoken wish of bettering their lives with the income from their new apartments. Still, they all determineed to transmit the pangs of conscience, and the responsibility for this shameful business, to other members of the family.

The population of Istanbul went from one to ten million in a very short space of time, and if you were to view it from above you would see at once why all this family strife, this greed, guilt, and remorse, served no good purpose. Below you would see the concrete legions, as great and unstoppable as the army in Tolstoy's *War and Peace,* as they roll over all mansions, trees, gardens, and wildlife in their way; you see the tracks of asphalt that this force leaves in its wake; you can see it coming ever closer to the neighborhood where once you led a timeless and heavenly life. If, after studying the map and the statistics, and tracking the movements of this unstoppable force, we consider the idea that one individual might be able to resolve a family quarrel, one might very well remember Tolstoy's dark thoughts on the role of the individual in history. If we happen to be part of a relentless, expanding city, the rooms and gardens and streets in which we have made our lives—the walls that have given shape to our memories and our very souls—are doomed to be destroyed.

For those who resisted, or who tried to delay the inevitable, the final blow was expropriation. During my childhood, when many of Istanbul's narrow little Ottoman streets were being cleared to make way for avenues, to be expropriated meant to be evicted, to be unjustly made homeless. Over the past fifty years, Istanbul has gone through two major road-making, or expropriation, drives, and I was six or seven years old during the first. I remember the scary walks I took with my mother in 1950 along the opposite shore of the Golden Horn, amid the dust of Ottoman ruins. The demolition area looked like a war zone; as each empty lot stood there awaiting its new life, it filled with endless fears and rumors. There was talk of some lot owners being favored over others when it came to compensation, of unnecessary expropriations, of maps indicating future expropriations, and of certain powerful politicians pulling strings to save a particular street or have the map changed. Wherever the roads along the Bosphorus and the Golden Horn diverted into a narrow lane passing through a village market, it would emerge that someone very rich or close to power lived in a house the road had swerved to avoid. This was much remarked by old ladies riding in a *dolmuş* and old barbers shaving customers and taxi drivers ever grateful for wider roads—vehemently in favor of the demolition, these last would always insist that it had not gone far enough. There was more to this than the desire for wide Parisian boulevards, expressing as it did the anger Istanbul's new arrivals felt for the old city and its culture and the grudge they held against all that had come before them, and the Republic's wish to forget the city's Christian and cosmopolitan buildings, the city's Byzantine and even Ottoman remains. In the 1970s, when the domestic automobile industry began to turn out cars that the middle classes could afford, the demand for fast roads decreed that the past would soon be hidden under concrete and asphalt.

There are two ways of looking at cities. The first is that of the tourist, the newly arrived foreigner who looks at the buildings, monuments, avenues, and skylines from outside. There is also the inside view, the city of rooms in which we have slept, of corridors and cinemas and old class-rooms, the city made up of the smells and lights and colors of our most cherished memories. To those viewing them from the outside, one city can seem much like the next, but a city's collective memory is its soul, and its ruins are its most eloquent testimony.

During the great demolition drive of the 1980s, I happened to be walking down Tarlabaşı Avenue as the bulldozers were shunting along, observed by a modest crowd. The work had been going on for months by then; everyone had become accustomed to it, so the anger and resistance had died down. Despite the drizzle, the walls kept coming down, dis-solving into dust as they fell, and as we stood watching it seemed to me that what disturbed us more than seeing other people's houses and mem-ories destroyed was seeing Istanbul twist this way and that as it changed shape and knowing how even more fragile and transitory our own lives were in comparison. As children wandered among the wrecked walls, gathering up doors, windows, and pieces of wood, I understood how much these piles of rubble represented a loss of memory that would, in time, seem like second nature.

A few years earlier I had gone to visit the empty and soon-to-be-demolished building that had once housed Şişli Terakki Lycée, where I had been enrolled from the last years of primary school until the end of middle school. I have now been walking the same streets for fifty years, and when I pass the site of my old school, which is now a parking lot, I remember both my days at the school and my last stroll through its empty classrooms. At first its ruination pierced me like a knife, but now it is something to which I am slowly becoming accustomed. A city's ruins also help it to forget. First we lose a memory, but we know we've lost it and we want it back. Then we forget we have forgotten it, and the city can no longer remember its own past. The ruins that cause us such pain and open the road to forgetfulness become, in the end, the lots on which others can found new dreams.

CHAPTER TWENTY-FOUR

Frankfurter

I t was a cold day in January 1964, in the early afternoon. I was standing in a corner of Taksim Square (which at that time was not yet a six-
lane highway and was much more run-down than it is today), just outside
a buffet that occupied the ground floor of one of the old Greek apartment
buildings. I was awash in guilt and fear but also euphoric; in my hand
was a frankfurter I'd just bought at the buffet. I took a big bite, but as I
stood there, chewing amid the great chaos of the city, watching the cir-
cling trolleybuses and the swarms of women shoppers and young people
rushing off to the movies, my joy abandoned me; I had been caught. My
brother was walking down the pavement and, what's more, he had seen
me; as he came closer I could see at once that he was very happy to have
caught me red-handed.

"What do you think you're doing, eating that frankfurter?" he asked,
with a supercilious smile.

I lowered my head and finished my sandwich as surreptitiously as if
engaged in a criminal act. At home that evening, it was just as I had foreseen: My brother told my mother of my transgression in superior tones
tinged with compassion. Eating frankfurters outside the house in the
street was just one of many activities my mother had proscribed.

Until the early sixties, frankfurter sandwiches were known to İstan-
bullus as very special fare served only in the German-type beer halls that
were brought to the city in the early years of the twentieth century. From
the sixties on, thanks to the arrival of compact butane stoves, the falling
prices of domestically produced refrigerators, and the opening of Coca-
Cola and Pepsi bottling plants in Turkey, there were suddenly "sandwich
buffets" opening up everywhere, and what they offered was soon part of
the national diet. In the sixties, when the *döner* (now popular in Europe

70

under this name and known in the United States by its Greek name, gyro) had yet to be invented, the frankfurter was the height of fashion and the most important food for those of us who had taken to eating in the streets. You would gaze through the glass at dark red tomato sauce that had been simmering all day and pick out one of the frankfurters that had been swimming like so many happy water buffaloes wallowing in the mud; you would point it out to the man with the tongs, and then you would wait impatiently for him to assemble the sandwich. He would, if requested, slip the bread into the toaster, spread it with the dark red sauce, place tomatoes and thin translucent slices of pickle over the frank- furter, before finally adding a layer of mustard. Some of the fancier places also spread the mayonnaise once known as Russian dressing but now referred to as American dressing because of the Cold War.

Most of these pretentious buffets and sandwich shops opened first in Beyoğlu and, having changed the fast-food eating habits of the local res- idents, went on, over the next twenty years, to do the same for the rest of Istanbul and all of Turkey. Istanbul's first sandwich-toasting machines arrived in the mid-fifties; at about the same time, the bakeries began to produce special bread for toasted cheese sandwiches. Once these toasted cheese sandwiches had become a staple, the buffets of Beyoğlu went on to reinvent the hamburger. The first big sandwich shops of the era had names invoking other lands and seas, magic realms like the "Atlantic" and the "Pacific," and their walls were decorated with paintings of the heavenly islands of Gauguin's Far East. Each establishment offered a very different-tasting hamburger. This suggests that Turkey's first ham- burgers were, like so much else in Istanbul, a synthesis of East and West. Inside the sandwich whose name spoke of Europe and America to a young man walking through Beyoğlu was a hamburger patty that the nice head-scarf-wearing matron in the kitchen, a woman who took pride in feeding all young men, had made according to her own special recipe with her own loving hands.

This was the basis of my mother's objection: With great disgust, she had declared the minced meat in these hamburgers to be from "unknown parts of unknown animals" and forbade our eating not just hamburgers but frankfurters, salami, and garlic sausages, because it was hard to know the provenance of their meat also. Occasionally we would read in the papers that an illegal garlic-sausage factory had been raided and that they had found the sausages to contain horse or even donkey meat. Let me not confess that the tastiest sandwiches of my life were the ones I bought from the vendors who served up bread stuffed with meatballs and garlic sausages outside the sports halls and stadiums where I went to watch football matches and basketball games. My own interest in football had to do less with the fate of the ball or the team than with the crowd and the sense of occasion; while waiting in line for my ticket, the thick dark-blue smoke from the meatball vendors would seep into my nose, my hair, and my jacket until it was impossible to resist. After promising each other that we would not speak of it at home, my brother and I would each buy a sausage sandwich. The sausage would have been roasted over the coals until it was like leather and it would be stuffed into half a loaf of bread with a piece of onion. It went well with a glass of the yogurt drink, *ayran*.

These sausages and hamburgers of uncertain origin were the stuff of nightmares not just for my mother but for all other middle-class mothers too. This was why street vendors hawking garlic-sausage sandwiches would always cry, "Apik! Apik!" This referred to Apikoğlu brand sausages, famous for never using horse or donkey meat. From the time they enjoyed their first toasted sandwiches outside their first buffets, the *İstanbullus* of the 1960s were bombarded every time they went to the cinema with advertisements for the sausage and frankfurter companies whose products were used in those sandwiches. One of the first of these advertisements, itself one of the first domestically produced cartoons, is still lodged in my mind: Into the mouth of a gigantic hand-drawn meat grinder walk various cows, all wearing beatific expressions, so happy are they at the prospect of serving humanity as they parachute down from the sky. But what's this? A sweet, toothy, craftily smiling donkey has somehow infiltrated this herd of airborne cows. The audience grows uneasy as the donkey arrives at the mouth of the meat grinder, but just before he is turned into sausage a large fist comes out of that mouth to send the donkey flying, and a female voice assures us that we can buy such and such a brand of sausage with "peace of mind."

In Istanbul as elsewhere, people ate fast food on the streets not just because they were short of time, money, or other opportunities but also, in my view, to escape that "peace of mind." To leave behind Islamic tradition, whose ideas about food were embedded in ideas about mothers, women, and sacred privacy—to embrace modern life and become a city dweller—it was necessary to be ready and willing to eat food even if you didn't know where, how, or why it was made. Because this act of will required willfulness, even bravery, the first to take the plunge were students, the unemployed, the disaffected, and those fools who were ready to stuff anything into their mouths for the sake of novelty. Such crowds first gathered at the entrances of football stadiums, on Istiklâl Avenue, near lycées and universities, and in the city's poorest neighborhoods; the pleasure they took in finding themselves thus assembled (together with the thrill of conveniences like refrigerators and butane burners) changed the eating habits not just of Istanbul but of the entire country almost overnight. In 1966, at the Turkey–Bulgaria match, at Galatasaray's Ali Sami Yen Stadium, the pushing and shoving in the cheap open stands set a frankfurter vendor's cart on fire, a blaze that quickly spread, and before my terrified eyes the huge crowds that had been eating frankfurters as they waited for the match began to undulate and drop off the second story, crushing others as they fell to their deaths.

Though it may have been "modern" and "civilized" to eat food made by unknown hands in dirty streets so far from home, those of us who embraced this habit at the exact same moment still found ways to avoid the solitary individualism that modernity so often brought with it. Before the *döner* craze swept Turkey in the seventies, quickly establishing a new standard, there was a similar craze for *lahmacun*. A better name might have been Arab pita bread, though twenty years later I would see it described in one store as "Turkish pizza" (as for whether or not *pide* and *pizza* share an etymology, this is a subject for another day); but it was not Istanbul's buffets and kebab restaurants that won the country over to *lahmacun;* it was a new army of vendors slipping through the city streets to conquer it with their familiar elliptically shaped boxes. Now you didn't even have to go to the buffet on the corner to fill your stomach. A *lahmacun* seller would appear in a white apron wherever you stood, and when he opened his box, out would come a warm and mouthwatering steam carrying the aroma of stewed onions, ground meat, and red pepper. To scare us, my mother would say, "They don't make those *lahmacuns* from horsemeat, they made them from cats and dogs," but when we'd look at the *lahmacun* men's boxes, each distinctively painted, with brilliant flowers and branches and pictures of *lahmacuns* and the names of cities like Antep and Adana, we'd succumb to desire.

The best thing about Istanbul street food is not that each vendor is different, offering specialties and chasing fashions, it is that each sells only the things he knows and loves. When I see the men who have taken a village dish—something their mother or their wife makes for them at home—out into the streets of the big city, certain that everyone else will love it too, it's not just their chickpea pilaf or grilled meatballs or fried mussels or stuffed mussels or Albanian liver that I savor but the proud beauty of their decorated stands, three-wheeled cars, and chairs. These men are fewer than they once were, but at one time they would roam the streets of Istanbul, and even as its multitudes swarmed around them, in their souls they were still living in the "clean" world of their wives and mothers. Another street food that has resisted the trend toward factory-made uniformity is, of course, "fish and bread." In the old days, when the sea was clean and fish were plentiful and cheap and the pavements were full of bonito from the Bosphorus, you'd see fish-and-bread vendors not just on rowboats tied to the shore but in neighborhood centers and outside football stadiums.

In the sixties, a childhood friend of mine who was crazy about street food would sometimes smile with his mouth full of it and pronounce the defiant mantra: "It's the dirt that gives it flavor!" In so saying he was offering a defense against the sadness and guilt of eating food made far from your mother's kitchen.

When I've been eating and enjoying street food, what I feel most strongly is the sin of solitude. The mirrors they put along the walls of these long narrow counters to make them seem larger make my sin seem larger too. When I was fifteen and sixteen and stopped in these places on my way to see a film alone, I would look at myself standing there, eating my hamburger and drinking my *ayran,* and see that I was not handsome, and I would feel alone and guilty and lost in the city's great crowds.

CHAPTER TWENTY-FIVE

Bosphorus Ferries

When I take a ride on an Istanbul ferry, I never feel as if I am traveling through the city; rather, I sense my place inside it; I see the way my life fits in with the other lives around me. I know that my place is on the shores of the Bosphorus, the Golden Horn, and the Sea of Marmara, the great masses of water that give Istanbul its shape. All those buildings—windows and doors—that make this city what it is: Their meaning depends on their closeness to these seas and waterways, their height, their points of view. It's the same with all those people who live in its houses and walk its streets: In one corner of their minds they know how near or how far they are from those waters. As for those who can see those waters from their windows (and in the old days, they weren't just a happy minority), whenever they look at the city ferries going up and down, they feel as if the city is a center, a threshold, a whole; they sense that everything is going to turn out more or less all right.

So this is why, when we step onto one of those ferries that we watch night and day, to go from one side of the city to the other or to set out on an excursion, we enjoy the pleasure of seeing from the outside our place in the city's inner world. So if forty years earlier, my brother and I were on a ferry going from the islands to Karaköy, we'd breathlessly wait to see which of us would first see the tall buildings of our neighborhood and the windows of our own house. To get a better view of the streets we knew, the high-rise buildings and the billboards, we would go to the ferry's top deck, to a place near the captain's bridge, but when we caught sight of them our spirits would drop. Seen from the decks of a moving ship, the streets in which we had spent our entire lives, those great buildings we'd seen so many times that their shapes were engraved together in our memories, those billboards we read over and over from morning till night—they all seemed less important and more ordinary. The childish excitement of seeing your own street and your own house from a distance (and I still feel this excitement every time I step onto a ferry) was overshadowed by a bleak thought: If the city's millions of windows and its hundreds of thousands of buildings all resemble one another, your life is more like other lives than you ever could have imagined.

If the sight of the city from the deck of the ferry reminded us how much we were like others, the sight of the city from one of those millions of identical windows told us the exact opposite; it awakened in us the desire to be different, to be unique. For when we watched the city ferries darting up and down its waterways, moving all alone through the middle of the city, we felt free. My uncles and my father knew the names and numbers of each of the forty-odd to my eye identical vessels, and they could identify them from their silhouettes even from very far away. One chimney stack was just a little longer than the others, or else it sloped just a bit more; some had captain's bridges that were set a bit higher or their stern was a bit broader. When my father guessed the name and number of an approaching ferry that was still no more than a silhouette on the horizon and, awestruck, we asked him to tell us his secret, we soon found out how hard it was to master these tiny differences. My father and my uncles each had one particular ferry he thought of as his own, and when he saw this ferry chugging down the Bosphorus, he would be as glad as if he'd seen his lucky number, and he'd proceed to tell us children about the history of this ferry and what distinguished it. Were we able to notice and appreciate the fine lines of its smokestack and the elegance in its curves? Could we see how it listed slightly to the rise when riding with the current? When the ferry came very close to the shore, when it turned around Akıntıburnu, where we were standing, we would all wave to the captain. In those days there was an official who stood on Akıntıburnu and signaled to the city-line ferries with green and red flags.

These ferries ran on coal, and from their smokestacks came thick black smoke. On windless days, this dark smoke would hang in the sky, tracing the curves of a journey down the Bosphorus. In my childhood and youth, when my dream was to become a painter, after I finished a watercolor of a Bosphorus view, the ultimate joy was in adding the smoke that poured from the ferries to spread across the sky.

After our father's and our uncles' examples, my brother and I each marked a ferry of our own. The ferries that we so rejoiced to see, wherever we caught sight of them, and that we would report seeing to each other, were roughly the same age as we were, and they had been traveling between the Bosphorus and the islands since the 1950s. The *Paşabahçe,* which had been brought from Liverpool and could be distinguished from its two brothers by its flat smokestack, was "my" ship, and on one summer evening in 1958, following a request my uncle made to its captain, it blew its horn twice just as it was passing our house in Heybeliada. My uncle, having met the captain but one day before this and talked him into it, alerted me in advance, and I spent the whole day in anxious waiting before the evening the *Paşabahçe* was to pass before us. In that early evening of late summer, when I looked through the pine trees and saw the ship emerging from the lights of the island behind it, I rushed toward the shore, to wait trembling at the top of the garden steps. I shall never forget the two blows of its horn when it was between the two islands—the first somber, the second time angry—in exactly the place that I expected. The blast, which had come from deep within the ferry, echoed between the mountains and the islands in the still and windless night, and then there was a silence, and for a moment I was at one with all nature, with all the world, as if in a dream, before I heard the cries coming from twenty yards away, from the table among the trees next to the kitchen where my large family (my grandmother, my uncle, my mother, my father, and the others) were eating supper, cries applauding the ferry that had sent me its greetings. I can still see the *Paşabahçe* from my office windows once or twice a day.

Though the *Paşabahçe* has been traveling out to the islands and up and down the shores of the Bosphorus for fifty years now, the sense of continuity and elegance that the ferries gave us is slowly disappearing. Many of the old Bosphorus landing stages have been closed, some have been turned into restaurants, and a few others were mercilessly ripped up and demolished. As for the ferries that my uncles and my father knew by their numbers and their silhouettes, except for one or two that have been converted into restaurants for tourists, they are all gone, disappeared, sent to the scrapyard. But there are still some old ferries working the Bosphorus, and there are still hundreds of thousands of passengers who, lining their sides, watch the city slip past house by house, who go out on deck to breathe in the bracing Bosphorus air, who sit in these ferries drinking tea on their way to work every morning. Behind the Bosphorus ferries that I can see from my office, especially on winter days, I can see a welcome mass of white spots. The seagulls are masters at catching the *simits,* or sesame rings, and bread crumbs that are thrown to them. There is always someone on the Bosphorus ferries in winter throwing crumbs to the seagulls. What is disappearing are the one-to-one relationships these ferries forged with people who saw them not as ships but as characters. In the old days, when these three-deck ferries passed in front of *yalıs,* the captain on the uppermost deck would come eye to eye with the daydreaming housewife stoking her stove. Now, passengers traveling in the fast catamarans that were brought from Norway, whose interiors all resemble silent airless cinemas, do not look out the windows but at the television inside.

I love the Bosphorus ships most when they are docked at night to nest. If we are sitting at a *meyhane* next to the landing station, the ferry will poke its long high nose into our conversation like a curious authoritarian father, or so we think, as we glance every so often in its direction. Then, while the captain smokes a cigarette in his cabin, the crew hoses down the deck. If it's very late and very hot, a crew member will be sleeping in his pajamas on a bench on a landing stage across which thousands raced all day long, while another sits on the bench opposite and smokes a cigarette as he gazes into the darkness of the Bosphorus. At that time of night, the silence—and the ferry, moored to the landing stage with ropes—calls to mind a beautiful person, asleep in good health.

CHAPTER TWENTY-SIX

The Islands

A week after I was born, I was taken to Heybeliada; here I spent the summer of 1952. My grandmother had a large two-story house surrounded by a garden, in the middle of the forest and very near the sea. A year later I was photographed taking my first steps on the balcony of this house, which was as wide as a veranda. In 2002, the date of this essay, I rented a house in Heybeliada as I had before, not far from the one at which I stayed as a child. I have spent many of the fifty summers between then and now on the Princes Islands—in Burgaz, Büyükada, and Sedefada as well as Heybeliada—writing many novels. There is a corner on the wall of the balcony of that first house in Heybeliada on which my cousins and I would mark our heights every summer. Although it was sold after a string of family feuds, business failures, and inheritance disputes, I still go to see that house from time to time, to find the marks we made on that wall to see how much we'd grown.

For me, the Istanbul summer begins with the departure for the islands. Before this can happen, school has to close and the sea has to be warm enough for swimming—and the price of cherries and strawberries has to have fallen substantially. In my childhood the preparations for going to the islands would take much longer than they do today. Because there was no refrigerator in the island house—for in those days a refrigerator was an expensive Western luxury—my grandmother would first defrost her Nişantaşı refrigerator and then porters would come to the house, wrap it up in sacking, and, with blocks and pulleys, lower it onto their shoulders; pots and pans would be wrapped in newspapers, carpets would be mothballed and rolled up, and over the continuous roars of the washing machine, the vacuum cleaner, arguments, and repair work, the armchairs, wooden furniture, and curtains of the winter house would be covered with newspaper to protect them from the summer sun. When, after all this, we finally rushed onto one of those ferries whose particular shape we knew on sight, I would be unbearably agitated. That ninety-minute trip we took at the start of every summer felt endless. As we breathed in the cool sea air, the smell of moss and spring, my brother and I would walk the full length of the ferry once or twice, next we would beg my grandmother or my mother to buy us each a soda from one of the white-shirted vendors wandering about with their trays, and then we would go down below to chat with our cook—who would be waiting with our suitcases, trunks, and refrigerator, and when the ferry made its first stops at Kınalı and Burgaz, we would watch the ropes being tied and the quayside goings-on, giving grave attention to every last detail.

Every city has a sound that can be heard in no other, a sound that all those living in the city know well and share like a secret—the metro whistle in Paris, the buzz of motorcycles in Rome, and the strange whir of New York—and Istanbul too has a sound that all its residents know intimately; it is the metallic whine they have been hearing for sixty years whenever a ferry docks at any of the little wooden tire-ringed landing stations. When the ferry at last reached Heybeliada, my brother and I would rush across the quay to the island, paying no attention to our grandmother and our mother, calling from behind for us to take care not to trip and take a spill.

It was in the middle of the nineteenth century that the Istanbul rich and the city's upper middle classes began taking excursions to and building summer homes on the islands. Until the end of the eighteenth century, it was only large oared freight caïques that made the trip, which took half a day from the Tophane shore. In earlier days, the islands were places of exile for defeated Byzantine emperors and politicians; except for the prisons, monasteries, monks, vineyards, and small fishing villages, these were empty places. From the beginning of the nineteenth century, the islands began to serve as summer resorts for Istanbul's Christians and Levantines, as well as for those connected to various embassies. In 1894, after the English-made steam ferries were put into daily summertime service, the travel time between Istanbul and Büyükada went down to between an hour and a half and two hours. With the arrival of "express" service in the 1950s, the Istanbul rich were able to return to their islands every evening in forty-five minutes—a far cry from the half-day journey that Byzantine emperors, empresses, and princes would take by caïque perhaps once in a lifetime, not to mention would-be sovereigns whose eyes had been burnt out after a botched attempt to seize the throne. In the 1960s and 1970s, when the rich of Istanbul had yet to discover Antalya, Bodrum, or the southern coast, it was so difficult to find a place on the evening ferry leaving from Karaköy that men of importance would send along a manservant to hold a place, ceding it to his esteemed employer when he arrived. Whether they were Jewish, Christian, or Muslim, members of the city's wealthy classes were unlikely to have been in the habit of reading; left to pass the time by smoking and gazing at the sea and one another, these naturally entrepreneurial commuters would also liven things up by organizing lotteries and raffles. The prizes were enormous pineapples or bottles of whiskey—both symbols of luxury as they were not generally available. I remember my uncle returning to the Heybeliada house one evening, smiling and holding the huge lobster he had won.

From the beginning of the 1980s, when the Sea of Marmara became polluted, the largest of the islands, Büyükada, slowly ceased to be a place where the rich could stroll about in the evening, heedlessly flaunting the class credentials that were their European clothes. One afternoon in the summer of 1958, we were picked up in a flashy yacht and taken with our mother and father to a party on the shores of Büyükada. I remember seeing beautiful women stretched out along the shore in their bathing suits, rubbing oil on themselves, and rich men hailing one another and joking so confidently, and white-coated waiters offering them drinks and canapés on trays. Heybeliada was the home of the Naval Academy and favored by military families and bureaucrats, and perhaps this is why Büyükada always seemed richer to me; as I walked down its streets, looking at the cheese imported from Europe and the black-market whiskey, listening to the music and the happy chatter pouring out of the Anatolian Club, I sensed that this was the place where the "truly rich" spent their time. It was during my childhood, when shame and greed caused me to notice all degrees of difference, between the horsepower of one outboard motor and another, between the gentlemen who stepped into horse-drawn carriages after arriving and those who walked, between the women who went out to do the shopping and those fine ladies who had others to do this for them.

Aside from their sumptuous mansions, their beautiful gardens, and their palm and lemon trees, the thing that lends these resort islands an atmosphere altogether different from the rest of Istanbul is their horse-drawn carriages. When I was a child, I'd rejoice whenever I was allowed to sit next to the driver; as I played in our garden, I would imitate the bells on the reins, the clop of horseshoes, and the driver's gestures. Forty years later, I would play the same games with my daughter on these same islands. The horse-drawn carriages are the same today as they were then, cheap, quiet, and practical, and to love them you must learn to accept the strong smell of horse manure in the markets, the crowded streets, and the depots—learn, even, to love it enough to seek it out, so that when, in the course of a journey, the tired (and sometimes cruelly whipped) horse elegantly raises his tail to drop a steaming hot load on the avenue, you are happily childish enough to smile.

Until the start of the nineteenth century, the islands were mainly where Greek priests, seminarians, and fishermen wintered. When, after the 1917 revolution, White Russians started settling on some of the islands, the villages began to grow, filling up with flashy restaurants and nightclubs. The Heybeliada Naval Academy was founded, as were several TB clinics; the city's Jewish community moved en masse to Büyükada and the Armenian community to Kınalı. There followed another influx of people to serve the tourists, and though the islands grew more crowded, their essential character did not change.

Since the powerful İzmit earthquake of 1999 made itself felt on the islands, and it became widely known that the next great one would very likely strike even closer, the islands have progressively emptied out. I love imagining them in the autumn, when the primary and middle schools reopen and the high season comes to an end, allowing me to enjoy the sadness of the empty gardens; I love imagining the early evenings and the winters.

Last year, on one of those very autumn days, I was wandering among the empty gardens and verandas of Heybeliada when I remembered how, as a child, I would gobble up the figs and the grapes that families had not managed to pick before returning to Istanbul. It was a sad joy to enter the empty gardens of families we had known from afar, never having had the opportunity to become acquainted—to climb their stairs, swing on their swings, and view the world from their balconies. After this walk last year, so much like the ones I had taken as a child, jumping from wall to wall, I went into İsmet Pasha's house, which I had visited only once before—a vague memory of having come with my father forty-five years earlier and of the former president taking me on his lap to kiss me. The walls of this house were now adorned with photographs from the pasha's days as a politician and statesman, alongside holiday photographs of him jumping into the sea from a caïque in his black swimsuit with its single suspender. What unnerved me was the silence and the emptiness, so much like the end of summer on Heybeliada, surrounding the house. Its bathtubs, sinks, and kitchen fittings, its well, its cistern, its floor cover-ings, its old cupboards, its window moldings, and so many other details, amid the faint smell of mold, dust, and pine—everything reminded me of the family home that was no longer ours.

Each summer, at the end of August and the beginning of September, the flocks of storks flying south from the Balkans go straight over the islands. Now, as in my childhood, I go out to the garden to admire the mysterious fortitude in the unheard flapping of these pilgrims' wings. When I was a child it would be two weeks after the passing of the last flock when we would make our forlorn return to Istanbul. Once we reached home, I would pick the sun-bleached newspapers from the win-dowpanes, and as I read the news now three months old, I would fall into a trance and think how very slowly time passed.

CHAPTER TWENTY-SEVEN

Earthquake

I was awoken between midnight and dawn—at 3 a.m., as I was later to discover—by the first jolts. It was August 17, 1999, I was in my study in our stone house on Sedef, the little island just next to Büyükada, and my bed, which was three yards from my desk, was swaying violently like a rowboat caught in a storm at sea. A terrifying groan came from underground, from what seemed to be right under my bed. Without pausing to find my glasses, following instinct more than reason, I rushed outdoors and began to run.

Outside, behind the cypress and pine trees just before me, among the lights of the distant city, and on the surface of the sea, the night was juddering. It was as if everything was happening at once. While one part of my mind was registering the earthquake in all its violence and listening to the noise coming from the earth, another confused part was asking, Why has everyone started shooting at this time of night? (The bombs, assassinations, and nighttime raids of the 1970s may have caused me to associate gunfire with disaster.) Afterward I thought a great deal but without success about what could have sounded so much like automatic weapons fire.

The first tremors lasted forty-five seconds, claiming thirty thousand lives; before they were over, I had climbed the side steps to the upper floor where my wife and daughter were sleeping. They were awake and waiting in the darkness, afraid and not knowing what to do. The electricity had failed. Together we went out into the garden and the enveloping silence of the night. The awful roar had stopped, and it was as if everything around us were likewise waiting in fear. The garden, the trees, this little island surrounded by high rocks—silence in the dead of night, but for the light rustling of the leaves and my pounding heart, which spoke of something terrifying. In the dark under the tress, we whispered with a strange hesitance—fearful, perhaps, of provoking another earthquake. There followed a few gentle tremors; these did not scare us. Later, lying in the hammock with my seven-year-old daughter sleeping in my lap, I heard the sirens of ambulances coming from the Kartal shore.

In the days that followed, through the endless succession of after-shocks, I listened to many others recounting their movements during those lethal first forty-five seconds. Twenty million had felt the first quake and heard that roar from underground, and later, when they got in touch with one another, it wasn't the astonishing casualty figures they discussed but those forty-five seconds. Most of them said, "You can't understand it unless you've lived through it."

A pharmacist emerged untouched from an apartment building that had been reduced to rubble, and what he said was consistent with the testimony of two others who also emerged unharmed from the same building; he hadn't hallucinated. His five-story building had jumped into the air—he had felt this very distinctly—and then it had fallen back in place and crumbled. Some had awoken to find themselves and their houses lurching surreally from side to side; as the structures began to topple the inhabitants prepared to die, but when the building next door broke its neighbor's fall these people found themselves clinging to a corner of something. In relief they threw their arms around one another; some corpses later recovered from the rubble would attest to this too. Every-thing—pots, televisions, cupboards, bookcases, ornaments, wall hang-ings—was wrenched from its moorings, so the mothers, sons, uncles, and grandmothers who went frantically searching for one another were hit by they knew not which of their own belongings and were bumping into new walls they did not recognize. These walls, which had changed shape in an instant, shedding all their objects; the overturned furniture; the clouds of dust and the darkness—all this turned the houses into very different places, causing many to lose their bearings, though within the space of forty-five seconds some did manage to race down several flights and escape to the street before the building collapsed.

I heard stories about a grandfather and a grandmother lying in bed awaiting death, of people who walked out onto what they thought was a fourth-floor balcony only to find themselves on a ground-floor terrace, of people who were opening their refrigerators just as the first tremors began and wound up spitting out whatever they had put into their mouths before they even had the chance to chew it. A surprising number reported being awake and standing somewhere inside their houses just before the first tremor hit. Others reported struggling though the darkness until fear at the violent shuddering got the better of them and they fell to the floor, not daring to move a muscle. Quite a few people claimed not even to have risen from their beds; with peaceful smiles, they told me they had put the sheets over their heads and left it to Allah—and many of the dead were found in this position.

All these stories came to me by word of mouth, via Istanbul's rapid gossip networks; people talked of nothing but the earthquake all day long. The morning after the fact, all the leading private television stations had helicoptered camera teams into the stricken areas; they ran the footage continuously. On my little island, and on the larger and more populated ones around us, there were very few casualties, but the epicenter was only twenty-five miles away as the crow flies. On the shore just across from us, many badly constructed buildings had collapsed and many people had died. All day, in the Büyükada market, a fearful, guilty silence reigned. I could not take in the fact that the earthquake had been so close and taken so many lives, that it had struck places where I had spent large parts of my childhood, and my disbelief frightened me all the more.

Most of the damage occurred in the Gulf of İzmit. It is crescent-shaped, and if we were to imagine it as the crescent on the Turkish flag, the group of islands to which my little one belongs would be located where the star sits. I was brought to one of these islands a week after I was born, and over the next forty-five years have visited and stayed on several of them and at many varied places along the gulf. The city of Yalova, much loved by Atatürk for its thermal springs and famous during my childhood for its ersatz Western hotel, was now in ruins. The petrochemical plant where my father had once been the director—I could remember when it was just a field and how the empty plot sprouted refineries—was in flames. The little towns along the crescent-shaped gulf, the villages we'd visit, on car trips or in a motorboat, to do our shopping, the entire shoreline would go on to be filled with huge apartment houses, while the districts I described with sad affection in *The Silent House* were later turned into huge summer resorts. Now many of these buildings had been razed or rendered uninhabitable. If, for two days, my mind refused to take all this in, struggling to deny the enormity of the catastrophe, perhaps the novel I was working on at that time was to blame. For its sake I did not wish to leave my little island, where life carried on as silently as before.

On the second day, I could not hold myself back any longer. First we crossed over to Büyükada in a little motorboat, and then we made the hour-long crossing on a scheduled ferry to Yalova, on the opposite shore. No one had asked me or the friend accompanying me, the author of a book entitled *In Praise of Hell,* to make this trip; neither of us intended to write about what we saw or even tell anyone about it. We were moved only by the desire to draw near to the dead and dying, to leave our happy little island and observe, perhaps mitigate, the horror. On the ferry, as everywhere else, people were reading the papers and talking in hushed tones about the earthquake. The retired postmaster sitting next to us said he had a little shop on Büyükada that sold dairy products from Yalova, where he lived. Now, two days after the earthquake, he was returning home to see whether there were any cupboards or other furnishings that had collapsed in a dangerous way.

Once Yalova was a small town whose shores were lined with trees and whose meadows provided Istanbul with its fruits and vegetables. Over the past thirty years, the greenery has given way to earth and concrete; the fruit trees have been chopped down, making way for thousands of apartment buildings; and the city's summer population has swelled to almost half a million. The moment we set foot in the city, we saw that nine in ten of these concrete monoliths had either been reduced to rubble or were so badly damaged as to preclude entry. We were soon to see the hopelessness of the dream we had secretly nurtured—that we might be able to help someone, grab on to the corner of a piece of debris and help to lift it: After two days there were hardly any people still alive underneath the rubble. What few there were could be reached only by the German, French, and Japanese teams who'd come with the necessary expertise. More important still, the disaster's effect had been so pervasive that unless someone took you by the arm and begged a particular service, it was impossible to see what you could do.

There were many people like us, wandering in shock, up and down the street: With them we walked among the collapsed, overturned, and pulverized buildings; the cars crushed by rubble; the toppled walls, electric poles, and minarets; stepping over pieces of concrete, broken glass, and the telephone and electric wires that covered every street. In small parks, empty lots, and the gardens of lycées, we saw pitched tents. We saw soldiers, some blocking streets and some picking up rubble. We saw people wandering about bewildered, looking for now nonexistent addresses, people looking for lost loved ones, people parsing blame for this disaster, people fighting over a place to pitch a tent. Through the streets came a continuous stream of traffic: emergency vehicles with boxed milk and tinned food, trucks full of soldiers, cranes and bulldozers to remove the pulverized debris that had sunk into the cobblestones. Just as children immersed in a game will forget the rules of the real world, so strangers struck up conversations that broke all rules of etiquette. The disaster had made everyone feel they were living in an alien world. It was as if the most secret and cruel laws of life had been exposed like the furniture in those houses whose walls had been destroyed or toppled.

I gazed for a long time into the buildings lying on their sides, buildings that had half disappeared or were leaning against those beside them as in a toy model of a city some child had mischievously arranged, buildings whose tops had crashed into buildings across the street and whose facades had fallen away. Machine-made carpets, hanging from their perches like flags on a windless day, broken tables, divans, chairs, and other sitting room furnishings, pillows faded with dust and smoke, over-turned televisions, flowerpots and flowers sitting in perfect condition on the balconies of completely ruined houses, awnings that had buckled and bent like rubber, vacuum cleaners whose hoses stretched out into the void, bicycles crushed into corners, open wardrobes displaying dresses and shirts in brilliant colors, robes and jackets hanging on the backs of closed doors, tulle curtains, rustling in the breeze as if nothing had happened. . . . As we wandered from one house to the next, staring trans-fixed at the exposed interiors, the cross section exposed how fragile life is, how ill defended against the works of evil. We sensed how much our lives depended on the decisions of men whom we mostly despised. All those filthy contractors, those crooked bribe-taking councils and unregu-lated construction firms, those lying politicians we had been complain-ing about for so many years—they'd come from among us, from inside us, and our censure had not protected us from their evil.

We walked for a long time from street to street, feeling that the disas-ter had changed history and our hearts in a way that could never be undone. Sometimes we would enter a small street whose houses were half standing—not yet totally collapsed but condemned all the same—or a back garden blanketed with fragments of glass, concrete, and crockery, where a pine tree had been pinned down but not snapped by a toppled building, a scene I would imagine the lady of the house beholding as she looked out at the garden through a back window while she worked in her kitchen. The familiar sights—the old lady at the kitchen window oppo-site; the old man watching television in the same corner every evening; the girl behind the half-open curtain—they were gone now, because the kitchen across the way, the corner, the tulle curtain, which we'd been watching from this angle for so many years, were themselves gone. Most probably, those who had once enjoyed these views were gone too.

The survivors—those who had managed to hurl themselves out of these buildings without killing themselves—were now sitting on walls and street corners and chairs salvaged from who knows where, waiting for those still inside to be rescued. "My parents are over there," said one young man, pointing at an indistinct pile among the slabs of collapsed concrete. "We're waiting for them to be pulled out." Another said that he had come from Kütahya to find his mother's apartment house shattered; after pointing out where it had once stood, he said, "We'll be going as soon as we have claimed the body!"

Everyone who is walking the city streets—standing in front of the ruins; helplessly watching the emergency aid teams, the cranes, the soldiers; sitting dazed among the refrigerators, televisions, furniture, and boxes full of clothes recovered from their houses—everyone is waiting for something. Waiting for news of lost acquaintances, waiting to be sure their mother really is inside the building (perhaps she left the building in the middle of the night—before the earthquake—and went somewhere else, even though this would have been entirely out of character); waiting for the body of an uncle, a brother, a son, so they can put this place behind them; waiting to see whether, when the team gets here with digging equipment, they can extract some of their belongings, some of their valuables, from the heaps of dust and broken concrete; waiting for someone to find a pickup truck so they can cart off whatever they've been able to salvage; waiting for the aid workers to arrive and for the roads to open, so that some serious emergency teams can get through and rescue the wife or the brother who is still alive under that rubble. Though television and the press have done much to exaggerate such miracles, the truth is that by the end of the third day, there is little hope of rescuing anyone still alive. This despite the voices that can be heard, the noises by which those hanging on make their presence known.

There are two types of ruins. There are the ones that are lying on their sides like discarded boxes, that still recall their original form, though some of their floors have collapsed into one another like the folds of an accordion; in buildings like these, it is still possible to find survivors in the air pockets. In the other type of ruin, there are no layers, no blocks of concrete, and it is impossible to guess the shape of the building as it once was; it is just a heap of powder, iron, broken furniture, tiny scraps of concrete. It is impossible to believe there could be any still-living survivor inside it. One by one, they pluck out the bodies from these piles of rubble; it's slow work, like digging a well with a needle. As the soldiers slowly lift up a slab of concrete with a crane, the building's former inhabitants and those looking for the bodies of their loved ones look on with sleep-deprived eyes. When a body emerges, they say, "He was in there crying all day yesterday, but no one came!" Sometimes there is digging equipment, sometimes there are only car jacks, iron rods, or picks to probe the empty spaces. Before they find the body, they find the deceased's personal effects: a framed wedding photograph, a box with a necklace inside, clothes, and the dense stink of a corpse. Whenever they open up a hole in the concrete, and an expert or a heroic volunteer goes in to search with a flashlight, a ripple goes through the crowd waiting around the ruin; everyone starts talking, and there are cries and shouts. The volunteer who has gone inside, who usually has no personal relation to the building but who just happened to hear a noise coming from somewhere inside it, now asks for help from the front-end loader or the men who are digging by hand, but because of all the noise it's impossible to hear what he is asking for. All this takes such a long time, people soon realize that to lift each stone and each body out of this rubble could take months. But with the corpses stinking so, and the fear of epidemic, this will be impossible. Most probably, there will come a moment when the remaining corpses will be shoveled up with the rest of the rubble—the broken concrete, the household goods, the stopped clocks, the bags, the shattered televisions, the pillows, curtains, and carpets—and carted off to some distant place for burial. Part of me wishes to act as if none of this is happening, to forget everything I have seen, while another part wants to witness everything I can and then tell others.

We saw people walking down the street talking to themselves, people sleeping in cars they had moved to an empty lot, and people who had taken furniture and food out of half-wrecked houses and arranged it along the pavement. In the center of the stadium, which the helicopters we saw flying back and forth over our heads used for a landing field, we saw people lying in a makeshift hospital; just next to this hospital were row after row of buildings turned to dust. We ran into a friend who is a photographer and married to a writer; he was heading toward the home of his wife's father, taking pictures as he went. That old house was safe and sound; the father-in-law told us about the noise he had heard coming from the dust and rubble in the middle of the night. We ran into other people we knew, and in the empty garden of a little half-wrecked house we plucked sweet dusty grapes and ate them.

Seeing us, seeing the cameras, everyone cried, "Journalists, write this down!" and then they vented their complaints about the state, the councils, the thieving contractors; their voices were loudly echoed in the media but it was all too likely that the politicians, state officials, and bribe-taking mayors being railed against would again run for office and again find favor with these voters. It was also likely that these people complaining so bitterly had at some point in their lives paid bribes to the city council to circumvent the construction codes and would have considered it stupid not to do so. In a country where presidents speak well of bribes, calling them "practical," in a culture that runs on informal arrangements and in which swindles are bemoaned but tolerated, one can hardly expect contractors to eschew substandard iron and concrete, stay within the law, and thereby sustain higher costs, all in the name of preparing for a hypothetical earthquake that might harm others in the future. According to one earthquake myth—disseminated widely by word of mouth and popular because it cast homeowners as innocent victims—all but one of the buildings put up by a certain contractor were destroyed, the sole surviving building being the one in which the contractor himself lived.

Having taken no precautions whatsoever before the earthquake, and having failed to mobilize a proper rescue effort afterward, the state has lost a great deal of popular respect. But because so many have, in their helplessness, a deep commitment to the dream of a higher power that will look after them, as Allah does, we can expect the state to regain its standing without undue exertion to earn it. One might say the same of the army, which was late in bringing help and was not much in evidence in the beginning, partly because many of its own buildings were destroyed. The national pride, the country's self-confidence—these too were badly shaken in the quake. In quite a few places, I heard people saying, "The Germans and the Japanese got help to us on time, but not our own state!" I read the same words in the press. What reasons were adduced? "We're just not organized," said one old man, for he knew resignation heals better than anger; when bread was going moldy in one part of the city, in another part there was a bread shortage. As people lay under concrete, crying for help and slipping away, rescue vehicles were stranded without fuel or stuck in faraway traffic jams.

We saw one man driving his dusty old car very slowly through the back streets; upon approaching a ruin that had caught his eye, he stopped and shouted at the crowd through his window. "How many times did I tell you that Allah's wrath was upon you, that you should renounce sin?"

Some people in the crowd gave him a lecture fierce enough to send him on his way, and off he went in angry triumph to the next ruin. I read an article by a like-minded analyst who held that the army and the state were being punished for interfering too much in religious matters, and I heard others ask why, if that was the case, had so many mosques and minarets had been destroyed?

Amid all this devastation—these ruins and corpses—there were of course moments of elation. To see a survivor step out of the rubble, even after so much time had passed! To see help coming from all over the country, and help also coming from countries that the state had always tarred as enemies! But the main and unspoken source of joy: to have somehow survived. There were those who by the end of the third day had come to terms with the disaster and begun to think of the future; despite all warnings and prohibitions, they were neatly and cautiously removing their belongings from their former homes. We watched two young men walk into a ground-floor apartment that was lurching 45 degrees to one side and remove a chandelier from the ceiling.

At the quayside, the coffeehouse beneath the big chestnut tree was full to bursting. There, despite all the dead and missing, people allowed themselves the exultation of having survived a disaster. The manager had found a generator and managed to chill refreshments in his refrigerator. The young men who came to our table did not want to talk about the earthquake but about literature and political memories.

On our return, we again saw the retired postmaster who had gone back to check on his property. "I went into our street and looked down it; our house is gone," he said quietly. "There was a twelve-year-old girl beneath the rubble, apparently." He spoke softly, as if this were somehow his fault, and he complained very little.

Later, my friend remarked that an Englishman would complain if it rained during his annual holiday, while a man whose house had disappeared made no complaint at all. We went on to conjecture that it was perhaps because people didn't complain at all that earthquakes in Turkey took so many lives, but we didn't like where our thoughts were taking us. That evening, fearing (along with the entire nation) that there might be another earthquake, we slept outside in our gardens.

When our ferry was in the middle of the crescent-shaped gulf, I noticed how many new inhabitants these shores had accumulated since my childhood, and how, with their identical concrete apartments, the towns had merged to become one continuous city. The entire area now lived in fear of what the scientists assured us would be an even deadlier earthquake, whose epicenter would be even closer to Istanbul. It was not clear when this earthquake would strike, but according to the maps in the papers, the all-destroying fault line ran directly underneath the little island we were now approaching.

CHAPTER TWENTY-EIGHT

Earthquake Angst in Istanbul

In the old days, I never stopped to wonder whether the towering minaret I can see from my desk might fall on me. The mosque was built in memory of Süleyman the Magnificent's son, Prince Cihangir, who died at a young age; since 1559 it has stood with its two high minarets at the top of a steep slope overlooking the Bosphorus, serving as a symbol of continuity.

It was my upstairs neighbor who first broached the subject when he came to share his earthquake angst with me. Half in panic and half in jest, we went out to the balcony to estimate the distance. In the space of four months, there had been two major earthquakes in Istanbul and countless aftershocks; these and the death toll of thirty thousand were still very much on our minds. What's more (and I could read this in the eyes of my engineer neighbor), we both believed what the scientists were telling us: that in the near future, somewhere in the Sea of Marmara and closer to Istanbul, another major earthquake would kill 100,000 people instantaneously.

The crude measurements of the minarets we made with the naked eye did not reassure us. After perusing a few books and encyclopedias, we were reminded that over the past 450 years, the Cihangir Mosque (that "symbol of continuity") had twice been destroyed by earthquakes and fires, and there was no trace of the original mosque in the dome or the minarets standing across from us. A bit more research, and we discovered that most of Istanbul's historic mosques and monuments had been destroyed at least once by earthquakes (including Hagia Sophia, whose dome collapsed in an earthquake that struck the city twenty years after it was built) and that quite a few of them had been destroyed more than once and later rebuilt "to withstand more pressure."

As for minarets, the story was much worse. In all of the worst earthquakes that had struck the city in the past five hundred years—including the "little day of judgement" that hit the city in 1509 and the great earthquakes of 1766 and 1894—fallen minarets greatly outnumbered collapsed domes. After the two recent quakes, my friend and I had seen countless fallen minarets, not just on television and in the newspaper but during our visits to the earthquake zone. In most cases, they'd fallen onto neighboring buildings: student hostels where sleepy watchmen were playing backgammon late into the night, houses where mothers had risen from their beds to feed their babies, or (in the case of the second big earthquake in Bolu) families that had gathered around a television to watch on the evening news a discussion of the likelihood of another earthquake, only for a minaret to come down like a cake knife, slicing the room in two.

Of the minarets that had not fallen, most were damaged. Those that were beyond repair were lifted with chains and cranes and destroyed. Because we had watched many minarets fall in slow motion on television, both my neighbor and I knew how minarets fell. The tremors from the next earthquake were expected to come from the Bosphorus and the Sea of Marmara, as I've said. So my neighbor and I set out to calculate the angle at which our minaret would fall, trying to factor in past mishaps: The section just above the balcony had buckled slightly during the August earthquake; an earlier bolt of lightning had struck the stone just beneath the star and crescent, sending it flying into the courtyard below.

All factors considered, it was clear to us that, if the minaret were indeed to fall at the angle we had divined using our hands and a bit of string, it would not hit us: Our building, which looked out on the Bosphorus, was simply too far from the minaret, farther than the height of the structure. "So there's no chance that the minaret would fall on us," said my neighbor, as he took his leave. "Actually, it's far more likely that our building will fall onto the minaret."

In the days that followed—as I carried on with my research, trying to determine whether the building in which I worked would collapse onto the minaret, and whether the building in which I lived with my family was as likely to fall as the building in which I worked—I did not seek out my neighbor. This was not because he, like so many other acquaintances, tempered his earthquake angst with dark humor. It was because he, like the rest of us, was engrossed in his own particular way of addressing his fear of death. My neighbor had chipped a corner off our six-story building and sent it to Istanbul Technical University so that the strength of the concrete could be analyzed, and now he was waiting for the results, as were thousands of others who had done the same thing. Having done all that could be done, he found the wait calming; this much I know.

As for me, I assumed that peace of mind would come only with greater knowledge. My visits to the earthquake zones had taught me that buildings had collapsed mainly for two reasons: shoddy construction and poor soil. So, like many others, I set out to discover what sort of soil my home and my office building stood on and how sturdily they'd been built; this I did by speaking to construction engineers, examining maps, and exchanging notes with the many others who, like me, had developed a taste for worry and fear.

Though both epicenters were more than ninety miles outside the city, the two recent earthquakes had shaken all the inhabitants of Istanbul from their sleep; the death toll of thirty thousand had laid bare the construction sector's practice of building shoddily on poor soil without any effort at earthquake proofing. For the twenty million living in the environs of the city, nightmares sprang from the well-founded fear that their homes would be unable to withstand an earthquake of the intensity that the scientists had now forecast. Even if the houses and apartments had been constructed according to the building code (highly improbable), it was not cheering to remember that these rules and regulations had been drawn up to protect against earthquakes far milder than the one we were all now expecting. And so even those homes, put up not by careless and dishonorable contractors, using too little iron and low-quality concrete, but by their own fathers and grandfathers, could not be presumed to be safe. Also, in many apartment buildings, bribes to city councils had made it possible for numerous extra floors to be added and columns and support walls heedlessly removed to create space for shops, making weak buildings even weaker. Furthermore, even if you had definitive proof that your building could not withstand what was expected, even if you had resolved to undertake repairs costing typically a third of the value of your apartment, you would still have to convince your other-minded, cynical, apathetic, depressed, brainless, opportunist, and most probably penniless neighbors to do likewise.

And so, despite the magnitude of the looming danger, I have not met many apartment dwellers in Istanbul who have faced reality and set about making their buildings safe. I do know quite a few earthquake worriers who have failed to persuade not only their neighbors but their wives, husbands, and children. Then there are those who cannot afford to make their homes safe; resigned to their fate, while also stricken with fear, they take refuge in cynicism, saying, "Well, even if I did spend all that money to make my building safe, what if the building across the street fell on us?" It's because of this helplessness, this hopelessness, that millions of *İstanbullus* see earthquakes in their dreams.

My own dreams resemble a great many that others have reported to me. In the dream, you see the bed in which you are sleeping and recall the anxious thoughts you had about earthquakes just before getting into that bed. All at once an earthquake hits; it's huge. You watch as the bed sways back and forth, an earthquake in slow motion as your little room, your house, your bed, and all the things around you lose all sense of place; as they sway, they change shape. Slowly, your perspective widens beyond the room to encompass scenes inspired by the helicopter views of flattened towns ubiquitous on television; it is now that the enormity of the disaster begins to dawn on you. But despite the Judgment Day atmosphere, you are—in the dream as in waking life—secretly happy, because witnessing the earthquake is proof that you survived it. The same holds true for the mother, the father, the spouse who blames the earthquake on your mistaken priorities: They scold you, but they too are still alive. These dreams stem partly from dread and the desire to get it over with, which may explain why so many people recall that, in spite of the terror they felt, they'd also felt cleansed of sin, as they might after a religious observance. Many of those who quake in terror, wafting through that dark zone between wakefulness and sleep, assume that there must have been a real earthquake while they were sleeping, that actual tremors prompted the dream, and if there is no one next to them to wake up and consult, if they are not able to work out whether it was just a dream or the real thing, they'll be sure to scan the newspapers the next morning for the latest reports on aftershocks.

Having convinced ourselves that we cannot ensure the safety of our houses, we have decided that there is only one way to shake off that sense of impending disaster afflicting all earthquake survivors: Go back to the scientists and professors who have warned us that Istanbul is soon to suffer a great earthquake and make them reconsider.

It was Professor Işıkara, the director of Turkey's only big observatory, who first informed us that our fault line was much like the one in California, stretching from one tip of northern Turkey to the other, and that if you charted the big earthquakes of recent times you could see that they'd begun in the east and were coming closer and closer to Istanbul. After the first big earthquake in August 1999, when the entire press

corps was seeking Professor Işıkara out and he spent every evening racing from one television station to the next, reiterating views to which no
one had paid the slightest attention for so many years, the presenters
would all ask him the same question: "So tell me, sir, is there going to be
another earthquake tonight?" In his early appearances, the answer had
always been, "An earthquake can strike at any time." Later—having
scared millions of people out of their wits and seen hundreds jumping
from their windows when a much smaller earthquake hit the city, and having heard complaints from the state about the chaos born of desperation—
he edited himself, and his line became, "It is impossible to say when the
next earthquake will hit." Even so, two days after the great earthquake
that killed thirty thousand people, when the aftershocks became more
intense and the entire nation was watching him on television, we still took
him to be insinuating that there might be another quake that very night, so
we all moved outside to sleep in parks, gardens, and streets. This charming professor, with Einstein's look of disheveled absentmindedness
(though lacking his genius), came to be greatly loved by the people of
Istanbul, because during the days of greatest hopelessness, with the fear
of earthquakes at its height, he bent to the will of its sleepless inhabitants
and gave us a brighter if not very convincing picture (suggesting, for
example, that the fault line might be farther away from Istanbul than previously thought) and smiling whenever he imparted bad news, at all times
speaking in very sweet tones.

Then there were the scientists who stood by their predictions, refusing
to sugarcoat; Professor Şengör was one such expert. He greatly angered
everyone by acting like an unfeeling clinician, describing that first earthquake, the one that killed thirty thousand people, as a "beauty." But the
greater reason to resent scientists like this who refused to soften their
prognostications was the irrefutability of their proof that the impending
earthquake would be enormous and the scolding, almost cruel manner in
which they presented it. Behind this demonic professorial anger was not
just the fact that unsafe buildings housing ten million people had gone up
in the earthquake area without anyone's paying the weak warnings of science any heed, but also that no one had listened to the international press,
which had quoted him 1,300 times. This is why he took on the air of an
angry imam prophesying the punishments that the godless were soon to
suffer.

These scientists were speaking on entertainment programs whose
typical guests were beauty queens and champion bodybuilders, and the

hosts would always interrupt the scientists' detailed analyses to ask, "Sir, is there going to be an earthquake in the near future, and how strong will it be?" On one of the most important news programs on November 14, there was such a ferocious exchange about the latest data on the fault in the Sea of Marmara that Bill Clinton's arrival in Turkey that day was mentioned only briefly in the forty-fifth minute of the show. That program, like so many others, ended by offering no definitive answers to the questions that the host had asked so insistently, so many times, and with the understanding that, for precisely that reason, we could only expect more inconclusive discussions, interrogations, and public declarations.

No scientists showed themselves willing to offer a hope to the public by saying that the earthquake might never come, barring the handful whose science was clearly unreliable, so very slowly the millions of *İstanbullus* living in unsound buildings on unsound soil have come to understand that they have to find their own way of fending off terror. This was how some came to leave the matter to Allah or, with time, simply to forget it, while others now take false comfort in precautions they adopted after the previous earthquake.

Many sleep with gigantic flashlights covered in plastic next to their beds, so that, in the event of an earthquake and a power failure, they can find their way out before fire overtakes them. Next to these flashlights are whistles, to alert rescue teams searching the rubble, and mobile phones. Some hang whistles (and in one case, a harmonica) around their necks. Others also wear their house keys, so that when the earthquake hits they needn't waste time looking for them. Some have stopped shutting their doors, so they can flee without impediment from their two- or three-story houses, while others have suspended ropes from their windows so they can shimmy down to their gardens. During the first months, some were so unnerved by the continual aftershocks that they took to wearing miners' helmets inside their homes. Because the first big quake struck at night, the desire to be prepared was so strong—even among those who lived in apartments so high up that getting downstairs and out with any speed was all but impossible—that they would go to bed fully dressed. I even heard of some so worried about being caught with their pants down that they rushed whenever they were in the toilet or taking a bath, and that some couples, afflicted by a similar worry, lost interest in making love, while others created shelters in which they stored food, drink, hammers, lamps, and so on—everything to escape a big burning city and survive without benefit of electricity and with roads and bridges collapsed. After the earthquake, some took to carrying large quantities of cash. In many homes, corners were deemed unsound and beds were pulled away from walls, clear of overloaded shelves and wardrobes. Shelters were erected next to the vital appliances of refrigerator and oven; in these one was theoretically protected from the ceiling caving in, or so it was claimed in the guides published by newspapers for constructing these "life triangles."

I did much the same thing at one end of the long desk at which I have been writing novels for twenty-five years. With the heaviest books in my library—among them a forty-year-old *Encyclopedia Britannica,* an even older volume of the *Islam Encyclopedia,* and the *Istanbul Encyclopedia* that was one of my sources for the earthquakes of times past—I built a shelter beneath my desk. Having assured myself that it was strong enough to withstand falling concrete, I lay down there for a few earthquake drills, assuming a fetal position as instructed to protect my kidneys. The little earthquake guides also recommended storing biscuits, bottled water, a whistle, and a hammer in a secure corner, but I didn't do any of those things. It was enough that my everyday life was full of these little precautions, bottled this and that. Was my reluctance to bring them to my desk rooted in some vague awareness that such accommodation might sink my morale even faster?

No, my reason was deeper and more mysterious. I've seen glints of it in many people's eyes, though they rarely express it; I'd call it shame, a shame tinged with guilt and self-blame. It is something akin to what you might feel if you had a relative who was an alcoholic criminal or if you'd just suffered sudden financial ruin—your wish to protect yourself would be as strong as your wish to hide the necessity from others. When my friends and publishers outside Turkey wrote to me after the first big earthquake to ask me how I was, it was shame that kept me from giving any sort of answer; I turned in on myself, like a man just diagnosed with cancer, whose first concern is that no one find out. In the early days, if I wanted to discuss the subject, it was only with those who shared my predicament and anxiety about the next big one, people who took the same view of it as I did. Though most of these conversations were more like serial monologues, as we parroted, in anger and agitation, the views of experts whose respective degrees of pessimism and optimism had quickly become common knowledge.

For a while I limited my research to the neighborhoods in which my home and my office are located, seeking to determine how well the ground beneath them had withstood tremors in the past. I was relieved to discover that only a few buildings had collapsed in these neighborhoods in the 1894 earthquake. But when I studied the full inventory of collapsed houses, when I read the names of those whose roofs had fallen in on them—the Greek butchers, the milkmen, the Ottoman soldiers in their barracks—when I learned that all those markets and historic buildings I had visited on so many occasions had been destroyed and later rebuilt, I was overcome with sadness at the brevity of life and the fragility of men and minarets.

There was one little map published by a magazine that had undertaken to depict a disaster gradient for the earthquake to come, and it filled me with fury. It colored my neighborhood the dark shade indicating one of the districts expected to suffer the worst damage. Or was that just how it looked to me? Was it even possible to conclude anything from a map so small and crude? Armed with a magnifying glass, I examined the deadly blot that spread across this wordless map, as far as my street and my house, and tried to determine how it corresponded with more detailed maps. No other map in any other paper, no other source, said my neighborhood was in particular jeopardy. I decided it must be a mistake and tried to forget it. I knew I would have an easier job of this if I mentioned it to no one.

A few days later, I found myself at midnight poring over the same crude map, examining that dark blot through my magnifying glass. My landlord, who had discovered that I was worried about soil quality at the foundation of the building, dug out the photograph he'd proudly had taken with the workmen as they were laying it forty years earlier. Because I'd lived for forty years in that same neighborhood, the photograph brought back many memories, but when I picked up my magnifying glass it was to look for bedrock in the earth. The contradictory statements of the scientists, as well as the media's irresponsible ratings war, had kept the inhabitants of Istanbul caught between anxious despair and excited relief—sleepless one night with a new piece of bad news, and sleepless the next night with an intimation of reprieve (according to the latest satellite pictures, the earthquake would only measure 5 on the Richter scale!). So it was, back and forth, with my research into soil quality under the blot on the map. I yielded to the urging of that magazine's editors not to give so much importance to their crude little map, but I still thought long and hard about how that black spot might have come to fall on my house and my life.

Throughout this period, I'd also kept an ear out for the suspicions and rumors circulating like so many packs of wild dogs through the city. When, in the days following the earthquake, I heard that the sea had grown warmer, proof that another earthquake was imminent, and when I heard of strange correspondences between the earthquake and the previous week's solar eclipse, I merely laughed. "Don't laugh so loud," one angry young girl scolded me, "If there's an earthquake, we won't hear it." One rumor had it that the earthquake was the work of Kurdish separatist guerrillas, another that it was caused by Americans who were now coming to our aid with a huge military hospital ship ("How do you suppose they made it here so fast?" the conspiracy theory went). In one outrageous version, the commander of said ship had looked sadly from the deck and guiltily sighed. "Look what we've done!"

Later on, the paranoid delusions took on a more domestic slant: The janitor who rang your doorbell every morning to deliver your milk and newspapers would announce (in the same voice he used to warn you that the water would be turned off for an hour) that a massive earthquake was predicted for ten past seven that evening, which would destroy the entire city. Or a demonic scientist who'd made no provisions of his own for the upcoming disaster had fled to Europe. Or it would be said that the state, knowing full well what was to come, had secretly imported a million body bags. You would also hear that the military had already sent out earth movers to dig mass graves in open fields outside the city, and that a friend who had doubts about the construction of his house—and of course the soil underneath it—had moved to another building on the same street, only to discover that his new apartment was even more unsafe. In Yeşilyurt, one of Istanbul's richest neighborhoods built on some of its poorest soil, the homeowners attending a meeting to discuss the earthquake had divided into two opposing camps: those who wished to discuss how to protect themselves and those who said that such talk would depress real estate values. It was around the same time that a journalist friend of mine told me that they'd not been able to print the maps I'd wanted to consult while investigating the black stain on that little map, for fear of angering real estate agents and homeowners.

Two months later, my upstairs neighbor at home told me that the university to which he'd sent his concrete sample had sent back a report. The conclusion—as in the case of the inquiry concerning the building in which I had my office—was neither wholly discouraging nor wholly confidence-inspiring. It was up to each of us to decide how to take it, just as it had been a subjective decision on that day to determine whether or not the minaret would fall on us.

At around the same time, I heard that an old friend who worked in the music business had decided, after passing through Gölçük, the town worst hit by the August earthquake, that he could never again set foot in his Istanbul home; he had moved into the Hilton Hotel, which he thought to be of sounder construction, until that place no longer seemed safe enough either and he took to spending his days outside, doing all his business on his mobile phone, racing up and down the street as if he were in a great hurry. It was said that while he hurried along, never stopping, he would mutter, "Why aren't we leaving this city, why aren't we leaving?"

When it had been impressed on us all that, though the epicenter of the first earthquake was sixty-two miles outside the city, thousands of *İstanbullus* had died, there was an exodus from the poorer neighborhoods, and that brought down the rents. But most of Istanbul remains in its mostly unsound buildings, taking no precautions. At this point, everything—the importuning of scientists, the credited rumors, the act of forgetting, the deferment of millennium celebrations, the embrace of lovers, the resignation—everything naturalizes the idea of an earthquake and helps us "live with it," as people now say. The other day, a fresh-faced, recently married, and very cheerful young woman came to my office to discuss a book cover and with great conviction explained her own way of coping.

"You know an earthquake is inevitable, and that makes you fearful," she said, raising her eyebrows. "But you live through each moment by acting as if it's not going to happen at that exact moment. If you don't, you can't do anything. But these two thoughts contradict each other. For example, we all know by now that it is very dangerous to be on a balcony after an earthquake. Even so, I'm now stepping out to the balcony," she told me in a teacher's voice, and then, opening the door slowly and with care, she stepped out onto the balcony. I stayed where I was, and she stood there looking at the mosque across the street and the view of the Bosphorus behind it. "As I stand here," she said more volubly, a few moments later through the open door, "I cannot believe that the earthquake will hit at this precise moment. Because if I did believe this, I would be too frightened to stay here." A while later, she came in from the balcony, shutting the door behind her. "So that's what I do," she said, with the faintest of smiles. "I go out onto the balcony, and while I'm there I manage to score a small victory against the earthquake in my head. It's with little victories like these that we'll defeat that big earthquake still to come."

After she left I went out to the balcony, to admire the minarets and the beauties of Istanbul and the Bosphorus rising from the mist. I've lived in this city my entire life. I've asked myself the same question as that man pacing the streets, about why a person might not be able to leave.

It's because I can't even imagine not living in Istanbul.

BOOKS AND READING

CHAPTER TWENTY-NINE

How I Got Rid of Some of My Books

During the second of the two recent earthquakes—the one that hit Bolu in November—a knocking sound was heard from one end of my library; then for the longest time the bookshelves creaked and groaned. I was lying on the bed in the back room, a book in my hand, watching the naked lightbulb sway above me. That my library should conspire in the earthquake's wrath, that it should confirm and dignify its message—this frightened me, and the apocalyptic intimations made me angry. The same thing had happened during the aftershocks of the previous weeks. I decided to punish my library.

This was how, with a strangely clear conscience, I picked 250 books from my shelves and disposed of them. Like a sultan pacing among a crowd of slaves, singling out the ones to be lashed, like a capitalist pointing out the lackeys to be sacked, I made my selection summarily. What I was punishing was my own past, the dreams I'd nurtured when I'd first found these books and picked them up, bought them, taken them home, hidden them, read them, and labored over them so lovingly, imagining what I would think when reading them in the future. On reflection, this seemed less like punishment than liberation.

The happiness it gave me? This is a good place to begin a discussion of my books and my library. I want to say a few things about my library, but I don't wish to praise it in the manner of one who proclaims his love of books only to let you know how exceptional he is, and how much more cultured and refined than you. And neither do I wish to seem like those ostentatious booklovers who will tell you they found such and such a rare volume in a little secondhand bookstore in the back streets of Prague. Still, I live in a country that views the nonreader as the norm and the reader as somehow defective, so I cannot but respect the affectations, obsessions, and pretensions of the tiny handful who read and build libraries amid the general tedium and boorishness. All that having been said, the matter I wish to discuss here is not how much I love books but how much I dislike them. The best and quickest way to tell this story is to remember how and why I got rid of them.

Since we do—to some degree—arrange our libraries so that our friends will see our books as we want them to be seen, an easy way to clear them out is to decide which books we'd prefer to, shall we say, hide or banish altogether, so that our friends won't see them at all. We can throw large numbers of books away just so no one will know you ever took such nonsense seriously. As we pass from childhood to adolescence and from adolescence to youth, this particular obsession takes hold. When my elder brother gave me the books he was ashamed he'd read as a child, and the bound collections of soccer magazines (like *Fenerbahçe*) that had ceased to interest him, he was killing two birds with one stone. I used the same technique to get rid of many Turkish novels, Soviet novels, bad poetry collections, and sociology texts, not to mention middling examples of village literature, and the left-wing pamphlets I'd collected in the same way as the archivist in *The Black Book*. In the same manner, I dealt with the popular science books I'd bought periodically and the vanity memoirs about how so-and-so found success, which I could not help reading, and various works of refined pornography, without illustrations, first consigning them anxiously to an obscure corner before throwing them away.

When I've decided to throw a book away, the thrill of degradation masks deep grievances not immediately apparent. What is degrading is not the disquieting thought that this book (a Political Confession, a Bad Translation, a Fashionable Novel, a Collection in Which All the Poems Are Alike and Like All Other Poems) is in my library at all, it is knowing that there was a time when I took this book seriously enough to pay money for it, kept it sitting on my shelves for years, and even read some of it. I'm not ashamed of the book itself, I'm ashamed of having once accorded it importance.

Here we come to the real issue: My library is not a source of pride but of self-revenge and oppression. Like those who take pride in their education, I too sometimes take pleasure in looking at these books, passing my hand over them, and picking up some of them to read. In my youth, I would imagine myself posing in front of my books, once I'd become a writer. But now there is only the crushing embarrassment of having invested time and money in them, in having carted them home like a porter and then hidden them away; what makes me most miserable is to know I have been "attached" to them. As I've grown older, I have perhaps begun to throw away books to convince myself that I possess the sort of wisdom to be expected in the owner of a library made up of books he himself has read. But I keep buying books at a faster rate than I throw them away. And so if I were to compare my library to that of a well-read friend in a rich Western country, his would have many fewer books than mine does. Fortunately, for me the imperative is not to own good books but to write them.

A writer's progress will depend to a large degree on having read good books. But to read well is not to pass one's eyes and one's mind slowly and carefully over a text: it is to immerse oneself utterly in its soul. This is why we fall in love with only a few books in a lifetime. Even the most finely honed personal library is made up of a number of books that are all in competition with one another. The jealousies among these books endows the creative writer with a certain gloom. Flaubert was right to say that if a man were to read ten books with sufficient care, he would become a sage. As a rule, most people have not even done that, and that is why they collect books and show off their libraries. Because I live in a country almost devoid of books and libraries, I at least have an excuse. The twelve thousand books in my library are what compel me to take my work seriously.

Among them there are perhaps ten or fifteen books I truly love, but I'm not sentimental about this library. As an image, a collection of furniture, a pile of dust, a tangible burden, I don't like it at all. To feel an intimacy with its contents is like having relations with women whose chief virtue is their being always ready to love us; the thing I love most about my books is that I can pick them up and read them whenever I wish.

Because I fear "attachments" as much as I fear love, I welcome any pretext to get rid of books. But in the past ten years I've found a new excuse, something that never occurred to me before. The authors whose books I bought in my youth and kept and sometimes even read, because they were "our nation's writers," and even quite a few of the writers I read in the years that followed—in recent years they have colluded to assemble proof of how bad my own books are. In the beginning I was happy that they took me so seriously. But now I am glad to have a pretext even better than an earthquake for clearing them out of my library. This is how my Turkish literature shelves are quickly losing works by half-witted, mediocre, moderately successful, bald, male, degenerate writers between the ages of fifty and seventy.

CHAPTER THIRTY

On Reading: Words or Images

To carry a book in your pocket or in your bag, particularly in times of sadness, is to be in possession of another world, a world that can bring you happiness. During my unhappy youth, the thought of such a book—a book I looked forward to reading—was a consolation that helped me through the school day, as I yawned so much my eyes would fill with tears; later on in life, it helped me bear the boring meetings I attended out of obligation or a desire not to be rude. Let me list the things that make reading something I do, not for the purposes of work or for my edification, but for pleasure:

1. The pull of that other world I mentioned earlier. This could be seen as escapism. Even if only in your imagination, it is still good to escape the sadness of everyday life and spend some time in another world.

2. Between the ages of sixteen and twenty-six, reading was central to my efforts to make something of myself, elevate my conscious-ness, and thereby give shape to my soul. What sort of man should I be? What was the meaning of the world? How far could my thoughts stretch, my interests, my dreams, the lands I could see in my mind's eye? While following others' lives, dreams, and rumina-tions in their stories and their essays, I knew I would keep them in the deepest recesses of my memory and never forget them, the way a small child never forgets his first sight of a tree, a leaf, a cat. With the knowledge I gathered from my reading, I would chart my path to adulthood. Having set out with such childish optimism to make and shape myself, my reading during those years was an intense and

playful enterprise that drew deeply from my imagination. But these days I almost never read this way, and perhaps this is why I read so much less.

3. Another thing that makes reading so pleasurable for me is self-awareness. When we read, there is a part of our minds that resists total immersion in the text and congratulates us on our having undertaken such a deep and intellectual task: in other words, reading. Proust understood this very well. There is, he said, a part of us that stays outside the text to contemplate the table at which we sit, the lamp that illuminates the plate, the garden around us, or the view beyond. When we notice such things, we are at the same time savoring our solitude and the workings of our imagination and congratulating ourselves on possessing greater depth than those who do not read. I understand how a reader might, without going too far, wish to congratulate himself, though I have little patience for those who take pride in boasting.

This is why, when I talk of my own reading life, I must say this at once: If the pleasures I describe as 1 and 2 were pleasures I could find in film, television, or other media, perhaps I would read fewer books. Perhaps one day it will be possible. But I think it would be difficult. Because words (and the works of literature they make) are like water or like ants. Nothing can penetrate into the cracks, holes, and invisible gaps of life as fast or as thoroughly as words can. It is in these cracks that the essence of things—the things that make us curious about life, about the world—can first be ascertained, and it is good literature that first reveals them. Good literature is a piece of wise counsel that has yet to be given, and as such it has the same aura of needfulness as the latest news; that is mainly why I still depend on it.

But I think it would be wrong to talk about this pleasure as running counter to—or competing with—the pleasures of watching, of seeing. This may be because, between the ages of seven and twenty-two, I wanted to become a painter and spent those years painting obsessively. For me, to read is to create one's own mental film version of a text. We may raise our heads from the page to rest our eyes upon a picture on the wall, the scene outside the window, or the view beyond, but our minds do not take these things in: We are still occupied with filming the imaginary world in the book. To see the world imagined by the author, to find happiness in that other world, one must bring one's own imagination into play. By giving us the impression of being not just spectators of an imaginary world but in part its creators, a book offers us the creator's bliss in seclusion. And it's that bliss-in-seclusion that makes reading books, reading great works of literature, so alluring to all and so essential to the writer.

CHAPTER THIRTY-ONE

The Pleasures of Reading

This summer I reread Stendhal's *Charterhouse of Parma*. After finishing certain pages of this wondrous book, my eyes would pull back from the old volume in my hand to gaze at its yellowing pages from afar. (In the same way, when I was drinking a favorite soft drink as a child, I would stop from time to time to gaze lovingly at the bottle in my hand.) As I was carrying the book around with me this summer, I asked myself many times why it was such pleasure just to know the book was at my side. Afterward I would ask myself whether it was even possible to speak about the joy I took in it—to do so without first speaking of the novel itself would be like speaking about my love for a woman I had fallen for without first describing her. This is what I'm trying to do now. (Those who wish to separate the novel from the love of reading novels should skip over every parenthetical below.)

1. While following the events described in the story (the Battle of Waterloo, the intrigues of love and power in a small principality), I was overtaken by intense emotion. The source of my happiness lay not in the events themselves but in the spiritual and emotional responses they provoked. I experienced the events as emotions, a sort of synesthesia. I experienced the joy of youth, the will to live, the power of hope, the fact of death, and love, and solitude.

2. As I savored the writer's nuances, the force of his prose, his powers of observation, his élan, his way of going straight to the heart of the matter, and the sharpness of his intelligence, it seemed to me as if he were whispering all his wisdom in my ear, just for me. Though

I knew millions had read this book before me, I felt—for reasons I have not been able to fathom—that in this book there were many passages, many little details, refinements, and understandings, that the writer and I shared and that only the two of us could appreciate. To be so close in mind and spirit to a writer this brilliant gave me confidence, and on this account, as with all happy people, my self-esteem was buoyed up.

3. Certain details of the writer's life (his solitude, his disappointments in love, and the fact that his books were not as well loved as he wished them to be) and the legendary tale about the writing of this novel (Stendhal was said to have based it on old Italian chronicles and dictated it to a secretary over fifty-two days) seemed to me to be the story of my own life.

4. It was not just the affinity I felt with Stendhal that left its mark on me; many of the scenes he narrates, his descriptions of the landscape, and his portrayal of the epoch (the palace interiors, the figure of Napoleon, the lakes outside Milan and its environs, the scenery of the Alps refracted through the author's urban sensibilities, as well as the arguments, the murders, and the political intrigues) stayed with me too. Unlike Proust's hero, I never assumed the identities of other characters or believed these events were happening to me. I was not present in the novel. But from the beginning I enjoyed the excitement of entering a space altogether different from my everyday world, and I studied the interior world of the novel in much the same way as I once studied the liquid inside my soft-drink bottle. This was why I carried the book around with me.

5. I first read this book (*The Charterhouse of Parma*) in 1972. When I looked at the passages I had underlined and the notes I had written in the margins on that first reading, I laughed, a sad laugh at my youthful enthusiasm. But I still felt affection for the young man who had picked up this book then and who, to open his mind to a new world and to become a better person, had read it so eagerly. I preferred that optimistic and still half-formed young man, who thought he could see everything, to the reader I'd become. So whenever I sat down to read the book, we were a crowd: my twenty-year-old self, my confidant Stendhal, his heroes, and me. I liked this crowd.

6. Because it reminded me of the person I had been then, I treasured this book as an object. Its badly produced cover was tattered, and from time to time I would fiddle with the ribbon that served as a page marker. I had written notes inside the back cover all those years ago. I kept going back to them.

7. In this way, the pleasure I derived from reading merged with my enjoyment of the book as an object. That's why I carried it like an amulet that might bring me happiness, even when I was going to places where I would have no time to read. If I was somewhere and feeling bored or upset, I would open the book at random, read a paragraph, and calm down. By now the book's pages and its cover were giving me as much happiness as the words themselves. The book gave me as much happiness as reading it.

8. When, as I sometimes did of an evening on Heybeliada, the small island where we spent our summers, I sat down on a bench on a road no one else used and began to read the book by the light of the streetlamp, I felt the book to be as much part of the natural world as the moon, the sea, and the clouds, trees, bushes, and stone in the walls. Perhaps because it was set in the distant past, the book seemed as natural and as unmannered as a tree or a bird. It cheered me to be so close to nature, and I felt as if the book was improving my character, cleansing me of all life's stupidities and evils.

9. During one such happy moment, as I was gazing at the book from a certain distance—gazing actually not at its yellowed pages but the trees and the dark sea beyond it in the distance—I asked myself what meaning this book could have to make me so happy. Realizing that to ask this question was like asking the meaning of life itself, I felt as if this book had brought me closer to understanding that meaning, close enough to be able to say a thing or two on the subject.

10. The meaning of life is intimately linked with happiness, as are all great novels. As in novels, there is in life a genuine wish, an impulse, a race toward happiness. But there is more to it than that. A person wishes to reflect on that desire, that impulse, and a good novel (like *The Charterhouse of Parma*) is well suited to this purpose. In the end a wondrous novel becomes an integral part of our lives and the world around us, bringing us closer to the meaning of life; it comes in place of the happiness we may never find in living to offer us a joy that derives from its meaning.

11. What makes me happy now is to read a page while keeping all these thoughts somewhere in mind—this despite the fact that I begin to feel as if my happiness threatens to destroy the mystery of the novel.

CHAPTER THIRTY-TWO

Nine Notes on Book Covers

- If a novelist can finish a book without dreaming of its cover, he is wise, well-rounded, and a fully formed adult, but he's also lost the innocence that made him a novelist in the first place.

- We cannot recall the books we most love without also recalling their covers.

- We would all like to see more readers buying books for their covers and more critics despising books written with those same readers in mind.

- Detailed depictions of heroes on book covers insult not just the author's imagination but also his readers'.

- When designers decide that *The Red and the Black* deserves a red and black jacket, or when they decorate books entitled *Blue House* or *Château* with illustrations of blue houses or châteaux, they do not leave us thinking they've been faithful to the text but wondering if they've even read it.

- If, years after reading a book, we catch a glimpse of its cover, we are returned at once to that long-ago day when we curled up in a corner with that book to enter the world hidden inside.

- Successful book covers serve as conduits, spiriting us away from the ordinary world in which we live, ushering us into the world of the book.

- A bookshop owes its allure not to its books but to the variety of their covers.

• Book titles are like people's names: They help us distinguish a book from the million others it resembles. But book covers are like people's faces: Either they remind us of a happiness we once knew or they promise a blissful world we have yet to explore. That is why we gaze at book covers as passionately as we do at faces.

CHAPTER THIRTY-THREE

To Read or Not to Read:
The Thousand and One Nights

I read my first tales from the Thousand and One Nights when I was seven. I had just finished my first year of primary school, and my brother and I had gone to spend the summer in Geneva, Switzerland, where my parents had moved after my father took a job there. Among the books my aunt had given us on leaving Istanbul, to help us improve our reading over the summer, was a selection of stories from the Thousand and One Nights. It was a beautifully bound volume, printed on high-quality paper, and I remember reading it four or five times over the course of the summer. When it was very hot, I would go to my room for a rest after lunch; stretching out on my bed, I would read the same stories over and over. Our apartment was one street away from the shores of Lake Geneva, and as a light breeze wafted in through the open window and the strains of the beggar's accordion drifted up from the empty lot behind our house, I would drift off to lose myself in the land of Aladdin's Lamp and Ali Baba's Forty Thieves.

What was the name of the country I visited? My first explorations told me it was alien and faraway, more primitive than our world but part of an enchanted realm. You could walk down any street in Istanbul and meet people with the same names as the heroes, and perhaps that made me feel a little closer to them, but I saw nothing of my world in their stories; perhaps life was like this in the most remote villages of Anatolia but not in modern Istanbul. So the first time I read the Thousand and One Nights, I read it as a Western child would, amazed at the marvels of the East. I was not to know that its stories had long ago filtered into our culture from India, Arabia, and Iran; or that Istanbul, the city of my birth, was in many ways a living testament to the traditions from which these magnificent stories arose; or that their conventions—the lies, tricks, and

deceptions, the lovers and betrayers, the disguises, twists, and surprises—were deeply woven into my native city's tangled and mysterious
soul. It was only later that I discovered—from other books—that the first
stories I read from the Thousand and One Nights had not been culled
from the ancient manuscripts that Antoine Galland, the French translator, and the tales' first anthologizer, claimed to have acquired in Syria.
Galland did not take Ali Baba and the Forty Thieves or Aladdin's Magic
Lamp from a book, he heard them from a Christian Arab named Hanna
Diyab and only wrote them down much later, when he was putting
together his anthology.

This brings us to the real subject: The Thousand and One Nights is a
marvel of Eastern literature. But because we live in a culture that has
severed its links with its own cultural heritage and forgotten what it owes
to India and Iran, surrendering instead to the jolts of Western literature, it
came back to us via Europe. Though it was published in many Western
languages—sometimes translated by the finest minds of the age and
sometimes by the strangest, most deranged, and most pedantic—it is
Antoine Galland's work that was the most celebrated. At the same time,
the anthology that Galland began to publish in 1704 is the most influential, most widely read, and most enduring. One could go so far as to say
it was the first time this endless chain of tales had appeared as a finite
entity, and the edition was itself responsible for the worldwide fame
these stories achieved. The anthology exerted a rich and powerful influence on European writing for the better part of a century. The winds of
the Thousand and One Nights rustle through the pages of Stendhal,
Coleridge, De Quincey, and Poe. But if we read the anthology from cover
to cover, we can also see how that influence is bounded. It is preoccupied
mostly with what we might call the "mystical East"—the stories are
replete with miracles, strange and supernatural occurrences, and scenes
of terror—but there is more to the Thousand and One Nights than that.

I could see this more clearly when I returned to the Thousand and
One Nights in my twenties. The translation I read then was by Raif
Karadağ, who reintroduced the book to the Turkish public in the 1950s.
Of course—like most readers—I didn't read it from cover to cover, preferring to wander from story to story as my curiosity took me. On second
reading, the book troubled and provoked me. Even as I raced from page
to page, gripped by suspense, I resented and sometimes truly hated what
I was reading. That said, I never felt I was reading out of a sense of duty,
as we sometimes do when reading classics; I read with great interest,
while hating the fact that I was interested.

Thirty years later, I think I know what it is that was bothering me so much: In most of the stories, men and women are engaged in a perpetual war of deception. I was unnerved by their never-ending round of games, tricks, betrayals, and provocations. In the world of the Thousand and One Nights, no woman can ever be trusted. You can't believe a thing women say; they do nothing but trick men with their little games and ruses. It begins on the first page, as Sheherazade keeps a loveless man from killing her by entrancing him with stories. If this pattern is repeated through the book, it can only reflect how deeply and fundamentally men feared women in the culture that produced it. This is quite consistent with the fact that the weapon women use most successfully is their sexual charm. In this sense, the Thousand and One Nights is a powerful expression of the most potent fear gripping men of its era: that women might abandon them, cuckold them, and condemn them to solitude. The story that provokes this fear most intensely—and affords the most masochistic pleasure—is the story of the sultan who watches his entire harem cuckold him with their black slaves. It confirms all the worst male fears and prejudices about the female sex, and so it is no accident that popular Turkish novelists of the modern period, and even politically committed "social realists" like Kemal Tahir, chose to milk this tale for all they could. But when I was in my twenties, and awash in typically male fears about never-to-be-trusted women, I found such tales suffocating, excessively "Oriental," and even somewhat coarse. In those days, the Thousand and One Nights seemed to pander too much to the tastes and preferences of the back streets. The crude, the two-faced, the evil (if they weren't ugly all along, they dramatized their moral depravity by becoming ugly) were unremittingly repugnant, acting out their worst attributes over and over, just to keep the story going.

It could be that my distaste upon reading the Thousand and One Nights for the second time arose from the puritanical streak that sometimes afflicts Westernizing countries. In those days, young Turks like me who considered themselves modern viewed the classics of Eastern literature as one might a dark and impenetrable forest. Now I think that what we lacked was a key—a way into this literature that preserved the modern outlook but still allowed us to appreciate the arabesques, pleasantries, and random beauties.

It was only when I read the Thousand and One Nights for the third time that I was able to warm to it. But this time I wanted to understand what it was that had so fascinated Western writers through the ages— what had made the book into a classic. I saw it now as a great sea of stories—a sea with no end—and what astounded me was its ambition, its secret internal geometry. As before, I jumped from story to story, abandoning one midway if it started to bore me and moving to another. Though I had decided it wasn't a story's content that interested me so much as its shape, its proportions, its passions, in the end it was the stories' back-street flavor that most appealed to me—those same evil details I had once deplored. Perhaps with time I grew to accept that I had lived long enough to know that life is made of treachery and malice. So on my third reading, I was finally able to appreciate the Thousand and One Nights as a work of art, to enjoy its timeless games of logic, of disguises, of hide-and-seek, and its many tales of imposture. In my novel *The Black Book,* I drew upon the magnificent story of Harun al Rashid, who goes out in disguise one night to watch his double, the false Harun al Rashid, impersonate him; I changed the story only to give it the feel of one of those black-and-white films of 1940s Istanbul. With the help of commentaries and annotated editions in English, I was able, by the time I was in my mid-thirties, to read the Thousand and One Nights for its secret logic, its inside jokes, its richness, its beauties tame and strange, its ugly interludes, its impudences, and its vulgarities—it was, in short, a treasure chest. My earlier love-hate relationship with the book no longer mattered: The child who could not recognize his world in it was a child who had not yet accepted life as it was, and the same could be said of the angry adolescent who dismissed it as vulgar. For I have slowly come to see that unless we accept the Thousand and One Nights as it is, it will continue to be—like life, when we refuse to accept it as it is—a source of great unhappiness. Readers should approach the book without hope or prejudice and read it as they please, following their own whims, their own logic. Though perhaps I am already going too far—for it would be wrong to send a reader into this book with any preconceived ideas at all.

I would still like to use this book to say something about reading and death. There are two things people always say about the Thousand and One Nights. One is that no one has ever managed to read the book from start to finish. The second is that anyone who does read it from start to finish is sure to die. Certainly an alert reader who has seen how these two warnings fit together will wish to proceed with caution. But there's no reason for fear. Because we're all going to die one day, whether we read the Thousand and One Nights or not.

A thousand and one nights . . .

CHAPTER THIRTY-FOUR

Foreword to *Tristram Shandy:* Everyone Should Have an Uncle Like This

Prelude

We'd all like an uncle like Tristram Shandy, an uncle who is always telling tales and losing his way inside them, even as he nimbly pulls us in with his jokes, word games, indiscretions, follies, quirks, obsessions, and hilarious affectations; who, despite his cunning, culture, and worldliness, is still a mischievous child at heart. Whenever this uncle has gone on for too long or strayed beyond the limit, our father or our aunt will say, "Enough! You're frightening the children; you're making them sick!" Although it's not just the children who have been hanging on every word and are now addicted to this uncle's meandering tales, it's the grown-ups too. Because once we've grown accustomed to this uncle's voice, we want to hear it all the time.

There are many other stages in life when we become attached to a voice, to the words of a storyteller. In crowded offices, in the army, at school, and at reunions, we recognize these special people first from the color of their voices. Sometimes we grow so accustomed to hearing them that when we wish to speak to them it is not because we're curious to know what they have to say but simply because we long to hear their voices again. We depend on this uncle as we might a busybody neighbor, or the sort of actor who can make an audience laugh the moment he walks onstage, before he's even opened his mouth. In Turkey, uncles like this remind us, too, of our favorite columnists, who can make stories out of whatever happens to them. In real life, whenever we have accustomed ourselves to this sort of voice—this sort of storyteller—what we most long for is to hear our own thoughts expressed, our own experiences, but in the storyteller's voice and from his unique point of view. It's much the same with a relative who lives upstairs and sees you every day, or an army buddy with whom you share all your waking hours: Your need for his voice is so great it is almost as if the world and life itself would not exist without it. We should all have uncles like this.

But you run into an uncle like Laurence Sterne only once in forty years. When I was little, my own uncle amused us, with not literary but mathematical riddles. As reluctant as I was to put myself to an unwelcome test, I still wanted to prove how bright I was, and in this frenzy I would struggle to find an answer. But there was something else going on too: My uncle had a very beautiful wife. When I was five I would often go to visit my aunt, whose beauty could not be dulled by my grandmother's old furniture, tulle curtains, and dusty ornaments. Forty years on, my aunt still reminds me of my visits. Her sons, both of them, have, God bless them, become dentists, with practices in Nişantaşı. When I was leaving the older brother's practice one day, I discovered that the building's front door was locked from the outside. I stood there watching, savoring the aftertaste of cloves, as a striped cat squeezed through a gap in the grillwork and went into the grocery store across the street. The grocery store into which the cat had gone still sold the best *mezes* in Nişantaşı, most especially the stuffed dolmas.

Getting off the Subject

What I did in that last paragraph is what is known as getting off the subject. Tristram Shandy weaves together his story with digressions and, because it's something we all do, we have felt no need to give it a new name in the language we use every day. In the book—*The Life and Opinions of Tristram Shandy, Gentleman*—we never get around to the life and opinions of Tristram Shandy. Only at the end do we hear of Tristram's birth, and then he disappears from the scene before anyone takes much notice of him. Sterne's hero acts as if he could talk forever about the history of the world into which he was born, his father's views on birth, and life in general. But he never rests on one subject for long. He's like a happy monkey, swinging from one branch to the next, never stopping, leaping from subject to subject, always moving forward.

Most of the time the reader is left with the impression that Sterne has no idea where his story is going. But there are illustrious critics, like Victor Shklovsky, who have set out to prove that certain clues in the text, along with the book's narrative structure, indicate that Sterne planned his novel with the utmost care. So let us look at what our storyteller says on this subject, in the second section of the eighth book: Today there exist on this earth several ways of beginning a book, and I am certain that the path I've chosen is the best of these—at least it is the one closest to religion—because what I do is to write the first sentence and leave the second to God the All-knowing.

The entire story follows the same logic, forever digressing—so often that we could say the book's very subject is digression. But had Sterne ever guessed that someone like me might be able to pin him down on this, he would have changed the subject at once.

So What's the Subject?

When novelists get off the subject we get bored. That's our complaint, after all, whenever we're bored with a novel; we say it got off the subject. But there are many reasons why a novel may cease to amuse. Long descriptions of nature make some readers yawn; some become bored because there is not enough sex, and others because there is too much; some are annoyed by minimalists and some by authors who go into too much detail about confused family backgrounds. What makes a novel compelling is not the presence or absence of the above-mentioned qualities, it is the novelist's skill and style. In other words, a novel can be about anything. That's what sort of book *Tristram Shandy* is: a book about anything.

Let us not forget that this "anything" follows a defined logic. It may well be that a writer can put everything and anything into a novel, but even so, we readers are quick to grow bored and lose patience whenever the author strays from the subject, takes too long to say what he has to say, or includes needless detail. (Impatience is an important concept in *Tristram Shandy;* Sterne was fond of saying that he wrote to stave off boredom.) What makes it possible for Sterne to write about anything and everything (and what it is that piques our interest despite the unusual narrative shape) is the strange voice I described earlier. This book is a miscellany of outlandish tales and tongue-in-cheek sermons—one minute we are hearing of Uncle Toby's adventures and the next we are watching Tristram's father wind his grandfather clock of a Sunday—and as the still-unborn Tristram Shandy slowly merges with Sterne the novelist, we learn of everything that happened to be going on in the author's mind when he set out to relate Tristram's story.

So Tell Us the Author's Story

Laurence Sterne was the son of an impoverished noncommissioned officer. He was born in Ireland in 1713 and spent his early years with his family in various garrison towns in Ireland and England. After the age of ten he never again returned to Ireland. When he was eighteen, his father died, impoverishing the family further, but with the help of a distant relative who hoped the boy might find a position in the church, he went on to study theology and classics at Cambridge. Upon graduating, he entered the Church of England, rising quickly through the ranks with the help of certain distinguished clerics to whom he was related. At the age of twenty-eight he married Elisabeth Lumley; of their children, only their daughter Lydia survived. Until he published *Tristram Shandy* in 1760 at the age of forty-seven, nothing of note happened in Sterne's life, apart from his wife's melancholia.

Be it Anglican or Sunni in origin, a cleric's tale naturally contains a clear moral code that derives from scripture. So the tales clerics tell have a purpose, the sort of purpose our own moralist and socially responsible critics want to find in literature. We listen to Imam Nurullah Efendi's Friday sermon because he has an aim, a moral lesson to impart; his skill, his tears, his ability to move and scare us, his voice, and his powers of narration are of secondary importance. This is what makes Sterne so startlingly fresh and original: Although he was a cleric, he invented a form that one might call "the story with no purpose." He does not write toward a particular end, or to teach a lesson, but just for the pleasure of telling a story. What's more, he engages in this modern passion knowingly; to have no purpose is not a failing but a purpose in and of itself. That is what separates him from a man who is just prattling on. This despite the fact that there is, in his voice and his demeanor, a great deal that brings to mind empty gossip.

Needless to say, Sterne—living as he did in a society unaccustomed to clerics who wrote novels for no purpose and sent them to London to be published and read widely—provoked both anger and envy. He was attacked by those who did not appreciate his playful wit and by the sort of angry, jealous busybodies who are always too numerous; he was denounced for writing pornography, for writing too trivially for a cleric, for writing a novel that made no sense, for mocking religion, and for using bad grammar, broken sentences, and made-up words of uncertain meaning.

As the attacks continued, he also had to grapple with domestic problems and failing health (he contracted tuberculosis at an advanced age). But his wit remained as sharp as ever, and he never stopped making fun of things. Sterne was only too happy for it to be known that he was racing off to London when his books began to sell well, following up his first success with new volumes, and forging "sentimental attachments" with women. Because Sterne (as strange as it may sound in a country like Turkey, with its religious conservatives, traditionalists, nationalists who cannot take a joke, and joyless Jacobins) would have been pleased for it to be known that there were readers clever enough to appreciate *Tristram Shandy* and writers who were influenced by him.

So All Right, Then, What Is the Subject of Tristram Shandy?

Let me make it clear that if you are already feeling impatient, and asking yourself when this introduction will end, you will never find the patience to finish the book itself. In response to your insistent pleas, I now offer a breakdown of the chapters in the first book:

1. The narrator, speaking from a place somewhere between the author and Tristram himself, describes the sad circumstances of his birth.

2. The author talks about the Homunculus—the little Man—that is, the replica of the sperm responsible for his conception.

3. We discover that the story that will appear in the next chapter was told to the author by Uncle Toby.

4. I am very pleased with the way I have begun my story, the author says, and he goes on to tell us about the night he was conceived.

5. The author informs us that he was born on the fifth of November, 1718.

6. The author warns the reader, If I play games along the way and if from time to time I don a clown suit—even if it has bells on its toes—don't fly off and leave me.

7. The difficulties encountered by a vicar and his wife in their search for a midwife.

8. He acquaints us with his Hobby-Horses—Depending on my fancy, I sometimes play the violin and sometimes paint—and provides a dedication.

9. An explanation of this dedication.

10. A return to the midwife story.

11. An introduction to Mr. Yorick, who takes his name from the jester whose skull Shakespeare examines.

12. Yorick's jokes and his sorry end.

13. Yet another return to the midwife story.

14. In which the author explains why he has not reached the end of the story and keeps turning off onto side roads: a digression about a digression.

15. The author's mother's wedding certificate and its story.

16. His father's return from London.

17. His father's wishes upon returning to the house.

18. Preparations for birth in the provinces and various reflections.

19. His father's hatred of the name Tristram and his various philosophical obsessions.

20. The author scolds his inattentive readers—something that the author of this introduction has himself done on occasion. Of course this does not imply that he is an attentive author.

21. We approach the birth, though the digressions continue in abundance.

22. The author's reflections on his mode of narration: If it necessary to summarize it in a single word, my creation leans to digression, while also facing forward—and both at the same time.

23. I am inclined to begin this chapter with nonsense, and I am not inclined to impede my imagination. On pastimes.

24. On Uncle Toby as a pastime.

25. The groin wound suffered by Uncle Toby in the war and the boast with which the first book ends: If the reader has not been able to guess a single thing about any of these goings-on, the responsibility largely rests with me, because I am possessed of such a temperament that if I thought you could entertain the smallest idea or hypothesis as to what you might find on the next page, I would rip the page out of my book.

So What Is the Subject Then?

The subject is the impossibility of ever getting to the point, the center, the heart of the story: hence the disorder, the slipshod narration, and the easy pursuit of any distraction, any new thought, any pretext for digression—for if Sterne is fascinated with events of little import and with the very logic of digression (and let us remember how determined our author is to keep the reader from guessing what will happen on the next page), if he is only too willing to engage with those who complain that the beginning and the end are meaningless, that the meaning of the middle is obscure, and that the whole is both taxing to the brain and full of pointless excess—it is because that is the point. In its subject as in its shape, *Tristram Shandy* exactly reflects real life.

So You're Saying What, That This Is What Life Is Like?

Especially when it is asked in anger, this question is the novelist's best friend, and I would go so far as to suggest that novelists write their books with the express purpose of provoking it. Novels are only as valuable as the questions they raise about the shape and nature of life. Great novelists (and there are only a few) stay in our thoughts not because they quiz their heroes on this question directly, or engage their narrators in discussions with those who think like them, but because, as they go about describing life's petty and extraordinary details, and its problems large and small, they evoke these questions in their structure, their language, their atmosphere, their voice and tone. Until reading a particular novel, we've had our own ideas about life—ideas confirmed by ordinary novels (romantic melodramas that are assumed to evoke the true feeling of love, political melodramas in which complaints masquerade as politics, and all those tales that have for the last thousand years been telling us over and over that the good people who once populated the earth have been replaced with evil-minded mercenaries)—but in a great novel, the author offers us a new way of understanding life.

On first inspection, *Tristram Shandy* is hard to read, as books that defy our fundamental views of life and writing so often are. We get angry and rail against them. We say, "Nothing made sense, I gave up in the middle." The most brilliant readers will make the same complaint as those with simple tastes: "It's unreadable, because life's not like that," they both say. But while the birdbrained reader boasts of having understood nothing and condemns the book for defying his narrow rules (much was written about Sterne's narrative confusion, his immorality, and his refusal to abide by the rules of grammar), the reader of refined sensibilities feels more uneasy. Behind the smoke and noise of his anger, there is the knowledge that great literature is what gives man his understanding of his place in the scheme of things, and so, reminding himself that writing is one of the deepest and most wondrously strange of human activities, he picks up the book again in a moment of solitude.

Books like this touch on truths that natural readers will always find—and that literary poseurs will never understand. Even as they quarrel with the book's strange wilderness, intelligent readers who happen on its treasures and its moments of brilliance will recognize the foundations of true literature in a way that joyless legislators of literary law never can do. But the recognition can never be presumed. Even the brilliant wit Samuel Johnson allowed his schoolmasterly side to prevail when speaking about the novel in your hands: Impatiently grasping for words, he declared, "Nothing strange lasts. *Tristram Shandy* will never last." It is an honor and a pleasure to be writing the foreword for the Turkish translation of *Tristram Shandy* two hundred and forty years after it was first published.

So What Has This Book Taught Me?

As I am forever reminding myself (and I apologize for reminding you too), I live in a poor country where it is the habit to read great books not for pleasure but for their utility, and where the literate are conditioned to serve those less fortunate; this being my lot, I have found an easy but deceptive way of endearing books to readers, which begins by pointing out how books will improve them. For example: Like all great novels, *Tristram Shandy* is rich with the stuff of life—its rituals, states of mind, and refinements. Thus, *War and Peace* gives us the details of the Battle of Borodino and *Moby-Dick* offers an encyclopedic account of whaling, while *Tristram Shandy* offers invaluable insights into the life and times of a boy born in Ireland in the eighteenth century who went on to become an English vicar. In addition, *Tristram Shandy* is a leading examplar of "scholarly wit" or "philosophical humor," along with Robert Burton's *Anatomy of Melancholy,* Cervantes's *Don Quixote* (which we can even write in Turkish as *Don Kişot,* this term having entered our vocabulary), and Rabelais's *Gargantua and Pantagruel.* The encyclopedic knowledge that impatient readers call digression, the sweeping philosophical statements, the extravagant shows of erudition, the studies of character and the human soul—yes, they are all here in this book, but they are balanced by the fine wit and mock solemnity that Sterne brings to these grave subjects and by a hero whose adventures mock, overturn, and cast doubt on those very philosophical assertions. These great, encyclopedic, magnificent books are before all else books about books, and they show us that a deep and fundamental knowledge of life only comes from reading books and then writing new books that contradict them. The first example of this sort of philosophical novel, narrated by a hero whose life has been poisoned by dreams garnered from books, was *Don Quixote,* himself a victim of chivalric romances; the last of them (and possibly literature's first realist novel) was *Madame Bovary,* in which the heroine, having been poisoned by romantic novels and failed to find what she was seeking in love, chooses to poison herself further.

The "realist" scene at the end of the novel (in which Emma Bovary succumbs not to a book but to a deadly drug) had a huge effect on literature the world over; this overdose of "realism" was to poison Turkish literature too, by condemning it to a superficial reality. Living as we did on the periphery of Europe and believing Europe to be the source of all truth, we remained convinced that this kind of flat realism was the only way forward; so much so that sixty-five years later, when *Ulysses* was first published, we were still busy forgetting our own literary traditions—ignoring our ways of writing and feeling. We forgot that the realist novel was not a homegrown tradition but a narrative form we had recently imported from the West in the example of Flaubert, who came in person to Istanbul in 1850. Today, we are saddled with a new generation of narrow-minded, humorless, nationalist critics, come to denounce any narrative not superficially realist as "alien to our traditions." Had books like *Gargantua and Pantagruel* and *Tristram Shandy* been translated earlier, they might have exercised an influence on our small literary world, and the puny Turkish novel might have been more receptive to the complexities of our lives. (By now you ought to have learned not to get angry at Orhan, who has given his life to this cause, when he utters such things.) As for *Ulysses,* this novel did the most to save the world from superficial realism. Emerging from the birdcage of realism, the puny Turkish novel should spread the wings of its own traditions and its own dreams and fly!

O reader who, having learned so much from the foreword alone, is seized by love and joy! Now let me whisper in your ear what is most useful in this book, what it has to teach you. Listen carefully, and don't try to pass it off as your own idea in six years' time.

So Here It Is, the Fundamental Lesson This Book Teaches

The logic behind all great legends, religions, and philosophies is to teach us the great and fundamental truths. Let us call such an exercise a *grand narrative,* for it takes the form of a detailed story and is more literary than is commonly thought. In the literary novel, there are many ways to draw people's daily lives and adventures into these grand narratives. They present us with characters whose minds are set on an essence, a quest, a point in the distance. We may judge a character overly consumed by carnal pleasures or the pursuit of money to be one-dimensional, a caricature, but the character who lives in the service of this grand narrative (for love, national pride, or a political ideal) basks in its glory and so never seems one-dimensional. Don Quixote is not a caricature but a rounded person. But what *Tristram Shandy* tells us is that whatever a person's aims and personality, and however stable his character, his mind and his life will be much more untidy.

In other words, it doesn't matter if we believe in a grand narrative or indeed in its shadow; both are too clearly delineated to convey the shape of reality. Our lives do not have a center, a single focal point; what goes on inside our heads is too chaotic for us ever to achieve such focus. Life's like that too: Like Tristram, we spend our lives jumping from one subject to another, telling stories, following our fancies, and saying *If only* to ourselves, whatever happens to come into our heads. We are forever open to—disposed to—distraction, and our thoughts wander; we will stop a story midway to launch into a joke, and in so doing we reflect the surprises and coincidences of life in ways that a grand narrative never

can. Though we live mostly in the moment, struggling to protect ourselves, struggling to stay on our feet, there arrives a time—perhaps as we
lie dying or, as in the case of this novel, as we await the moment of our
birth—when we ask ourselves what life means; rather than assume the
grand shapes suggested by religion, philosophies, and legend, our
thoughts will reflect the shape of this book.

Summary: Life does not resemble that which is narrated in great novels, it resembles the shape of that book in your hands.

But beware: Life doesn't resemble the book itself, just its shape.
Because this book cannot bring any story to a conclusion and cannot, in
fact, make sense.

Finale

Life has no meaning, only this shape.

We knew that already, so why did Sterne have to write a six-hundred-
page book to prove it? If that's what you're asking, my answer is this:

All great novels open your eyes to things you already knew but could
not accept, simply because no great novel had yet opened your eyes to
them.

CHAPTER THIRTY-FIVE

Victor Hugo's Passion for Greatness

Some authors we love for the beauty of their texts. This is the purest sort of reader-writer relationship, the closest to perfection. Other writers leave their imprint on us because of their life stories, their passion for writing, or their place in history. For me, Victor Hugo belongs to that second group. In my youth I knew him as a novelist, as the author of *Les Misérables.* I loved him for the way he conveyed the chemistry of great cities, the high drama of their streets, and for the way he could show the logic by which two entirely unrelated things could happen in a city at the same time (as Parisians are attacking one another's barricades in 1832, we have the sounds of billiards coming from two streets away). He influenced Dostoyevsky; when I was young, and wedded to a melodramatic vision of cities as dark and dirty places where the poor and defeated congregate, he influenced me too. When I grew a bit older, Hugo's voice began to annoy me: I found it pompous, affected, ostentatious, and artificial. In his historical novel *Ninety-Three,* he spends a great many annoying pages describing a loose cannon rolling back and forth on a ship in a storm. When he took Faulkner to task for being influenced by Hugo, Nabokov offered a cruel example: *"L'homme regardait le gibet, le gibet regardait l'homme."* What has influenced me the most—and disturbed me most about Hugo's life—was his use of emotion (in the negative sense of this romantic word!) to confect greatness through rhetoric and high drama. All French intellectuals, from Zola to Sartre, owe a debt to Hugo and his passion for greatness; his concept of the politically engaged writer as champion of truth and justice has exerted a deep influence on world literature. Overly aware of his passion for greatness—and mindful of the fact that he had achieved it—Hugo became a living symbol of his ideal, thereby turning himself into a statue. His self-conscious moral and political gestures gave him an artificial air, and that cannot help but make a reader uneasy. In his discussion of "Shakespeare's genius," Hugo himself said that the enemy of greatness was falseness.

In spite of all his posturing, Hugo's triumphant return from political exile endowed him with a certain authenticity, as did his flair for public speaking, and his heroes live on in Europe's—and the world's—imagination. Perhaps this is simply because France and French literature were for so long at the forefront of civilization. Once upon a time, and no matter how nationalistic they were, France's writers spoke not just to France but to all of humanity. But it's not that way today. Perhaps that is why France's continuing affection for this strangest of great authors speaks above all of nostalgia for her lost days of glory.

CHAPTER THIRTY-SIX

Dostoyevsky's *Notes from Underground:*
The Joys of Degradation

We all know the joys of degradation. Perhaps I should rephrase
that: We must all have lived through times when we discovered
it was pleasurable, even relaxing, to run ourselves down. Even as we tell
ourselves we are worthless—over and over, as if repetition will make it
true—we are suddenly freed from all those moral injunctions to conform
and from the suffocating worry of having to obey rules and laws, of having to grit our teeth as we strive to be like others. When others degrade
us, we arrive at the same place as we do when we take the initiative in
humiliating ourselves. Then we find ourselves in a place where we can
wallow blissfully in our existence, our smell, our filth, our habits, the
place where we can abandon all hope of self-improvement and stop trying to nurture optimistic thoughts about other human beings. This resting
place is so comfortable that we cannot help feeling grateful for the anger
and selfishness that has brought us to this moment of freedom and solitude.

It was this recognition that most struck me when I returned to Dostoyevsky's *Notes from Underground* thirty years after my first reading.
But when I read the book as a young man, I was not so much alert to the
joys and logic of degradation as inspired by the anger of the hero wandering alone through the great city of St. Petersburg, flaying all he saw
with his razor-sharp wit. I saw the Underground Man as a variant of
Raskolnikov in *Crime and Punishment,* a man who had lost all sense of
guilt. Cynicism gave the hero a beguiling logic and a compelling tone.
When I first read it at the age of eighteen, I valued *Notes from Underground* because it openly expressed many of my own as-yet-unvoiced
thoughts about my life in Istanbul.

As a young man I could easily and instantly identify with one who

136

had removed himself from society and retired into himself. Particularly resonant was his insistence that "to live beyond the age of forty is shameful" (Dostoyevsky put these words into his forty-year-old hero's mouth when he himself was forty-three)—though I also agreed that he had been cut off from life in his own country owing to poisoning by Western literature, and that excessive self-consciousness—or, indeed, any form of consciousness—was a type of illness. I understood how he assuaged his pain by blaming himself, why he found his own face rather idiotic, and why he indulged in the game of asking himself, "How long can I bear this man's gaze?" I shared all these idiosyncrasies; they bound me to the hero without my needing first to interrogate his "strange and alien nature." As for the deeper thing that the book and its hero whispered between the lines, I may have sensed it at the age of eighteen but, disliking it—indeed, finding it disturbing—I refused to engage with it and soon erased it from my memory.

Today, I can at last speak more comfortably about the book's true subject and wellspring: It is the jealousy, anger, and pride of a man who cannot make himself into a European. Earlier I had confused the Underground Man's anger with his personal sense of alienation. Because, like all Westernized Turks, I liked to think of myself as more European than I really was, I was inclined to believe that the philosophy expounded by the Underground Man I so admired was an eccentricity reflecting a personal despair. In no way had I connected it to his spiritual unease with Europe. Turkish literature, like Russian, had been influenced by European thinkers. In the late sixties, existentialism from Nietzsche to Sartre was as popular in Turkey as it was in Europe, so to me the words of the Underground Man expounding his strange philosophy seemed not idiosyncratic but quintessentially "European"—which distanced me even further from the things the book was whispering into my ear.

To better understand the secrets that *Notes from Underground* whispers to those who, like me, live on the edge of Europe, quarreling with European thought, we need to look at the years during which Dostoyevsky was writing this strange novel.

A year earlier, in 1863, Dostoyevsky had embarked on his second journey to Europe, spurred on by deep unhappiness and failure. He had in mind to escape his wife's illness, the failure of *Time* (the journal of which he was an editor), and St. Petersburg itself. Also, he was planning a secret meeting in Paris with his lover, Apollinaria Suslova, who was twenty years his junior. (When at last they finally met in the same city, he would hide her from Turgenev.) In a burst of typically Dostoyevskyan indecision, he did not go straight to Paris to join his lover; he went first to Wiesbaden to gamble and lost a great deal of money. The delay precipitating this piece of bad luck also revealed the young and cruel Suslova's true colors. For while waiting for Dostoyevsky, she had found another lover, and when Dostoyevsky arrived in Paris, she made no effort to hide this from him. Tears, threats, slurs, and entreaties; hatred, chronic anxiety, and misery—everything endured by the heroes in *The Gambler* and *The Idiot:* their self-abasement before strong, proud women, their total loss of self, their vain pantomines of suffering—Dostoyevsky first endured himself.

Having admitted defeat and ended the affair, he returned to Russia to learn that his wife, who'd been suffering from tuberculosis, was on the brink of death. His brother Mikhail was struggling for permission to publish a new magazine to succeed one that was foundering, but he too kept meeting with failure. In the end he did gain permission, but money was scarce, and the January issue of *Epoch* did not come out until March; there were not enough subscriptions, and the typesetting was dreadful.

It was in these straitened and undisciplined conditions that *Epoch* published *Notes from Underground;* it did not attract a single review in all of Russia.

Notes from Underground was originally conceived as a critical essay. Dostoyevsky's idea had been to write a critique of Chernishevky's *What Is to Be Done?,* which had been published a year earlier. This book had a large following among the Westernizing, modernizing younger generation; it was not a novel so much as a textbook promoting a rosy version of positivist enlightenment. When in the mid-1970s it was translated into Turkish and published in Istanbul, it was accompanied by a preface that was highly critical of Dostoyevsky (calling him a dark and backward petit bourgeois); because this preface reflected the childish determinism and utopian illusions of Turkey's young pro-Soviet Communists, Dostoyevsky's anger against Chernishevsky was as real to me as if it had sprung from my own heart.

But his anger was not a simple expression of anti-Westernism or hostility to European thinking: What Dostoyevsky resented was that European thought came to his country at second hand. What angered him was not its brilliance, its originality, or its utopian leanings but the facile pleasure it afforded those who embraced it. He hated seeing Russian intellectuals seize upon an idea just arrived from Europe and believe themselves privy to all the secrets of the world and—more important—of their own country. He could not bear the happiness this grand illusion gave them.

Dostoyevsky's quarrel was not with the Russian youths who read Chernishevsky and drew upon this Russian writer to elaborate a crude, juvenile, secondhand "determinist dialectic," what bothered him was the way this new European philosophy was celebrated with such an aura of easy success. Though he was fond of castigating Westernizing Russian intellectuals for being cut off from the people, I see this as an evasion. For Dostoyevsky to believe an idea, the important thing was not that it be logical but that it be "unsuccessful"; not that it be believable but that it touch on some sort of injustice. Behind Dostoyevsky's great anger and hatred for the Westernizing liberals and the modernizers who propagated Fourier's determinist utopianism in Russia during the 1860s was his fury at the way they basked in the limelight of their ideas, embracing success unabashedly and without question.

Here the matter becomes even darker and more confused—as it always does in places that waver between East and West or between the local and the European. For though Dostoyevsky hated Western liberals and materialists, he accepted their reasoning. Let us remember that Dostoyevsky had grown up with these very ideas; he'd had a modern education and had trained to be an engineer. His mind had been shaped by Western thought and he knew no other. We can suppose that he may have wished to reason in another way, to have recourse to another, more "Russian" logic, but Dostoyevsky did not choose to undergo this sort of education. Even at the very end of his life, when he was writing *The Brothers Karamazov,* we can see in the notes he made when he began to take an interest in the lives of Russian Orthodox mystics that his first discovery was how little he knew on such subjects. (Still, I like the pragmatic pose he strikes when blaming himself for being "cut off from the people.") Following the same line of thought, it would not be wrong to conclude that Dostoyevsky accepted all these ideas coming from Europe, that his own views on individualism came from the same source, that he knew European ideas were sure to spread throughout Russia, and that he opposed them for these very reasons. But let me repeat that it wasn't the content of Western ideas that Dostoyevsky opposed, it was their necessity, their legitimacy. He hated his country's modernizing intellectuals because they used these ideas to legitimize their own importance; it was this that fed their pride. Let us remember that, in Dostoyevsky's lexicon, pride was the greatest sin; he used the word *proud* only as a pejorative. In *Winter Notes of Summer Impressions* (published in *Time*), chronicling his first European journey two years earlier, he linked all the evils of the West (individualism, addiction to wealth, and bourgeois materialism) with conceit and pride. In one burst of anger, he declared that English priests were as proud as they were rich. In another, he described French families walking down the streets arm in arm as conceited, derisively declaring it a national characteristic. Eighty years later, in *Nausea*—a novel written with the soul of an Underground Man—Sartre would create an entire world from this single observation.

The originality of *Notes from Underground* issues from the dark space between Dostoyevsky's rational mind and his angry heart— between his acceptance that Russia stood to benefit from Westernization and his fury at the proud Russian intellectuals who peddled impartial materialist ideas. Let us remember what all Dostoyevsky scholars agree: *Notes from Underground* is the starting point for *Crime and Punishment* and the great novels that were to follow; it is the first book in which he finds his true voice. This makes it all the more interesting to explore the ways in which Dostoyevsky would reconcile the tension between his knowledge and his anger at this point in his life.

Dostoyevsky never wrote the anti-Chernishevsky essay he had promised his brother. He was manifestly unable to write a critique of a philosophy that he himself accepted. Like all imaginative writers, who draw less from reason than from the imagination, he preferred to act out his ideas in stories and novels. That said, the first half of *Notes from Underground* is as much a sort of long essay as it is a novel; sometimes it is published separately.

It takes the form of an angry monologue of a forty-year-old man from St. Petersburg who, having come into a small inheritance, leaves his job and rejects ordinary society, only to suffer from an anguished isolation he calls "underground." Our hero's first target is what Chernishevsky calls "reasonable egotism." Chernishevsky views human beings as innately good; if with the help of science and reason they are "enlightened," they will see that it is in their interest to behave reasonably; even when they are pursuing their own interests, they can create a perfectly rational utopian society. But the Underground Man maintains that human beings—even if they are in full possession of their reason and can clearly understand their own interests—remain creatures who cannot always act according to their interests. (This can be read as meaning, "Westernization might be in Russia's interest, but I still want to stand against it.") Later on, the Underground Man portrays the human uses of "reason" as even more confused. "The full strength of a person proves not that he is a cog in a machine but a person. . . . For this reason, we do not do what is expected of us; instead, we succumb to unreason." The

Underground Man resists even Western thought's most powerful weapon, logic, disputing even that two times two is four.

The thing we must note here is not the Underground Man's cogent (or at least mature) argument against Chernishevsky but the fact that Dostoyevsky has created a character who can embrace and defend other ideas convincingly. The discoveries he makes while creating this character—so central to Dostoyevsky's later works—are what make him a true novelist. To act against one's own interest, to take pleasure in pain, to begin suddenly to defend the exact opposite of that which is expected of you—all these impulses that defy European rationalism, the pursuit of demands of an enlightened ego, and so on? It is perhaps difficult to appreciate how original this program was in its day, for it has been copied so often.

Let us look at one experiment that the Underground Man performs to prove himself a creature who refuses to conform to the idea that all people act in their own best interest.

One evening, he is passing by a lowly tavern when he sees a fight break out around the billiard table. Later he sees a man thrown from the window. At once a great jealousy rises up in the Underground Man: He wants to be similarly degraded; he too wants to be thrown out of the window. He goes inside, but instead of getting the beating of his dreams, he is degraded in an entirely different way. An officer decides he's blocking the way and so pulls him into the corner, but he does this in a manner to suggest he's handling a nonentity, a thing not even worthy of contempt. It is this unexpected humiliation that will prey on him.

I see all the elements that characterize Dostoyevsky's later novels in this small scene. If Dostoyevsky went on to become a writer who, like Shakespeare, changed our understanding of humanity, it is in *Notes from Underground* that this new point of view begins to emerge, and if we study it closely, we can see how his great discovery was made. Failure and unhappiness had greatly distanced Dostoyevsky from the complacent winners and the spiritual world of the proud, and he had begun to feel anger toward the Western intellectuals who looked down on Russia. But though he wished to quarrel with Westernization, he was still a product of his Western education and upbringing and still practicing a Western art, the art of the novel. *Notes from Underground* was born of a desire to write a story that took the hero through all these states of spirit and consciousness, or an urgent wish to create a hero and a world that could hold together all these contradictions in a convincing way.

When he began the book, Dostoyevsky wrote to his editor brother, "I have no idea what will come of this; perhaps it will be bad art." The great discoveries of literary history are (like style) rarely planned and hard to account for. They are shocking, liberating discoveries that occur only when creative writers use the full force of their imagination to penetrate the surface of their fictive worlds, to extract all that seems contradictory and impossible to reconcile.

When he first sits down to write, an author cannot know where his work will lead. But if we accept today that it might be possible to want to embrace our own smell, our filth, our defeat, and our pain—if we understand there is a logic to the love of degradation—we owe a debt to *Notes from Underground*. It is from Dostoyevsky's gloomy, damning ambivalence—his familiarity with European thought and his anger against it, his equal and opposite desires to belong to Europe and to shun it—that the modern novel derives its originality; and how comforting it is to remember this is so.

CHAPTER THIRTY-SEVEN

Dostoyevsky's Fearsome Demons

*D*emons is, in my view, the greatest political novel of all time. I first read it when I was twenty, and I can describe its impact only by saying I was stunned, awed, terrified, and utterly convinced. No other novel had affected me so deeply; no other story had given me such distressing knowledge of the human soul. Man's will to power; his capacity for forgiveness; his ability to deceive himself and others; his love for, hatred of, and need for belief; his addictions, both sacred and profane— what shocked me was that Dostoyevsky saw all these qualities as existing together and rooted in a common tangled tale of politics, deception, and death. I admired the novel for the speed with which it conveyed its all-embracing wisdom. This may be literature's primary virtue: Great novels draw us into their trance as fast as their heroes race into the thick of things; we believe in their worlds as deeply as we believe in their heroes. I believed in Dostoyevsky's prophetic voice as ardently as I believed in his characters and in their addiction to confession.

What is harder to explain is why this book struck such fear in my heart. I was particularly affected by the excruciating suicide scene (the snuffing of the candle and the dark other, observing events from the next room) and by the violence of an ill-conceived murder born of terror. Perhaps what shook me was the speed with which the novel's heroes switched back and forth between grand thoughts and their small provincial lives, a boldness Dostoyevsky saw not just in them but in himself. When we read this novel, it seems as if even the smallest details of ordinary life are tied to the characters' grand thoughts, and it is by seeing such connections that we enter the fearful world of the paranoid, in which all thoughts and great ideals are linked to one another. So it is with the secret societies, intertwined cells, revolutionaries, and informers who inhabit this book. This fearsome world in which everyone is connected to everyone else serves both as a mask and a conduit to the great truth lurking behind all thoughts, for behind this world is another, and in this other world it is possible to question man's freedom and God's existence. In *Demons,* Dostoyevsky offers us a hero who commits suicide to confirm both these grand ideas—man's freedom and God's presence—and he does so in a way no reader is likely ever to forget. There are very few writers who can personify or dramatize beliefs, abstract thoughts, and philosophical contradictions as well as Dostoyevsky.

Dostoyevsky began work on *Demons* in 1869, at the age of forty-eight. He'd just written and published *The Idiot;* he'd written *The Eternal Husband.* He was living in Europe (Florence and Dresden), where he'd gone two years earlier to escape his creditors and work in relative peace. He had in mind a novel about faith and the lack of it, which he called *Atheism, the Life of a Great Sinner.* He was full of rancor for the Nihilists, whom we might define as half anarchist, half liberal, and he was writing a political novel that mocked their hatred of Russian traditions, their enthusiasm for the West, and their lack of faith. After working on this novel for some time, he began to lose interest in it and coincidentally became fired up (as only an exile can be) about a political murder that he read about in the Russian papers and also heard about from a friend of his wife's. That same year a university student named Ivanov had been murdered by four friends who believed him to be a police informer. This revolutionary cell in which the youths were killing one another was headed by the brilliant, devious, devilish Nechayev. In *Demons,* it is Stefanovich Verhovensky who serves as the Nechayev figure, and as in real life, he and his friends (Tolchenko, Virginski, Shigalev, and Lamshin) kill the suspected informer Shatov in a park and throw his body into a lake.

The murder allowed Dostoyevsky to look behind the revolutionary and utopian dreams of Russian Nihilists and Westernizers and to discover there a powerful desire for power—over our spouses, our friends, our surroundings, our entire world. And so, when as a young leftist I read *Demons,* it seemed to me that the story was not about Russia a hundred years earlier but about Turkey, which had succumbed to a radical politics deeply rooted in violence. It was as if Dostoyevsky was whispering into my ear, teaching me the secret language of the soul, pulling me into a society of radicals who, though inflamed by dreams of changing the world, were also locked into secret organizations and taken with the pleasure of deceiving others in the name of the revolution, damning and degrading those who did not speak their language or share their vision. I remember asking myself at the time why no one talked about the revelations in this book. It had so much to tell us about our own times, yet in leftist circles it was ignored, and that may be why, when I read it, the book seemed to be whispering a secret to me.

There was also a personal reason for my fears. For at the time—in other words, about a hundred years after the Nechayev murder and the publication of *Demons*—a similar crime was perpetrated in Turkey, at Robert College. A revolutionary cell to which a number of my classmates belonged became convinced (with the encouragement of a clever and devilish "hero" who then vanished into the mist) that one of their number was a traitor; they killed him one night by smashing his head with a cudgel, stuffed the body into a trunk—and were caught while taking it across the Bosphorus in a rowboat. The idea that drove them, the idea that made them willing to go as far as murder, was that "the most dangerous enemy is the one closest to you, and that means the one who leaves first"—it was because I had read this first in *Demons* that I could feel it in my heart. Years later I asked a friend who'd been in this cell if he'd read *Demons,* whose plot they'd unwittingly imitated, but he had no interest in the novel whatsoever.

Though suffused with fear and violence, *Demons* is Dostoyevsky's most amusing, most comic, novel. Dostoyevsky is a consummate satirist, especially on crowded sets. In Karmazinov, Dostoyevsky has created a biting caricature of Turgenev, for whom he felt both friendship and hatred in real life. Turgenev troubled Dostoyevsky by being a wealthy landowner who approved of the Nihilists and Westernizers and (in Dostoyevsky's view) looked down on Russian culture. *Demons* is to some degree a novel he wrote as a way of arguing with *Fathers and Sons.*

But angry as he was at left-wing liberals and Westernizers, Dostoyevsky, knowing them from within, also could not help discussing them with affection from time to time. He writes of Stephan Trofimovich's end—and of his meeting just the sort of Russian peasant he'd always dreamed of—with such heartfelt lyricism that the reader, who has been smirking at this man's pretensions throughout the novel, cannot help but admire him. This could in some sense be seen as Dostoyevsky's way of saying farewell to the Westernizing all-or-nothing revolutionary intellectual, dispatching him to indulge his passions, his mistakes, and his pretensions in peace.

I have always seen *Demons* as a book that proclaims the shameful secrets that radical intellectuals (who live far from the center, on the edge of Europe, at war with their Western dreams and racked by doubts about God) wish to hide from us.

CHAPTER THIRTY-EIGHT

The Brothers Karamazov

I have a vivid memory of reading *The Brothers Karamazov* at the age of eighteen, alone in my room in a house that looked out on the Bosphorus. This was the first book of Dostoyevsky's I'd ever read. In my father's library there was, along with the famous English translation by Constance Garnett, a Turkish translation from the 1940s, and its title, which so powerfully evoked Russia's strangeness—its difference and its power—had been calling me into its world for some time.

Like all great novels, *The Brothers Karamazov* had two instant and opposite effects on me: It made me feel as if I was not alone in the world, but it also made me feel helpless and cut off from all others. It was when I was engrossed in the visible world of the novel that I felt I was not alone; because (as is always the case with great novels) I felt as if its most shocking revelations were thoughts I'd entertained myself; the scenes and phantasmagoria that most affected me seemed to come from my own memories. But at the same time the book revealed to me the rules that govern the shadows, the things no one speaks about, so it also made me feel lonely. I felt as if I were the first person who had ever read this book. I felt as if Dostoyevsky were whispering arcane things about life and humanity, things no one knew, for my ears only—so much so that when I sat down with my parents for our evening meal, or when I tried to chatter about politics in the normal way in the crowded corridors with my friends at Istanbul Technical University, where I was studying architecture, I would feel the book quivering inside me and knew that, from here on, life would never be the same: Next to the book's shocking world, my own life and troubles were small and unimportant. I felt like saying, I am reading a book that shocks me deeply and will change my entire life. As Borges says somewhere, "Discovering Dostoyevsky is like discovering love for the first time, or the sea—it marks an important moment in life's journey." My first reading of Dostoyevsky has always seemed to mark the moment when I lost my innocence.

What was the secret that Dostoyevsky whispered to me in *The Brothers Karamazov* and his other great novels? Was it that I would always feel a longing for God or faith, though we would never have it in us to believe in anything to the last? Was it the acceptance that there was a devil inside us, railing against our most deeply felt beliefs? Or was it that, as I imagined in those days, happiness would come not just from the colors of the deep passions, attachments, and great thoughts that made life what it was but also from the humility that was the exact opposite of those ostentatious concepts? Or was it that human beings are creatures who oscillate between the polar opposites of hope and hopelessness, love and hate, the real and the imagined, faster and more uncertainly than I had previously thought? Was it accepting that, as Dostoyevsky showed in his portrayal of Father Karamazov, people were not even sincere when they cried; even then a part of them was playing a game? If Dostoyevsky struck such terror in me, it was because he refused to offer up his wisdom in the abstract: Instead, he locates these truths inside characters that give every impression of being real. When we read *The Brothers Karamazov,* we find ourselves wondering whether people can really swing so fast between such extremes, and whether the all-or-nothing mood reflects Dostoyevsky's own frame of mind—and perhaps that of Russia's intellectuals—during the third quarter of the nineteenth century, when the country was in a social crisis. At the same time, however, we can feel aspects of the heroes' spiritual malaise inside ourselves. To read Dostoyevsky, especially when young, is to make one awesome discovery after another. *The Brothers Karamazov* (like all his novels) is meticulously plotted, and once inside its web of finely woven events we discover, somewhat to our dismay, that it is set in a world still in the process of becoming.

For some writers, the world is a place that has fully matured, a finished state. Novelists like Flaubert and Nabokov are less interested in unearthing the fundamental rules and structures that govern the world than in displaying its colors, symmetries, shadows, and half-hidden jokes, less concerned with the rules of life and the world than with its surfaces and textures. The joys of reading Flaubert and Nabokov are not of discovering the great idea in the authors' minds but of observing their attention to detail and their expert narration.

I wish I could say there was a second group of writers, of which Dostoyevsky was one. But I cannot say that Dostoyevsky is the most lucid and interesting member of such a group, for he is its only member. For a writer like Dostoyevsky, the world is a place that is in the process of becoming; unfinished, it is somehow lacking. It resembles our own world, which is also in the process of becoming, so we want to dig deep: to understand the rules that govern this world, to find inside it a corner wherein we might live by our own ideas of right and wrong. But as we do so, we begin to feel as if we ourselves are part of this half-finished world that the book is trying to fathom. As we struggle with the novel, we do not just sense the terror and uncertainty of this world still in progress, we begin to feel almost responsible for it, as if our struggle with the book has become part of a personal struggle to decipher our own beings. This is why, when we read Dostoyevsky, the things we learn about ourselves make us so fearful: The rules are never quite clear.

The impassioned questions that consume most people when they are young—what it means to believe in something, where faith in God or in religion leads, what it means to embrace a creed to the end, how to reconcile such metaphysical questions with society and everyday life—these matters occupied Dostoyevsky throughout his life, and in *The Brothers Karamazov* he examines them more deeply than ever before and on all fronts. *The Brothers Karamazov* is a fundamental text, best read while young. Reflecting as it does the agonies, fears, and hidden desires that afflict us most keenly in our early years—I am thinking here of the patricide at the heart of the book and the guilt to which it gives rise—it is a shocking experience for the young reader. In his famous essay on Dostoyevsky, which underlines the greatness and importance of *The Brothers Karamazov,* Freud notes the parallels with Sophocles (*Oedipus*) and Shakespeare (*Hamlet*), noting that the element that makes all these stories so shocking is patricide.

But we can still enjoy this novel later in life, when our understanding has matured. What I admired most on my second reading was the way in which Dostoyevsky pitted the local culture and its humble traditions against the sacred values of the modern age—enterprise, authority and war, the rights to question and to rebel. Various ideas entertained in *The Idiot* are dealt with in a richer way here: Dostoyevsky has Ivan Karamazov inform us that the intelligent are doomed to humility and guilt, while the stupid will tend to purity and steadfastness. On my second reading, I could not find it in myself to hate Father Karamazov in the way Dostoyevsky intended: His coarse manners, his interest in his children, his addiction to pleasure, and his propensity for lying made me smile—he seemed drawn from life and close to life as I knew it. Most great writers write against their beliefs, or at least unwittingly interrogate them to such a degree that they sometimes seem to be writing against them. It is in *The Brothers Karamazov* that Dostoyevsky puts his beliefs to the greatest test, in the heroes' conflicts and spiritual anguish. One cannot but feel awe for Dostoyevsky's ability to create so many characters who are so distinct from one another and to bring them to life in the reader's mind in such detail, color, and convincing depth. Other writers—Dickens, for example—create memorable characters, but mostly we remember them for their strange, sweet peculiarities. In Dostoyevsky's world, the heroes' tormented souls haunt us. Because the three Karamazov brothers are also, in a strange sense, brothers of the spirit, the reader tries to choose among them, to identify with them, to talk about them, to argue with them—and before long to argue with each of the Karamazov brothers is to argue about life.

In my youth I identified most with Alyosha: His purity of heart, his desire to see the good in everyone, and his struggle to understand all those around him spoke to the moralist in me. But a part of me knew that—as with Prince Mishkin of *The Idiot*—this sort of purity took great effort to attain. That was how I came to understand that Ivan, the theory-addicted, book-addicted absolutist, was closer to my own nature. All angry young men who live in poor non-Western countries and bury their moralizing selves in books and ideas have something of Ivan's merciless sangfroid. We can see in Ivan shades of the political conspirators whom Dostoyevsky studied in *Demons* and who went on to govern Russia after the Bolshevik revolution—people willing to go to any extreme, and resort to the worst cruelty, in pursuit of a great ideal. But he's still a Karamazov, this brother; in spite of all his anger, passions, and excesses, his hunger for love has left him wounded, and he is softened by a sweet compassion that Dostoyevsky sensitively conveys. The eldest, Dimitri, I saw as a distant hero, and that is how I still see him. He is too worldly, and in this way he resembles his father; his rivalry with his father over a woman makes him more real than his brothers, but for the same reason he is more easily forgotten. Having noted how similar he is to his father, we don't, in the end, feel involved in Dimitri's problems—by which I mean we don't feel these problems inside us. It's another brother (an illegitimate half brother) who frightens me, and that is the servant boy, Smerdyakov. He prompts the frightening thought that our fathers might have other lives, also awakening middle-class fears about the poor: the anxieties about being spied on, judged, and condemned by them. Judging from the honest, merciless, and precise logic he deploys after the murder, Smerdyakov shows how a marginal character can sometimes, through exercise of wit and intuition, take control.

As Dostoyevsky was writing *The Brothers Karamazov,* a story of a family in the provinces, he was grappling with the political and cultural dilemmas that would beset him all his life. During the years he was writing this book, he was (along with Tolstoy) the greatest of Russia's novelists, and by the end of his life the public had at last accepted this as fact. Just before he wrote this novel, he was publishing a magazine, *The Diary of a Writer,* in which he collected his ideas, bêtes noires, and literary sketches on politics, culture, philosophy, politics, and religion. With his wife's help he published his last books and this magazine by himself, and because the magazine was at this point the country's most popular literary intellectual journal, he was even earning a decent living from it. In his youth he'd been a left-wing Westernizing liberal, but in the last years of his life, Dostoyevsky defended Pan-Slavism, going so far as to praise the czar, who by freeing the serfs in 1861 had made a youthful dream of Dostoyevsky's come true (and who also had pardoned Dostoyevsky himself, in 1849, just before he was to have been executed for a political offense); Dostoyevsky was proud of the small personal connection he had established with the czar's family. Upon hearing that the 1877–78 Russian-Ottoman war, launched under the influence of Pan-Slavism, had begun, he went to the cathedral to pray tearfully for the Russian people. (It has been the custom in Turkey to remove or change, in various translations of *The Brothers Karamazov,* the words he utters against the Turks in the fever of war.) By the age of seventy, Dostoyevsky, now receiving many letters from readers and admirers, respected even by his enemies, had become a tired old man; a year after publishing *The Brothers Karamazov,* he died. Years later, his wife would recall how her husband would continue to climb four flights of stairs to a regular literary meeting, although the effort would leave him exhausted and panting for breath, all for the sake of the immoderate pride he felt when the meeting fell silent at his arrival. Despite bouts of jaundice owing to liver ailments, Dostoyevsky refused to give up the joy of writing till dawn while smoking and drinking tea.

Dostoyevsky's career is a succession of literary miracles; that he wrote one of the greatest novels ever at a time of failing health was his final coup de grâce. There is no other novel that goes back and forth between a person's daily life—his family quarrels, his money problems—and his grand ideas, no other novel that seizes the mind as this one does. Along with orchestral music, the novel is Western civilization's greatest art, and so it is a notable irony that Dostoyevsky, who wrote one of the greatest novels ever, hated the West, and Europe, as much as today's provincial Islamists.

CHAPTER THIRTY-NINE

Cruelty, Beauty, and Time:
On Nabokov's *Ada* and *Lolita*

There are, as I've said, writers who—though they teach us many things about life, writing, and literature, and though we read them with love and ardor—remain in our past. If we return to them in later years, it is not because they still speak to us but out of nostalgia, the pleasure of being taken back to the time when we first read them. Hemingway, Sartre, Camus, and even Faulkner belong to this camp. Today, when I take them up, I do not expect to be overwhelmed with new insights; all I wish is to *remember* how they once influenced me, how they shaped my soul. They are writers I may from time to time crave, but not writers I still need.

On the other hand, every time I pick up Proust, it is because I wish to remind myself how boundlessly attentive he is to his heroes' passions. When I read Dostoyevsky, it is because I need to be reminded that, whatever other anxieties and designs he might have, the novelist's main concern is depth. It is almost as if the greatness of such writers stems in part from our profound longing for them. Nabokov is another writer whom I read over and over, and I doubt I will ever be able to give him up.

When I am going on a trip, preparing my suitcase for a summer holiday, or setting off for a hotel to write the last pages of my latest novel, when I pack my dog-eared copies of *Lolita, Pale Fire,* and *Speak, Memory* (which in my view shows Nabokov's prose at its finest), why do I feel as if I am packing a box of my medicines?

It is the beauty of Nabokovian prose. But what I call *beauty* cannot explain this. For lurking beneath the beauty in Nabokov's books there is always something sinister (he used this word in one of his titles), a whiff of tyranny. If the "timelessness" of beauty is an illusion, this is itself a reflection of Nabokov's life and times. So how have I been affected by this beauty, underwritten as it is by a Faustian pact with cruelty and evil?

When we read his famous scenes—Lolita playing tennis; Charlotte's slow descent into Hourglass Lake; Humbert, after he has lost Lolita, standing on the roadside at the top of a little hill, listening to children playing in a small town (a snowless Breughel) and then meeting with someone he loved as a youth in the woods; the afterword for *Lolita* (which he says took him a month to write, though it is only ten lines); Humbert's visit to the barber in the city of Kasbeam; or the crowded family scenes in *Ada*—my first response is that life is just like this; the writer is telling us things I already know, but with a shocking and resolute honesty that brings tears to my eyes at just the right moment. Nabokov—a proud and confident writer with an exact knowledge of his gifts—once noted that he was good at putting "the right word in the right place." His flair for *le mot juste,* Flaubert's term for this brilliant selectivity, gives his prose a dizzying, almost supernatural quality. But there is cruelty lurking behind the pristine words that his genius and imagination have given him.

To better understand what I call Nabokov's cruelty, let us look at the passage in which Humbert pays a visit to the barber in the city of Kasbeam—just to kill some time, shortly before Lolita so cruelly (and rightfully) leaves him. This is an old provincial barber with the gift of gab, and as he shaves Humbert he prattles on about his baseball-player son. He wipes his glasses on the apron over Humbert and puts down his scissors to read clippings about the son. Nabokov brings this barber to life in a few miraculous sentences. To us in Turkey he is as familiar as if he lived here. But at the last moment, Nabokov plays his last and most shocking card. Humbert takes so little interest in the barber that not until the last minute does he realize that the son in the newspaper cuttings died thirty years earlier.

In two sentences—sentences that took two months to perfect—Nabokov evokes a provincial barbershop and the garrulous barber's boasts about his son with an élan and an attention to detail worthy of Chekhov (a writer whom Nabokov explicitly admired); then, having drawn the willing reader into the melodrama of the "dead son," he immediately drops it and we return to Humbert's world. We understand from this cruel and satirical rupture that our narrator has not the least interest in the barber's woes. What's more, he is assured that, because we too are caught up in Humbert's amorous panic, we will dwell on the barber's son, who has been dead for thirty years, no more than he does. And so we share the guilt for the cruelty that is beauty's price. In my twenties I always read Nabokov with a strange sense of guilt and with a Nabokovian pride at developing a shield against that guilt. This was the price I paid for the beauty of the novels and also for the pleasure I took from them.

To understand Nabokov's cruelty and its beauty, we must first remember how cruelly life treated Nabokov. Born into an aristocratic Russian family, he was dispossessed of his estates and all his wealth after the Bolshevik revolution. (Later he would proudly claim indifference.) Leaving Russia for Istanbul (where he stayed one day in a Sirkeci hotel) he went first to live in exile in Berlin; from there he went to Paris, emigrating to America after the Germans invaded France. Though he perfected a literary Russian in Berlin, once in America he lost his mother tongue. His father, a liberal politician, was destroyed by a botched murder like the one described with such satirical heartlessness in *Pale Fire*. Coming to America in his forties, he lost not just his mother tongue but his father, his patrimony, and his family, whose members were spread across the world. If we do not wish to judge him too harshly for his curious brand of malice—what Edmund Wilson called "kicking the underdog"—or the pride with which he eschewed all interest in politics, or the way he ridiculed and even degraded ordinary people for their coarse manners and kitsch tastes, we must bear in mind the losses that Nabokov suffered in real life, particularly in relation to the great compassion he showed his heroes and heroines, like Lolita, Sebastian Knight, and John Shade.

As is clear from his description of the Kasbeam barber, Nabokov's cruelty emerges in finely detailed expositions which show that nothing in life—in nature, in other people, in our surroundings, our streets, our cities—answers to our pains, to our troubles. This awareness reminds us of Lolita's remark about death ("you are completely on your own"), which her stepfather also admired. The deep joy in reading Nabokov comes from our seeing the cruel truth: Our lives do not fit at all into the logic of the world. Having come to terms with this truth, we can begin to appreciate beauty for its own sake. Only when we have discovered the deep logic governing the world—the world we can appreciate only through great literature—can we be consoled by the beauty in our hands; in the end, our only defense against life's cruelties is Nabokov's fine symmetries, his self-referential jokes and mirror games, his celebration of light (to which this always exceedingly self-aware writer referred to as a "prismatic Babel"), and his prose, as beautiful as the fluttering wings of a butterfly: After losing Lolita, Humbert tells the reader that all he has left is words and, in a half-mocking way, talks airily of "love as the last refuge."

The price of admittance to this refuge is cruelty, which gives rise to such feelings of guilt as I've described. Because Nabokov's prose owes its beauty to cruelty, it is crippled with the same guilt, and so too is Humbert as he searches for timeless beauty with all the innocence of a small child. We sense that the author—the narrator, the speaker of this wondrous prose—is forever trying to conquer this guilt, which quest only fuels his fearless cynicism, his brilliant diatribes, and his frequent returns to the past, to his memories of childhood.

As we can see in his memoirs, Nabokov looked back on his childhood as a golden age. Though writing with the example of Tolstoy's *Childhood, Boyhood, Youth* in mind, Nabokov shows no interest in the sort of guilt that Tolstoy derived from Rousseau. It is clear that for him guilt is a pain that came after childhood, after the Bolsheviks forced him from his Russian idyll, a pain he was suffering at the time he was honing his style. "If all Russian writers write about their lost childhoods," Pushkin once said, "who will speak of Russia itself?" Though Nabokov is a modern instance of the tradition of which Pushkin was complaining—the literature of the landowning aristocrat—there is a great deal more to him than that.

Nabokov's quarrels with Freud, and the pleasure he took in needling him, suggest that he was trying to defend himself against the terrible guilt he felt about the golden age of his childhood. To put it differently, he was trying to protect himself from prohibitions and pronouncements of guilt and not from Freud's idiocies (as Nabokov himself described them). For when he began to write about *time, memory,* and *eternity*—and his pages on these themes are among his most brilliant—Nabokov was also attempting sorcery of a Freudian sort.

Nabokov's concept of time offers an escape from the cruelty that attends beauty and engenders guilt. As he elaborates the concept at length in *Ada,* Nabokov reminds us that our memories allow us to carry our childhood with us, and with it the golden age we thought we had left behind. Nabokov brings this simple, self-evident idea into being with a fine lyricism, showing how the past and the present can coexist in a single sentence. The encounters with belongings evoke the past at the most unexpected moments; the images are laden with wondrous memories, opening our eyes to the golden age that is always with us, even in the ugly material world of the present. Memory—according to Nabokov, the writer's and the imagination's greatest resource—envelops the present with the halo of the past. But this is not a Proustian narrator who, nearing the end of his life, with no future, returns to the past. Nabokov's insistent explorations of memory and time speak of a writer who is certain of the present and the future, and who knows that his memories are born of games and shaped by the vicissitudes of experience. *Lolita*'s balanced vitality derives from the sometimes serene and sometimes agitated flitting back and forth between the past and the present: Humbert's narration darts from memories of his childhood (long before Lolita) to memories after her flight of the happy times he spent with her. When Nabokov speaks of these wondrous memories, he uses the word *paradise* repeatedly; in one passage he even refers to the *icebergs of paradise*.

Ada is, by contrast, Nabokov's attempt to carry the lost paradise of the past into the present. Because Nabokov knew that a world made up of memories from a lost golden age could survive neither in the America in which he then lived (Lolita's America, a land wavering between freedom and coarseness) nor in Russia (by then part of the Soviet Union), he blended his memories of these two worlds to create a third country, a wholly imagined literary paradise. Compounded of a surfeit of details from a childhood he viewed as sinless, it is a strange and wondrous world of unbridled narcissism that is thoroughly childish. We have here not an elderly writer gathering childhood memories; in an elegant, arrogant tour de force, Nabokov sets out to transplant his childhood into his old age. We see his lovelorn heroes not just realizing their childhood loves but preserving the states of being that will allow them to carry those loves with them until death. Humbert might spend his life searching for the lost love of his childhood, but Van and Ada want to live forever in the paradise that radiates from their childhood love. First we learn that they are cousins, later that they are brother and sister. Like Freud, whom he so loved to hate, Nabokov makes this disclosure guardedly, suggesting that taboos are what banish us from the paradise of childhood.

The Nabokovian childhood is a paradise far from guilt and sin; we can feel true admiration for the egoism in Ada and Van's love. This in turn will cause us to identify with poor Lucette, whose great love for Van is unrequited. As Van and Ada enjoy the enchanted heaven that the narrator has created for them, Lucette (the book's most modern, troubled, and unhappy character) becomes the victim of Nabokovian cruelty, excluded from the major scenes in the book and from the great love that many readers feel for it.

This is the point at which the author's greatness depends on the reader's. As Nabokov struggles to bring his paradise into our own times—to create for himself a refuge from reality—his will to indulge his private jokes and puns, his secret pleasures and games, and to elaborate his awe at the boundlessness of the imagination—this impulse produces moments in *Ada* when he loses the impatient reader. This is the point at which Proust, Kafka, and Joyce also refuse their readers, but unlike these other writers, Nabokov, father of the postmodern joke, has foreseen the reader's response and so embroils him in a game: He speaks of the difficulty of Van's philosophical novel, of how "in the drawing-room prattle among fan-wafting ladies" he is viewed as conceited for his indifference to literary fame.

In my youth, when everyone around me expected novelists to engage in social and moral analysis, I used this proud Nabokovian stance as my shield. Seen from Turkey, the characters in *Ada* and in Nabokov's other novels from the 1970s looked like fantasies of a nonexistent world "cut off from the present." Fearing I might be smothered by the cruel and ugly demands of the social milieu in which I planned to set my novels, I felt a moral imperative to embrace not just *Lolita* but also the books like *Ada*, in which Nabokov took to the outer limit his puns, sexual fantasies, erudition, literary games, self-referential jokes, and taste for satire. This is why for me great literature lives in a nearby place, cooled by the alienating wind of guilt. *Ada* is a great writer's attempt to eradicate that guilt, to use the power and will of literature to bring paradise into the present. This is why, once you lose your faith, in this book and in the incestuous union of Van and Ada, the book is drowned in a sin that is the opposite of what Nabokov intended.

CHAPTER FORTY

Albert Camus

A s time goes on, therefore, we cannot remember reading writers
without also revisiting the world as we knew it when we first read
them and recalling the inchoate longings they awoke in us. When we are
attached to a writer, it is not just because he ushered us into a world that
continues to haunt us, but because he has in some measure made us who
we are. Camus, like Dostoyevsky, like Borges, is for me this kind of ele-
mental writer. Such a writer's prose ushers one into a landscape waiting
to be filled with meaning, suggesting, nonetheless, that any literature
with metaphysical designs has—like life—limitless possibilities. These
authors, read when you're young and reasonably hopeful, will inspire
you to want to write books as well.

I read Camus sometime before reading Dostoyevsky and Borges, at
the age of eighteen, under the influence of my father, a construction engineer. In the 1950s, when Gallimard was publishing one Camus book
after another, my father would arrange for them to be sent to Istanbul, if
he was not in Paris to buy them himself. Having read the books with
great care, he enjoyed discussing them. Though he tried, from time to
time, to describe "the philosophy of the absurd" in words I could understand, it was not until much later that I came to understand why it spoke
to him: This philosophy came to us not from the great cities of the West,
or the interiors of their dramatic architectural monuments and houses,
but from a marginalized part-modern, part-Muslim, part-Mediterranean
world like ours. The landscape in which Camus sets *The Stranger, The
Plague,* and many of his short stories is the landscape of his own childhood, and his loving, minute descriptions of sunny streets and gardens
belong neither to the East nor to the West. There was also Camus the literary legend: My father was as enthralled by his early fame as he was

shaken when the news came that he had died, still young and handsome, in a traffic accident the newspapers were only too eager to call "absurd."

Like everyone else, my father found an aura of youth in Camus's prose. I sense it still, though the phrase now reflects more than the age and outlook of the author. When I revisit his work now, it seems to me as if Europe in Camus's books was still a young place, where anything could happen. It is as if its cultures had not yet fissured; as if contemplating the material world you could almost see its essence. This may reflect the postwar optimism, as a victorious France reasserted its central role in world culture and most particularly in literature. For intellectuals from other parts of the world, postwar France was an impossible ideal, not just for its literature but for its history. Today we can see more clearly that it was France's cultural preeminence that gave existentialism and the philosophy of the absurd such prestige in the literary culture of the 1950s, not just in Europe but also in America and non-Western countries.

It was this kind of youthful optimism that prompted Camus to regard the thoughtless murder of an Arab by the French hero of *The Stranger* as a philosophical rather than a colonial problem. So when a brilliant writer with a degree in philosophy speaks of an angry missionary, or an artist grappling with fame, or a lame man mounting a bicycle, or a man going to the beach with his lover, he can spiral off into a dazzling and suggestive metaphysical rumination. In all these stories, he reconstitutes life's mundane details like an alchemist, transforming its base metals into a filigree of philosophical prose. Underlying it there is, of course, the long history of the French philosophical novel to which Camus, no less than Diderot, belongs. Camus' singularity lies in his effortless melding of this tradition—which relies on acerbic wit and a slightly pedantic, somewhat authoritarian voice—with short sentences à la Hemingway and realistic narration. Though this collection belongs to the tradition of the philosophical short story comprising Poe and Borges, the stories owe their color, vitality, and atmosphere to Camus the descriptive novelist.

The reader is inevitably struck by two things: the distance between Camus and his subject and his soft, almost whispering mode of narration. It is as if he seems unable to decide whether or not to take his readers deeper into the story and ends up leaving us suspended between the author's philosophical worries and the text itself. This may be a reflection of the draining, damning problems that Camus encountered in the last years of his life. Some find expression in the opening paragraphs of "The Mute," when Camus alludes, somewhat self-consciously, to the problems of aging. In another story, "The Artist at Work," we can sense that Camus at the end of his days was living too intensely and that the burden of fame was too great. But the thing that truly damned and destroyed Camus was without a doubt the Algerian War. As an Algerian Frenchman, he was crushed between his love for this Mediterranean world and his devotion to France. Whereas he understood the reasons for the anticolonial anger and the violent rebellion it had unleashed, he could not take a hard stance against the French state as Sartre did, because his French friends were being killed by the bombs of Arabs—or "terrorists," as the French press called them—fighting for independence. And so he chose to say nothing at all. In a touching and compassionate essay he wrote after his old friend's death, Sartre explored the troubled depths concealed by Camus's dignified silence.

Pressed to take sides, Camus chose instead to explore his psychological hell in "The Guest." This perfect political story portrays politics not as something we have eagerly chosen for ourselves but as an unhappy accident that we are obliged to accept. One finds it difficult to disagree with the characterization.

CHAPTER FORTY-ONE

Reading Thomas Bernhard
in a Time of Unhappiness

I am hopelessly miserable and reading Thomas Bernhard. Actually, I did not have it in mind to read him. I did not have it in mind to read anyone—I was too unhappy to think so clearly. To open a book, to read a page, to enter someone else's dreams—these were all excuses for dwelling on my own wretchedness, reminders that everyone else in the world had managed to avoid the well of misery into which I had fallen. Everywhere were people who flattered themselves about their successes and tiny refinements, their interests, their culture, and their families. It seemed that all books had been written in such people's voices. No matter what they described—a nineteenth-century Parisian ball, an anthropological tour of Jamaica, the impoverished environs of a great city, or the determination of a man who had dedicated his life to the study of art—the books concerned lives whose experience bore no relation to my own, so I wanted to forget them all. Because I could find nothing in these books that remotely resembled my mounting misery, I felt anger both at the books and at myself: at the books because they ignored the pain I was suffering, at myself because I had been so stupid as to throw myself into this senseless pain. I wanted nothing other than to escape my mindless misery. But books had prepared me for life, books were mostly what kept me going, so I kept telling myself that if I wished to pull myself out of my black cloud, I would have to keep reading. Yet whenever I opened a book to hear the voice of an author who accepted the world as it was, or who, even if he wished to change it, still identified with it, I would feel myself alone. Books were remote from my pain. What's more, it was books that had brought me to the idea that the misery into which I had fallen was unique, that I was an idiotic wretch like no other. This was why I kept telling myself, "Books are not for reading, but for buying and selling." After the earthquakes, whenever books annoyed me, I found a reason for throwing them out. And so I was bringing my forty-year war with books to an end in a spirit of loathing and disillusionment.

This was my frame of mind as I leafed through a few pages of Thomas Bernhard. I was not reading them in the hope that they might save me. A magazine was doing a special issue on Bernhard and had asked would I please write something. There was a debt I needed to discharge, and once upon a time I'd liked Bernhard very much.

So I began to read Bernhard again, and for the first time since the dark cloud had descended, I heard a voice saying that the wretchedness I called my unhappiness was not as great or as bad as I thought. There was no particular sentence or paragraph that made this particular point; they talked about other things—a passion for the piano, solitude, publishers, or Glenn Gould—but I still felt that these were merely pretexts; they were speaking to my misery, and this perception lifted my spirits. The problem was not the misery itself but the way I perceived it. The problem was not that I was unhappy but that I felt so in particular ways. To read Bernhard in this time of unhappiness was like a tonic, though I knew that the pages I read had not been written to serve as such, or even as a consolation for readers grappling with depression.

How to explain all this? What made reading Bernhard at a time of unhappiness seem like taking an elixir? Perhaps it was the air of renunciation. Maybe I was soothed by a moral vision, wisely suggesting that it is better not to expect too much of life. . . . But it might have had nothing to do with morality, for a dose of Bernhard makes clear that the only hope lies in remaining oneself, in clinging to one's habits, to one's anger. There is in Bernhard's writing the suggestion that the greatest stupidity is to give up one's passions and habits in the hope of a better life, or the joy of attacking others' idiocies and stupidities, or of knowing that life can never be more than what our passions and perversions make of it.

But I know that all attempts at formulation will be fruitless. This is not just because it is hard to find in Bernhard's words confirmation of what I've said. It is also because every time I return to Bernhard's books I see that they defy reduction. But before I begin again to doubt myself, let me say this, at least: What I enjoy most in Bernhard's books is not their settings or their moral vision. I enjoy just being there, inside those pages, to embrace his unstoppable anger and share it with him. That is how literature consoles, by inviting us to fulminate with the same intensity as the writers we love.

CHAPTER FORTY-TWO

The World of
Thomas Bernhard's Novels

The history of literary bias goes back more than two thousand years, and between the two world wars there arrived a new fashion for "economy" that continues to hold sway in the aphoristic tendencies of those who write introductions to writers. Hemingway, Fitzgerald, and other American writers who set the style of the interwar era established the literary precept according to which any right-thinking writer should write a scene in the shortest way possible, using the fewest words, without repetition.

Thomas Bernhard is not a writer who wishes to seem right-thinking or economical. Repetition is the brick of his world. It is not only that his lonely and obsessed heroes repeat the same perversions over and over as each wanders back and forth, obsessively venting some furious passion; as he describes their progress with a shocking energy, Bernhard too will repeat the same sentences over and over. So when Bernhard speaks of the hero of *Concrete,* who gives many years over to writing a treatise on hearing, he does not, as a traditional novelist might, say, "Konrad often thought that society was nothing and the work he was writing was everything"—instead, he conveys this idea through his hero's endless repetitions.

His circular thoughts—these are not thoughts so much as angry shouts, curses, screams, and expletives ending in exclamation points—are hard for rationalist readers to absorb. We read that all Austrians are idiots and, later, that the Germans and the Dutch are too; we are told that doctors are uniformly monstrous and most artists idiotic, superficial, and crude; we read that the world of science is inhabited by charlatans and the world of music by fakes; aristocrats and the rich are parasites, while the poor are opportunistic swindlers; most intellectuals are birdbrains addicted to their affectations, and most young people are imbeciles prepared to laugh at anything; we read that the abiding human passion is to deceive, oppress, and destroy others. Such and such a city is the most disgusting city in the world, such and such a theater is not a theater but a brothel. Such and such a composer is the greatest so far, and so-and-so is the greatest philosopher, but since there are no other composers or philosophers to reckon with, they are all "would-be" composers and philosophers . . . and so on.

When we read Tolstoy or Proust, who protect themselves and their heroes with aesthetic armor—thus safeguarding their fictive worlds from this sort of excess—we might see these attacks, in Bernhard's words, as "the affectations of an anguished aristocrat or of a conceited but still sympathetic hero," but in the world of Thomas Bernhard they serve as supporting columns. In the work of "balanced" writers like Proust or Tolstoy, we might view such obsessive repetition as "a leaf in the world of human virtues and frailties," but here it serves the instantiation of an entire world. Most writers concerned with portraying "life in its fullness" consign "obsessions, perversions, and excesses" to the margins, but Bernhard places them in the center, while the rest of the experience we describe as life gets pushed into the margins, evident only in the little details involved to insult it.

If I am drawn to these attacks and curses that draw their power from obsession, it is partly owing to Bernhard's endless verbal energy, but the attraction also derives from the heroes' situation. Anger offers Bernhard's heroes protection against the evil, idiocy, and misery of the world. Bernhard's heroes spout not such belittling curses as confident, successful, and refined people deploy to look down on those around them; this is anger born of face-to-face familiarity with catastrophe that may strike at any time, of having accepted the painful truth about what people are really made of—and it is their anger that keeps his heroes from collapsing, that keeps them on their feet. We read again and again that this or that person "has not been able to stay on his feet," "was destroyed in the end," "withered away in a corner," "was crushed in the end, too." For Bernhard's heroes, hemmed in as they are by cruelty and idiocy, the destruction of others serves as warning of danger. In their language, this notion might be expressed thus: For those who would endure, carry on, forbear, and remain standing, the first imperative is to curse the world and the second is to turn this passion into a deep, philosophical, meaningful enterprise—or at the very least to give ourselves over to obsession. Once the obsessions come to define the world in which we live, we are reduced to those things we cannot give up.

In *Correction,* the hero, who resembles Wittgenstein, is preoccupied with an unwritten biography that will take him long years to research, but his hatred of his sister, who thinks he is impeding his own efforts, preoccupies his thoughts. So it is with the hero of *Concrete:* Concerned as he is with his work on "hearing," he is just as obsessed with the conditions under which he writes it. Similarly, the engaging hero of *Woodcutters,* having invited to dinner all the intellectuals of Vienna he most detests, directs all his hospitable energy to detesting them even more.

Valéry once said that people who rail against vulgarity are really expressing their curiosity and affection for it. Bernhard's heroes return continually to the things they hate most; they devise ways of fanning the hatred; indeed, they could not live without disgust and contempt. They hate Vienna, but they run to be there; they hate the world of music, but they could not live without it; they hate their sisters, but they seek them out; they abhor newspapers but couldn't bear not to read them; they deride intellectual chatter, only to mourn its absence; they detest literary prizes, but they don new suits and rush off to accept them. In their struggle to set themselves above reproach, they recall the hero of *Notes from Underground.*

Bernhard has something of Dostoyevsky in him. In his heroes' obsessions and passions—their defenses against the hopeless and the absurd—there are shades of Kafka as well. But Bernhard's world is closer to Beckett's.

Beckett's heroes do not rail so much against their surroundings; they are less interested in the disasters they suffer than in their mental anguish. No matter how they struggle to escape it, Bernhard's heroes remain open to the outside world; to escape the suffering in their minds, they embrace the anarchy of the outside world. Beckett tries to erase, as much as possible, the chain of cause and effect, while Bernhard fixates on these causes down to the last detail. Bernhard's characters refuse to surrender to illness, defeat, and injustice; they carry with them a mad anger and a blind will to fight on to the bitter end. Even if they are ultimately defeated, it is not their defeat and surrender that we read about but their obsessive quarrels and struggles.

If we were to look for another writer who might serve as an introduction to the world of Thomas Bernhard, Louis-Ferdinand Céline would be the best candidate. Like Céline, Bernhard was raised in a poor family that had to struggle to survive. He grew up without a father, suffered privation during the war, and contracted tuberculosis. Like Céline's, his novels are largely autobiographical, chronicling a constant battle, full of obstacles, resentments, and defeats. Like Céline, who lambasted authors like Louis Aragon and Elsa Triolet, and who railed against Gallimard, his publisher, Bernhard fumes at the old friends and institutions that take him in hand and give him prizes. Wholly autobiographical, *Woodcutters* is about a dinner party Bernhard actually organized in Austria for some friends and acquaintances with the express purpose of insulting them. But while Céline and Bernhard burn with flames from their inner hells, they use words very differently. Where Céline offers up ever shorter sentences ending in three dots, Bernhard's innovation is the sentence whose endless repetition of circular or, more accurately, elliptical insults refuses to submit to the paragraph block.

When the mist clears, what we see is a string of lovely, cruel, amusing little anecdotes. Despite their endless diatribes, Bernhard's books are not dramatic; instead, they pile one story on top of the other; the sense we get of the book comes not from the whole but from the little stories scattered inside it. If we recall that these are mostly made up of gossip, insult, and cruel descriptions of "so-called" artists and intellectuals, we can think that the world of Bernhard's novels is not only shaped much like our own but that it is—at times—close to its spirit too. Voicing the cruel attacks and obsessive hatreds that we all indulge in when angry, he goes on to fashion them into "good art."

But this is the point at which his hatred of art runs into trouble. For the newspapers on which he rained insults take note of him more and more often, while the prize juries on whom he spat keep giving him more prizes, and the theaters on which he poured scorn are only too eager to stage his plays—and when readers come to see that the story they so desperately wanted to believe is in reality just a story, they cannot help feeling duped. So perhaps this is a good moment to remind the reader that the world in which a novelist lives is a different realm entirely from the world inhabited by his characters. But if you insist that this other world is autobiographical, and that it takes all its power from an anger that is real, you will, after reading each Bernhard novel, need to ask yourself why, when you search for a "moral vision," you feel as if you've been pulled into a game with the novel's caricatures, and even the novel itself.

CHAPTER FORTY-THREE

Mario Vargas Llosa and Third World Literature

I s there such a thing as Third World literature? Is it possible to establish—without falling prey to vulgarity or parochialism—the fundamental virtues of the literatures of the countries that make up what we
call the Third World? In its most nuanced articulation—in Edward Said,
for example—the notion of a Third World literature serves to highlight
the richness and the range of the literatures on the margins and their relation to non-Western identity and nationalism. But when someone like
Fredric Jameson asserts that "Third World literatures serve as national
allegories" he is simply expressing a polite indifference to the wealth and
complexity of literatures from the marginalized world. Borges wrote his
short stories and essays in the 1930s in Argentina—a Third World country in the classic sense of the term—but his place at the very center of
world literature is undisputed.

It is clear, nonetheless, that there is a sort of narrative novel that is
particular to the countries of the Third World. Its originality has less to
do with the writer's location than with the fact that he knows he is writing far from the world's literary centers and he feels this distance inside
himself. If there is anything that distinguishes Third World literature, it is
not the poverty, violence, politics, or social turmoil of the country from
which it issues but rather the writer's awareness that his work is somehow remote from the centers where the history of his art—the art of the
novel—is described, and he reflects this distance in his work. What is
crucial here is the Third World writer's sense of being exiled from the
world's literary centers. A Third World writer can choose to leave his
own country and resettle—as Vargas Llosa did—in one of the cultural
centers of Europe. But his sense of himself may not change, for a Third

World writer's "exile" is not so much a matter of geography as a spiritual state, a sense of exclusion, of being a perpetual foreigner.

At the same time, this sense of being an outsider frees him from anxieties about originality. He need not enter into obsessive contest with fathers or forerunners to find his own voice. For he is exploring new terrain, touching on subjects that have never been discussed in his culture, and often addressing distinct and emergent readerships, never seen before in his country—this gives his writing its own sort of originality, its authenticity.

In a youthful review of Simone de Beauvoir's *Les belles images,* Vargas Llosa suggests what the guiding principles of such a career might be. He praises de Beauvoir not just for writing a brilliant novel but for refusing the purposes of the *nouveau roman* then fashionable (the 1960s). According to Vargas Llosa, Simone de Beauvoir's greatest achievement was to take the novelistic forms and writing strategies of writers like Alain Robbe-Grillet, Nathalie Sarraute, Michel Butor, and Samuel Beckett and to use them to entirely different ends.

Vargas Llosa elaborates his ideas about the "use" of other writers' strategies and forms in another essay on Sartre. In later years, Vargas Llosa would complain that Sartre's novels are devoid of wit and mystery, that his essays are clearly written but politically confused (or confusing), and that his art is outdated and trite; he would express dismay that in his own Marxist days he had been deeply influenced, even undone, by Sartre. Vargas Llosa has dated his disillusionment with Jean-Paul Sartre to an article he read in *Le Monde* in 1964. In this infamous article (it made waves even in Turkey), Sartre set literature alongside a black child dying of hunger in a Third World country like Biafra, declaring that as long as such suffering went on it was a "luxury" for poor countries to engage with literature. He even went so far as to suggest that Third World writers would never be able to enjoy the so-called luxury of literature with a clear conscience, and to conclude that literature was the business of rich countries. Vargas Llosa does admit that certain aspects of Sartre's thinking, his careful logic and his insistence that literature is too important ever to be a game, have proved "serviceable"—it was thanks to Sartre that Vargas Llosa found his way through the labyrinths of literature and politics—so in the end, Sartre was a "useful" guide.

To be forever aware of one's distance from the center, to discuss the mechanics of inspiration and also the ways in which other writers' discoveries can be useful, one must be possessed of a lively innocence (and there is, according to Vargas Llosa, nothing innocent or naïve in Sartre). Vargas Llosa's own lively innocence is reflected not just in his novels but in his criticism, his essays, and his other work.

Whether he is writing about his son's involvement with the Rastafarians, or offering up a political tableau of Nicaragua's Marxist Sandinistas, or describing the 1992 World Cup, he never fails to engage, never holds himself apart; he is particularly good on Camus, whom he recalls having read in a desultory manner, as a young man—so great was Sartre's influence on him at that time. Many years later, after surviving a terrorist attack in Lima, he read *The Rebel,* Camus's long essay on history and violence, and decided he preferred Camus to Sartre. Still, he praises Sartre's essays for getting to the heart of the matter, and the same can said of Vargas Llosa's essays.

Sartre is a vexed figure for Vargas Llosa, perhaps even a father figure. John Dos Passos, who so influenced Sartre, is important too for Vargas Llosa; he praises him for his refusal of easy sentimentality and for his experimentation with new narrative forms. Like Sartre, Vargas Llosa would take up collage, juxtaposition, montage, cut-and-paste, and similar narrative strategies to orchestrate his novels.

In another essay, Vargas Llosa praises Doris Lessing for being the sort of writer who was "engaged" in the Sartrean sense of the word. For him the engaged novel is one immersed in the quarrels, legends, and violence of its time, and Vargas Llosa's early leftist fiction is a good example of the genre. But it is an imaginative, playful leftist we see in these early novels. Of all the writers Vargas Llosa discusses in his essays— Joyce, Hemingway, and Bataille among them—the one to whom he owes the greatest debt is Faulkner. What Vargas Llosa praises in *Sanctuary*—its juxtaposition of scenes and leaps in time—is in even greater evidence in Vargas Llosa's own novels. He makes masterful use of this strategy—the ruthless crosscutting of voices, stories, and dialogues—in *Death in the Andes.*

This novel takes place in the abandoned and disintegrating small towns of the remote Andes—in empty valleys, mineral beds, mountain roads, and one field that is anything but deserted—and follows an investigation into a series of disappearances that may be murders. The investigator, Corporal Lituma, and his opposite number in the civil guard, Thomas Correno, will both be familiar to readers of Vargas Llosa's other novels. As the two men roam the mountains interrogating suspects, they tell each other about their past love affairs, ever watchful for an ambush by the Maoist Shining Path guerrillas. The people they meet along the way, and the stories that they tell, blend with their personal histories to create a vast tableau of contemporary Peru in all its pain and misery.

Of course, the murder suspects turn out to be Shining Path guerrillas and a couple who run a canteen in the area and put on strange performances recalling Incan customs. As the Shining Path's ruthless local political murders are described, and the evidence of old Incan sacrificial rituals builds, the mood grows steadily darker. Blowing through the wild landscapes of the Andes is a strong wind of irrationality. Death is everywhere in this book; in the poverty of Peru, the grim realities of guerrilla warfare, and the general hopelessness.

But the reader is left wondering if Vargas Llosa the modernist has lost his nerve, for he almost seems to have turned himself into a postmodern anthropologist, returning to his native land to study its irrationality, its violence, its preenlightenment values, and its rituals. This book is packed with legends, old gods, mountain spirits, devils, demons, and witches—more than the story needs. "But of course we make a mistake when we try to understand these killings with our minds," says one character. "They have no rational explanation."

Surprisingly, there is no trace of the irrational in the texture of the novel itself. *Death in the Andes* has two contradictory ambitions: to be a detective novel that displays Cartesian intellect and logic, and to create an atmosphere of irrationality that hints at the hidden roots of violence and cruelty. Because of those cross-purposes, there is no space in which a new vision might emerge. Ultimately *Death in the Andes* is a typical Vargas Llosa novel. Despite its moments of confusion, the narration is controlled throughout. The characters' voices are carefully modulated. The novel's power and beauty inhere in the tightness of its composition.

Though *Death in the Andes* skirts tired modernist hypotheses about the Third World, it is still not a postmodern novel in the manner of, say, Pynchon's *Gravity's Rainbow*. It sees the "other" as an irrational being, embedding in typical pursuits and settings: sorcery, strange rituals, savage landscapes, and brutality. But it would be wrong to dismiss it as a coarse statement about inscrutable cultures, for it is a playful and mostly witty realist text about everyday life in Peru: in short, a trustworthy history. Its account of the activities of guerrillas in a small town, and of their subsequent trials, and its portrait of the melodramatic love affair between a soldier and a prostitute have the credibility of reportage. If the Peru of *Death in the Andes* is a place "no one can understand," it is also a country where everyone complains all too understandably of a poor wage and the stupidity of risking one's life to earn it. Although always experimental, Vargas Llosa is one of the most realistic of Latin America's writers.

His hero, Corporal Lituma, was the central figure in *Who Killed Polomino Molero?* This, too, is a detective novel. In *The Green House,* which takes its name from a brothel, Lituma enjoys a double life, and he has a cameo in *Aunt Julia and the Scriptwriter.* In Lituma, Vargas Llosa offers us a well-founded and sympathetic portrayal of a soldier, with his down-to-earth pragmatism and his steadfast sense of duty that keeps him safe from extremism, his honest prudence, his instinct for survival, and his caustic humor.

His own schooling in a military lycée in Peru gave Vargas Llosa an insight into military life that he has used to great advantage, as in his descriptions of the rivalries and quarrels among young cadets in *The Time of the Hero* and in *Captain Pantoja and the Special Service,* a satire of bureaucracy and sex in the army. He is particularly brilliant on male friendships, locating the points of fragility in macho poses, and portraying tough men hopelessly in love with prostitutes, or the crude joke that dispels male sentimentality. His cruel wit is always very entertaining, and it is never without purpose. If one reads all his work, beginning with his first novels, one can see that Vargas Llosa has always preferred brilliant realists and mocking moderates to utopians and fanatics.

Soldiers are the heroes of *Death in the Andes.* There is little effort to understand the Shining Path guerrillas. They figure as representatives of unadulterated irrationality and an evil that borders on the absurd. This has much to do with the political changes that the author underwent as he grew older. As a young man, the modernist Marxist Vargas Llosa was entranced by the Cuban revolution, but as he matured he became a liberal, and in the 1980s, he was scathing about those who, like Günter Grass, said that "all of Latin America had to use Cuba as an example." Half in jest, Vargas Llosa defined himself as "one of the two writers in the world who admire Margaret Thatcher and hate Fidel Castro," adding that "the other writer, more accurately described as a poet, was Philip Larkin."

After reading his account of the Shining Path guerrillas in *Death in the Andes,* it is quite a surprise to read, in one of Vargas Llosa's youthful essays, a tribute to a Marxist guerrilla, a friend who was killed during a "clash with the Peruvian army." One is left wondering whether the humanity in guerrillas is impossible for people like us to see once our own youth has passed, or is it that after we have passed a certain age people like us have no friends who are guerrillas? Vargas Llosa is such a fine writer and his views are so compelling that even in those places where one's politics part from his, his voice still possesses the sincerity of a small boy for whom one cannot help but feel affection.

In an early article about Sebastian Salazar Bondy, one of Peru's most brilliant writers, who died a broken man at a very young age, he asks, "What does it mean to be a writer in Peru?" It is a question that must bring sorrow to us all, and not just because Peru lacks a proper body of readers and a serious literary publishing culture. It is easy to share Vargas Llosa's fury when he writes of the poverty, indifference, ignorance, and hostility that Peruvian writers are forced to endure; even if they survive all this, they are assumed to live outside the real world, leading Vargas Llosa to say that "all Peruvian writers are in the end doomed to defeat." When one reads of Vargas Llosa's youth and his hatred for the Peruvian bourgeoisie (which he describes as "more stupid than all the others"), when he bemoans its total lack of interest in books and its paltry offerings to world literature, when he describes his own great hunger for foreign literature, the sorrow in his voice is unmistakably that of remoteness from the center, a state of mind that people like us understand all too well.

CHAPTER FORTY-FOUR

Salman Rushdie: *The Satanic Verses* and the Freedom of the Writer

The exaggerated scenes that once marked Salman Rushdie as a quintessential magical realist, and the dreams this writer once invented for his books, have now come to resemble real life: His own novel has been banned in India, Pakistan, and most Islamic countries. There is as much anger against the English and American publishers as against the author and the novel. There have been protests and demonstrations in the West as well as in the East. Booksellers who stock the book have been threatened. When the book is burned in public places, so too is the author in effigy, and now the Ayatollah Khomeini has put a price on Rushdie's head. Some say he will have to spend the rest of his life in hiding, while others say that with plastic surgery and a new identity he might be safe to walk among us again. While the world media continue to go to astounding lengths to give us live coverage of the manhunt, which door or chimney an assassin might use, we have heard discussions about freedom of thought here—or, rather, the ways in which the imaginary world of a novelist might be rightfully limited. As we in Turkey live in a secular republic that puts strict curbs on both Islam and freedom of expression, we are always content to sit on the sidelines as the game plays itself out just beyond our borders, amusing ourselves with the details we can glean from the foreign press.

No, I am not saying that there is a total lack of interest, but as in Iran, those who are most eager to launch into the subject tend to be those who have not read one word of the novel and do not in fact read novels at all: The Religious Affairs Directorate is ordered to convene an emergency meeting, as if the matter posed a theological challenge to the history of Islam, whereupon imams who never read novels give sermons to congregations who never read novels, and journalists who have not read *this*

174

novel pose theological questions to professors—who have not read it either—and then go on to devise headlines whose deep shamefulness has nothing to do with theology: SHOULD HE BE KILLED OR SHOULD HE NOT BE KILLED?

Like his second novel, *Midnight's Children,* Salman Rushdie's *Satanic Verses* bears the stamp of "magical realism," which has informed world literature for twenty years now, though the lineage can be traced back to Rabelais. As we can see in Günter Grass's *The Tin Drum* and Gabriel García Márquez's *One Hundred Years of Solitude*—the two finest books in this mode, both already available in Turkish—the author's characters and their world do not obey the laws of the physical world. In these novels we see animals speaking, people flying, dead people standing, charming ghosts and spirits strolling about, objects coming to life, and—as in *The Satanic Verses*—natural events taking supernatural turns. Though *The Satanic Verses* has characters who quarrel with djinns, demons, and devils, changing from people into devils or goats, it also relates two intertwined tales that would fit easily into a realist novel: These follow the fortunes of two Indians from Bombay who move to London and become English.

Gibreel Farishta is a film star who grew up in a Bombay that resembles our own Istanbul, coming to public notice in a film industry that resembles our own Yeşilçam and thereafter gaining fame playing Hindu gods. Saladin Chamcha is a Bombay Muslim who, like Rushdie himself, is sent to England by his wealthy businessman father to study at a public school. (At one point the narrator defines him as "an Indian translated into English.") The two heroes come together during an Air India flight to London. The Air India plane (to which Rushdie, as fond as ever of wordplay, gives the name *Garden*) is hijacked by Sikh terrorists, forced to land and then take off again, and as it is approaching London it vanishes into space. Though everyone else on board dies, the two heroes fall as if from heaven into a snow-covered England, safe and sound but, like Kafka's Gregor Samsa, transformed. Saladin Chamcha, now a musician, turns into a horned and hairy-legged goat. Racing before him, Gibreel Farishta remains the same physically but undergoes a change of personality. With a megalomaniacal fury that will be tamed by medical intervention, Gibreel believes himself to be the archangel of the same name who delivered the Koran to the Prophet Muhammad. The journey that the two heroes make over English soil to London (called Eloven Diyoven in the novel) is in essence the story of Indian and Pakistani emigration to the same city.

Starting out together like twins, the heroes find each other again after every separation, for better or for worse. Their progress is unsure: Now they side with the angels and now with the devils. But—and this is always the case for me with magical realism—it was not the supernatural adventures that kept me reading. The texture emerges from a weaving together of flashback, reminiscence, digression, and subplot, so it is the narrator we heed first: He offers the reader long orations here and there (as for example a long critique of Thatcherism politics). What impresses me most is the myth-laden language that he and his heroes use to describe their early years in Bombay. (Like Nabokov, Rushdie loves word games, internal rhymes, seldom-used words, and neologisms.) As the narrator distances himself and his heroes from their "Muslim youth" to go in search of transformation, to shed one language, one culture, a certain anger seeps in. Years later, when the narrator returns to his own country, his father will give his anglicized son his own views on anger and its consequences: "If you went abroad to hate your own kind, then you will have nothing but hatred from your own kind!"

With Khomeini's fatwa, it is not just the translation of *The Satanic Verses* that has been stopped but the translation of Rushdie's previous works.

At this point, we must ask the public, which has witnessed the killing of Turan Dursun for his work on the Koran, to do some soul-searching about the threat against Rushdie.

POLITICS, EUROPE, AND OTHER PROBLEMS OF BEING ONESELF

CHAPTER FORTY-FIVE

PEN Arthur Miller Speech

In March 1985, Arthur Miller and Harold Pinter made a trip together to Istanbul. At the time, they were perhaps the two most important names in world theater but, sadly, it was not a play or a literary event that brought them to Istanbul, it was the ruthless limits being set on freedom of expression in Turkey at that time, and the many writers languishing in prison. In 1980 there had been a coup in Turkey. Hundreds of thousands were thrown into prison and, as always, it was writers who were persecuted the most vigorously. Whenever I look through the newspaper archives and the almanacs of that time to remind myself what it was like in those days, I soon come across what for us is the most emblematic image: men sitting in a courtroom, flanked by gendarmes, their heads shaven, frowning as their case proceeds. There were many writers among them, and Miller and Pinter had come to Istanbul to meet with them and their families, to offer assistance, and to bring their plight to the attention of the world. Their trip had been arranged by PEN—the International Association of Poets, Playwrights, Editors, Essayists and Novelists—in conjunction with Helsinki Watch. I went to the airport to meet them, because a friend of mine and I were to be their guides.

I had been proposed for this job, not because I had anything to do with politics in those days but because I was a novelist who was fluent in English. I happily accepted, not just because it was a way of helping writer friends in trouble, but because it meant spending a few days in the company of two literary giants. Together we visited small, struggling publishing houses, the dark and dusty headquarters of small magazines always on the verge of shutting down, and cluttered newsrooms, as well as afflicted writers and their families, their houses, and their restaurant

haunts. Until then I had stood on the margins of the political world, never entering unless coerced, but now, as I listened to suffocating tales of repression, cruelty, and outright evil, I felt drawn in by guilt—drawn in, too, by feelings of solidarity—while at the same time feeling an equal and opposite desire to protect myself from all this and to aspire to nothing but to write beautiful novels. As my friend and I took Miller and Pinter by taxi from appointment to appointment through the city traffic, we discussed the street vendors, the horse carts, the cinema posters, and the scarfless and scarf-wearing women, that distinction always so interesting to Western observers. One image was so deeply engraved in my mind I see it still, and it takes place at the Hilton Hotel, where our guests were staying. At one end of a very long corridor, my friend and I are whispering to each other in some agitation, while at the other end, Miller and Pinter are whispering in the shadows with an equally dark intensity.

The same tense gloom was evident in every room we visited—room after room of troubled, chain-smoking men—an atmosphere fed by both pride and guilt. Sometimes the feeling was expressed openly, and sometimes I felt it myself or sensed it in other people's gestures and expressions. The writers, thinkers, and journalists with whom we were meeting mostly defined themselves as leftists in those days, so it could be said that their troubles had much to do with affinities for the freedoms held dear by Western liberal democracies. Twenty years on, when I see that half of these people—or thereabouts, I don't have the precise numbers—

now align themselves with a nationalism that is at odds with Westernization and democracy, I of course feel sad, but recent events in the Middle
East have given pause to those who believe democracy to be the future.

Nevertheless, my experience then as a guide, and similar experiences
in later years, impressed upon me something that we all know but that I
would like to take this opportunity to emphasize: Regardless of national
circumstances, freedom of thought and expression are universal human
rights. These freedoms, which modern people long for as the starving
yearn for bread, can never justifiably be limited by nationalist sentiment,
moral sensitivities, or hoped-for international gain. If many nations outside the West suffer poverty in shame, it is not because they have freedom of expression but because they don't. As for those who emigrate
from these poor countries to the West or the North to escape economic
hardship and brutal repression, we know they sometimes find themselves further brutalized by racism in rich countries. We must be alert to
the xenophobia these immigrants encounter in the West and most particularly in Europe. We must be alert to the tendency to denigrate immigrants and minorities for their religion, their ethnic roots, or the
oppression visited upon them by the governments of the countries
they've left behind. But to respect the human rights of minorities, and to
respect their humanity, is not to suggest that we should accommodate all
manner of belief or tolerate those who attack or seek to limit freedom of
thought in deference to the moral codes of those minorities. Some of us
have a better understanding of the West, some of us have more affection
for those who live in the East, and some, like me, try to do the two things
at the same time, but these attachments, this desire to understand, should
never stand in the way of our respect for human rights.

I always have difficulty expressing my political judgments with
emphatic clarity—I feel pretentious, as if I'm saying things that are not
quite true. This is because I know I am bound to reduce my thoughts
about life to the music of a single voice and a single point of view; I am,
after all, a novelist. Living as I do in a world where, in a very short time,
someone who has been a victim of tyranny and oppression can suddenly
become one of the oppressors, I know also that holding strong beliefs is
itself a difficult and sometimes treacherous exercise. I do also believe
that most of us entertain contradictory thoughts simultaneously; much of
the pleasure of writing novels comes from exploring this peculiarly modern state of mind whereby people are forever contradicting themselves.
This is why I believe freedom of expression to be so important—because
it allows us to discover the hidden truths of the societies in which we

live. At the same time, as I know from personal experience, the shame and pride I mentioned earlier also play their part.

Let me tell another story that might cast some light on the shame and pride I felt twenty years ago while I was taking Miller and Pinter around Istanbul. In the ten years following their visit, and largely because of coincidence, good intentions, anger, guilt, and personal jealousies, not at all because of my books but because of issues to do with freedom of expression, I found myself developing a far more powerful political persona than I had ever wanted. About this time, the Indian author of a UN report on freedom of expression in my part of the world—an elderly gentleman—came to Istanbul and looked me up. As it happened, our meeting was at the Hilton Hotel. No sooner had we sat down at a table than the Indian gentleman asked a question that still echoes strangely in my mind:

"Mr. Pamuk, what is going on in your country that you would like to explore in your novels but shy away from, for fear of prosecution?"

There followed a long silence. Thrown by his question, I thought and thought and thought. I was plunged into a Dostoyevskyan despair. Clearly, what the gentleman from the UN wished to ask was, "Given your country's taboos, legal prohibitions, and oppressive policies, what is going unsaid?" But because he had—out of a desire to be polite, perhaps?—asked the eager young writer sitting across from him to consider the question in terms of his own novels, I, in my inexperience, took his question literally. Ten years ago there were many more subjects closed off by laws and oppressive state policies than there are today, but as I went through them one by one, I could find none that I wished to explore "in my novels." I knew, nonetheless, that if I said, There is nothing I wish to write in my novels that I am not able to discuss, I'd be giving the wrong impression. For I'd already begun to speak often and vociferously about all these dangerous subjects *outside* my novels. Moreover, didn't I often and angrily fantasize about raising these subjects in my novels, just because they happened to be forbidden? As I thought all this through, I was at once ashamed of my silence and yet again made deeply aware of the fact that freedom of expression was linked with pride and human dignity.

Many writers we respect and value have chosen to take up forbidden topics purely because the very fact of the prohibition was an injury to their pride; I know this from my own experience. Because when another writer in another house is not free, no writer is free. This, indeed, is the spirit that informs the solidarity felt by PEN writers all over the world.

Sometimes my friends rightly tell me or someone else, "That was wrong, what you said; if only you had worded it like this, in a way that no one would find offensive, you wouldn't be in so much trouble now." But to change one's words, to package them in a way that will be acceptable to everyone, and to become skilled in this arena is a bit like smuggling contraband through customs, and much the same way, even when successfully accomplished, it produces a feeling of shame and degradation.

Freedom of thought, the happiness that comes of the ability to express the anger deep inside us—we have already mentioned how honor and human dignity depend on it. So let us now ask ourselves how "reasonable" it is to denigrate cultures and religions or, more to the point, to bomb countries mercilessly in the name of democracy and freedom of thought. The theme of this year's PEN festival is reason and belief. In the war against Iraq, the heartless and tyrannical murder of almost a hundred thousand people has brought neither peace nor democracy. Quite to the contrary, it has served to ignite nationalist anti-Western anger. Things have become a great deal more difficult for the small minority struggling for democracy and secularism in the Middle East. This savage, cruel war is the shame of America and the West. Organizations like PEN, and writers like Harold Pinter and Arthur Miller, are its pride.

CHAPTER FORTY-SIX

No Entry

This man wandering so languorously through the streets—he may be just killing time before an appointment, or perhaps he got off the bus one stop before his destination because there was no need to rush, or perhaps he is just curious about the neighborhood, never having seen it before. As this traveler wanders through the streets, lost in thought but still taking an interest in his surroundings, gazing at the drapery shops, the pharmacy display windows, the crowded coffeehouses, the magazines and newspapers strung along the wall, he happens onto a sign that says NO ENTRY. It doesn't concern him, this sign; it's not addressed to him, because even if it were not there, this is not the sort of door that would ever interest or attract him. He is occupied with his own affairs, living in his own world; he has no interest in walking through this door.

But still, the notice has reminded him that aimless wandering has its limits. It might not have seemed so at once, but this door that previously meant nothing to him is now a rude reminder that there are limits beyond which his imagination cannot go; the imaginary world in which he had been traveling so blissfully is now cast in shadow. Maybe he should just forget it. But why did they write that? It's a door, after all, and doors are for people to enter. So the notice is there to remind him that, while some people pass through this door, others cannot. Which means the NO ENTRY sign is a lie. Actually, what it should say is NOT EVERYONE WHO WANTS TO ENTER IS ALLOWED DO SO. By implying that certain privileged people can pass through, all those who do not possess the requisite privileges are barred, even if they wish to enter. At the same time it accords to those who have no wish to enter the same fate as those who do.

After the man in the street has pursued this line of thought to its logical conclusion, he cannot help but wonder who the others might be who might have wished to go through that door, only to be kept out. Who exactly *is* allowed to enter that door, anyway? What is it that lets them through? What is it that gives some people this privilege and not others? At this point, the wanderer reminds himself that entry may not depend on privilege. Perhaps this is a door for undistinguished people who don't wish others to look inside and see how miserable their lives are. But when the traveler, who is now coming out of his daydream, remembers that most people fit the doors of their homes with keys for just this reason, he is returned to the thought that the door provides a covert way of maintaining privilege. Instead of arranging to furnish keys to all admissible individuals, with which they might lock the door when they leave before pocketing the key like any ordinary citizen, the privileged owners have written NO ENTRY.

If the daydreamer can think all this as he takes two steps forward, then these people must have been following the same line of thought when they put this sign on their door. Perhaps a few said, "Instead of putting up a NO ENTRY sign, let's have keys made for us all!" but those in favor of the sign must have insisted that this was not an option. Why? Because the problem was too complex to be solved with a few keys. Perhaps a lot of people would not obey the NO ENTRY sign, a lot of people who know this sign is not addressed to them—too large a group for keys. This would be the most logical conclusion: One day, the people inside sat down to discuss it among themselves—whom in this crowd to let inside and whom to keep out. "There are too many people coming in from the outside," they probably said. "Let's not let them all in! Which ones shall we keep out?" Then they crossed their legs and sipped their coffee and began to argue about which outsiders to admit and which to exclude. Some of the insiders were most certainly troubled by this discussion. Maybe they too would be evicted by the time this discussion was concluded.

The man outside, looking at the door, has witnessed tense situations like this before, so he can imagine the people who have nailed the sign up and he can guess how their discussion will proceed. It will first be dominated by those agitated souls who wish to protect their property, their pleasures, and their privileges, but because such anxieties are boring, the language will soon change. Those who ask, "What do you mean when you talk about our property, our pleasures, and our habits?" will themselves be asked, "What do you mean by the word *we*?" This very simple question causes instant ferment. These people have now discovered how much fun it is to pretend they don't know who they are. There will be those who find the discussion troubling, who have to object to four or five people joining them from the crowd outside. Under their guidance, the discussion turns into a riddle, a question of identity. This is the most fun of all. They all take pleasure in finding ingenious ways to enumerate the virtues that set them apart from all others, but without actually saying so. It is all so entertaining that they begin to wonder why they didn't hang up the NO ENTRY sign sooner. In an instant, the street on the other side of the door has become a gathering place for all those who oppose those virtues which they have assigned themselves. However they now define themselves, the people outside are their opposite. It could even be said that they are only able to define themselves by saying what they are that the people outside their door are not. Many idiots passing by the door without thinking are not aware of this. A few people feel indebted to these idiots. It wouldn't be a bad idea to take some of them in, they think. It could be a way of teaching them how we became people like us, and maybe when they become like us we'll be stronger.

This is the point at which some people will realize that the sign is intended to direct the attention of the idiots outside to the privileges enjoyed by insiders. What this sign does—what it does to our traveler— is to give all those who pass in front of the door the sense of being outsiders. Some people can feel this without even wanting to pass through the door. All they need to do is see the sign.

As he begins to feel as if he has stood longer than necessary in front of this door, our traveler sees how the sign has somehow divided the world in two. There are those who can enter and those who cannot. The world is full of pointless divisions like this, so many passersby will give this one no particular importance, but the fact remains that there are still some people who give it enough importance to take the trouble of nailing such a sign on their door. At this point, the traveler, having now emerged from his daydream, decides that all this talk of identity is really shameful boasting and self-aggrandizement. A great anger rises up from deep inside him. Who is it behind this door—who could it be? For the first time he feels the urge to enter. But what is to be gained from playing into the hands of the smug? Because it will take no more than two or three seconds for him to predict what will pass through their minds. At the same moment, it occurs to him that it should be easy to open the door. Two or three people could kick it in easily, or push it open with their shoulders. If this were not the case, they would not have put up the sign in the first place. If he wants to get inside, all he has to do is go get one or two of his brothers and ask for their help. Hadn't he already divined—

thanks to this sign—that he and all these other outsiders share a common fate? So now the man standing outside the door begins to imagine the new world unfurling before him. He could, if he wished, seek out all those with whom he shares his fate and draw them into a discussion of character. Now it has become important for him to know who, and what, he is. He must establish an identity that rejects all that the arrogant insiders stand for.

So it is that the traveler begins to think about his own particular virtues, pleasures, belongings, and relationships; one by one he turns them into things he must proudly claim and protect. So heady is this celebration of his character that he has even begun to feel anger against those who do not possess the same virtues, those who are unlike him. At the same moment it seems to him as if those inside might have foreseen this turn of events. But he is not about to give up all the traits that make him who he is simply because this is their game plan. There is a move he can make—an inspired move—against them. Before he undertakes to work out this move, he is well advised to ask himself what his purpose is. "Is my aim to go inside?" asks the man who, until only a few minutes ago, was wandering the streets lost in thought. "Or is my aim to discover what characteristics I share with all the others who are not allowed in?" But he does not wish to trouble himself with thoughts so cold-blooded and analytical. What he wants now more than anything else is to vent the anger he feels rising up inside him. If he does so, he'll calm down, maybe even forget the sign, but because he does not know of a way to vent his anger, he becomes more agitated still. As the pain of exclusion grows slowly stronger, it feeds the flame of his anger. Perhaps his pain comes from feeling that he belongs to the same class as all the other outsiders, is made from the same material, shares the same soul. There is something belittling about this—a reality that neither his mind nor his soul wishes to accept.

By now the man standing outside the door, staring at the sign, is well aware that he has fallen into a trap, allowed himself to be demeaned by the door, which had not concerned him in the least only moments earlier, when he was wandering so happily down the street. He is almost tempted to laugh at his own fragility, at the ease with which he can take offense. He has enough of a sense of humor to do this; but still he feels compelled to show that this small and unnecessary insult, this distressing prohibition, is uncalled for. The people who put up this NO ENTRY sign—did they realize, when they set out to safeguard their security, their virtue, their uniqueness, that their act would insult and trouble others? The man looking at the sign now decides that those who put it up had just this aim in mind. It was to cause people like himself just this sort of disquiet that they had hung a NO ENTRY sign on their door. They'd achieved their aim: There is a growing disquiet on the other side of the door. Then, in an instant, he sees the bigger picture. Yes, it's possible that the people who hung up the sign might not have foreseen this disquiet, that all they had wanted was to protect themselves, distinguish themselves from those outside. But they must have known that this would cause heartbreak and greatly upset people. In that case, there was a certain heartlessness to it all—these people thought too much of themselves, giving no thought to the disquiet, the misery, that their actions might cause.

Above all, I dislike people who think only of themselves, thinks the man, who is still troubled by the sign. We might say that he is not so much troubled by the sign as by his own nature, by things hidden deep in his soul. If we can entertain this thought, then he can too, and perhaps he is doing so at this very moment. But this is not the sort of thinking that comes easily—for it leads to the thought that the reason for the disquiet you feel inside might be your own inadequacy, your own shortcomings. For now the man standing outside the door is thinking that the people who hung up the sign foresaw that it would be insulting enough to stop someone like him in his tracks, and this makes the anger inside him grow stronger. But still he is thinking clearly enough to think that his anger is not wholly justified.

CHAPTER FORTY-SEVEN

Where Is Europe?

I'm walking down a street in Beyoğlu, the most European neighborhood on the European side of Istanbul, when I happen upon a used bookseller. I know this narrow, meandering street, with its modest repair shops, its little mirror and furniture stores, and its humble restaurants. This is a new place, so I go inside.

What I find is nothing like the old Istanbul secondhand booksellers who dealt in dusty manuscripts as well as other printed matter; there are no dusty book towers, no mountains waiting to be priced. Everything is as clean and beautifully arranged as in the antiques shops that have begun to proliferate in the area; the books have even been classified. So this is an "antiquarian" bookseller of the type that has begun to replace the old merchants in this area. I gaze disconsolately at the shelves, on which bound books stand to attention like soldiers in a modern, disciplined army.

In one corner I notice a long shelf of Greek lawbooks. They must have belonged to a Greek lawyer who died or moved to Athens long ago, and as there are not very many Greeks left in the city who might be interested in buying these old lawbooks, I guess that the bookseller has chosen to display them on his empty shelves because of their handsome bindings. I pick them up and caress them, impressed not so much by their bindings or their contents as by the fact that the original owners might have traced their lineage as far back as the Byzantine Empire; then I notice the books sitting next to them. Here are all eight volumes of Albert Sorel's early twentieth-century opus, *L'Europe et la révolution française.* I come across this one often in secondhand bookshops. Having discovered their relevance to our times, the novelist Nahit Sirri Örik translated these thick tomes into Turkish, and they were then published

by the Westernizing republic's National Education Ministry. No matter
what language they speak in their homes—be it Greek, or French, or
Turkish—a good many Istanbul intellectuals have read this work, but, as
I know only too well, they did not read them as a French reader might,
seeking connection with their memories and their own pasts, but rather
searching within the pages for some sense of their future, of their European dreams.

For people like me, who live uncertainly on the edge of Europe with
only our books to keep us company, Europe has figured always as a
dream, a vision of what is to come; an apparition at times desired and
at times feared; a goal to achieve or a danger. A future—but never a
memory.

So too my own memories of things European, to the degree that I am
able to dramatize them, are less memories than figments of a dream: I
have no real memory of Europe. What I have are the European dreams
and illusions of a man who has lived out his life in Istanbul. When I was
seven, I spent a summer in Geneva, where my father was working as an
engineer. Our house stood among the roofs rising above the eponymous
fountain, and the first time I heard church bells, I felt myself not inside
Europe but within Christendom. Like Turks who go to Europe to spend
the money they've earned in the tobacco trade, and like so many others
who go seeking political or economic refuge, I too walked the streets of
Geneva in amazement and admiration, unaccustomed, perhaps, to feeling quite so free, but my recollections of what I saw in shop windows,
cinemas, people's faces, and the streets of the city are memories of my
first glimpse of an imagined future. For people like me, Europe is only
interesting as a vision of the future—and as a threat.

It is because I am one of many intellectuals on the edge of Europe
obsessively engaged with this future that I am able to find Sorel's history
for sale in Istanbul's booksellers. When Dostoyevsky published his
impressions of Europe in a Russian newspaper a hundred and thirty
years ago, he asked, "Of Russians who read magazines and newspapers,
who does not know twice as much about Europe as Russia?" and then he
added, half in anger, half in jest, "Actually, we know Europe ten times
better, but I said 'twice as much' so as not to offend." This troubled interest in Europe is, for many intellectuals living on its periphery, a tradition
that goes back centuries. To some, it was a sort of overreaching that Dostoyevsky deemed offensive, while others saw it as a natural and
inevitable process. The quarrel between these two approaches has fos-
tered a literature that is at times ill-tempered and at times philosophical

or ironic, and it is to this literature, and not the great traditions of Europe and Asia, for which I feel greatest affinity.

The first rule of this tradition is that everyone must take a side. The debate about Europe has a long history in Turkey and was revived in 1996—after the Islamist Refah Party became part of a coalition government—and each new round begins with an attempt to define and reject both the dream version of Europe and the nightmare. Everyone—be he liberal or Islamist, socialist or socialite—has something to say on the matter, and I have heard so many admonishments about *which* Europe we should be discussing—humanist Europe, racist Europe, democratic Europe, Christian Europe, technological Europe, rich Europe, the Europe that respects human rights—that I often feel like the child so bored by dinner table discussions about religion that he abandons all faith in God; there have been times when I've wished to forget everything I've ever heard on this subject. But I would still like to share a few memories with my European readers and a few secrets about the private lives of people living on the edge of Europe. Here are a few ways in which we who live in Istanbul assert our European selves:

1. An expression I've heard in my upper-middle-class Westernized family since childhood: "This is how they do it in Europe." If they're drafting a new law on fishing, if you're choosing new curtains for your home, or hatching an evil plan against your enemies, utter these mysterious words, and you can bring any discussion of method, color, style, or content to an abrupt end.

2. Europe is a sexual paradise. Relative to Istanbul, this is a pretty accurate guess. As with many bookish compatriots, my first sight of a naked woman was in an illustration in a magazine imported from Europe. This is surely my first and most striking memory of Europe.

3. "If a European saw this, what would he think?" This is both a fear and a desire. We are all afraid that when they see how we do not resemble them, they will castigate us. This is why we want there to be less torture in prisons, or at least torture that leaves no trace. Sometimes we want to take pleasure in showing them just how different we are from them: as when we want to meet an Islamist terrorist, or when we want the first person to shoot the pope to be a Turk.

4. After saying, "Europeans are very courteous, refined, cultured, and elegant," people will often add, "But when they don't get what they want . . ." and the example they offer will reflect the degree of their nationalist anger: "When my Paris taxi driver found my tip to be too small . . ." or "Didn't you know that they also organized the Crusades?"

The Europe that figures in all such propositions is a place of all-or-nothing. For those like myself who live on its edge and sustain an obsessive interest in it, it is before all else a dream forever changing its face and character. My generation, and the generations that came before us, have for the most part believed in this dream more fervently than Europeans themselves. This was before Turkey's negotiations with the European Union became so intense and troubled.

Since I have lived all my life on the European shores of Istanbul—in other words, in Europe—it is not at all hard for me to feel myself a European in the geographical sense. But in Istanbul booksellers like the one I explored while writing this essay, the only sign of this identification is the book of Albert Sorel's, translated into Turkish in the last century. Do people now refrain from asking for *La question d'Orient au dix-huitième siècle* because this book was published in the Arabic script, which none of us can read now, on account of Turkey's having adopted the Latin alphabet in the early years of the Republic, so as to be more European? Or is it because we have come to see Europe as far too troubling and problematic in ways undreamt of before? I cannot say.

CHAPTER FORTY-EIGHT

A Guide to Being Mediterranean

I t was the early sixties; I was nine years old. My father was driving the whole family—my mother, my brother, everyone—from Ankara to Mersin in an old Opel. After traveling for many hours, I was told that in a short while I would have my first glimpse of the Mediterranean, and I would never forget it. As we passed among the last peaks of the Taurus Mountains, I kept my eyes on the road that our map described as stabilized; as I watched it snake across the yellow hills, it happened: I caught sight of the Mediterranean, and I've never forgotten it. In Turkish we call it the white sea, but this was blue, and one I'd never seen before—perhaps because I'd been expecting it to conform to its Turkish name. I'd imagined something tinged with white: an imaginary sea, perhaps, a sea that, like a desert, made people see mirages. Whereas this sea looked utterly familiar. That familiar sea breeze had floated all the way up to the mountains, to rush through the car window. The Mediterranean was a sea I recognized. Its Turkish name was what had fooled me into thinking it would be something I'd never seen before.

Years later, when I read the famous historian Fernand Braudel's writings on the Mediterranean, I realized that this encounter with the Mediterranean was not in fact my first. Braudel includes the Dardanelles, the Sea of Marmara, the Bosphorus, and the Black Sea in his map. In his view, these bodies of water are extensions of the great Mediterranean Sea. For Braudel, the Mediterranean is what it is by virtue of a shared history, shared trade, and shared climate. The proof is in the fig and olive trees that grow along the shores of the Black Sea, the Sea of Marmara, and the Bosphorus.

I remember how this simple line of reasoning troubled and confused me. All these years I'd been living in Istanbul—had I actually been liv-

ing in the Mediterranean without knowing it? How could I not know I
was Mediterranean, or even what it meant to be Mediterranean?

Perhaps the best way of belonging to a city, a country, or a sea is to
have no knowledge whatsoever of its boundaries, its image, or even its
existence. The best *İstanbullu* is the one who has forgotten that he is one.
The most authentic Muslim has no idea of what is Islamic and what is
not! It was when the Turks did not know they were Turks that they were
pure Turks! This was the right way to look at things, but for me it did not
work, because I did have an image of the Mediterranean and it had nothing to do with the Istanbul in which I lived. It was not just because Istanbul was in my view a darker, grayer, and more northern city than the
notion of "Mediterranean" could accommodate; it was also because the
Mediterranean belonged to peoples below us, to the south, in countries
and cultures very different from our own. It now seems to me that this
illusion, this confusion, reflects Turkey's awkwardness and uncertainty
about the Mediterranean.

The always westward-moving Ottoman Turks reached the Balkan
shores of the Mediterranean in the fourteenth century. Having conquered
Istanbul and entered the Black Sea, they were well aware that the
Mediterranean could be used for further conquest. By the height of the
Ottoman Empire, when it had the entirety of what is now called the Middle East in its possession, it had earned the right to think of the Mediterranean as a mare nostrum. As our lycée textbooks boasted, it was by now
an *inland sea*. The militarist bravado suggests a simpler logic than the
one put forth by those who wish to see the Mediterranean as culturally
distinct. For the Ottomans, the Mediterranean was a geographical entity:
a body of water, a string of routes, straits, and passageways. I must admit
I like this thoroughly geometrical approach, and I am to some degree its
victim.

Even so, this inland sea was fraught with danger. It was home to
Venetian galleons, Maltese ships, corsairs, storms of uncertain origin,
and disasters. When the mists began to clear, the Ottomans did not find a
warm and sunny paradise, they found themselves up against the ships,
flags, and general menace of the enemy, the other. In my early youth,
when I read the much-loved historical novels of Abdullah Ziya
Kozanoğlu, I could see that, for Barbaros and Dragut and the other sea
warriors (all of whom were born Christian), the Mediterranean figured
only as a hunting ground.

If this hunting ground, this war zone we call the Mediterranean, had a certain natural allure, it was its shape; its place on the map was what endowed it with mystery. The sea that Coleridge's Ancient Mariner might associate with God, crime, punishment, death, and the dream of immortality was for the Ottomans a sea to be conquered. Their concern was not with the legendary beasts and mysterious animals that might be lurking beneath the surface, but rather with the strange, worrisome sea creatures they saw with their own eyes. When looking at them, a person wanted to laugh and make up stories, as did Evliya Celebi. The Ottomans looked at the Mediterranean as an encyclopedia, a shape on the map, a place to visit. Far from the legends, monsters, and secrets of the unknown world, this was a military region, a place to wage war. So it is not by accident that it figures as such for the seventeenth-century Turks and Italians who come face-to-face to fight and take captives in *The White Castle*.

The idea of the Mediterranean as a single entity is artificial, and the single Mediterranean character that derives from it is, likewise, a thing that had to be invented and elaborated before it was discovered. But this dream of the Mediterranean—this mostly literary fantasy—has come exclusively from the North. It was from the writers of northern Europe that the peoples of the Mediterranean discovered they were Mediterranean. The origins of the Mediterranean temperament lie not in Homer or Ibni Haldun but in the Italian sojourns and Mediterranean journeys of Goethe and Stendhal. To be open to the literary and erotic possibilities of the Mediterranean, to explore Mediterranean sensibility, one must share the boredom of, say, Gustave von Aschenbach, the hero of Thomas Mann's *Death in Venice*. Paul Bowles, Tennessee Williams, and E. M. Forster explored the sexuality of the Mediterranean temperament long before today's Mediterranean writers discovered it. Cavafy embraced this dream more completely than any other, but if he now figures as the quintessential Mediterranean poet, it is because a poet like Cavafy is one of the heroes of Lawrence Durrell's Alexandria Quartet. It was from northern writers like these that the peoples of the Mediterranean discovered that they were Mediterranean, that they were different and not of the North.

There is not yet a single Mediterranean nation or Mediterranean flag, and there has been no wholesale humiliation or murder of those who are not Mediterranean, and this allows us to look at Mediterranean identity as an innocent literary game.

Even the most intelligent thinker will, if he talks too long about cultures and civilizations, begin to spout nonsense. We must never forget when we speak about Mediterranean identity to consider the enterprise only a jeu d'esprit.

So here are some ground rules for those wishing to acquire Mediterranean identity:

1. Foster the view of the Mediterranean as a unified entity; it would be a good thing if such it were. This would provide a new doorway to the place of which we are a part for those of us who cannot travel to Spain, France, and Italy without visas.

2. The best definitions of Mediterranean identity are in books written by non-Mediterraneans. Don't complain about this; just try to become like the Mediterraneans they describe, and you'll have your identity.

3. If a writer wants to see himself as Mediterranean, he must give up certain other identities. For example, a French writer who wants to be Mediterranean must give up a part of his Frenchness. By the same logic, a Greek writer wishing to be Mediterranean must give up part of his Balkan and European identities.

4. For those who want to become real Mediterranean writers, whenever you write about it, don't say "the Mediterranean," just say "the sea." Speak of its culture and its particularities without naming them and without using the word *Mediterranean* at all. Because the best way to become a Mediterranean is never to talk about it.

CHAPTER FORTY-NINE

My First Passport and Other European Journeys

In 1959, when I was seven years old, my father went missing under mysterious circumstances; several weeks later, we received word that he was in Paris. He was living in a cheap hotel in Montparnasse, filling up the notebooks that he would, at the end of his life, leave to me in a suitcase, and from time to time, when he was sitting in the Café Dome, he would see Jean-Paul Sartre passing in the street outside.

My grandmother was in the habit of sending him money from Istanbul. My grandfather, a businessman, had made a fortune in railroads. My father and his uncles had not managed to squander their entire inheritance under my grandmother's fretful gaze; not all of the apartments had yet been sold. But twenty-five years after her husband's death, my grandmother decided that the money was running out and she stopped sending money to her Bohemian son in Paris.

This is how my father joined the long line of penniless and miserable Turkish intellectuals who had been walking the streets of Paris for a century. Like my grandfather and my uncles, he was a construction engineer with a good head for mathematics. When his money ran out, he answered an ad in a newspaper; having been hired by IBM, he was dispatched to their office in Geneva. In those days computers were still operated with punch cards, and little was popularly known about them. That is how my Bohemian writer father went on to become one of Europe's first Turkish guest workers.

My mother joined him soon afterward. She left us in our grandmother's plush and crowded home and flew off to Geneva. My older brother and I were to wait until school closed for the summer, and in the meanwhile we both had to get passports.

I remember that we had to pose for a very long time while the pho-

tographer fiddled under a black cloth behind a three-legged wooden con-
traption with a bellows. For the light to strike upon the chemically
treated glass plate, he had to open the lens for a split second with an elegant flick of the wrist, but before he did this, he would look at us first and
say, "Yeeeees," and it was because I found this old photographer so
ridiculous that my first passport picture shows me biting my cheeks. The
passport says that my hair, which had probably not been combed all year
except for this passport picture, was chestnut brown. I must have flipped
through the pages of the passport too quickly to have noticed that it got
my eye color wrong, a mistake I would notice only when I opened up the
passport thirty years later. What this taught me was that—contrary to
what I'd thought—the passport was not a document of who we were but
of what other people thought of us.

Flying into Geneva, our new passports in the pockets of our new jackets, my brother and I were overcome with terror. The plane had banked
as it came in for a landing, and to us this country called Switzerland
became a place where everything, even the clouds, was on a steep incline
stretching to infinity. The plane finished its turn and straightened itself
out, and when we remember our relief at seeing that this new country
was, like Istanbul, built on level earth, my brother and I still laugh.

The streets in this new country were cleaner and emptier. There was
more variety in the shop windows and there were more cars in the roads.
The beggars didn't beg empty-handed, as in Istanbul; they would stand
under the window playing the accordion. Before we threw one of them
money, my mother would wrap it up in paper. Our apartment—a five-
minute walk from the bridges over the Rhône at the point where it flows
into Lac Léman—was "furnished."

This was how I came to associate living in another country with sitting at tables where others had sat before, using glasses and plates on
which strangers had dined, and sleeping in beds that sagged after years
of cradling other sleepers. Another country meant a country that
belonged to other people. We were to accept that these things we were
using would never belong to us, and that this old country, this other land,
would never belong to us either. My mother, who had studied at a French
school in Istanbul, would sit us down at the empty dining-room table
every morning all summer and try to teach us French.

It was after we were enrolled in a state primary school that we found
out we had learned nothing. My parents had been mistaken in hoping
that we might learn French just by listening to the teacher day in and day

out. At recess, my brother and I would wander among the crowds of children playing until we found each other and held hands. This foreign land was an endless garden full of happily playing children. My brother and I would watch this garden of happiness with longing and from a distance.

Although he didn't know French, my brother was top in the class at counting backward by threes. But the only thing that set *me* apart in this school where I couldn't understand the language was my silence. Just as one might refuse a dream in which no one speaks, I refused to go to school. Carried to other cities and other schools, this tendency to turn inward would protect me from life's difficulties, but it also deprived me of its riches. One weekend, they took my brother out of school too. Putting our passports into our hands, they sent us away from Geneva and back to our grandmother in Istanbul.

I never used this passport again—though it bore the words "Member of the Council of Europe," it became a memento of my first failed European adventure, and such was the vehemence of my decision to turn inward that it would be another twenty-four years before I left Turkey again. When I was young, I was full of admiration and longing at the thought of those who acquired passports and traveled to Europe and beyond, but in spite of all the opportunities, I remained fearfully certain that it was my lot to sit in a corner in Istanbul and give myself over to the books that I hoped might complete me as a person and others that might one day make my name. In those days, I believed one could best understand Europe by contemplating its greatest books.

In the end it was my books that prompted me to apply for a second passport. After years shut up in a room, I had managed to turn myself into an author. Now they had invited me to go on tour in Germany, where many Turks had taken political asylum, and it was thought that they would appreciate hearing me read from books that had yet to be translated into German. Though I applied for my passport in the happy hope that I would get to know Turkish readers in Germany, it was during my travels that I came to associate the document with the sort of identity crisis that would go on to afflict so many others in the years that followed.

The first story I need to tell about identity: In the mid-1980s and afterward, I returned to those wonderfully punctual German trains in recurring dreams, speeding from city to city past dark forests, distant village church towers, and platforms of passengers lost in thought. At each destination I would be met by my Turkish host, who would apologize for any number of things I had not noticed as lacking, and as he took me on a tour of the city he would tell me who was expected at that evening's event.

I remember those readings fondly: They were attended by political refugees and their families, teachers, young people who were half German and half Turkish—people who wished to know more about intellectual life in Turkey—and at every meeting there were a few Turkish workers and a few Germans who had decided it would be a good thing to take a warm interest in things Turkish.

At every reading, in every city, the scene would play itself out in much the same way. After I had read from my book, an angry youth would raise his hand to be recognized, and then he would heap scorn on me for daring to write books that spoke airily of abstract beauty when there was still oppression and torture in Turkey, and though I rejected such harsh words, they would awaken in me feelings of guilt. The angry youth would be followed by a woman trembling with the desire to protect me, and her question would have to do with the symmetries in my books or some other such refinement. This would be quickly followed by broad questions about my hopes for Turkey, politics, the future, and the meaning of life itself—these I'd answer as an eager young writer would. Sometimes someone would make a long speech laden with political terminology, though the intent here would not be to blame me but to address others in the audience, and afterward the directors of the association that had invited me would tell me which left-wing faction this particular orator came from; they would go on to explain what meaning he had intended members of other splinter groups to take from his words. From the excitement of the young people who would ask me to share with them the secrets of my success, it became clear to me that young Turks in Germany were less ashamed than their peers in Turkey to have ambitions in life. Then all at once, someone would ask a question that either stemmed from their own broken dreams—"What do you think about Germany's Turks?"—or else touched upon mine—"Why don't you write more about love?"—and as the eighty or ninety people in the hall would begin to titter and smile, I would understand that I was speaking to a group who knew one another, if not intimately then from a distance. As the reading drew to a cosy, friendly close, an elderly gentleman, perhaps a teacher approaching retirement, would praise me excessively, then turn an admonishing eye on one of the half-Turkish, half-German youths laughing and smirking in the back row; for their benefit he would go on to make a nationalist speech, proud but gloomy, about how there were writers of distinction in Turkey—their mother-land—and why it was important to read them and acquaint themselves with their own culture, which fine words would only make the youths laugh a little more.

So these conversations about identity, and the endless questions about nationality, only added to the family atmosphere. When the reading was over, the organizers would take me and ten or fifteen others out for a meal. Usually it was a Turkish restaurant. Even if it wasn't, the questions I'd be asked at the table, the jokes the others started among themselves, and the subjects they brought up would soon give me the impression that I was still in Turkey, and because I was more interested in discussing literature than in talking about Turkey, this would depress me. What I realized later was that even when we seemed to be discussing literature, we were really discussing Turkey. Literature, books, and novels were simply pretexts for broaching—or evading—the troubled uncertainties of self from which our deep unhappiness stemmed.

During these journeys, and all the others I made later on, when my books became better known in German, I would look at the people who had come to hear me read and it was as if I could see in their faces a per-petual distraction, the preoccupation with questions about Turkishness and Germanness. Because my books were partly about the contradic-tions between East and West, and because I was the sort of writer who explored the indecisions and hesitations that such contradictions bred, in allegorical games that turned them on their head, my audiences assumed I must be as exercised by questions of identity and as intrigued by those dark areas as they were, but the truth was that I was not. When, after try-ing for an hour to draw me out, they would retreat silently to the secret world of Germany's Turks, arguing endlessly about the degree to which they were either German or Turkish, I would begin to feel lonely on account of being just a Turk and not a German Turk, and then I would come to see the unhappiness in the room in my own way.

Was this unhappiness, or was it a source of riches? I can't decide. No matter how passionate they are, or how sincere, no matter how much light they may cast on the dreams and fears from which our anxieties stem, such conversations leave me feeling hopeless and thinking that life has no meaning.

Let me illustrate this point with my favorite kind of scale. As I sat around those tables, listening to the talk grow more heated as the night wore on, I noticed that there were quantitative differences in degrees of Turkishness and Germanness, which my Turkish-German tablemates all demanded that I adopt. Among these, let us assign the number 10 to those who believed that it was important to become fully German (if indeed such a thing is possible; in any case, this sort of person shies away from any memories of Turkey and sometimes even calls himself a German). To those who are unwilling to contemplate any dilution of their Turkishness, let us assign the number 1 (this sort of person is proud to be living like a Turk, even though he is in Germany). Among those at the table who found themselves between the two extremes, there were several varieties. Some dreamed of one day returning to Turkey forever but spent their holidays in Italy, others refused to fast during Ramadan but still watched Turkish television every night, while a few grew ever more distant from their Turkish friends even as they nurtured a deep resentment of Germans. When I considered the choices (or, rather, vows) that these people had made, it was clear enough what lay beneath them: fears of humiliation, unfulfilled desires, pain, and isolation.

But what surprised me the most—what made me feel as if I were watching the same mysterious scene play itself out over and over and no matter where the people at my table might find themselves on my scale—was the absolute and fanatical certainty with which each would defend the rightness of his own degree and reject all others. So for a person who would be a 5 on the scale, it was not enough to believe that his only path was to be both German and Turkish; he would go after all the 4s as being closed-minded and backward and all the 7s and 8s as being cut off from their true identities. Later in the evening, it would not be enough to promote their own relative degrees of Turkishness and Germanness as the best way to be; in fiery tones, they would proclaim them an article of faith too sacred to be questioned.

This reminds me of the famous sentence with which Tolstoy began *Anna Karenina,* to the effect that all happy families are alike but that all unhappy families are unhappy in their own way. The same applies to nationalism and obsessions with identity: Happy nationalists expressing their love for flags or celebrating victories in soccer matches and international competitions are the same all over the world. It is when national difference is not a cause for celebration that a terrible variety emerges. It is the same with our passports, which sometimes bring us joy and sometimes sadness: As for the miserable ways they cause us to question our identity, no two are alike.

It was because we stood in that school playground in Geneva in 1959, holding hands and watching at an envious remove as the other children laughed and played, that my brother and I were sent back to Turkey with our passports. In the years that followed, hundreds of thousands of other children settled in Germany, with or without passports, destined to sink into a much deeper despair. Ten or fifteen years after I first met them, these same people will now be trying to lighten their misery with the German passports they are now almost certain to be granted. It may be a good thing to know that a passport—a document that records how others stereotype and judge us—can lighten our sorrows, if only a little. But our passports, which are all alike, should never blind us to the fact that each individual has his own troubles with identity, his own desires, and his own sorrows.

CHAPTER FIFTY

André Gide

When I was eight, my mother gave me a diary with a lock and a key. I treasured it greatly. That this beautifully produced notebook was not a foreign import but was made in Turkey is interesting in and of itself. Until I received my elegant green diary it had never occurred to me that I could have a private notebook in which to record my own thoughts, or that I could lock it and keep the key, probably the first I had ever owned, in my pocket. It implied that I could produce, own, and control a secret text. A very private sphere indeed, then: It made the idea of writing more appealing and so encouraged me to write. Up to that time, it had never occurred to me that writing was something you did in private. People wrote for newspapers, for books, for publication, or so I thought. It was as if my locked notebook were whispering, Open me up and write something down, but don't let anyone else see.

In the Islamic world there is no habit of keeping diaries, as historians sometimes like to remind us. No one else pays the matter much attention. The Eurocentric historian sees this as a shortcoming, reflecting a reduced private sphere and suggesting that social pressures stamp out individual expression.

But the journal was probably in use in many parts of the Islamic world unmarked by Western influence, as some published and annotated texts seem to indicate. Their authors would have kept these diaries as an aide-memoire. They would not have been writing for posterity, and since there was no tradition of annotating or publishing diaries, most would have later been destroyed, either deliberately or accidentally. At first glance, the idea of publishing a diary or even showing it to others would seem a mockery of the privacy embodied in the very notion of a diary. The idea of keeping a diary for publication suggests a certain self-conscious artifice and pseudo-privacy. On the other hand, it expands the concept of the private sphere, and in so doing it extends the power of writers and publishers. André Gide was among the first to exploit the possibilities this practice afforded.

In 1947, just after the Second World War, Gide was awarded the Nobel Prize for Literature. The decision did not come as a surprise; the seventy-eight-year-old Gide was at the height of his fame, hailed as the greatest living French writer at a time when France was still seen as the center of world literature. He was not afraid to speak his mind, and he took up political causes as dramatically as he dropped them; his passionate insistence on the central importance of "the sincerity of mankind" had won him many enemies and admirers.

Many Turkish intellectuals admired Gide, especially those who looked to Paris with reverence and longing. The most illustrious of these was Ahmet Hamdi Tanpınar, who wrote an article for the republican and pro-Western newspaper *Cumhuriyet* when Gide was awarded the Nobel Prize. I am aware than many of you will not have heard of Tanpınar, so I would like to say a few words about him before I read you an extract from this article.

Tanpınar was a poet, essayist, and novelist who was thirty years Gide's junior; today his works are seen as classics of modern Turkish literature. He is as well thought of by leftists, modernists, and Westernizers as he is by conservatives, traditionalists, and nationalists; all champion Tanpınar as their own. Tanpınar's poetry was influenced by Valéry, his novels by Dostoyevsky, and his essays are informed by Gide's logic and lack of inhibition. But what endeared him to Turkish readers, most particularly intellectuals—what made his work indispensable in their eyes—was not that he was inspired by French literature but that he was just as passionately bound to Ottoman culture, and above all to its poetry and music. He was as preoccupied with the tranquil dignity of the premodern culture as he was with European modernism, and this gave rise to a fascinating tension that Tanpınar bore with guilt. In this respect he calls to mind another non-European writer, Junichiro Tanizaki, who also knew the tension between his country's tradition and the West as a source of bitterness. But unlike Tanizaki, Tanpınar derived no pleasure from violence or suffering and the perpetration of suffering that this tension engendered, preferring to explore the sorrow and poignancy of a people torn between two worlds.

I shall quote now from Tanpınar's article, published in *Cumhuriyet* fifty years ago:

Of the news that has come to us from abroad since the end of the war, few have given me more pleasure than the announcement that André Gide had won the Nobel Prize. This honorable gesture, this wholly deserved tribute, has quelled our fears: for it proves to us that Europe still stands.

Though it has been ravaged by the storms of disaster, though its homelands have been destroyed, though its wretched peoples continue to wait for the peace that has so far eluded them, though eight of its capitals still languish under occupation, and France and Italy remain locked in civil strife, Europe still stands.

Because André Gide is one of those rare people whose name alone can conjure up a civilization at its finest.

During the war years there were two men who visited me often in my thoughts. In that vanquished and desolated Europe, in that hopeless darkness pregnant with a future no one could foresee, they were my two stars of salvation. The first was Gide—I had no idea where he was—[and] the second, Valéry, was, I'd heard, living in Paris without wine, without cigarettes, and even without bread.

Tanpınar goes on to compare the writing of Valéry and Gide, concluding that "these two friends alone were keeping Europe alive in its purest form and broadest sense. By reinventing old stories, and reestablishing their value, they saved a culture that was the essence of humanity from the maw of the aggressor. . . . They gave this culture its human form."

When I first read this article many years ago, I remember finding it quintessentially "European," if also somewhat affected. What I saw as affected and even callous was that he should give so much attention to one writer's lack of wine and cigarettes when millions had died and millions of others had lost their families, homes, and countries. What I admired as European was not that Gide represented Europe but that a writer could be singled out from the crowd—that Tanpınar could see him as the "human form" of an entire culture and that he could wonder and worry about what he had done during the war.

Gide's celebrated *Journal,* into which he poured all his thoughts with an essayist's abandon, allows us easy entry into his lonely world, to share in his fears and uncertainties and meandering thoughts. These notes recording his most private and personal thoughts Gide gave to his publisher, and they were published while he was still living; though it may not be the most famous journal of modern times, it is the most highly regarded. Its first volumes contain some angry and derisive comments on Turkey, which he visited in 1914, after the Balkan War.

First Gide describes meeting a Young Turk on the train to Istanbul. This pasha's son had been studying art in Lausanne for six months and was now returning to Istanbul with Zola's popular novel *Nana* tucked under his arm; finding him superficial and pretentious, Gide turns him into a figure of fun.

When he reaches Istanbul he quickly takes exception to it, finding it just as loathsome as Venice. Everything has come here from elsewhere, brought by money or by force. The only thing that makes him happy about Istanbul is leaving it.

"Nothing sprang from the soil itself," he wrote in his diary, "nothing indigenous underlines the thick froth made by the friction and clash of so many races, histories, beliefs, and civilizations."

Then he changes the subject. "The Turkish costume is the ugliest you can imagine, and the race, to tell the truth, deserves it."

He goes on to declare with loud honesty a thought shared by many travelers before him, though most chose to keep to themselves: "I'm unable to lend my heart to the most beautiful landscape in the world if I cannot love the people who inhabit it."

So great is his desire to be true to his honest opinion that it negates the country that he is visiting: "The very educative value that I derive from this trip is in proportion to my disgust for the country," he writes. "I am glad not to like it more."

The Swedish Academy praised Gide's writings as "a form of the passionate love of truth that since Montaigne and Rousseau has become a necessity in French literature." His passion for the truthful recording of his thoughts and impressions prompted Gide to say something else that no one else had the courage to voice. Here is what he said about Europe after his return from Turkey:

For too long I thought that there was more than one civilization, more than one culture that could rightfully claim our love and deserve our enthusiasm. . . . Now I know that our occidental (I was about to say French) civilization is not only the most beautiful; I believe—I know—that it is the only one.

Gide's words could easily win him a prize for political incorrectness at an American university, illustrating that a passionate love for truth does not always lead to political rectitude.

But my object here is not to dwell on Gide's startling honesty or to condemn his inelegant racism. I love Gide—his work, his life, and his values—as much as Tanpınar did. His books were much loved in Turkey when I was young. My father had all of them in his library, and Gide was as important to me as he was to earlier generations.

I know that I can best grasp Europe as a concept if I approach it with two contradictory thoughts in mind: first, the dislike that Gide felt for other civilizations—for my civilization—and, second, the great admiration that Tanpınar felt for Gide and through him for all of Europe. I can only express what Europe means to me if I fuse the contempt with the admiration, the hate with the love, the revulsion with the attraction.

Though Tanpınar concludes his article by praising Gide's "pure thought" and his "sense of justice," earlier he drops a hint that he is aware of the *Journal*'s offending lines. But with justifiable modesty, he does not go into detail. That Yahya Kemal, Tanpınar's teacher and mentor and one of Turkey's greatest twentieth-century poets, had also read Gide's account of his visit to Turkey is clear from a letter he wrote to A. Ş. Hisar, published after his death; in this letter he described Gide's notes as "a travel diary which sets out to revile the Turkish character with the most poisonous invective." He goes on to complain that "of all the defamatory writing against us ever written, this is the most venomous. . . . To read it was to shatter my nerves." An entire generation read these pages by Gide, passing over the insults in silence as they might an indiscretion, whispering about them now and again but mostly acting if the words had never been written or had been kept locked in a diary. When selections from Gide's *Journal* were translated into Turkish and published by the Ministry of Education, his remarks about Turkey were silently omitted.

In other articles Tanpınar talks about the unmistakable influence on Turkish poetry of Gide's book *Les nourritures terrestres* (*Fruits of the Earth*). It is Gide who started the vogue among Turkish writers of keeping a diary and publishing it while one is still alive. Nurullah Ataç, the early Turkish Republic's most influential critic, was first to undertake a Gide-like *Journal*—less a confession than a tirade—and the form found a following among the next generation of critics too.

I am beginning to wonder if I am losing sight of the real question by going into all this detail. Is it necessary to see Gide's account of his jour-

ney to Istanbul and Turkey after the Balkan War, and his dislike of the
Turks, as contradicting the admiration of Tanpınar and an entire generation of Turkish writers? We admire writers for their words, their values,
and their literary prowess, not because they approve of us, our country,
or the culture in which we live. In his *Diary of a Writer,* serialized in a
newspaper, Dostoyevsky describes what he saw on his first journey to
France; he talks at length of the hypocrisy of the French, claiming that
their sublime values were being eroded by money. But having read these
words, Gide was not prevented from admiring him or from writing a
brilliant book about Dostoyevsky. By refusing to retreat into a narrow
patriotism, Tanpınar (who was also an admirer of the French-hating Dostoyevsky) displayed what I would call a European attitude.

　　In 1862, when a furious Dostoyevsky declared that the spirit of fraternity had abandoned France, he went on to generalize about "French
nature and . . . western nature in general." When he identifies France
with the West, Dostoyevsky is no different from Gide. Tanpınar's outlook is the same, though he did not share Dostoyevsky's growing anger
toward France and the West; instead, he maintained a troubled and somewhat guilt-ridden regard. Now I am ready to answer the question I asked
earlier: It may not be contradictory to admire a writer who scorns the culture, the civilization, the nation in which you live, but the two states of
mind—the disdain and the admiration—are strongly linked. Viewed
from my window, Europe is an idea that plays upon both. My image of
Europe or the West is not a sunny, enlightened, grandiose idea. My
image of the West is a tension, a violence born of love and hate, longing
and humiliation.

　　I do not know if Gide had to travel to Istanbul and Anatolia before he
could naïvely declare his own France, his own Western civilization, to
be "the most beautiful of all." But I have no doubt that the Istanbul Gide
visited was in his eyes a civilization utterly differently from his own. For
the past two centuries Westernized Ottoman and Turkish intellectuals
have been convinced, like Gide, that Istanbul and Anatolia were places
with no connection to the West. But where Gide feels irritation and
scorn, they feel reverence and longing, and this sends them into an identity crisis. When, like Tanpınar, they identify too closely with Gide, they
are obliged to pass over his disparaging comments in silence; as they
stand on the edge of Europe, torn between West and East, they are
obliged to put even more faith in Europe than André Gide did. Perhaps
this explains why Gide's derisive comments did not stop him from exerting a powerful influence on Turkish literature.

In my view, the West is not a concept to be explored, analyzed, or enlarged through a study of the history and great ideals that created it; it has always been an instrument. It is when we use it as instrument that we can participate in a "civilizing process." We aspire to something that does not exist in our own history and culture because we see it in Europe, and we legitimize our demands with Europe's prestige. In our own country, the concept of Europe justifies the use of force, radical political change, the ruthless severing of tradition. From improvement of women's rights to violations of human rights, from democracy to military dictatorship, many things are justified by an idea of the West that stresses this concept of Europe and reflects a positivist utilitarianism. Throughout my life I've heard all our daily habits, from table manners to sexual ethics, criticized and changed because "that's how they do it in Europe." It is something I have heard over and over: on the radio, on television, from my mother. It is not an argument based on reason and indeed precludes reason.

Tanpınar's elation on hearing of Gide's Nobel Prize can be better understood if we remember that the Westernizing intellectual depends on an ideal of the West rather than on the West itself. Even if he is someone who regrets the loss of traditional culture, the old music and the poetry, and the "sensitivity of former generations," a Westernized intellectual like Tanpınar can only criticize his own culture and can only move from a conservative nationalism to a creative modernity to the extent that he clings to a fairy-tale image of an ideal Europe or the West. At the very least, this grip allows him to open up an inspiring and critical new space between the two.

On the other hand, embracing a fairy-tale image of the West can lead even a deep and complex writer like Tanpınar to share Gide's naïve and vulgar idealization, as betokened in "occidental civilization is the most beautiful." This is a European dream that relies on a contradictory and hostile other. It may be that Westernized Ottoman and Turkish intellectuals failed to object openly to Gide's crude and humiliating remarks because of their own silent guilt, perhaps unacknowledged even by themselves: It is possible that they privately agreed with him. But they hid these thoughts in their own locked journals.

Many Westernized Young Turks did share Gide's opinions. They whispered them in secret or shouted them aloud, depending on the circumstances. Here we begin to see where the idea of Europe becomes interwoven with the nationalism that was to nourish it and give it shape. The views of Gide and the other Westerners who wrote about the Turks, Islam, East, and West were adopted not just by the last Young Turks but incorporated into the founding concept of the Turkish Republic.

Atatürk, founder of the Turkish Republic and father of the nation, instituted an extraordinarily ambitious program of reforms during the early years of the Republic, from 1923 to the mid-1930s. After changing from the Islamic to the Latin alphabet, and from the Islamic to the Christian calendar, and declaring Sunday, not Friday, to be the day of rest, he introduced other reforms, such as improvements in women's rights, which left even deeper marks on society. The debate between the Westernizers and Modernists who defended the reforms and the nationalists and conservatives who attacked them still forms the basis for most ideological discussion in Turkey today.

One of Atatürk's first reforms was the statutory adoption of Western dress in 1925, two years after the establishment of the Republic. Though it obliged everyone to dress like a European, it was at the same time a continuation of the traditionally regimented Ottoman dress code requiring one to dress according to religious affiliation.

In 1925, exactly one year after the publication of Gide's remarks about the Turks, Atatürk was to express similar views when he announced the clothing revolution during a tour of Anatolia:

For example, I see a person [indicating with his hand] in the crowd before me wearing a fez on his head, a green turban wound around the fez, a *mintan* [collarless shirt], and over that a jacket like my own. The lower part I am unable to see. Now what kind of costume is that? Would a civilized person let the world hold him up to ridicule by dressing so strangely?

To set these remarks alongside Gide's is to wonder whether Atatürk shared Gide's low opinion of Turkish national dress. We have no idea if Atatürk read Gide's remarks, though we know that Yahya Kemal, a member of his inner circle, had read them and expressed strong indignation in a letter. However, what matters here is that Atatürk, like Gide, viewed dress as a measure of civilization:

When the citizens of the Turkish Republic declare that they are civilized, they are obliged to prove that they are so in their family life and in their lifestyle. A costume which, if you will excuse the expression, is half flute, half rifle barrel is neither national nor international.

Atatürk's views of private life may reflect Gide's or they may not. Either way, it is evident that Atatürk identifies Europe with civilization; it follows that that which is not European is humiliatingly uncivilized. This humiliation is closely bound up with nationalism. Westernization and nationalism come from the same source, but (as we see in Tanpınar) there is guilt and shame mixed in. In my part of the world, the idea of Europe draws from these same sentiments in a profound but also very "private" way.

Both Gide and Atatürk see the ugly clothing worn by the Turks in the early years of the twentieth century as placing Turks outside European civilization. Gide sums up the relationship between a nation and its costume with the words "and the race, to tell you the truth, deserves it."

But Atatürk believed that Turkish apparel misrepresented the nation. During the same tour of the country, at the time when he was launching reforms of dress, he declared:

Is there any point in displaying a valuable jewel to the world when it is smeared with mud? Is it reasonable to inform them that there is a gem hidden beneath the mud, but that they are not aware of it? Of course it is essential to dispose of the mud in order to reveal the jewel. . . . A civilized and international style of dress is for us bejeweled, a costume worthy of our nation.

By presenting traditional costume as mud enveloping the Turkish people, Atatürk found a way of confronting the shame suffered by all Westernized Turks. It was, in a sense, a way of striking at the heart of shame.

Atatürk draws a line between the costume that he rejects (with Gide and other Westernizers) and the people who wear it. He sees dress not as part of a culture shaping the nation but as a stain smeared like mud on the race. So it was to bring the Turkish people closer to his idea of Europe that he undertook the difficult task of forcing them to discard their traditional dress. Even seventy years after Atatürk's dress revolution, the Turkish police were still chasing people going about the conservative neighborhoods of Istanbul in traditional dress, as journalists and television cameras record.

So let us speak openly now of shame, which has underpinned the idea of Europe from Gide to Tanpınar, from Yahya Kemal's affront to Kemal Atatürk's palliative measures.

The Westernizer is ashamed first and foremost of not being European. Sometimes (not always) he is ashamed of what he does to become European. He is ashamed that he has lost his identity in his struggle to become European. He is ashamed of who he is and of who he is not. He is ashamed of the shame itself; sometimes he rails against it and sometimes he accepts it with resignation. He is ashamed and angry when his shame is exposed.

It is rare when such confusions and humiliations are exposed in the "public sphere." When Gide's *Journals* are published in Turkish, the aspersions on Turkey are edited out and discussions of Gide are carried on in whispers. We admire Gide for sending his private journal into the public sphere, but then we use it to justify the state regulation of what must be the most private of concerns, the way we dress.

CHAPTER FIFTY-ONE

Family Meals and Politics
on Religious Holidays

I enjoy visiting my relatives on holidays, and most especially my uncles, aunts, distant relations, elders, and betters. My aunts and aged uncles make a disciplined effort to be "good" during these visits, and with all they offer us—sweet words, reminiscences, and refined conversation—in the end, they are. This suggests that, contrary to what we like to believe, it requires quite an effort to be good. But this year, even as I listened to the jokes about cuckoo clocks that reminded me so much of my childhood, and enjoyed the silence that the holiday had brought to the Istanbul streets, and bit into the Turkish delight that tasted the same as ever, I felt the presence of evil. Let me try to describe it. It stems, I think, from hopelessness and jealousy. All those uncles and distant relations and sweet relatives who kiss my daughter, all those august heroes of my childhood holidays: They once saw themselves as Western, but now it seems as if they have lost their faith. They are angry at the West.

The Festival of Sacrifice is meant to be a wholly religious holiday, one that should link us to the present and the past. But throughout my childhood I experienced these and the other Islamic holidays not as religious traditions but as celebrations of Westernization and the Republic. In upper-middle-class circles—in Nişantaşı and Beyoğlu—the emphasis was on the holiday, not the sacrifice of lambs, much less of Isaac. Because it was a holiday, everyone wore their most formal Western clothes; they'd put on jackets and ties, offer their guests liqueurs, and then all the men and women would sit down, Western style, at one big table, to eat a "Western-style" meal. It was not a coincidence that when I read Thomas Mann's *Buddenbrooks,* at the age of twenty, I was struck by the strange similarities and shocking differences between the family meals in the novel and the holiday meals at my grandmother's house. It was with these impressions in mind that I sat down to write *Cevdet Bey and Sons*. When we see that other writers have had experiences similar to our own, we are inspired not just to read but to write and, most particularly, to explore the differences. I was at the same time telling a story about the Republic and about Westernization. Like my grandmother, the characters in that first novel are anxiously innocent about the West, even if they retain the old communal spirit and its sense of a common aim. I no longer like that communal spirit or that common aim, but I still yearn for the childish innocence with which my relatives once expressed their longing for and interest in the West. During this holiday visit, however, I noticed, amid the discussions and reminiscences of everyday matters, newspaper headlines, and anger expressed by elderly relatives—in the flow of ordinary conversation—a certain disquiet; the Turkish bourgeoisie was suffering pain and anger, having lost hope in their dreams.

It seemed they are having second thoughts about Westernization: that the previous blind faith in Western enlightenment was a bad idea, because it encouraged us to denigrate tradition and turn away from our own history! Gone are the childhood days at the old holiday meals, with their hope and innocence and childish curiosity. Among those who wished to be Western, there was a sincere desire to learn how it was done. The belief that there were things to be learned from the West was much stronger in those days, and the mood was optimistic. But everyone I visited in 1998—the elderly relatives grumbling so miserably in front of their television sets, their affluent middle-aged children, the Istanbul bourgeoisie that has taken the lion's share of Turkey's riches but prefers to shop in Paris and London—were all cursing Europe with one voice. The old interest in what Europe was; that had gone. So too had the jackets and ties that they'd worn to the holiday meals of my childhood. Perhaps this is as it should be, for over the past century we have learned a fair amount about the West. But the anger is real, and it comes from watching the negotiations with the European Union, seeing that for all our efforts to be Western, they still don't want us, discovering that they intend to dictate terms on democratic structures and human rights. The anger that afflicts old people whose childhood dreams have come true—these days it's everywhere.

They say there is "also" torture in the West. They say that the history of the West is full of oppression, torture, and lies. They say that Europe's real interest is not in human rights but in its own advancement. In such and such a European country they "also" persecute minorities in such and such a way; in a certain European city the police "also" quell vociferous discontent among the citizenry with brute force. What they mean to say is that if they do commit an evil in Europe, we should also be permitted to go on doing it here, and perhaps do it even more. What they mean, perhaps, is that if Europe is to be our model, then we should emulate its torturers, inquisitors, and two-faced liars. The optimistic Kemalists of my childhood holidays admired Europe's culture, its literature, its music, its clothes. Europe was the fountain of civilization! But in the seventy-fifth year of the Republic, it has come to be seen as a source of evil.

This anti-European sentiment has been growing fast over the past few years, faster than I could ever have imagined, and I have no doubt that it has much to do with the rapidly rising number of newspaper columnists who take an anti-European stance—the ones who write that Europe "also" has torture, that "they" also persecute their minorities and abuse human rights; those who take every opportunity to remind the public how much "they" look down on Turks and our religion. It is clear that these columnists are doing this to cover up, and to legitimize, the human rights abuses, the banning of books, and the imprisonment of journalists in our own country. Instead of using their energies and their pens to criticize these homegrown outrages, they vent against the Europeans who have drawn attention to them. Perhaps this is understandable. But it has had consequences they could never have dreamed of. In the wake of all this anti-European, anti-Western, ever-more-nationalist invective, holiday meals have become gatherings at which everyone sits around talking about the devils of the lying West. I found uncles like this in three successive houses! In the old days, they would talk brightly about how we would all be more Western one day, but now they go on and on about the evils of the West, using the sort of broken, coarse language one might expect from the neighborhood thug. After a lifetime of going to Europe to do their shopping, drawing upon European ideas about everything from art to clothing, and using Western culture to distinguish themselves from the lower classes and so legitimize their superiority, they have now turned against Europe because of its perceived double standard on human rights. Now they want Europe to serve as the bogeyman, so they can say that when people are tortured and minorities persecuted here, it is happening not here alone but in Europe too.

In the old days, too, there were East-West tensions; as we drank our liqueurs and nibbled our sweets, our polite chat would sometimes descend into spats about the left and the right. But even if you found them superficial and naïve, you could not feel too angry, if only because these well-meaning people had their eyes fixed on the West. I see no sign of the old optimism today. After drinking two glasses of liqueur, let us prepare ourselves for the evil things my angry and unhappy relatives have to say about the devils of Europe.

CHAPTER FIFTY-TWO

The Anger of the Damned

I used to think disasters brought people together. During the great Istanbul fires of my childhood and after the 1999 earthquake, my first impulse was to seek out others, to share my experiences with them. But this time, as I sat across from a television screen in a small room near the ferry station—in a coffeehouse frequented by horse and carriage drivers, porters, and tuberculosis patients—and watched the twin towers crumbling, I felt desperately alone.

Turkish television went live just after the plane hit the second tower. The small crowd inside the coffeehouse watched in amazed silence as those hard-to-believe images flashed before their eyes, but they seemed not to be overly affected by them. At one point I felt like standing up and saying, I too once lived among those buildings, I walked penniless through those streets, I met with people in those buildings, I spent three years of my life in that city. But instead I remained silent, as if dreaming my way into an ever deeper silence.

No longer able to bear what I saw on the screen, and hoping to find others who felt the same way, I went out into the street. Sometime later, I saw a crying woman in the crowd waiting for the ferry. From the woman's demeanor and the looks she was getting, I could see at once that she was crying not because she had loved ones in Manhattan but because she thought the world was coming to an end. As a child, I had seen women crying in the same distracted way when the Cuban missile crisis was threatening to turn into the Third World War. I'd watched as Istanbul's middle-class families stocked their pantries with packets of lentils and macaroni. Returning to the coffeehouse, I sat down and as the story unfolded on the television screen I watched as compulsively as everyone else all the world over.

Later, when I was again walking down the street, I ran into one of my neighbors.

"Orhan Bey, did you see? They've bombed America." He angrily added, "And quite right too."

This old man is not at all religious; he makes his living by gardening and doing small repairs and spends his evenings drinking and arguing with his wife; he had not yet seen the shocking scenes on television; he'd simply heard that there'd been a hostile act against America. Though he was later to regret his initial angry remarks, he was far from being the only one I heard expressing them. This despite the fact that—as in so many other parts of the world—the revulsion for this savage act of terrorism was unanimous. Yet after cursing those who had brought about the deaths of so many innocents, they would utter the word *but* and launch into veiled or open critiques of America as a global power. It is perhaps neither fitting nor morally acceptable to debate America's role in the world in the shadow of terror, after terrorists wishing to engineer a false divide between Christians and Muslims have savagely killed so many innocent people. But in the heat of their righteous anger, some people can find themselves venting nationalist views that could lead to the killing of still more innocent people: As such, they invite a response.

We all know that the longer this campaign continues, the more the U.S. Army seeks to satisfy its own nation by killing innocent people in Afghanistan and elsewhere, the more it will exacerbate the manufactured tension between East and West, thereby playing into the hands of the very terrorists it wishes to punish. It is at present morally reprehensible to suggest this savage terrorism is a response to America's world domination. But it is nevertheless important to understand why millions of people living in poor and marginalized countries that have lost even the right to shape their own histories might feel such anger against America. This is not to imply that we must see their anger as justified. It is important to remember that many Third World and Islamic countries use anti-American sentiment to occlude their democratic shortcomings and shore up dictatorships. Muslim countries that are struggling to establish secular democracies are not helped in the least when America allies itself with closed societies like Saudi Arabia, which claim democracy and Islam to be irreconcilable. In much the same way, the more superficial variety of anti-Americanism that one sees in Turkey allows those at the top to waste and misappropriate the money given to them by international financial bodies and to conceal the ever-growing gap between rich and poor. There are many in the United States who support the offensive unconditionally, just because they wish to demonstrate their military dominance and give the terrorists a symbolic "lesson," and some who discuss the likely locations of the next bombing raids as cheerfully as if they were playing a video game, but they should understand that decisions taken in the heat of battle can only intensify the anger and humiliation that the millions in the world's poor Islamic countries feel against a West that sees itself as superior. It is not Islam that makes people side with the terrorists, nor is it poverty; it is the crushing humiliation felt throughout the Third World.

At no point in history has the gap between rich and poor been so wide. One might argue that the wealthy nations of the world are responsible for their own success and so bear no responsibility for world poverty. But there has never been a time when the world's poor have been as exposed to the lives of the rich as they are today through television and Hollywood films. One might say that the poor have always entertained themselves with legends about kings and queens. But never before have the rich and powerful asserted their reason, and their rights, with such force.

An ordinary citizen living in a poor, Muslim, nondemocratic country will, like a civil servant struggling to make ends meet in a former Soviet satellite or any other Third World nation, be only too aware what a small share of the world's wealth his country has; he will know, too, that he lives under much harsher conditions than his counterparts in the West, and that his life will be much shorter. But it does not end there, for somewhere in his mind is the suspicion that it is his own father and grandfather who are to blame for his misery. It is a great shame that the Western world pays so little attention to the overwhelming sense of humiliation felt by most people in the world, a humiliation that those people have tried to overcome without losing their reason or their way of life or succumbing to terrorism, ultranationalism, or religious fundamentalism. Magical-realist novels sentimentalize their silliness and their poverty, while travel writers in search of the exotic are blind to their troubled private world, where indignities are suffered day in and day out with compassion and pained smiles. It is not enough for the West to figure out which tent, which cave, or which remote city harbors a terrorist making the next bomb, nor will it be enough to bomb him off the face of the earth; the real challenge is to understand the spiritual lives of the poor, humiliated, discredited peoples who have been excluded from its fellowship.

Battle cries, nationalist speeches, and impulsive military ventures achieve the opposite ends. The new visa restrictions that Western countries have imposed on those living outside the European Union, the police measures that limit the movements of those coming from Muslim and other poor non-Western countries, the widespread suspicion of Islam and all things non-Western, the coarse diatribes that equate terrorism and fanaticism with Islamic civilization—with every new day, they take us further away from clear-headed reason and from peace. If a destitute old man on an Istanbul island can momentarily approve of the terror attack on New York, or if a young Palestinian worn down by the Israeli occupation can look with admiration as the Taliban throws acid into women's faces, what drives him is not Islam or this idiocy people call the war between East and West, nor is it poverty; it is the impotence born of a constant humiliation, of a failure to make oneself understood, to have one's voice heard.

When they met with resistance, the wealthy modernizers who established the Turkish Republic made no effort to understand why the poor did not support them; instead, they enforced their will with legal threats, prohibitions, and military repression. The result was that the revolution was left half finished. Today, as I listen to people all over the world calling for the East to go to war with the West, I fear that we will soon see much of the world going the way of Turkey, which has endured almost continuous martial law. I fear that the self-congratulatory, self-righteous West will drive the rest of the world down the path of Dostoyevsky's Underground Man, to proclaim that two plus two equals five. Nothing nurtures support for the "Islamist" throwing nitric acid in the faces of women more than the West's refusal to understand the anger of the damned.

CHAPTER FIFTY-THREE

Traffic and Religion

We were driving through a poor neighborhood on the southern outskirts of Tehran. Through the window I could see a string of bicycle and car repair shops. Because it was Friday, all the shops had their shutters down. The streets, the pavements, even the coffeehouses were deserted. Just then we pulled up to a huge empty square that had been fashioned into a roundabout of a type I'd seen all over the city. To enter the street that was just to our left, we would have to turn right and drive all the way around the circle.

I could see at once that our chauffeur was wondering whether he should just turn left. He was looking over both shoulders to see if any other car was entering the square: Should he obey the law, or should he use his head to find a way around it, the way he liked to think he always did whenever life threw him an unexpected challenge?

I remembered how often I'd faced this same dilemma as a young man driving through the streets of Istanbul. I was a model driver on the main avenues of the city (which journalists liked to describe as "traffic anarchy"), but as soon as I'd taken my father's car into the empty cobblestoned back streets, I ignored the rules and did as I pleased. To obey a NO LEFT TURN sign on a back street when there wasn't another car in sight, to sit in an out-of-the-way square in the middle of the night, patiently waiting for the light to turn green, was to bow down to an authority that made no allowances for the intelligent pragmatist. We had little respect for those who obeyed the letter of the law in those days; people only did that if they lacked brains, imagination, or character. If you were prepared to sit out a red light at an empty intersection, you were probably the sort of person who squeezed toothpaste tubes from the bottom and never took medicine without reading the entire label. Our contempt for this approach to life is well illustrated by a cartoon I remember seeing in magazines from the West during the 1960s: a lone driver waiting for the green light in the middle of an American desert

When I think back to Istanbul as it was between 1950 and 1980, it seems to me that our contempt for the highway code was more than a simple longing for anarchy. Rather, it was a subtle form of anti-Western nationalism: When we were all by ourselves, without any strangers in our midst, the old order prevailed and we went back to our old tricks. In the sixties and seventies, a man could feel a surge of pride just by holding a rickety phone together with one well-placed nail or getting an unrepairable German radio to work by pounding it with a fist. Feats like this made us feel different from Westerners, who so venerated the rules of technology and culture; they reminded us of how worldly we were, and how wily.

But as I sat on the edge of this square on the outskirts of Tehran, watching the driver waver between obedience and pragmatism, I could tell that this man, whom I knew well enough by then, had not the slightest interest in making a nationalist statement. His problem was much more mundane: Because we were in a hurry it seemed a waste of time to go all the way around the circle, but he was glancing anxiously at all the other roads that led into it, because he knew that if he rushed the decision he might end up crashing into another car.

The day before, when we were snarled in traffic anarchy, watching one unimaginable tie-up after another, this man had complained to me that no one in Tehran obeyed the law. Granted, he was smiling as he said it, but all day we'd been sitting in bumper-to-bumper traffic, staring at the dented sides of domestic Peykan cars, their drivers shouting abuse at one another, and we'd been laughing at them darkly as if we were thoroughly modern people who sincerely believed in the highway code. Now, though, I could sense a certain anxiety beneath my driver's smile as he tried to decide whether he should make the illegal turn.

I remembered feeling just as anxious, struggling through the Istanbul traffic of my youth, and just as lonely. As our driver considered giving up on the benefits and protections offered by the rule of law in order to save a bit of time, he too knew he was going to have to make the decision alone. He would have to run through all the possibilities as quickly as he could, pursue all channels open to him, and then decide on the spot, knowing full well that he was taking his own life and perhaps the lives of those around him into his hands.

You could argue that our driver was, by breaking the rules and choosing freedom, bringing this loneliness upon himself. But even if he was not making a free choice, he knew the city and its drivers well enough to realize that he was doomed to feel lonely for as long as he remained a driver in Tehran. Because even if you decide to obey the laws of modern traffic, others—pragmatic people just like you—will pay them no mind. Outside the city center, every driver in Tehran has to approach every intersection paying attention not just to the lights and the laws but also to any driver who might have chosen to ignore them. A driver in the West can change lanes feeling so sure that everyone around him is obeying the rules that he can listen to music, let his mind wander; a driver in Tehran feels freedom of a different order, and it offers him no peace.

When I went to visit Tehran and saw the chaos and destruction these drivers brought upon themselves as they fought the highway code with furious ingenuity for the preservation of their autonomy, it seemed to me that their little bursts of lawless individualism were strangely at odds with the state-imposed religious laws that dictate every other aspect of life in the city. It is, after all, to convey the impression that everyone in public life and anyone walking down the street is sharing the same thought that an Islamist dictatorship feels it must veil its women, censor its books, keep its prisons full, and plaster all the highest walls in the city with huge posters of heroes who have martyred themselves for their country and their religion. Oddly, it's when you're battling your way through the mad traffic, fighting it out with the city's lawless drivers, that you feel the presence of religion most keenly. Here's the state, proclaiming that all must bow to the laws laid down in the Holy Book, mercilessly enforcing those laws in the name of national unity and making it clear that to break them is to end up in prison, when meanwhile the city's drivers, knowing the state is watching, flout the highway code and expect everyone else to do likewise; they see the road as a place where they can test the limits of their freedom, their imagination, and their ingenuity. I saw reflections of the same contradiction in my meetings with Iranian intellectuals, whose freedoms were so severely restricted by the Sharia laws the state has imposed in the streets, the markets, the city's great avenues, and all other public spaces. With a sincerity I cannot help but admire, they set out to prove they were not living in Hitler's Germany or Stalin's Soviet Union by showing me they could discuss whatever they wanted, wear whatever they liked, and drink as much bootleg alcohol as they pleased in the privacy of their own homes.

In the final pages of *Lolita,* after Humbert has killed Quilty and is driving away from the scene of the crime in the car the reader has come to know so well, he suddenly swerves into the left lane. Fearful of being misunderstood, Humbert swiftly warns the reader against seeing this as a symbolic gesture of rebellion. Having already seduced a girl who is no more than a child and then committed murder, he has, after all, broken the greatest laws of humanity. This is the genius of Humbert's story and of the novel itself: From the very first page we share his lonely guilt.

When, after his brief attack of indecision on the outskirts of Tehran, my friend the driver took the shortcut—went into the wrong lane and made the turn without causing an accident, just as I had done so many times myself as a young man in Istanbul—we both felt the rush that can only come from breaking a rule and getting away with it, and we could not help but exchange smiles. The sad thing was knowing that (like Humbert, who was so brilliant at veiling his misdeeds with language, and like the inhabitants of Tehran who have found so many ways to circumvent the Sharia in the privacy of their own homes) the only time one could break the law in public was behind the wheel of a car, and that the law we broke governed traffic and nothing else.

CHAPTER FIFTY-FOUR

In Kars and Frankfurt

I t is a great pleasure to be in Frankfurt, the city where Ka, the hero of my novel *Snow,* spent the last fifteen years of his life. My hero is a Turk and therefore no relation of Kafka's; they are related only in literary terms (I shall be saying more about literary relations later on). Ka's real name was Kerim Alakuşoğlu, but he was not very fond of it, so he preferred the shorter version. He first came to Frankfurt in the 1980s as a political refugee. He was not particularly interested in politics—he didn't even like politics; his whole life was poetry. My hero was a poet living in Frankfurt. He saw Turkish politics as someone else might see an accident—something that he got mixed up in without ever meaning to. I would, if I have enough time, like to say a few words about politics and accidents. It is a subject about which I have thought a great deal. But do not worry: Though I write long novels, today I shall keep my comments brief.

It was in the hope that I might describe Ka's stay in Frankfurt during the eighties and early nineties without making too many mistakes that I came here five years ago, in the year 2000. Two people in the audience today were particularly generous in their help, and it was while they were showing me around that we visited the little park behind the old factory buildings near Gutleustrasse where my hero would spend the last years of his life. To better imagine the walk Ka made each morning from his home to the city library, where he spent most of his days, we walked through the square in front of the station, down the Kaiserstrasse, past the sex shops and the Turkish greengrocers, barbers, and kebab restaurants of Münchnerstrasse as far as Clocktower Square, passing just in front of the church where we are gathered today. We went into the *Kaufhof,* where Ka bought the coat he would draw such comfort from wearing for so many years. For two days, we roamed around the old poor neighborhoods where Frankfurt's Turks have made their homes, visiting the mosques, restaurants, community associations, and coffeehouses. This was my seventh novel, but I recall taking such needlessly extensive notes that I might as well have been a novice, agonizing over every detail, asking questions like, Did the tram really pass this corner during the eighties?

I did the same thing when I visited Kars, the small city in the northeast of Turkey where most of my novel takes place. Because I knew very little about Kars, I visited it many times before using it as my setting; during my stays there, I met many people and made many friends as I explored the city street by street and shop by shop. I visited the most remote and forgotten neighborhoods of this, Turkey's most remote and forgotten city, conversing with the unemployed men who spent their days in coffeehouses without even the hope of ever finding another job; conversing, too, with lycée students, with the plainclothes and uniformed policemen who followed me wherever I went, and with the publishers of the newspaper, whose circulation never rose above 250.

My aim here is not to relate how I came to write a novel called *Snow.* I am using this story as a way into the subject that I am coming to understand more clearly with each new day, and that is, in my view, central to the art of the novel: the question of the "other," the "stranger," the "enemy" that resonates inside each of our heads—or, rather, the question of how to transform this being. That my question is not central to all novels is self-evident: A novel can, of course, advance the understanding of humankind by imagining its characters in situations that we know intimately and care about and recognize from our own experience. When we meet someone in a novel who reminds us of ourselves, our first wish is for that character to explain to us who we are. So we tell stories about mothers, fathers, houses, streets that look just like ours, and we set these stories in cities we've seen with our own eyes, in the countries we know best. But the strange and magical rules that govern the art of the novel can open up our families, homes, and cities in a way that makes everyone feel as if they can see their own families, homes, and cities reflected in them. It has often been said that *Buddenbrooks* is an excessively autobiographical novel. But when I first picked up this book, as a boy of seventeen, I read it not as Mann's account of his own family—for at the time I knew very little about him—but as a book about a universal family, one with which I could easily identify. The wondrous mechanisms of the novel allow us to take our own stories and present them to all humanity as stories about someone else.

So, yes, one could define the novel as a form that allows the skilled practitioner to turn his own stories into stories about someone else, but this is just one aspect of the great and mesmerizing art that has entranced so many readers and inspired writers for almost four hundred years. It was the other aspect that drew me to the streets of Frankfurt and Kars: the chance to write of others' lives as if they were my own. It is by doing this sort of research that novelists can begin to test the lines that mark off that "other" and in so doing alter the boundaries of our own identities. Others become "us" and we become "others." Certainly a novel can achieve both feats simultaneously. Even as it describes our own lives as if they were the lives of others, it offers us the chance to describe other people's lives as if they were our own.

Novelists wishing to enter into the lives of others do not necessarily need to visit other streets and other cities, as I did when preparing to write *Snow*. Novelists wishing to put themselves in others' shoes and identify with their pains and troubles will draw first and foremost from their imaginations. Let me try to illustrate my point with an example that will call to mind what I was saying earlier about literary relations: "If I woke up one morning to find that I had turned into an enormous cockroach, what would become of me?" Behind every great novel is an author whose greatest pleasure comes from entering another's form and bringing it to life—whose strongest and most creative impulse is to test the very limits of his identity. If I woke up one morning to find myself transformed into a cockroach, I would need to do more than research insects; if I were to guess that everyone else in the house would be revolted and even terrified to see me scuttling across the walls and the ceilings, and that even my own mother and father would hurl apples at me, I would still have to find a way to become Kafka. But before I try to imagine myself as someone else, I might have to do a little investigating. What I need most to ponder is this: Who is this "other" we are pressing ourselves to imagine?

This creature who is nothing like us addresses our most primitive hatreds, fears, and anxieties. We know full well that these are the emotions that fire up the imagination and give us power to write. So the novelist observing the rules of his art will recognize that only good can come of his managing to identify with this "other." He will also know that thinking about this other in whom everyone sees his own opposite will help to liberate him from the confines of his self. The history of the novel is a history of human liberation: By putting ourselves in another's shoes, by using our imaginations to shed our identities, we are able to set ourselves free.

So Defoe's great novel conjures up not just Robinson Crusoe but also his slave, Friday. As powerfully as *Don Quixote* conjures up a knight who lives in the world of books, it also conjures up his servant, Sancho Panza. I enjoy reading *Anna Karenina,* Tolstoy's most brilliant novel, as a happily married man's attempt to imagine a woman who destroys her unhappy marriage and then herself. Tolstoy's inspiration was another male novelist who, though he himself never married, found his way into the mind of the discontented Emma Bovary. In the greatest of all allegorical novels, *Moby-Dick,* Melville explores the fears gripping America in his day—and particularly the fear of alien cultures—whose intermediary is the white whale. Those of us who come to know the world through books cannot think of the American South without also thinking of the blacks in Faulkner's novels. Having failed to realize them credibly, his work would be found wanting. In the same way, we might feel that a German novelist who wished to speak to all of Germany, and who failed, explicitly or implicitly, to imagine the country's Turks along with the unease they cause, was somehow lacking. Likewise, a Turkish novelist who failed to imagine the Kurds and other minorities, and who neglected the black spots in his country's unspoken history, would have, in my view, produced something hollow.

Contrary to what most people assume, one's politics as a novelist have nothing to do with the societies, parties, and groups to which one might belong—or with a dedication to any political cause. A novelist's politics arise from his imagination, from his ability to imagine himself as someone else. This power not only allows him to explore human realities previously unremarked—it makes him the spokesman for those who cannot speak for themselves, whose anger is never heard, and whose words are suppressed. A novelist may, like me, have no real reason to take a youthful interest in politics, and if he does his motives may end up mattering very little. Today we do not read the greatest political novel, Dostoyevsky's *Demons,* as the author originally intended—as a polemic against Russian Westernizers and Nihilists; we read it instead as a reflection of the Russia of its day, one that reveals to us the great secret locked inside the Slavic soul. Such a secret only a novel can explore.

Obviously, we cannot hope to come to grips with matters this deep merely by reading newspapers and magazines or by watching television. To understand what is unique about the histories of other nations and other peoples, to share in unique lives that trouble us, terrifying us with their depths and shocking us with their simplicity—such truths we can glean only from the careful, patient reading of great novels. Let me add that when Dostoyevsky's demons begin to whisper into the reader's ear, telling him of a secret rooted in history, a secret born of pride and defeat, shame and anger, they are illuminating the shadows of the reader's own history too. The whisperer is the despairing writer who loves and despises the West in equal measure, a man who cannot quite see himself as a Westerner but is dazzled by the brilliance of Western civilization, who feels himself caught between the two worlds.

Here we come to the East-West question. Journalists are exceedingly fond of it, but when I see the connotations it carries in some parts of the Western press, I'm inclined to think that it would be better not to speak of the East-West question at all. Because most of the time it carries an assumption that the poor countries of the East should defer to everything the West and the United States might happen to propose. There is also a perceived inevitability that the culture, the way of life, and the politics of places like the one where I was raised will provoke tiresome questions, and an expectation that writers like me exist only to offer answers to those same tiresome questions. Of course there is an East-West question, and it is not simply a malicious formulation invented and imposed by the West. The East-West question is about wealth and poverty and about peace.

In the nineteenth century, when the Ottoman Empire began to feel itself overshadowed by an ever more dynamic West, suffering repeated defeats at the hands of European armies and seeing its power slowly wane, there emerged a group of men who called themselves the Young Turks. Like the elites that would follow in later generations, not excluding the last Ottoman sultans, they were dazzled by the superiority of the West, so they embarked on a program of Westernizing reforms. The same logic underlies the modern Turkish Republic and Kemal Atatürk's Westernizing reforms. And underlying the logic itself is the conviction that Turkey's weakness and poverty stem from its traditions, its old culture, and the various ways it has socially organized religion.

Coming as I do from a middle-class Westernized Istanbul family, I must admit that I too sometimes succumb to this belief, which is, though well-intended, narrow and even simpleminded. Westernizers dream of transforming and enriching their country and their culture by imitating the West. Because their ultimate aim is to create a country that is richer, happier, and more powerful, they also tend to be nativist and powerfully nationalistic; certainly we can see these tendencies in the Young Turks and the Westernizers of the young Turkish Republic. But as part of westward-looking movements, they remain deeply critical of certain basic characteristics of their country and culture; though they might not do so in the same spirit and the same style as Western observers, they too see their culture as defective, sometimes even worthless. This gives rise to another very deep and confused emotion: shame.

I see shame reflected in some responses to my novels and to perceptions of my own relations with the West. When we in Turkey discuss the East-West question, when we talk of the tensions between tradition and modernity (which to my mind is the essence of the East-West question), or when we prevaricate over our country's relations with Europe, the question of shame is always lurking. When I try to understand this shame, I always try to relate it with its opposite, pride. As we all know, wherever there is too much pride, whenever people act too proudly, there is always the specter of their shame and humiliation. For wherever another people feels deeply humiliated, we can expect to see a proud nationalism rising to the surface. My novels are made from these dark materials, from this shame, this pride, this anger, and this sense of defeat. Because I come from a nation that is knocking on Europe's door, I am only too well aware of how easily these emotions of fragility can, from time to time, take flame and rage unchecked. What I am trying to do here is to speak of this shame as a whispered secret, as I first heard it in Dostoyevsky's novels. For it is by sharing our secret shames that we bring about our liberation: This is what the art of the novel has taught me.

But it is at the moment of liberation that I begin to feel in my heart the complicated politics of representation and the moral dilemmas of speaking in another's name. This is a difficult undertaking for anyone, but particularly for a novelist who is himself riddled with such emotions as I was just describing. The freewheeling world of the imagination can seem treacherous, and never more so than in the mirror of a prickly and easily offended novelist consumed by nationalist pride. If we keep a reality secret, it will—we hope—shame us only in silence, but that hope is betrayed when a novelist uses his imagination to transform that same reality, to fashion it into a parallel world demanding notice. When a novelist begins to play with the rules that govern society, when he digs beneath the surface to discover its hidden geometry, when he explores that secret world like a curious child, driven by emotions he cannot quite understand, it is inevitable that he will cause his family, his friends, his peers, and his fellow citizens some unease. But this is a happy unease.

For it is by reading novels, stories, and myths that we come to understand the ideas that govern the world in which we live; it is fiction that gives us access to the truths kept veiled by our families, our schools, and our society; it is the art of the novel that allows us to ask who we really are.

We have all known the joy of reading novels; we have all known the thrill of going down the path that leads into someone else's world, engaging with that world body and soul, and longing to change it, engrossed in the hero's culture, in his relationship with the objects that make up his world—in the author's words, in the decisions he makes, and in the things he notices as the story unfolds. We know that what we have been reading is both the product of the author's imagination and of an actual world into which he has taken us. Novels are neither wholly imaginary nor wholly real. To read a novel is to confront both its author's imagination and the real world whose surface we have been scratching with such fretful curiosity. When we retire to a corner, when we lie down on a bed, when we stretch out on a divan with a novel in hand, our imaginations travel back and forth between the world in that novel and the world in which we still live. The novel in our hands might take us to a world we have never visited, never seen, and never known. Or it might take us into the hidden depths of characters who seem on the surface to resemble people we know best.

I am drawing attention to each of these possibilities singly because there is a vision I entertain from time to time that embraces both extremes. Sometimes I try to conjure up, one by one, a multitude of readers hidden away in corners, nestled in their armchairs with their novels; I try also to imagine the geography of their everyday lives. Then, before my eyes, thousands—tens of thousands—of readers will take shape, stretching far and wide across the streets of the city, and as they read they dream the author's dreams, imagine his heroes into being, and see his world. So now these readers, like the author himself, try to imagine the other; they too are putting themselves in another's place. These are the times we feel humility, compassion, tolerance, pity, and love stirring in our hearts, for great literature speaks not to our powers of judgment but to our ability to put ourselves in someone else's place.

As I imagine all these readers using their imaginations to put themselves in someone else's place, as I conjure up their worlds, street by street, neighborhood by neighborhood, all across the city, a moment arrives when I realize that I am really thinking of a society, a group of people, an entire nation—what you will—imagining itself into being.

Modern societies, tribes, and nations do their deepest thinking about themselves by reading novels; through reading novels, they are able to argue about who they are. So even if we have picked up a novel hoping only to divert ourselves, relax, and escape the boredom of everyday life, we begin, without realizing it, to conjure up the collectivity, the nation, the society to which we belong. This is also why novels give voice not just to a nation's pride and joy but also to its anger, its vulnerabilities, and its shame. It is because they remind readers of their shame, their pride, and their tenuous place in the world that novelists can arouse such anger, and what a shame it is that we still see outbursts of intolerance— that we still see books burned and novelists prosecuted.

I grew up in a house where everyone read novels. My father had a large library, and when I was a child he would discuss the great novelists I mentioned earlier—Mann, Kafka, Dostoyevsky, and Tolstoy—the way other fathers discussed famous generals and saints. From an early age, all these novelists—these great novelists—were linked in my mind with the idea of Europe. But this was not just because of my family, which believed fervently in Westernization and therefore longed, in its inno- cence, to believe itself and its country far more Western than they really were; it was also because the novel was one of the greatest artistic achievements to come out of Europe.

The novel, like orchestral music and post-Renaissance painting, is in my opinion one of the cornerstones of European civilization; it is what makes Europe what it is, the means by which Europe has created and made visible its nature, if there is such a thing. I cannot think of Europe without novels. I am speaking now of the novel as a way of thinking, understanding, and imagining and also as a way of imagining oneself as someone else. In other parts of the world, children and young people first meet Europe in depth with their first ventures into novels; so it was for me. To pick up a novel was to step inside Europe's borders; to enter a new continent, a new culture, a new civilization; to learn, in the course of these explorations, to express oneself with new desire and new inspira- tion; and to believe, as a consequence, that one was part of Europe—this is how I remember feeling. Let us also remember that the great Russian novel and the Latin American novel also stem from European culture . . . so just to read a novel is to understand that Europe's borders, histories, and national distinctions are in constant flux. The old Europe described in the French, Russian, and German novels in my father's library is, like the postwar Europe of my childhood and the Europe of today, a place that is forever changing. So, too, is our understanding of what Europe is.

I have one vision, however, that is constant, and that is what I shall speak of now.

Let me begin by saying that Europe is a very delicate, very sensitive subject for a Turk. Here we are, knocking on your door, asking to come in, full of high hopes and good intentions but also feeling rather anxious and fearing rejection. I feel such things as keenly as do other Turks, and what we all feel is very much akin to the "silent shame" I was describing earlier. As Turkey knocks on Europe's door, as we wait and wait and Europe makes promises and then forgets us, only to raise the bar—and as Europe examines the full implications of Turkey's bid to become a full member—we've seen a lamentable hardening of anti-Turkish sentiment in certain parts of Europe, at least among certain politicians. In recent elections, when they took a line against Turks and Turkey, I found their style just as dangerous as that adopted by certain politicians in my own country.

It is one thing to criticize the democratic deficits of the Turkish state or find fault with its economy; it is quite another to denigrate all of Turkish culture—or those of Turkish descent here in Germany whose lives are among the most difficult and impoverished in the country. As for Turks in Turkey: When they hear themselves judged so cruelly, they are reminded yet again that they are knocking on a door and waiting to be let in, and of course they feel unwelcome. It is the cruelest of ironies that the fanning of nationalist anti-Turkish sentiment in Europe has provoked the coarsest of nationalist backlashes inside Turkey. Those who believe in the European Union must see at once that the real choice we have to make is between peace and nationalism. Either we have peace, or we have nationalism. I think that the ideal of peace sits at the heart of the European Union, and I believe that the chance for peace that Turkey has offered Europe will not, in the end, be spurned. We've arrived at a point where we must choose between the power of a novelist's imagination and the sort of nationalism that condones burning his books.

Over the past few years, I have spoken a great deal about Turkey and its EU bid, and often I've been met with grimaces and suspicious questions, so let me answer them here and now. The most important thing that Turkey and the Turkish people have to offer Europe and Germany is, without a doubt, peace; it is the security and strength that will come from a Muslim country's desire to join Europe, and this peaceable desire's ratification. The great novelists I read as a child and a young man defined Europe in terms not of its Christian faith but of the yearning of its individuals. It was because these heroes were struggling to free themselves, express their creativity, and make their dreams come true that their novels spoke to my heart. Europe has gained the respect of the non-Western world owing to the ideals it has done so much to nurture: liberty, equality, and fraternity. If Europe's soul is enlightenment, equality, and democracy, if it is to be a union predicated on peace, then Turkey has a place in it. A Europe defining itself in narrow Christian terms will, like a Turkey that tries to derive its strength only from its religion, be an inward-looking place divorced from reality, bound more to the past than to the future.

Having grown up in a Westernized secular family in the European part of Istanbul, it is not at all difficult for me—or people like me—to believe in the European Union. Don't forget, since childhood, my football team, Fenerbahçe, has been playing in the European Cup. There are millions of Turks like me who believe wholeheartedly in the European Union. But what is more important is that most of today's conservative and Muslim Turks, and with them their political representatives, also want to see Turkey in the European Union, helping to plan Europe's future, dreaming it into being and helping to build it. Coming as it does after centuries of war and conflict, this gesture of friendship cannot be taken lightly, and to reject it outright would be cause for huge regret and chagrin. Just as I cannot imagine a Turkey without a European prospect, I cannot believe in a Europe without a Turkish prospect.

I would like to apologize for speaking at such great length about politics. The world to which I seek foremost to belong is, of course, the world of the imagination. Between the ages of seven and twenty-two, my dream was to become an artist, and so I would go out into the streets of Istanbul to paint cityscapes. As I describe in my book *Istanbul,* I gave up painting at the age of twenty-two and began to write novels. I now think that I wanted the same thing from painting as I did from writing: What drew me to both art and literature was the promise of leaving behind this boring, dreary, hope-shattering world for one that was deeper, richer, and more diverse. To achieve this other magical realm, whether I expressed myself in lines and colors, as I did in my early life, or in words, I've had to spend long hours by myself every day, imagining its every nuance. The consolatory world I have been constructing for thirty years as I sit alone in my corner is most certainly made from the same materials as the world we all know—from what I've been able to see of the streets and interiors of Istanbul, Kars, and Frankfurt. But it is the imagination—the imagination of the novelist—that gives the bounded world of everyday life its particularity, its magic, and its soul.

I shall close with a few words about this soul, this essence that the novelist struggles all his life to convey. Life can only be happy if we can manage to fit this strange and puzzling undertaking into a frame. For the most part, our happiness and unhappiness derive not from life itself but from the meaning we give to it. I've devoted my life to trying to explore that meaning. Or, to put it differently, all my life I've wandered through the clatter and roar of today's chaotic, difficult, fast-moving world, thrown this way and that by life's twists and turns, looking for a beginning, a middle, and an end. In my view, this is something that can only be found in novels. Since my novel *Snow* was published, every time I've set foot in the streets of Frankfurt, I've felt the ghost of Ka, the hero with whom I have more than a little in common, and I feel as if I am truly seeing the city as I have come to imagine it, as if I have somehow touched its heart.

Mallarmé spoke the truth when he said, "Everything in the world exists to be put into a book." Without doubt, the sort of book best equipped to absorb everything in the world is the novel. The imagination—the ability to convey meaning to others—is humanity's greatest power, and for many centuries it has found its truest expression in novels. I accept the Peace Prize of the German Book Trade in recognition of my thirty years of loyal service to this sublime art, and I thank you all from the bottom of my heart.

CHAPTER FIFTY-FIVE

On Trial

In Istanbul this Friday—in Şişli, the district where I have spent my whole life, in the courthouse directly opposite the three-story house where my grandmother lived alone for forty years—I will stand before a judge. My crime is to have "publicly denigrated Turkish identity." The prosecutor will ask that I be imprisoned for three years. I should perhaps find it worrying that the Turkish-Armenian journalist Hrant Dink was tried in the same court for the same offense, under Article 301 of the same statute, and was found guilty, but I remain optimistic. For, like my lawyer, I believe that the case against me is thin; I do not think I will end up in jail.

This makes it somewhat embarrassing to see my trial overdramatized. I am only too well aware that most of the Istanbul friends from whom I have sought advice have at some point undergone much harsher interrogation and lost many years to court proceedings and prison sentences just because of a book, just because of something they had written. Living as I do in a country that honors its pashas, saints, and policemen at every opportunity but refuses to honor its writers until they have spent years in courts and in prisons, I cannot say I was surprised to be put on trial. I understand why friends smile and say that I am at last "a real Turkish writer." But when I uttered the words that landed me in trouble, I was not seeking any such honor.

In February 2005, in an interview published in a Swiss newspaper, I said that a million Armenians and thirty thousand Kurds had been killed in Turkey; I went on to complain that it was taboo to discuss these matters in my country. Among the world's serious historians, it is common knowledge that a large number of Ottoman Armenians were deported, allegedly for siding against the Ottoman Empire during the First World

War, and many of them were slaughtered along the way; Turkey's spokesmen, most of whom are diplomats, continue to maintain that the death toll was much lower than the academics suggest, that the slaughter does not count as genocide because it was not systematic, and that in the course of the war Armenians killed many Muslims too.

This past September, however, despite opposition from the state, three highly respected Istanbul universities joined forces to hold a conference of scholars open to views not tolerated by the official Turkish line. Since then, for the first time in ninety years, there has been public discussion of the subject—this despite the specter of Article 301.

That the state is prepared to go to such lengths to keep the Turkish people from knowing what happened to the Ottoman Armenians qualifies the fact as a taboo. My words certainly caused a furor worthy of one: Various newspapers launched hate campaigns against me, with some right-wing (but not necessarily Islamist) columnists going as far as to say that I should be "silenced" for good; groups of nationalist extremists organized meetings and demonstrations to protest my treachery; and there were public burnings of my books. Like Ka, the hero of my novel *Snow,* I discovered how it felt to have to leave one's beloved city for a time on account of one's political views. Because I did not want to add to the controversy and did not want even to hear about it, I kept quiet at first, drenched in a strange sort of shame, hiding from the public and even from my own words. Then a provincial governor ordered a burning of my books; following my return to Istanbul, the Şişli public prosecutor opened the case against me; and I found myself the object of international concern.

My detractors were not motivated just by personal animosity, nor were they expressing hostility to me alone; I already knew that my case was an instance of a problem worthy of discussion in both Turkey and the outside world. This was partly because I believe that what denigrated a country's "honor" is not the discussion of the black spots in its history but the preclusion of any discussion at all. It was also because I believed that the prohibition against discussing the Ottoman Armenians was a prohibition against freedom of expression in Turkey today, and indeed that the two matters were inextricably linked. Comforted as I was by the interest in my predicament and by the generous gestures of support, there were also times when I felt uneasy about finding myself caught between my country and the rest of the world.

The hardest thing was to explain why a country officially committed to entry into the European Union would wish to imprison an author whose books were well known in Europe, and why it felt compelled to play out this drama (to use Conrad's expression) "under Western eyes." This paradox cannot be explained away as simple ignorance, jealousy, or intolerance, and it is not the only paradox involved. What am I to make of a country that insists that the Turks, unlike their Western neighbors, are a compassionate people, incapable of genocide, while nationalist political groups are pelting me with death threats? What is the logic behind a state's complaints that its enemies spread false reports about the Ottoman legacy all over the globe, while it prosecutes and imprisons one writer after another, thus propagating the image of the Terrible Turk worldwide? When I think of the professor whom the state asked to present his findings on Turkey's minorities and who, having produced a report that failed to please, was prosecuted, or the news that between the time I began this essay and embarked on the sentence you are now reading, five more writers and journalists have been charged under Article 301, I imagine that Flaubert and Nerval, the two godfathers of Orientalism, would call these incidents *bizarreries,* and rightly so.

That said, the drama we see unfolding is not, I think, a grotesque and inscrutable drama peculiar to Turkey; rather, it is an expression of a new global phenomenon that we are only just coming to acknowledge and that we must now begin, however carefully, to address. In recent years, we have witnessed the astounding economic rise of India and China, and in both these countries the rapid expansion of the middle class, though I do not think we shall truly understand the people who have been part of this transformation until we have seen their private lives reflected in novels. Whatever you call these new elites, the non-Western bourgeoisie or the enriched bureaucracy, they, like the Westernizing elites in my own country, feel compelled to follow two separate and seemingly incompatible lines of action in order to legitimatize their newly acquired wealth and power. First, they must justify the rapid rise in their fortunes by adopting the idiom and the attitudes of the West; having created a demand for such knowledge, they then take it upon themselves to tutor their countrymen. When the people berate them for ignoring tradition, they respond by brandishing a virulent and intolerant nationalism. The disputes that an foreign observer might call bizarreries may simply be the clashes between these political and economic programs and the cultural aspirations they engender. On the one hand, there is the rush to join the global economy; on the other, the angry nationalism that sees true democracy and freedom of thought as Western inventions.

V. S. Naipaul was one of the first writers to describe the private lives of the ruthless, murderous non-Western ruling elites of the postcolonial era. When I met the great Japanese writer Kenzaburo Oe in Korea, I heard that he too had been attacked by nationalist extremists after stating that the ugly crimes committed by his country's armies during the invasions of Korea and China should be openly discussed in Tokyo. The intolerance shown by the Russian state toward the Chechens and other minorities and civil-rights groups, the attacks on freedom of expression by Hindu nationalists in India, and China's discreet ethnic cleansing of the Uighurs—all are nourished by the same contradictions.

As tomorrow's novelists prepare to narrate the private lives of the new elites, they are no doubt expecting the West to criticize the limits that their states place on freedom of expression. But these days the lies about the war in Iraq and the reports of secret CIA prisons have so damaged the West's credibility in Turkey and in other nations that it is more and more difficult for people like me to make the case for true Western democracy in my part of the world.

CHAPTER FIFTY-SIX

Who Do You Write For?

Who do you write for? Over the last thirty-odd years—since I first became a writer—this has been the question I've heard most often from both readers and journalists. The motives depend on the time and the place, as does the extent of their curiosity, but they all ask in the same suspicious, supercilious tone of voice.

In the mid-seventies, when I first decided to become a novelist, the question reflected the widely held philistine view that art and literature were luxuries that a poor non-Western country struggling to join the modern age could ill afford. There was also the suggestion that someone "as educated and cultivated as yourself" might serve the nation more usefully as a doctor fighting epidemics or an engineer building bridges. (Jean-Paul Sartre gave credence to this view in the early 1970s when he said he would not be in the business of writing novels if he were a Biafran intellectual.)

In later years, those questioners were more interested in finding out which sector of society I hoped might read and admire my work. I knew this to be a trick question, for if I did not answer, "I write for the poorest and most downtrodden members of society!" I would be accused of protecting the interests of Turkey's landowners and its bourgeoisie—even as I was reminded that any pure-minded, good-hearted writer who claimed to be writing for peasants, workers, and the indigent would be writing for people who were barely literate. In the 1970s, when my mother asked who I was writing for, her mournful and concerned tone told me she was really asking, How are you planning to support yourself? And when friends asked me who I wrote for, the tinge of mockery in their voices was enough to suggest that no one would ever want to read a book by someone like me.

Thirty years on, I hear this question more frequently than ever. This has more to do with the fact that my novels have been translated into forty languages. Especially during the past ten years, my ever more numerous interviewers seem worried that I might take their words the wrong way, so they are inclined to add, "You write in Turkish, so do you write just for Turks or do you now also have in mind the wider audience you reach through your translations?" Whether we are speaking inside Turkey or outside it, the question is always accompanied by that same suspicious, supercilious smile, leaving me to conclude that, if I wish my works to be accepted as true and authentic, I must answer, "I write only for Turks."

Before we examine the question itself—for it is neither honest nor humane—we must remember that the rise of the novel coincided with the emergence of the nation-state. When the great novels of the nineteenth century were being written, the art of the novel was in every sense a national art. Dickens, Dostoyevsky, and Tolstoy wrote for an emerging middle class, who could in the books of its respective national author recognize every city, street, house, room, and chair; it could indulge in the same pleasures as it did in the real world and discuss the same ideas. In the nineteenth century, novels by important authors appeared first in the art and culture supplements of national newspapers, for their authors were speaking to the nation. In their narrative voices we can sense the disquiet of the concerned patriot whose deepest wish is for his country to prosper. By the end of the nineteenth century, to read and write novels was to join a national discussion on matters of national importance.

But today the writing of novels carries an entirely different meaning, as does the reading of literary novels. The first change came in the first half of the twentieth century, when the literary novel's engagement with modernism won it the status of high art. Just as significant have been the changes in communication that we've seen over the past thirty years: In the age of global media, literary writers are no longer people who speak first and only to the middle classes of their own countries but are people who can speak, and speak immediately, to readers of "literary novels" all the world over. Today's literary readers await a new book by García Márquez, Coetzee, or Paul Auster the same way their predecessors awaited the new Dickens—as the latest news. The world audience for literary novelists of this cohort is far larger than the audience their books reach in their countries of origin.

If we generalize the question—For whom do writers write?—we might say they write for their ideal reader, their loved ones, themselves, or no one. This is the truth, but not the whole truth. For today's literary writers also write for those who read them. From this we might infer that today's literary writers are gradually writing less for their own national majorities (who do *not* read them) than for the small minority of literary readers in the world who do. So there we have it: The needling questions, and the suspicions about these writers' true intentions, reflect an uneasiness about this new cultural order that has come into being over the past thirty years.

The people who find it most disturbing are the opinion makers and cultural institutions of non-Western nations. Uncertain as they are about their standing in the world, unwilling as they are to discuss current national crises or the black marks in their history in international arenas, such constituencies are necessarily suspicious of novelists who view history and nationalism from a nonnationalist perspective. In their view, novelists who do not write for national audiences are exoticizing their country for "foreign consumption" and inventing problems that have no basis in reality. There is a parallel suspicion in the West, where many readers believe that local literatures should remain local, pure, and true to their national roots; their secret fear is that becoming a "world" writer who draws from traditions outside his own culture will cause one to lose one's authenticity. The one who most acutely feels this fear is a reader who longs to open a book and enter a foreign country that is cut off from the world, who longs to watch that country's internal wrangling, much as one might witness a family argument next door. If a writer is addressing an audience that includes readers in other cultures speaking other languages, then this fantasy dies too.

It is because all writers have a deep desire to be authentic that—even after all these years—I still love to be asked for whom I write. But while a writer's authenticity does depend on his ability to engage with the world in which he lives, it depends just as much on his ability to understand his own changing position in that world. There is no such thing as an ideal reader unencumbered by social prohibitions and national myths, just as there no such thing as an ideal novelist. But—be he national or international—it is the ideal reader for whom all novelists write, first by imagining him into being, and then by writing books with him in mind.

MY BOOKS ARE MY LIFE

CHAPTER FIFTY-SEVEN

The White Castle Afterword

There are some novels that, though they might come to a satisfying finish, contain characters who continue their adventures in the author's dreams. Certain nineteenth-century writers would fill two or three additional volumes with such dreams, while others, not wishing to entrap themselves in the world of a previous novel, go to the other extreme: So intent are they on shutting down these dangerous afterlives that they sum them up in a hasty postscript, noting that "Years later Dorothea and her two daughters returned to Alkingstone" or "In the end, Razarov arranged his affairs, and now he has quite a good income." Then there is another class of writer, who returns to the world of an old novel not to relate the new adventures of his old characters but simply because the life of the story itself demands it. Memories, missed opportunities, perceived responses of readers and close friends, and new ideas may cause the book to change shape in the author's mind. A point arrives when his image of the book is utterly different from the book he originally intended—not to mention the book that is on sale in bookshops—and it is when that happens that the author wants to remind this strange and elusive new beast where it came from.

The inspiration for *The White Castle* visited me in its initial ghostly form as I was finishing my first novel, a long family saga set in the first half of the twentieth century entitled *Cevdet Bey and Sons*. It took the form of a soothsayer, called to the palace, walking down blue streets at midnight. That was my name for the novel then. My soothsayer was a well-meaning man of science who, seeing how little enthusiasm there was for science in the palace, set himself up as an astrologer—an easy switch, thanks to his interest in astronomy—and though his original idea had been to win others at court over to the cause of science, his head was soon turned by the power and influence his predictions brought him, and he began to use his art to devious ends. That was all I knew. In those days, I had begun to shy away from historical subjects; I had grown so tired of being asked why I wrote historical fiction that it had ceased to interest me.

Earlier—when I was twenty-three—I'd written three historical stories, and people even called my first novel historical; to understand my interest in history, it seemed I would need to examine not just my literary tastes but my childhood predilections. Once, when I was small—eight years old—I left the apartment where I lived with my family and went upstairs to visit the gloomy rooms of my grandmother's apartment, where every object and every bit of radio chatter duplicated our own, and as I searched among the yellowing newspapers and the medical books that once belonged to the uncle who had gone to America, never to return, I happened onto a large illustrated volume by Reşat Ekrem Koçu. For days I read the story of the wretched monkeys that people would buy from the monkey stores in Azapkapı and that were later strung from trees for committing immoral acts. On laundry days, as the washing machine wailed and angry grown-ups darted to and fro, boiling water and soft soap, I would crawl into a corner and look at black-and-white drawings of Where-Angels-Fear-to-Tread Street, where the harlots were punished with bubonic plague. While waiting for the great clock in the hallway to announce the next hour, a fearful impatience would grip me as I read the story of the condemned criminal whose legs and arms were broken so that he could be stuffed into the mouth of a cannon and shot into the sky.

After finishing *The Silent House,* my second novel, I found myself again preoccupied with daydreams drawn from history. Why don't I write something short between the long novels? I'd say to myself, since my story was already clear in my head. So to serve my soothsayer I happily immersed myself in science and astronomy books. Adnan Adıvar's amusing and unrivaled *The Science of the Ottoman Turks* gave me the colors I was looking for (as did books like Acaib-ül Mahlûkat's strange animal tales, which Evliya Çelebi liked so much). It was from Professor Süheyl Ünver's *Istanbul Observatory* that I first learned of the famous Ottoman astronomer Takiyüddin, who once tried to explain comets to the sultan; having read of this exchange and watched him instruct my hero by illuminating his scientific notes (which have since been lost), I could begin to understand just how blurred the line was between astronomy and astrology.

In another book I read this about astrology: "To advance a guess that the order of things might be disturbed is not a bad way of undermining the order of things." Later, when I turned to Naima, one of the most dramatic and readable Ottoman historians, I learned that the head soothsayer Huseyin Efendi had, like all politicians, made energetic use of this, the soothsayer's golden rule.

My reading had no other aim than to gather background detail for the story I meant to write, and from the books I had at hand emerged a theme that is very popular in Turkish literature: a hero who is aching to do good and help others! In some of those books, the noble and good-hearted hero is constantly up against evil traitors. In the better class of novel, we read that it is through suffering evil that he is able to change. Who knows, I may have been planning to write something along the same lines, but I could not find the source of his "virtue," nor could I trace the origins of his enthusiasm for science and discovery. Later, I decided that my soothsayer would acquire his science from a "Westerner." The slaves that came in shiploads from distant countries would serve my purposes perfectly. This was how the Hegelian master-slave relationship came into play. I thought my master and an Italian slave would have a great deal to tell and teach each other; to give them time to talk, I put them together in a room in a city bathed in darkness. The affinity and the tension between this pair at once became the book's imaginative center. I discovered that master and slave looked much alike. Perhaps it was my analytical side taking over, but this was how I happened onto the idea of their being identical. From then on I did not have to expend too much effort to immerse myself in that most celebrated of literary themes: identical twins changing places.

This is how my story came to take on—either through my difficulties with its internal logic or the laziness of my imagination—an entirely new shape. I was of course familiar with the tales of twins in E.T.A. Hoffmann, who was always dissatisfied with himself, and who, because he'd wished to be a musician, imitated Mozart, going so far as to add Mozart's name to his own; I knew the bloodcurdling stories of Edgar Allan Poe and Dostoyevsky's *The Other,* to whom I paid homage in the legend of the epileptic pope in the Slavic villages. When I was in middle school, our biology teacher boasted he could always tell the two ugly identical twins in the class apart, but in oral exams, they would switch places, unbeknownst to him. At first, when I saw Charlie Chaplin imitations in *The Great Dictator,* I liked them, but later I did not. When I was little, I was in awe of the comic-book character Onethousandandonefaces, who was forever changing identities: If he changed places with me, what would he do? I wondered. If he changed places with an amateur psychologist, he might say, "Actually, what all writers want is to become someone else." Robert Louis Stevenson put even more of himself into *Dr. Jekyll and Mr. Hyde* than Hoffmann put into his fairy tales: an ordinary citizen by day and by night a writer! Whenever my own identical twin changed places with me, he would try to remind my readers of my debt to doubles.

I am still not sure if it was the Italian slave or the Ottoman master who wrote the manuscript of *The White Castle*. When writing it, I decided to use the closeness I felt to Faruk, the historian in *The Silent House,* to safeguard against certain technical problems. Cervantes, whom I salute in the first and last sections of the book, must have suffered such anxieties at some point; to write *Don Quixote* he made use of a manuscript by the Arab historian Seyyit Hamit bin Engeli, and to make it his own he filled the gaps with word games. Those familiar with *The Silent House* will remember that after Faruk found the manuscript in the Gebze archives and undertook to render it in the language of the citizenry, he seems to have added passages from other books. At this point, I should like to point out to readers who imagine that I, like Faruk, worked in the archives, rummaging among the shelves of dusty manuscripts, that I am unwilling to take responsibility for Faruk's actions. What I did was use a few details that Faruk discovered. For these I borrowed a method from Stendhal's *Three Italian Chronicles,* which I read while writing my first historical books: I arranged for the discovery of an old manuscript by sprinkling the details into the foreword I wrote for Faruk. This perhaps opened the way for my using Faruk again (as his grandfather Selahattin Bey would) in another, subsequent, historical novel, while also sparing the reader the hazards of a costume ball arriving out of nowhere— always historical fiction's greatest danger point.

I chose to set my novel in the mid-seventeenth century, not just because it was historically convenient and a lively and colorful time but because this would allow my characters to make use of the writings of Naima and Evliya Çelebi; still, various little fragments gleaned from travel books from preceding and succeeding centuries also seeped into the novel. To make my hopeful and well-meaning Italian into my master's slave (these were the days of quack medicine and ships that took captives), I took a leaf from Cervantes and made use of a book presented to Philip II by a nameless Spaniard who had also been a captive of the

Turks. The memoirs of Baron W. Wratislaw, a galley slave in Ottoman ships at the time of Cervantes, served as a model for my own slave's incarceration. I also made use of certain passages from the letters of a Spanish traveler who visited Istanbul forty years before them, and who described the city succumbing to plague (when even a normal boil would spark terror) and the deportation of Christians to the Princes Islands. Other details that figure in the book come not from the period in which it is set but from accounts of witnesses from other times: Istanbul's scenic views, firework displays, and nighttime amusements (Antoine Galland, Lady Montagu, Baron de Tott); the sultan's beloved lions and his lion zoo (Ahmet Refik); the Ottoman army's Polish campaign (Ahmet Ağa's *Diary of the Siege of Vienna*); some of the child sultan's dreams (a book called *Strange Events from Our History,* made from the same stuff as the Reşat Ekrem Koçu book that I read in my grandmother's library); Istanbul's packs of wild dogs; precautions against the plague (Helmuth K. B. Von Moltke's Turkish letters); and the White Castle, from which I took my novel's name (in Tadeutz Trevanian's *Journeys in Transylvania,* illustrated with engravings, he mentions the chronicle of the castle and also a novel by a French author about a European changing places with a barbarian).

Evliya Çelebi also wrote a book about the lunatic asylum in the complex connected to the Beyazit Mosque in Edirne (the one who heard the mysterious music played for the patients was, of course, Evliya Çelebi), but I could only shiver in the gloom when my wife and I visited this beautiful monument on a muddy, cloudy, featureless spring morning. Also the sultan's beloved stork. Some of the dreams that Mehmet the Hunter sees and that my hero interprets are actually my own dreams (the dark men carrying sacks). Like my Italian hero, I once had a new outfit that my brother got to wear, because his was torn to pieces, but it wasn't red, as in the book (it was navy and white). On cold winter mornings, returning home from an excursion, if our mother bought us something to eat (not *helva* but bitter almond shortcake), she would say the same thing as the Master's mother: "Let's eat these before anyone sees us." The book's redheaded dwarf bears no relation to the classic from our childhood, *The Redheaded Child,* or any dwarf in any of my novels past and future; I saw him in 1972 in the Beşiktaş market. For a time I thought that the Master's long experiments toward a clock that might show the times of prayer was a daydream of my own, dating back to my bachelor years, but I was wrong. It turns out that many people have been interested in this idea, which makes it all the more surprising that such a clock still does not exist; someone told me that the Japanese have made a wristwatch along these lines, but I've never seen it.

Perhaps its time has come. That the East-West divide is one of the ideas cultures have used and will continue to use to classify and differentiate humanity is not, however, the subject of *The White Castle*. This divide is an illusion, but if it had not been made and remade with great enthusiasm over many centuries, my book would have lost much of the background color sustaining it. That the plague might be used as a litmus test for the East-West divide is another old idea. Somewhere in his memoirs, Baron de Tott says, "The plague merely kills a Turk, while a Frank suffers the greater torment of fearing death!" This sort of observation is not, in my view, a piece of nonsense or even a fragment of science; it is one of many little details I used to create the texture of the book. Perhaps they will help the writer remember how happy he was when writing and researching his book.

CHAPTER FIFTY-EIGHT

The Black Book: Ten Years On

M y most powerful memories of *The Black Book* are of the last days I spent working on it. In 1988, after three years of work, when the end was in sight, I shut myself up for a brief time in an empty apartment at the top of a newly constructed seventeen-story apartment building in Erenköy, where I did nothing but write. My wife was in America, no one knew my phone number so the phone never rang, and all of the others who might have pulled me away from Galip's adventures and the imaginary world in which I had sunk so deep were far away. I saw no one except the two relatives who lived in the same apartment building and kindly asked me over for supper now and again; as is always the case when I am so deeply and obsessively inside a book to my delight, I lost touch with the outside world.

But as I sat in my corner, I could not bring *The Black Book* to a close. It would take me almost five years to write it. As I sat in that distant place, working on this book that refused to end, a strange and miserable fear began to taint the joy of my writing, and my solitude, a fear that slowly came to resemble that suffered by the hero, Galip. As he searches fruitlessly for his wife all over Istanbul, he comes across all manner of surprise but cannot take real pleasure in the underground tunnels, the Türkan Şoray look-alikes, or all the old columns he peruses, so great is his grief at his loss. Likewise, as the writing progressed and the book grew broader, the pleasure of writing it grew deeper, but I was unable to take pleasure in that fact because of the obsessive goal that eluded me. I was mournfully alone, just like Galip. I neglected daily shaving and paid no attention to my clothes. I remember wandering like a ghost through the back streets of Erenköy of an evening, clutching a mangled plastic bag and wearing a cap, a raincoat that was missing a few buttons, and ancient gym shoes with rotting soles. I'd go into any old restaurant or buffet and wolf down my food, casting hostile looks about me. My father came to take me out to eat once a fortnight, and I remember his telling me how worried he was about the dirt and disorder of my apartment, my air of ruination, and this book that I could not seem to finish.

I felt all alone, like Galip—perhaps I felt like this so I could carry the emotion into the book—but he was subsumed by melancholy, while my isolation was in anger. Because they wouldn't understand this book that was becoming steadily stranger, because they would measure it against traditional novels, because it was hard to understand, because they would point to the book's more obscure parts to prove it a failure, and also, perhaps, because I was never going to finish it; I'd written the wrong book. *The Black Book* proved to me that the measure of a book is not its ability to solve the literary and structural problems set forth in it but the greatness and importance of the questions the author is address-ing and the degree to which he gives himself over to this task, however hopeless. As difficult as it is to write good books, it is just as difficult to concoct subjects to which a writer can devote all his creative energy, everything he has in him, for the rest of his life.

Books like these, books to which you can devote your entire life—like life itself—they take you where they want you to go, but very slowly. This new place, this foreign country, is no doubt made up of our past, our memories, and our dreams; during the days I was writing *The Black Book,* these blended with the fears and uncertainties, the harbin-gers of death and solitude that came to haunt me as I wrote through the night until morning, smoking cigarette after cigarette. This is your first intimation of what lies beyond; it is also your first consolation. Once again your helpless obstinacy has saved you, not your clever artistry. Despite the stubborn patience that I trusted so much more than I did the thing they call *skill,* there were times when I feared that the book was going nowhere, that all these pages I had written would lead neither me nor the reader anywhere but a state of confusion. This would plunge me into despair. As I was writing *The Black Book,* it seemed as if I was wavering between a deep personal quest for meaning, a superficial aim-lessness, and the sort of obscurity that can only come from the desire to write something great. During my time alone, what preoccupied me most were the worst-case scenarios that these tensions suggested: I might have spent five years of my life on a book that had no worth; I might have failed. I now think that for people like me such fears are therapeutic, in that such individuals can write only by experiencing disquiet and tension.

The original idea for *The Black Book* was something set in the very late seventies, evoking the poetry of the streets of my childhood and embracing the anarchy of Istanbul, past and present. In a journal I began to keep in 1979, I wrote about a thirty-five-year-old intellectual who flees from his home, of his experiences over a long weekend, of a football match that is being played during the same weekend and that turns into a national catastrophe, of power outages and Istanbul streets, of the atmosphere of Brueghel's paintings (snow) as well as Bosch's (devils), of the *Mesnevi,* of the *Shahname,* and of the Thousand and One Nights.

When these first thoughts were taking shape in my mind, I had not yet published *Cevdet Bey and Sons,* but I was thinking of an artist as the hero and I had even thought up a title, "The Shattered Miniature." Istanbul's endless noise and confusion, its intellectuals, the glittering parties they attended, family meetings, the funerals, beauty pageants, and football matches—I was imagining all these things at once, and as always I took more pleasure in my dreams and plans for this novel called *The Black Book* that I would write in the future than I did in the books I was writing at the time (a never-finished political novel, *The Silent House,* and *The White Castle*).

At around the same time, one day in particular influenced the shape and concept that the book would ultimately assume. In 1982, two years after the coup and just before the new constitution that severely limited freedom was being harshly imposed without a chance for public debate, my cousin rang to say that a Swiss television team had come to Istanbul to do a program on the new constitution and were looking for intellectuals willing to criticize it on camera: Did I know anyone with the courage to do so? I spent the next two days combing the city—its universities and its encyclopedia publishers, its advertising agencies and its newsrooms, going from house to house, trying to find intellectuals who might be willing to speak. Because telephone calls were—then as now—subject to continuous surveillance, I was obliged to visit each and every candidate, each and every one of whom turned me down. Because the persecution of intellectuals by the state and the army had reached Soviet proportions, I felt that the journalists, writers, and other decent people who turned me down were right to do so, and so I felt guilty for having forced them into a moral quandary. The foreign TV team, which was waiting in a room at the Pera Palas, had even told me they could backlight anyone who agreed to speak so all faces would be obscured in shadow. In the end they said that if there were no intellectuals willing to speak to them, they would interview me instead (as in *The Black Book,* when Galip, unable to find Celal, speaks in his stead), but I had no faith in myself and no courage.

There are so many fragments of memory that made their way into *The Black Book* in slightly altered form that it would be presumptuous to list them. But I would still like it to be known that I was at pains to replicate Nişantaşı as I knew it in those days, that I paid attention to the names of the streets, the avenues, their atmosphere. That Alaaddin is a real person who has a real shop next door to the police station is something many people know from the newspaper interviews he went on to give after the Turkish publication of the novel. I have always been glad to see the clippings that Alaaddin displayed on his windows and in corners of his shop, just as I have enjoyed introducing him to the translators ("Alaaddin, this is Vera; she's going to make you famous in Russia!") and the fact that there are curious readers who come from all over the world looking for him. As for those who solved the acrostic and found that there was a building called the Pamuk Apartments where the Heart of the City Apartments were located in the novel, they will also have guessed that I used many other details from my life in the same way, from the moaning of the lift to the smell of the stairwell and the domestic quarrels of that Westernized family. After the book was published, my relatives, taking issue with the novel down to its last sentence, continued the same domestic disputes as a sort of postmodern joke, first taking one another to court over property matters and then gathering together for holiday meals.

Because it is set in the places where I spent my childhood and because it tells the story of a man about my age, I am of course asked frequently how much of me there is in Galip. My life's minor details—shopping trips, looking at Alaaddin's shop from the window, talking to the real Kamer Hanım, spending Saturday nights alone, walking the streets at night—perhaps resemble Galip's. But Galip's essential loneliness, the melancholy that has seeped into him like an illness, and the mournful darkness of his life—I am glad to say that my wounds are not so deep. I am jealous of Galip's ability to bear his resignation, his gravity, and his pain, just as I admire his quiet affirmation of life in spite of all he must endure. It was because I am not as strong as Galip that I became a writer.

I began *The Black Book* in 1985 in my little dorm room at the University of Iowa. My window looked out into the woods, where the beech trees radiated an autumnal red. Then I went to join my wife in student housing at Columbia University, where I continued the book on a desk that I bought in Harlem and placed next to a window overlooking Morningside Park. Whenever I raised my eyes, I would gaze at the broad path running along the edge of the park where squirrels scampered and drug dealers robbed passersby (myself included) and killed one another before my eyes, and where once Dustin Hoffman was to be seen waiting to be called to the set of *Ishtar,* a film that would famously fail. After that I worked in a room measuring six feet by four feet in the Columbia University library, which is home to four million books. My room, which was always blue with cigarette smoke, was at the very top of the building and looked out over the central campus where hundreds of students were constantly strolling back and forth. I continued work on the book in the penthouse flat on Teşvikiye Caddesi that inspired Celal's secret office (the radiators and the parquet floors moaned and creaked in the same way) and on Heybeliada, in a summerhouse that was later sold (from my window I could see the forest and the darkness of the sea beyond). From the Erenköy apartment, where I wrote the last pages, I could see tens of thousands of windows, and on the nights I'd spend so joyfully writing and smoking pack after pack, I would watch the blue light of television disappear from the windows one by one. Thinking back on those days, when my ears were attuned to Istanbul's silence (and the distant packs of barking dogs, the swishing trees, the police sirens, the rubbish vans, and the drunks); when I could smoke as many cigarettes as I pleased, and write, I can see how very happy I was then—even as I lived through the pleasures and fears of the dizzying mental fatigue that would descend on me toward morning, when I lost my way inside the mysterious core of the novel, which was at times closed even to me.

CHAPTER FIFTY-NINE

A Selection from Interviews
on *The New Life*

I began *The New Life* in the midst of another novel, in a way I could never have predicted. I was writing the novel that would become *My Name Is Red*. I'd been invited to a festival in Australia, and after a long plane trip I arrived. They took me and a number of other writers to a motel. Three of us—the neurologist Oliver Sacks, the poet Miroslav Holub, and myself—then went out to the seashore. The coast was endless, the sky gray, the sea calm and almost gray. The air was still, close. I was standing on the edge of the continent that I had seen as a horse's head when I was a child. Sacks went off to the edge of the sea with his palette. Holub went off to look for stones and seashells and soon vanished from sight. I was left alone on the endless shore. It was a mysterious moment. "I am a writer!" I was oddly prompted to tell myself. I was happy to be alive, to be standing in this place, to be in this world. That evening they gave us writers a big party, but I was tired, and I didn't go. I watched the party from the hotel veranda; the sounds and lights in the distant garden filtered through the leaves of the trees. For me, watching a party from a distance bespeaks a writer's stance toward life. At just that moment, Oliver Sacks walked through the next door. I told him I had not been able to sleep after the long journey. He brought me a sleeping pill from his room. "I can't sleep either, let's share this," he said. "I never take sleeping pills," I said, in the way I might say, *I never take drugs*. "I don't take them either," said Sacks, "but it's the only remedy for jet lag."

He was a neurologist and a writer I admired, so I took the pill from the palm of his hand, thanked him, went back to my room, swallowed the pill, got into bed, and waited hopefully. But sleep did not come. The thought that had come to me earlier—that I was a writer—was now mixed with a longing for "purity," for truth. I was lying in my bed in the darkness, thinking about my life. I felt as if only happiness and writing something good would bring me peace. I rose from bed like a sleep-walker, took out the blank notebook that I always carry with me, sat down at the desk in that big room, and began to write: *I read a book one day and my whole life was changed.* This sentence had been in my mind for years. I had long wanted to begin a novel with that sentence. The hero would resemble me too. The reader would learn nothing of the book the hero had read, only of what happened to the hero after he finished reading it. The reader would then use this knowledge to figure out what book the young man had read. It was in this way that I wrote my first paragraph of *The New Life,* and it wasn't long before I was caught inside it. I was very happy about that. I took a break from *Red* and wrote this book in the space of two years, remaining faithful to the form, the poem, in which it had arrived.

When I was writing the book, I spent a lot of time traveling to small towns that were not too far from Istanbul—the towns of the Marmara region, where *The Silent House* is set. Actually, all of Turkey's big cities are coming to resemble provincial towns (as opposed to big villages), and in this sense, Istanbul is a small town too. Turkey's provincial towns reflect something other than the old Reşat Nuri Güntekin's provincial novels: "A governor, a director of land registry, a few leading citizens, a landlord, a Kemalist teacher, and an imam." The atmosphere of today's Anatolian town is created by its Arcelik and Aygaz chain stores, its betting parlors, its plexiglass panels, its televisions—all the same brand—and its pharmacies, pastry shops, post offices, and shabby hospital, where there is always a queue at the door. I may be insisting too much, but I'd like to add this: Ziya Gökalp, the architect and leading propagator of Turkish nationalism, defines a nation through its common culture, its common language, its shared history, and other such elements. In some sense, he is searching for the principles of the unified modern Turkey that he hopes to create. But today what unifies Turkey is not language, history, or culture. It is the Arçelik and Aygaz distributors, the football pools, the post offices, and the Butterfly furniture stores. These centralized concerns have networks that spread all across the country, and the unity it suggests is far stronger than the unity suggested by Ziya Gökalp.

Actually, we've all come across sales conventions somewhere. Most take place in five-star hotels. Whenever we go to such a hotel, we come across crowds of men with their hands in their pockets, looking at the tourists, looking for fun, and perhaps if it's the early hours of the morning and they have had a bit to drink, they'll grow a bit childish, as one does become when he is doing his military service. These salesmen who will spend two or three days a year at sales conferences. They see one another, meet one another, pass together through whatever indoctrination the company wants to give them about the company's identity, and there results a childish excitement, a feeling of brotherhood, and the air of male friendship that we know so well in this country. In general, spouses do not come to these conventions.

The company wants to acquaint its salesmen with its "promotions" and with the updates to its image. So if it is a television manufacturer, there will be a tower of televisions in the lobby; if it is a pharmaceutical company, there will be mountain of medicines or a similar monument to pill consumption. As in secret societies, the creation of an identity—a sense of "us"—is of the utmost importance, so you will see the name of the company emblazoned on key chains, fancy notebooks, envelopes, pencils, and lighters they give out as gifts to the rank and file. Those gifts also bear the symbols and logos that create that identity, that sense of "us."

The New Life caramels I describe in the book are real; they were still producing them when I was a child. There were other companies that produced imitations, and this is one of the details in the book that I enjoy the most, because *The New Life* is also the name of Dante's novel, and the winds from that book may be faintly felt in mine. In other words, *The New Life* refers to a caramel that was popular all over Turkey during the 1950s and also to a book by Dante.

In the middle of the night, when you are fast asleep, your bus enters a small town. The town's lights are pale, its buildings shabby. There is no one in the streets. But through the high windows of the bus you can see a house whose curtains are open. Perhaps that is where the bus stops for a traffic light. And in the midst of all this activity, you suddenly find yourself looking through the open curtains of a house on a side street in a small town where you know no one, where you see people smoking in their pajamas, reading newspapers, or watching the late news before turning off the television. Everyone who has taken a night bus through Turkey has experienced this. Sometimes we come eye to eye with these people in the privacy of their homes. In an instant, you go from sixty miles an hour to a full stop, to view the most awkward and most intimate details of their slow-moving lives. These are the unequaled moments, when life shows you, in such a mysterious way, that the world is made up of so many different lives, so many different people. When we open a refrigerator, we see pots and tomatoes that make us jealous of another life in the same way. We compare ourselves with these people. We are interested in this or that aspect of their lives, and we would like to be in those lives. We dream of being more like those people, of becoming them. To be attracted to another life is to understand how relative our own lives are, while also unique.

I am interested in Sufism as a literary source. As a discipline comprising positions and actions that train the soul, I cannot engage with it, but I look at the literature of Sufism as a literary treasure. As I sit at my table, the child of a republican family, I live like a man committed to Western Cartesian rationalism to the nth degree. Reason sits at the center of my existence. But at the same time, I try to open myself as much as I can to other books, other texts. I do not look at those texts as material, I take pleasure in reading them—they bring me joy. This joy lifts my spirit. Whatever it touches, it will have to reckon with the rationalist in me. Perhaps my books rise out of these two poles, attracting and repelling each other.

CHAPTER SIXTY

A Selection from Interviews
on *My Name Is Red*

Filiz Çağman, the director of Topkapı Palace, was the first person to read *My Name Is Red,* and she was also the most meticulous. Filiz Hanim was the director of the palace library when I began the book. Before I began writing, we had long conversations. It was Filiz Hanim who told me what we see in unfinished miniatures—that artists setting out to draw horses began with the feet, suggesting that they drew from memory.

Before *My Name Is Red* was published, Filiz Hanim and I met at Topkapı Palace one Sunday morning and went through the book page by page. Our work went on until late in the day. It was dark outside by then; the palace museum had closed. We went into the courtyard of the harem. Wherever we looked, it was dark, empty, ominous. Autumn leaves, wind, cold. Dark shadows flitted across the walls of the treasury I describe in the book. We stood there, watching in silence, for a very long time. In our hands were pages of the still-unpublished manuscript. It was worth writing *My Name Is Red* just to stand there in the palace on that dark and windy Sunday afternoon.

Until I began to imagine this novel, my understanding and love of Islamic miniatures was limited. To distinguish these paintings by period and to appreciate their styles, one needed a great deal of patience, and this patience needed love to sustain it. At the beginning, loving these paintings was the hardest thing for me. It was like loving the subject. In the Islamic section of the Metropolitan Museum of Art in New York, they used to exhibit miniatures much better than they do now, especially the Persian miniatures, and you could get very close to the pages and the paintings. In the early 1990s, when the showcases were accessible, I would go there and look at them for hours on end. Some of them bored me, of course; in others I found a sense of play, of rapture; and others still I learned to love by looking at them for a very long time. I learned that you had to work to appreciate them. At the beginning, it was a bit like trying to read a book in a language you don't know, with only a very bad dictionary to help you; you get only the slightest sense of what is going on; hours pass and nothing happens. It pains you to know that there are others well versed in this language, and you envy them, thinking that you yourself will never attain their level of proficiency or its attendant pleasures. But on the other hand there is a matter of pride to it. At first you don't know how to approach these strange and superficially indifferent, closed, difficult, slant-eyed, and identical people arranged with no perspective—how are you going to find it in yourself to love people whose clothes are so distant and Eastern?—but by looking at their faces, looking into their eyes, you learn to love them. It's not all the books I have read that I'm proud of but that over a period of ten years I learned to love them.

The real hero of *My Name Is Red* is the storyteller: Every night he goes to a coffeehouse to stand next to a picture and tell a story. The saddest part of the book is his sorry end. I know how this storyteller feels—the constant pressure. Don't write this, don't write that; if you're going to write that then put it this way; your mother will be angry, your father will be angry, the state will be angry, the publishers will be angry, the newspaper will be angry, everyone will be angry; they'll cluck their tongues and wag their fingers; whatever you do, they interfere. You might say, "So help me God," but at the same time you'll think, I am going to write this in such a way that it will make everyone angry, but it will be so beautiful that they'll bow their heads. In a cobbled-together demi-democracy like ours, in this society so riddled with prohibitions, writing novels puts me in a position not altogether different from my traditional storyteller's; and whatever the explicit political prohibitions might be, a writer will also find himself hemmed in by taboos, family relations, religious injunctions, the state, and much else. In this sense, writing historical fiction speaks of a desire to put on a disguise.

One of my main preoccupations in *My Name Is Red* was the question of style. Style as I understand it today is a post-Renaissance concept embraced by Western art historians in the nineteenth century, and it is what distinguishes each artist from all others. But to dramatize the singularity of a particular artist's style is to encourage a cult of personality. Persian artists and miniaturists of the fifteenth and sixteenth centuries are not known for their individual styles but for the reigning shah, the workshop, the city in which they worked.

The central issue of *My Name Is Red* is not the East-West question; it is the arduous work of the miniaturist: the artist's suffering and his complete dedication to his work. This is a book about art, life, marriage, and happiness. The East-West question is lurking somewhere in the background.

All my books are made from a mixture of Eastern and Western methods, styles, habits, and histories, and if I am rich it is thanks to these legacies. My comfort, my double happiness, comes from the same source: I can, without any guilt, wander between the two worlds, and in both I am at home. Conservatives and religious fundamentalists who are not at ease in the West, as I am, and idealist modernists who are not at ease with tradition, will never understand how this might be possible.

As in *The Silent House,* the characters speak in the first person. Everything talks, not just the characters but also the objects. The title sets the tone.

The title *My Name Is Red* came to me as I was finishing the book, and I immediately liked it. The book's original title was "Love at First Picture." This had to do with the theme of falling in love by looking at the picture of Hüsrev and Şirin that carried the caption "Love at first sight." *Hidden Face,* a film inspired by a story in *The Black Book* for which I wrote the script, explored the same theme: falling in love through looking at pictures.

Şirin falls in love with Hüsrev by looking at a picture, but why, when she goes to the forest, does she not fall in love at first sight of the picture? The second time she goes to the forest, she sees it again, and again she does not fall in love. It is when she sees him on her third visit to the forest that she falls in love. Shouldn't she have fallen in love with a man this handsome and enchanting the first time she saw him? asks my hero, Black. Shekure replies that, in legends, everything happens in threes. In legends everyone has three chances, but in the modern novel, each motif is used only once. The title I discarded was linked to the book's central issue. *My Name Is Red* circles around this question, addressing it from all angles: If Şirin falls in love with Hüsrev by looking at his picture, Hüsrev's picture must certainly have been done in the style of Western portraiture, because Islamic miniatures portray a much more generic type of beauty. After looking at the picture, she can recognize him on the street (as with a picture on an ID card). There were hundreds of pictures done of Tamburlaine and the sultans and khans of the period, but today we have no idea of what they actually looked like: It's always a picture of an ideal sultan or khan. Is it possible to fall in love with someone who looks so much like everyone else?

My books turn on these themes. Kara, who is to a degree modeled on Hüsrev, goes into exile when his love is not returned and for years thinks of his beloved's face. But after a point he can no longer remember it and reasons that if only he had a portrait in the Western sense he could bring her to life before his eyes. He knows that if we don't have a picture of the one we love, no matter how much we love her, her face will slowly be erased from our memory. Instead of her face, what we see are the ideas of various memories. This was another theme of the book: to remember someone's face, the uniqueness of people's faces. This is why the first title was Love at First Picture.

The story of Hüsrev and Şirin is the best-known and most frequently illustrated story in Islamic literature, and it served as a model for many scenes, gatherings, situations, and stances in my novel. We all share a culture; we've read novels, seen films. All these inform the narrative archetypes (in the Jungian sense) we have in our minds. A new story is measured against the template of the old story in our heads, and on that basis we like or dislike it. Like a film we will remember all our lives, a film we would have liked to star in: Shall we call it *West Side Story* or *Romeo and Juliet*? I find the story of Hüsrev and Şirin less romantic and more realistic. It's a story with more politics, more coyness, more intrigues, and in that sense it is more sophisticated.

My novel's central concern: to blend the more distilled and poetic style derived from works in the style of Persian miniatures with the speed, power, and character-driven realism of the novel as we understand it today. In this sense the story's characters—let's exaggerate this a little—suggest clues that play games with real full-blooded characters like Shekure in the novel, and from time to time they resemble us today. But in another sense, being taken from scenes portrayed in miniatures they become more distant from us. My novel travels between these two poles, of intimacy and recognition on the one hand, and remoteness and generalities on the other.

The characters in the book also view nature through pictures or archetypes. This is the part of the book I love the most. This comes from the part of me that burns with the desire to take the cultural past—our traditions—and play with it, to produce new effects. My book really has only one center, one heart: the kitchen! It is the place where Hayriye seeks to influence Esther the clothier with gossip and food; Shekure, too, comes downstairs to the kitchen to advance her intrigues, send off letters and notes, scold her children, and supervise the cooking. The kitchen and all that it contains are the platform on which everything stands. But when I was writing this book that has so much to do with pictures, I could not see nature through the eyes of the characters, not even through the eyes of the miniaturists. For my characters—and for modern readers too— what is of interest is not nature as we all know it but nature as miniaturists painted it. It would be true to say that my book rises out of that parody. There are many descriptions of horses. The horses talk, the horses spend pages talking about how they're painted. One horse even describes himself.

This is not a book about how I see a horse, it's about how miniaturists saw them. And my horse is not talking about real horses, but about how miniaturists depict them. When I see a horse with my own eyes, I'll immediately compare it to a picture of a horse, and there it will end.

I composed the mystery plot easily. It wasn't a problem, but I am not proud of it. When we write our books, and we ask people, Did you like it? and they say, Yes, I liked it, that's not all we want; we also want them to like it for a particular reason, and that reason was: "I liked *My Name Is Red* for echoing the paintings that are its subject and the world of the miniature." I wanted the reader to hear a few of my ideas on style, identity, and difference; I wanted to make him aware of these beautiful paintings and the strange and unique world they evoke. I wanted readers to see how these two beloved subjects become a whole. It was especially where I was describing the paintings and the characters' style, identities, and disquisitions on time that I felt myself growing stronger.

Some readers felt moved to go see Persian and Ottoman painting after reading the book. This was very natural because the book is all about miniatures and the joys of seeing and describing them. As much as I might have wanted the book to interest the reader in those paintings, however, I wrote it in order successfully to describe the paintings in words. Now I'm sorry to see that some of my more inquiring readers were very disappointed when they saw the actual miniatures. Because we have been educated in Western post-Renaissance art like so many other peoples in the world, and belong to the age of the mass-produced photographic image, somehow we can no longer understand or enjoy these paintings. This is why someone not educated in the art of the miniature will likely find it boring and even primitive. This is another central theme in my book.

There is a relation between the art of the miniature and the language of the book. But there's something more important: If you pay close attention, the people in miniatures are at once looking into the world of the painting and also looking at the eye observing them—in other words, at the painter or the person viewing the painting. When Hüsrev and Şirin come into the clearing, they look at each other, but actually their eyes don't meet, because their bodies are half turned toward us. In much the same way do my characters tell their stories, addressing each other and the reader at the same time. They'll say, "I am a picture and I mean something," and also, "Oh, reader, look over here; I'm talking to you." The miniatures are always telling us that they are pictures, just as the readers who are reading my novel are always aware that they are reading a novel.

The women characters, meanwhile, are only too much aware that the reader has invaded their privacy. Even as they speak, they are tidying the room, adjusting their clothes, and taking care not to say the wrong thing. The women are not comfortable being on view; they are not exhibitionists. Only when they turn the reader-observer into a confidante are they able to transform him from an outsider into a brother, creating a new plane for that relationship.

Of all the miniaturists in the book, only one, Zeytin (Velican), is based on a real historical figure. He was an important Persian-Ottoman painter, trained by the Persian portrait artist Siavush. The two other miniaturists are imaginary. I had to do some extensive research to find out how the law of the sixteenth century dealt with crimes of bearing false witness and with financial disputes and to discover what happened in cases where a husband disappeared, so I could work out the details of Shekure's divorce.

It was essential that Esther be a clothes peddler. The figure is not just central to novels about the Ottomans but a staple in novels about the Middle Ages, as it provides an arena for courtship. Social laws forbade male and female characters from being together. But in a novel set in a lively milieu, to describe the important decisions and the uncertainties, the changes of mind—to draw the zigzags of the plot, in other words— the man and the woman must balance each other—tease each other, express themselves to each other, chase and repudiate each other in equal measure—in love as in war, the armies must first stake out their positions on hills. In those days it was not possible for men to do such things, because their access to women was limited, especially in Islamic cultures.

In Ottoman times as in the Middle Ages, these maneuvers—what I describe as "a chess game of love" at one point, using Nizami's words—could only happen with the help of intermediaries carrying letters. In the Ottoman Empire, in Istanbul, it was clothiers who went from house to house to visit women. As women they could come face-to-face with their clients and be admitted to their private worlds, and because they belonged to a non-Muslim minority they were free to race about the city. For an Ottoman woman of the upper class, to go to the market to buy apples, tomatoes, and celery was out of the question. The Jewish merchant who carries the gossip is a staple of the literature of the Tanzimat reform period. We accept Esther as she is, a figure of fun. We don't have much interest in Esther's drama. She is an entertaining conduit of other people's dramas.

In every novel—no matter how much I resist it—there is a character whose thoughts, constitution, and temperament are close to my own and who carries a number of my sorrows and uncertainties. Galip, the hero of *The Black Book,* is in this sense much like Kara in this novel. Kara is the character in *My Name Is Red* to whom I feel closest. I'd like to move beyond using such characters, but I can't see the world without their lighting the way for me. They are the ones who make me feel as if I inhabit their world. Kara has bits of me in him. While other characters do too, Kara is more inclined to follow events from a distance.

It is a character's silences, uncertainties, and sorrows that bring me close to him, not his victories or acts of courage. I would like to be loved in the same way by my readers. I pay most attention to the shadowy patches and moments of fragility in my books, as miniaturists do in their paintings, and in much the same way I want readers to notice where I am troubled and sorrowful.

There is some of my mother in Shekure, which is my mother's name as well. The way she scolds Şevket, Orhan's brother in the novel, the way she watches over the brothers—these, like so many other little details, are copied from life. This is a strong and dominant woman who knows what she is doing—at least that is how she presents herself. But there the similarity ends. It is, in any case, a postmodern sort of similarity: acting as if she is the same but actually different. There is also an amusing play on chronology: I sometimes tell my mother and brother that I reimagined 1950s Istanbul in 1590, keeping everything the same. Her desires are entirely contradictory, and although she knows this, the prospect of their clashing does not send her into a panic. Calm in the knowledge that life is made up of such contradictions, that everything becomes a burden in the end, she sees them as an enrichment.

. . .

For quite a long time, as in *My Name Is Red,* our father lived far away from us (though the father in the book doesn't come and go as ours did). My mother, my brother, and I lived together. As in the book, we brothers fought. As in the book, we would talk of our father's return. Our mother would give us a hard time when we did. As in *My Name Is Red,* she would shout at us when she was angry. But there the similarity ends.

When I was a child, from the age of seven until the age of twenty-two, I wanted to become an artist. I spent much of my time at home painting. My parents brought out some basic pocket books, one of which was about Ottoman art, and I used to copy the Ottoman miniatures. I would do this with full concentration. When I was thirteen and in middle school, I could tell the difference between the sixteenth-century miniaturist Osman and the eighteenth-century miniaturist Levni. I had a strong but childish interest in this subject and bought other books to try to learn more.

I'd been thinking for years about a book about miniaturists. For a while I saw it as the story of a single miniaturist, but later I went off that idea. Anyway, by the age of twenty-four I was living a sort of miniaturist's life. If a miniaturist would sit at his drawing table year in and year out until he went blind, that was what I was doing at my own table from the age of twenty-four, sitting at a table, looking at the empty page, writing by hand with a pen (*kalem,* a word loved by painters), engulfed in books. Sometimes one wrote, sometimes one didn't. Sometimes one would lose hope and tell himself he'd never achieve anything. Sometimes one would write for three days running only to throw it all into the trash can. Sometimes a great black cloud would descend; sometimes I'd be very pleased and feel genuinely happy. Then I would bring all this out into the open. As I narrate in my books, artists are prey to jealousy, jubilation, hope, anger, and agitation about how people might respond; because I know many other writers socially, I have come to see these emotions as hardly particular to miniaturists but a way of describing "the artist's life."

If there is a sense of elegance and measure in the book, it is because my characters long for the unity, beauty, and purity of an earlier age. (My own world is not the measured, elegant, and godly world of *My Name Is Red;* the world of *The Black Book* is dark, chaotic, and of course modern.)

If you ask me, *My Name Is Red* at its deepest level is about the fear of being forgotten, the fear of art being lost. For 250 years, under the influence of the Persians, from the time of Tamburlaine to the end of the seventeenth century—after which Western influence changed things—the Ottomans painted, for better or worse. The miniaturists challenged the Islamic prohibition against representation from the sides and the corners. Because they did their small paintings to illustrate books produced for sultans, shahs, potentates, princes, and pashas, no one questioned this. No one saw them. They stayed inside books. The shahs were the greatest admirers of such work (like Shah Tahmasp, who rose and fell with the miniaturists and advanced the art to the point of doing it himself). Afterward, this fine art was cruelly lost and forgotten—such is the merciless power of history—supplanted by Western post-Renaissance ways of painting and seeing, especially in portraiture. This was simply because Western ways of seeing and painting were more attractive. My book is about the sorrow and tragedy of this loss, this erasure. It is about the sorrow and pain of lost history.

CHAPTER SIXTY-ONE

On *My Name Is Red*

These notes on My Name Is Red *were written on an airplane just after finishing the book.*

NOVEMBER 30, 1998

After reading and rereading *My Name Is Red* and correcting the commas for the thousandth time—after handing it in, what are my thoughts?

I'm happy, tired, at peace with myself, because the book is finished. I feel as relaxed and as happy as I did when I finished my lycée exams and my military service. I went to Beyoğlu and bought myself two expensive shirts; I ate chicken *döner,* looked at the shop windows. I rested at home for two days, tidying up here and there; I was glad I had given myself over to my work, my book, for so many years, and particularly happy about the last six months, when I'd worked with the incandescence of a mystic trying to leave his body. All those drafts that had failed to come together, all those cul-de-sacs and passages that ended badly—over the past two months I'd ruthlessly cut them out and thrown them away. I am sure that the prose is at last taut and well organized, and it flows.

What is there of my soul, of me, in this book? I would say that there is quite a lot here from my life and somewhat less from my soul. For example, my endless quarrels with my older brother, Şevket—I put these into the book though in an affectionate spirit. I did not convey the violence of the beatings I suffered or the deep desires and furies they provoked; this was because *My Name Is Red* was to be indebted to the hopefulness of beauty, to tolerance, to a Tolstoyan harmony, to a sensitivity worthy of Flaubert; these ambitions were with me from the very start. But still my

271

views on the mercilessness, coarseness, disorderliness of life found their way into the book. I wanted it to be a classic; I wanted the whole country to read it and each to find himself reflected in it; I wanted to evoke the cruelty of history and the beauty of a world now lost.

As I was finishing the book, it seemed to me that the mystery plot, the detective story, was forced, that my heart wasn't in it, but it was too late to make changes. I had worried that no one would be interested in my lovely miniaturists unless I found such a device to draw the reader in, but my speculations (on Islam and the prohibition against representational art) led to an assault on their world, their logic, and their fragile labors. That said, I cannot, in the presence of contemporary readers, close my eyes to Islam's historical intolerance of painting, its deep-seated opposition to creativity and visual expression. So this was why my poor miniaturists were forced to endure the intrusion of a political detective plot that would make my novel easy to read. I would like to offer them my apologies.

My Name Is Red was a huge labor, undertaken with childish enthusiasm and heartfelt seriousness, drawing many things from my own life, and designed as a classic that would speak to the whole country. If I now proudly claim to be sure I will succeed in this aim, am I being too sure of myself? My fragility, my filth, my depravity, and my shortcomings— they are not in the fabric of the book, in its language or its structure, but they can be made out in the characters' lives and stories.

The shape of the novel is hopeful, plain for all to see; far from challenging life, it affirms it; far from awakening suspicions, it calls the reader to enjoy what miracles life affords. I hope many readers will like this book. Though I wonder whether a writer's silly optimism is reason enough for a book to be liked.

CHAPTER SIXTY-TWO

From the Snow in Kars Notebooks

SUNDAY, FEBRUARY 24, 2002

I'm back in Kars for the fourth time. Manuel, a photographer friend, and I arrived at ten in the morning. After a day spent walking the city streets and taking photographs, my spirits dropped in an odd sort of way. Kars, on this fourth visit, was not exciting me the same way it had before. These streets, old Russian buildings, gloomy courtyards, broken-down teahouses—the city's deep melancholy, its isolation and beauty—I could no longer contemplate such things and look forward to putting them into a novel. I've written most of the novel, three-fifths of it; the novel (which I've sometimes called *Kar* (*Snow*) and sometimes *Kar in Kars*) has by now taken shape. I know what it can become, and what I will be able to draw from the city and from the loneliness and isolation it evoked in me. What I think about now is not the real city of Kars but the novel *Kar* (or *Kar in Kars*). I also know that the novel is made of the stuff of the city, of its streets, inhabitants, trees, and shops and even from some of its faces, but I also know that it does not resemble the real city.

This is partly because I did not write this novel to replicate the city: I wanted to project onto Kars my own sense of the city's atmosphere and the questions it posed to me. Then there was the snow, which has figured in my every dream during the years I have spent imagining this book. I needed this ever-falling snow to cut the city of the book off from the rest of Turkey. . . .

My memories of my first visit to Kars twenty-five years ago, the cold of the city, and its legendary snowy winters were what originally made me think I could set my book here. This was why, after I finished *My Name Is Red*, I came to Kars—with a press pass from *Sabah*, an Istanbul newspaper, in my pocket—for the city's beauty and its snow. Because I believed that my story could take place here. My motive was not to record the stories of Kars, to listen to the tales of woe and happiness that its residents might whisper in my ear, but to situate my original idea of the novel in this city.

From the day of my arrival I was telling myself I'd been very clever to come to Kars. I so loved this city: its beautiful old worn-out buildings, its wide Russian avenues, its provincial air, its sense of having been utterly forgotten by the rest of the world. This was why I had listened to the people and to their stories with such passion. With my little tape recorder and my video recorder I went from its shantytowns to its party headquarters, from its cockfights to its governor's offices, from its tiny newspaper offices to its teahouses, to interview all those prepared to speak to me. I ended up with between twenty-five and thirty hours of material. I photographed everything I encountered with my simple camera. I remember rushing around on the last day of my first visit to record as much as I could (with the civil police trailing behind me). During every visit, I would go every morning to the Birlik Kıraathanesi—Unity Teahouse—and dash off a few thoughts in my notebooks. Despite all this, despite gathering up all this material (I do not like that word), what I went on to tell is not based solely on my impressions of Kars and its people but is essentially the story in my head.

Above all, this was because of the snow, which no longer fell as it had during the days when Kars was beautiful, rich, and happy. The bourgeois families who had made their money doing business with the Russians of the pre- and post-Soviet eras, who had skated on the River Kars when it froze over, who had traveled about the city in sleighs and put on plays—these people had picked up and left, and when they did the snow left the city too. These days, there is not as much snow in Kars as there once was.

The political disasters in the novel—as well as the poverty and other evils—these are things that have afflicted all of Turkey, but they did not reach such extremes here, or perhaps they did, and everyone forgot: The streets make me feel this might be so. But this could be a mistake on my part.

Another impression, and it may be false too: that life here is so much humbler. And the people too: The people I met in the coffeehouses and while walking the streets were in my view much simpler and plainer than the characters in my novel, who come from the outside. Perhaps it is everyday life—the ordinariness of everyday life—that gave me this impression. Perhaps if at a particular moment someone commits suicide, or commits murder in the coffeehouse where I am sitting half asleep, life will continue to seem ordinary.

During the second half of the 1970s, Kars went through a period of extreme violence. Oppressive measures instigated by the state and its intelligence services changed the course of the city's history. In the mid-nineties, Kurdish guerrillas came down from the mountains. Despite all this (perhaps because of all this), it seems almost to be bad manners to mention political violence or political disasters, an almost shaming sense of having exaggerated—as if I've told a lie, yes, an actual lie.

A painter who has spent his entire life trying to paint a tree will—when finally able to paint that tree in an interesting and enchanting way, when he has brought that tree to life in the language of art and has returned to the painting in creative euphoria to look once more at the tree that inspired it—that painter will feel a certain defeat, a certain betrayal . . . this is what I felt while walking the streets of Kars today. I'll continue walking, feeling that deep sense of loneliness, of remoteness, that the streets still give me.

MONDAY, FEBRUARY 25

I'm back in the Unity Teahouse, where I have been writing since early in the morning. An old man is trying to draw me into conversation; I say old but he may not be much older than I am. Powerfully built, curly hair, wearing a cap and a gray jacket, healthy-seeming with a cigarette hanging from his mouth.

"So you're back again, are you?" he says.

I stand up and shake his hand. "Yes, I'm back," I say with a smile.

He takes a coat off the hook on the wall, and I return to my writing, to this notebook. As he is leaving the Unity Teahouse, his coat in hand, he says, loud enough for me to hear, "Go ahead, then, write how much they paid the officials! Write how much they charge for coal in Kars!"

As he says this, the busboy is opening the lid of the stove to shift the coal with a pair of tongs. Whenever I visit the teahouses of Kars and turn on my tape recorder, and the people around me begin to register their complaints, the price of coal is always high on the list. This tells you how people see me when I am wandering around the teahouses, notebook in hand. Few people know I am a novelist, and those who do know are not aware that I am writing a novel set in Kars. When I say I am a journalist, they immediately ask, "From what newspaper? I saw you once on television. Write, journalist, write!"

Without worrying about my being close enough to hear them, one will say, "Of course he's writing; he's a journalist," and the other will ask, "What is he writing?" In the mornings, the Unity Teahouse is almost empty. Across the room is a table where they started playing cards at around eight. And over there is a man not yet forty who is telling his own fortune. Two retired men sit across from each other at another table, watching this man as they converse. At one point, the man doing his fortune takes his eye off the cards and says some harsh things about Prime Minister Ecevit. His words have to do with the ridiculous fracas between him and the president, and Ecevit going on television to blame the president, and the ensuing stock market crash and the value of the Turkish currency plummeting. At that moment someone from a neighboring table offers a comment. The twelve men in the coffeehouse (I have counted them with my own eyes) gather around the stove, about three paces away from where I am sitting. Tired, lifeless joking and needling. The expression "early in the morning" comes up quite a lot. "Don't do something like that, don't say something like that, so early in the morning!" The stove heats up, casting its sweet warmth on my face. . . . Now silence has fallen over the Unity Teahouse.

The door opens, and a man comes in, and then another. "Good morning, friends!" "Good morning, friends, may things go well for you!"— because a game has begun at another table. It's now half past eight. There is a whole winter day to fill. The *börek* seller comes inside: *"Börek börek börek!"* Why do I love sitting in the teahouses of Kars, and most especially in the Unity Teahouse? (The *börek* seller has come in again with that tray of pastries he balances on his head.) I think it must be because I write so well here "early in the morning." In the morning, when I walk through the cold, wide, windy, and deserted streets of Kars, I feel as if I am able to write anything, that I will be able to write without ever having to stop, that everything I see will excite me, and that I will be able to express everything that excites me with the tip of my pen. A calendar on the wall. A portrait of Atatürk. A television—a moment ago, they cut off the sound (with God's will, the prime minister and the president will be able to come to some agreement at the meeting that was broken off halfway through). Hopelessly rickety chairs, the stovepipe, the playing cards, the dirty walls, the soiled carpets.

Later Manuel arrives with his camera and we walk the streets of Yusufpaşa, Kars's most beautiful neighborhood. The Ismet Pasha Primary School is housed in a beautiful old Russian building. Through an open window on the top floor comes the angry hectoring voice of a teacher scolding her pupils with all her might. "If we could get inside, I could take pictures." What if they throw us out? "Maybe they'll recognize you!" says Manuel.

They do. They offer us tea and cologne in the teachers' room. I shake quite a few teachers' hands. Walking down the high-ceilinged corridors past the closed classroom doors, we can sense the crowds inside. Looking at the gigantic poster of Atatürk that the art teacher has made, we think what it means to be a pupil in this school.

We visit the city's first "restored mansion," which is just next door. An Ankara builder bought this beautiful building and poured a lot of money into it, furnishing it in the style so loved by interior design magazines. It's strange to see such well-ordered affluence amid the poverty of the city: While you appreciate its beauty, you feel it's almost rude to say so.

We walk through the streets again, for a very long time, along the frozen Kars River and over those iron bridges. This is one of my favorite places in Kars. But still, whenever I walk here in the middle of the day, I am somehow overtaken by feelings of sadness and defeat. I've now written most of my novel; it's almost complete and now as compelling to me as the city itself; all I want to do now is work on my novel. The city has begun to look as if it holds no more secrets. We visit the building that once served as the Russian consulate. In the old days, it was the home of a rich Armenian. When the Russian armies conquered the city, they kicked out the Armenian and turned it into a military headquarters. Then the city passed into the hands of the Turks. In the early years of the Republic, the house passed into the hands of a rich Azeri who did business with the Russians. After that it was rented to the Soviets for their consulate. Then it passed to the family who lives there today. The well-meaning man who shows us around tells me that they're not renting the mansion, they own it.

In the novel I made this into a much bigger house and rented it not to the present owner but to the religious high school. The real religious high school is quite a long distance from here, down the hill. Why did I make this small adjustment? I don't know, I just wanted to. Because this made the story more believable, more real. Anyway, the location of the religious high school is not particularly significant in the novel. At the same time, it is small changes like these that take the novel out of the realm of "reality" and made it possible for me to write.

For me to believe in my own story, I was well aware that I would need, from time to time, to narrate not the real Kars but the Kars of my imagination—it is the story in my mind that I must tell—and it is when I narrate the legend inside me (laden though it is with political violence) that everything becomes beautiful to me. On the other hand, these alterations awaken lies and obsessions, faint pangs of conscience, and feelings of guilt whose hidden symmetry I have no desire to explore. Another cause for anxiety is knowing that my novel will upset my friends in Kars—for example, Sezai Bey or the courteous mayor—who both expect good things of me. I live with this constant contradiction. Whenever I turn on my tape recorder, whenever I try to find out what I should write about Kars, everyone complains vociferously about the poverty, the state's neglect and oppression, the injustices, the cruelties. As I thank them, they all say, "Write about it all!" then, "But say good things about Kars." The things they have told me are not "good things" at all.

In Kars, there is no "political Islamist movement" as powerful as the one in the book. On the other hand, only yesterday the mayor was telling us that the Azeris were slowly falling under the influence of political Islam, that those going to Qum in Iran for their education felt more tied to their Shiite identity, that the Hasan-Huseyin-Kerbala rituals were being performed here now, where before this had never happened.

TUESDAY MORNING, FEBRUARY 26

I woke up at half past five this morning. It was daylight but there was no one in the streets. So I sat down at the little table with the mirror in my hotel room and began to write. I felt only joy to be in Kars so early in the morning, to have awoken here, to know I would again walk its deserted streets, again go into its teahouses to jot a few things down in my notebooks. As always when the time of my return to Istanbul approaches, I long to record the whole of Kars—its mournful streets, its dogs, its teahouses, its barbershops—to fix it on film and to hide it away.

THE LAST MORNING IN KARS

My last hours in Kars. Perhaps I'll never come back. I walked for some time through the ice-cold streets. A deep melancholy overtakes me each time I've known I am soon to leave Kars. The simplicity of life, the gentle companionship, the intimacy, the fragility of life, its continuity, and the sense of being in a place where time moves so slowly: These are the things that bind me to Kars.

This morning, the same *börek* seller as before, with the same tray balanced on his head. When I am thinking all this, the friends sharing my table at the Unity Teahouse talk of unemployment, of being stranded in teahouses with nothing to do. "Have you written that down?" they ask. "Write it down. The president of the Republic supports us citizens. The president is a good man. The others keep thieving and building up their fortunes. Write that down. Deputies take a salary of two billion, and then they rob us of the right to earn a hundred million. Write that down, and write down my name too. Write, write."

The men sitting in the Unity Teahouse, despite their poverty, are not the worst off in Kars. For instance the man with whom I was speaking just now is a gentleman who once had a job, and others owned businesses that have since failed, or they were hospital directors, managers who've now retired, men who owned trucks; but now they are left with nothing to do, like the bankrupt tailor we interviewed on our last visit (he had a little garment factory with twelve machines). They were all once rich and successful. This is what distinguishes the Unity Teahouse from the teahouses of the most desperate among the city's unemployed—those who live out their unlettered lives in the city's shantytowns. What we see here is a continuation of the old Unity Club.

"Not a single person is happy here. And everything is forbidden," someone says. Everyone complains in Kars; no one is happy; they all seem on the verge of bursting from unhappiness. If there is a silence, a dullness, a strange sense of calm, it is because the streets are full of people who have made peace with misery and helplessness; the state has banned all other possibilities, and done so with some violence. Happiness is another matter. But this is what I felt when I was writing the novel. What I feel rising up inside me is not guilt at not sharing in these people's fate but a feeling of helplessness. I am pessimistic: There seem to be no prospects for significant change here in the near future. But let me write my novel as I believe it to be, and from the heart. The best thing I can do for the people of Kars is to write from the heart, to write a good novel.

PICTURES AND TEXTS

CHAPTER SIXTY-THREE

Şirin's Surprise

I am a novelist. However much I have learned from theory, having at times even been beguiled by it, I have quite often felt the need to steer clear of it. I now hope to entertain you with a few stories and, through them, to suggest a few ideas of my own.

If there is a garden in your dreams—a garden you have never seen in life, perhaps because it is on the other side of a high wall—the best way to imagine that unseen garden is to tell stories that evoke your hopes and fears.

A good theory, even one that has affected us deeply and convinced us, will remain someone else's theory and not our own. But a good story that has affected us deeply, and convinced us, becomes our own. Old stories, very old stories, are like this. No one can remember who told them first. We erase all memory of the way in which they were first expressed. With each new telling, we hear the story as if for the first time. I shall now tell you two such stories.

The first is one I tried to retell in my fashion in *The Black Book*. I would like to apologize to those of you who have already read it— though stories like this take on new meanings with each telling: Gazzali told the following story in Ihya-ul Ulum; Enveri compressed it into four verses; Nizami used it in the Iskendername, Ibni Arabi told it, and so too did Rumi in Mesnevi.

One day a ruler—a sultan, a khan, a shah—announced a painting competition, whereupon the Chinese artists and the artists from countries to the west began to challenge one another: We paint better than you do; No, we do. . . . After pondering the matter, the sultan—let's say he's a sultan—decided to put both sides to the test. He offered them two facing walls in two adjoining rooms, for this would allow him to compare their work. Between the two facing walls was a curtain; once this was closed and the artist camps could no longer see each other, they both went to work. The western artists took out their colors and their brushes and began to draw and paint. The Chinese, meanwhile, decided that they first needed to scrub away the dust and the rust, so they set about cleaning and shining the wall to which they had been assigned. The work continued for months. In one room there was now a wall filled with brilliantly colored paintings. In the other was a wall that had been so well polished that it had turned into a mirror. When the time was up, the curtain between the two rooms was opened. The sultan looked first at the work of the western artists. It was a beautiful painting, and the sultan was very impressed. When he looked at the wall on which the Chinese artists had been working, he saw the reflection of the wondrous paintings on the wall opposite. The sultan gave the prize to the Chinese artists, who had turned their wall into a mirror.

The second story is as old as the first. It too has many variations. It appears in the Thousand and One Nights, in the parrots' tales of Tutiname, and in Nizami's Hüsrev and Şirin, itself taken into various other books. I shall try to summarize the Nizami version.

Şirin is an Armenian princess and a great beauty. Hüsrev is a prince, the son of the Persian shah. Şapur wants to make his master Hüsrev fall in love with Şirin, and Şirin with Hüsrev. With this in mind he travels to Şirin's country. One day, when Şirin has gone to the forest with her courtiers to eat and drink, he hides among the trees. There and then, he draws a picture of his fine handsome master, hangs it on a tree, and makes himself scarce. As Şirin frolics in the forest with her courtiers, she sees the picture of Hüsrev hanging from the branch and falls in love with this person in the picture. Şirin does not believe in her love; she wants to forget the picture and her response to it. Then, during another excursion to another forest, the same thing happens. Şirin is again affected by the picture; she is in love but helpless. During a third excursion, when Şirin again sees Hüsrev's picture hanging from a branch, she knows she is helplessly in love with him. She accepts her love and begins to search for the person whose likeness, whose image, she has seen.

In the same way, Şapur makes his master fall in love with Şirin, but in this case he does not use pictures but words. After falling equally in love, one through pictures and the other through words, these two young people begin to search each other out. Each sets out for the other's country. Their paths cross on the banks of a spring, but they fail to recognize each other. Şirin, tired from her travels, undresses and steps into the water.

The moment he sets eyes on her, Hüsrev is besotted. Is this the beauty he has come to know through words and stories? At a moment when he is not watching her, Şirin also sees Hüsrev. She too is deeply affected. But Hüsrev is not wearing the red robes that might have helped her recognize him. She is sure of her feelings but surprised and confused enough to entertain these thoughts: It was a picture hanging from the tree, but the man before me is alive. What I saw hanging from the branch was a likeness, but this is a real man.

In Nizami's version, the story of Hüsrev and Şirin carries on with the utmost elegance. What I can identify with most easily here is Şirin's surprise, the way she wavers between image and reality. I see her innocence—her susceptibility to a painting, the way she lets an image give rise to desire—as something we can still understand today. And perhaps I can see it, too, in Nizami's affection for the tradition that makes things happen in threes. But the uncertainty Şirin feels when she first sets eyes on the handsome Hüsrev is also our uncertainty: Which is the "true"

Hüsrev? Like Şirin, we ask ourselves, Is it in reality that the truth lies, or in the image? Which one affects us more deeply, handsome Hüsrev's picture or the man himself?

Each of us answers such questions in his own way. When we hear or read these stories, these elementary questions come back to us. They come to us at times when we are deep in thought or reading a story, watching a film, or feeling fragile and naïve. Which has the stronger influence on us, the picture of the man or the man himself?

Eastern storytellers who take up the story of the artists' competition always offer sweet explanations as to why the Chinese artists win the sultan's prize. What interests me is not the wisdom these storytellers offer but something else that reflects the life of the story itself, something that the mirror in the story reveals: The mirror that multiplies, the mirror that expands, also makes us feel as if we are somehow lacking, as if we are a bit inauthentic or uninteresting. As if we are not whole. Then, depending on how much courage we have, we too set out on a journey: the same sort of journey on which Hüsrev and Şirin embarked for love. We each seek the "other" who will complete us. This is a journey that takes us beyond the surface, into the depths, closer to the center. The truth resides far away. Someone somewhere told us so, and now we have embarked on a journey to find it. Literature is the story of this journey. Though I believe in this journey, I do not believe that there is a center waiting to be discovered in a faraway land.

This may be a source of sadness or of optimism. You could call it a lesson we learn from life in countries like ours that are so far from the center. If I find myself believing in the dilemma suggested by the sultan's competition, or if I succumb to Şirin's surprise, I ask the very question I should most avoid: Then I am obliged to say that I have gone my whole life without ever reaching that center, without ever achieving that authenticity, that pure truth. But my story is the story of most people in the world.

Before reading Dante I heard funny stories inspired by *Inferno.* Before I saw Chaplin's *The Great Dictator,* I saw it copied in a Turkish film series known as *Vanished Ibrahim.* I came to know and love the Impressionists from reproductions torn from magazines and displayed on the walls of barbershops and greengrocers. I came to know the world through Tintin—as with most books, in the Turkish translation. I acquired my taste for history from countries whose histories do not resemble our own. I have gone through life convinced that the buildings in which I have lived and the streets I have walked are bad imitations of streets and buildings somewhere in the West. The chairs and tables at which I sat were copies of originals in American films; it was only much later, after I saw the films again, that I realized this. I have compared a great many new faces with those I have seen in films and on television, and I have confused them. I have learned more about honor, courage, love, compassion, honesty, and evil by reading about them than by knowing them in real life. I cannot say how much of my joy or my seriousness of purpose, my way of standing or speaking, is innate and how much I have unwittingly copied from other examples. Nor do I know how many of those examples are themselves copies of another original or copy. The same can be said of my own words. Perhaps this is why it may be best just to repeat what someone else has already said.

Oğuz Atay (1934–1977), one of Turkey's best novelists, who was heavily influenced by experimental European writers from Joyce to Nabokov, once said, "I am a copy of something, but I've forgotten what that something is." The center where the truth might lie is very far away indeed! Most of the non-Western world knew this already. We knew it without knowing we knew it. Now we are discovering what we already knew.

Literary modernism was one of the last responses to this search for authenticity; rooted in romanticism, it was in pursuit of purity. If its echo was heard here in Turkey, it was very faint. I cannot say that I found this upsetting. Like most people in the world, I have passed most of my life waiting for something to happen.

But what we have in hand now are endless fragments. Were there a philosopher king in the way Plato envisaged, he would not be able to provide a right or consistent reason for choosing between the artists who painted their wall and those who turned their wall into a mirror. The story of the artists' competition carries traces of Plato's famous shadow cave. In the non-Western world, and especially in their media, the question as to whether this or indeed any other story or image is the original or a copy of an original is at this point a matter only for old-fashioned philologists or art historians. The truth we once believed to be hiding far, far away, behind the curtains and the shadows, has perhaps vanished altogether. If the truth exists anywhere, it lies among our memories. I would be happier if we used these fragments at hand, these images and stories we have separated from one another, from their pasts.

In the nineteenth-century novel, detailed descriptions of faces and gestures serve as clues to fundamental truths lying beneath the surface. The narrator or his character would set out on a journey to this hidden truth in much the same way as did Hüsrev and Şirin. The meaning behind the faces and the objects is something that emerges from the book as a whole, and only after we have come to the end of the story. The book's meaning—the meaning of the nineteenth-century novel—would be the meaning of the world we have explored with the characters. This was a victorious Truth with a capital T.

But with the waning of the nineteenth-century novel, the world lost its unity and its meaning. As we set out to write novels today, all we have at hand are fragments and more fragments. This can be a source of optimism: By ridding ourselves of hierarchies, we can embrace the whole world and all of culture and life. But it can also be cause for fear and confusion, prompting us to narrate less, to push the centers of our stories from the center to the margins. That it allows for new narrative possibilities and points of view is irrelevant. We cannot use the fragments we have to make that vertical journey to meaning, to the center; what we make instead is a horizontal journey. Instead of traveling to the world's hidden depths, we explore its vastness. I enjoy going out in search of more fragments, in search of stories not yet told. This new continent of forgotten and heretofore unnamed stories, histories, peoples, and objects, of lands whose voices have yet to be heard, and stories yet to be told, is so vast, and so little explored, that the word "journey" is entirely apt.

But the journey that leads to the underlying meaning of a text still stands before us, and it demands individual effort. It is more personal than ever before, because we have neither a recipe nor a compass. The depth of a text resides in its complexity and its determination to address these fragments. Let me bring this discussion to an end by telling you a third tale. It is short and very personal.

I have been writing a novel about a group of artists—miniaturists—set in the classical age of Ottoman miniatures. This is why I came, at one point, to take a close interest in the story of Hüsrev and Şirin. This story is very popular in Islamic and Middle Eastern culture. This is why miniaturists were so often summoned to Persian and Ottoman palaces to illustrate it. What interested me the most was the scene in which Şirin looks at Hüsrev's picture and falls in love. The artists painting this scene were to depict more than just Şirin and her surroundings, for there was a painting inside the painting: the picture that caused Şirin to fall in love. This dramatic scene was well beloved as the story of which it was a part, and so I have seen it in many books, reproductions, and museums. But when I look at these pictures, I always feel disquiet: as if something is lacking, as if I'm not whole.

In these pictures, Şirin was always there, and though her clothes and her face varied, she was still Şirin. Whatever the colors, the clothes, the stance, her courtiers still surrounded her. There were trees, too, and the vastness of the forest. And somewhere, hanging from a branch, the picture inside the picture.

It took me a long time to understand what was making me uneasy. Though there was a picture inside the frame hanging from the tree, it never showed the Hüsrev I expected to see. Though I have searched for it everywhere, I have never found my own conception of Hüsrev reflected in any miniature. In all these miniatures, the picture inside the picture was so small that Hüsrev was an undistinguished, unrecognizable red spot rather than a character or a developed face.

Such rendering of course defeats the central point of the Hüsrev and Şirin story, that of falling in love by means of an image. Still I like the technical simplicity made possible by ignorance of the ways of Western portraiture. This simplicity evokes the fragile, naïve world I aim to explore in the novel I have been writing, a world whose stories and fragments I mean to integrate, proposing for it a new center.

CHAPTER SIXTY-FOUR

In the Forest and as Old as the World

I'm sitting, waiting, in the forest; my painting is done. Behind me is my horse, and I'm watching something . . . something you can't see. You will never know what it is, this thing that has brought me such disquiet, though you've seen the same look in Hüsrev's eyes as he spies Şirin bathing in the lake. In their paintings you can see them both: Hüsrev feasting his eyes on the naked Şirin. But the fifteenth-century miniaturist who was commissioned to paint this picture chose not to show what I see—only that there's something I'm watching. I hope you'll appreciate the painting for just this reason. See how beautifully he's painted me, lost in the forest, among the trees, the branches, the grass. As I wait, a wind begins to blow; the leaves tremble, one by one; the branches sway. I'm worried. How does the artist's pen manage to reach so far? The branches bend in the wind and rise up again, the flowers grow and fall, the forest swells like a wave, and the whole world trembles. We hear the hum of the forest, the world's lament. The artist patiently re-creates the world's lament, leaf by leaf. It is now, as I sit in this windswept forest, that you sense I am trembling with loneliness. If you look even closer, you will see how old that feeling is, to sit alone in the forest, a feeling as old as the world.

CHAPTER SIXTY-FIVE

Murders by Unknown Assailants and Detective Novels

The Columnist Çetin Altan and Şeyhülislam Ebussuud Efendi

A large part of *The Black Book* consists of columns ostensibly printed in *Milliyet,* one of Turkey's most important newspapers. In the novel they are presented as pieces written by a character who is a journalist. They appear at regular intervals, interrupting the novel's straight narrative, and because they determine the shape of *The Black Book,* they caused me a great deal of difficulty. Because I was having such a good time writing in the voice of a columnist, balancing fake erudition with a subtle buffoonery, the columns kept getting longer, dominating the book in a way that destroyed the balance and composition of the whole. Even today, when readers say to me, "I read *The Black Book;* the columns are wonderful," I am at the same time pleased and also troubled.

Those who have read the book in translation are the ones who say this most often. The Western reader is entranced by the strangeness and facile narration of the columnists I parody, who belong to a tradition that stretches beyond Turkey to include many other countries living within the same cultural contradictions. They are a dying breed, but we can still find echoes of them in columnists writing in Turkey today.

In Turkey a real columnist will write four or five times a week. He will take his subjects from every aspect of life, geography, and history. He will deploy every narrative shape and strategy, whether drawing upon the most mundane daily news or philosophy or memoir or sociological observation. Everything, from the city council—the shape of the new streetlamps—to questions of civilization—Turkey's place between East and West—are within the columnist's purview. (He is most likely to gain the reader's attention by linking something like the shape of streetlamps to the East-West question.) The most successful are the most quarrelsome and agile debaters; they make their names with their polemic, their courage, and their blunt language. Quite a few of them have spent parts of their lives in prisons and courthouses as a result of what they have written. Their readers admire and trust them, not for their ability to illuminate or explain but for their courage and intrusiveness. They are stars because they presume to be experts on everything, because they seem to have an answer to any question, because they discuss political enmities about which everyone has an opinion. At times when the country is politically polarized, they are the witnesses who can find their way into all parts of society: into the homes of the powerful; into coffeehouses, state offices, and everyday life. Because they enjoy the readers' trust and affection, one day talking about love and the next giving their views on Clinton and the pope, writing about a corrupt mayor with the same ease as they write about Freud's errors, they become "Professors of Everything." Ten or fifteen years ago—before television changed the country's newspaper-reading habits—Turkish readers considered newspaper columns to be the highest literary form. In those days, whenever I traveled by bus around Anatolia, anyone who found out I was a writer would ask me which newspaper I worked for.

When I was creating Celâl Salik, the columnist of *The Black Book,* and even more when I was writing his columns, my main concern was to ensure he bore no resemblance to the famous columnists of the day— each one of whom was as well known as the most powerful politicians— and thereby to escape the shadow cast by these illustrious writers. The real columnist I was most afraid of resembling, the columnist whose controversial stands made him the most famous of the past half century—was Çetin Altan.

Recently Çetin Altan was charged with "insulting the state," after speaking openly about its links with the Mafia and about certain murders in which the government had a hand. In one interview at the time of his trial, he revealed that he'd had roughly three hundred cases lodged against him. Because he was one of my great literary and political heroes when I was young, I remember both the days when he was sentenced to prison and the days of his release as high drama. During the time when he was a deputy for the Turkish Workers Party, his brilliant speeches in the National Assembly and his powerful columns caused him to lose his immunity, whereupon deputies from the then ruling conservative party subjected him to a beating in the National Assembly.

Much of the anger that the state and public opinion vented against Altan came, without a doubt, from his being a socialist in a country neighboring the Soviet Union during the Cold War. In any case, from the

1970s on, when Altan began to direct his criticisms at the state, the anger against him did not abate. My own view is that conservatives and nationalists on the right and the left hated him because he refused to blame Turkey's poverty and political and administrative inadequacies on the political experiments and manipulations of foreign powers, seeing the national problems as rooted in national conditions. When he criticized his own country, Altan never presented the reader with devils upon whom to heap all the blame, and neither did he offer recipes that might change the country's fate overnight. More than the regime his target was Turkey's culture, and this Altan observed with a sharp and ironic eye— its everyday habits, its way of thinking, its assumptions—ascribing to it the nation's ills. Not only could Altan write in the language of the very people he most infuriated, he could also count on those same people to read him every day, and in this sense he was a sort of Naipaul.

But Çetin Altan never succumbed to the pain that makes Naipaul seem so loveless and pessimistic. He remained optimistic about Westernization and modernization. This is why the West was not for him a center that caused pain because it was being imitated, or that was imitated because it caused pain and was responsible for all imaginable ills. His childish optimism came in part from the fact that Turkey had never suffered colonialism, and this allowed him to see Western civilization as a center that could be approached, if in a slow and measured way. Whatever it might be that makes "us" different from those living in the West, it is something we ourselves lack. Because we are not like Westerners, we must first establish what it is we lack and then make up for it. History, our history, is the history of all our shortcomings. Like so many Ottoman and Turkish intellectuals, and so many of our polemical columnists, Çetin Altan was given to long lists of dismal shortcomings that distinguish us from the West; they range from democracy to modern capitalism, from the art of the novel to individuality and piano playing, from the visual arts to prose, from the hat to which Atatürk gave so much importance to the table I jokingly proposed in *The Silent House*.

In the 1970s, when political terror had risen to its current furious levels, Çetin Altan noticed one other lack, and that is our subject today.

The detective story in Turkey is not as highly developed as it is in England, America, and France. Set against the complexities of life in industrial societies, their finely plotted murders have had a strong influence on the novels, plays, and films of these same societies, and as a consequence a great variety of creative talents have emerged in the detective genre.

But in our village-dominated society, there is nothing clever about murder. A husband whose judgment is clouded by jealousy takes out his knife and stabs his wife without further ado, and the business is over. Or a man who has entered into a blood feud will see his enemy and empty his bullets into his brain then and there. In the countryside, where there is a dispute about land or water rights, the custom is to take up a double-barreled shotgun and lie in wait. Everyone knows who was killed by whom, and why. If this sort of murder has failed to interest writers, it is due to the roughness of the execution, which calls to mind a man bludgeoning a pumpkin with an axe, and this is why the art of detective fiction is so undeveloped in our country.

On first reading, we cannot help but delight in the directness of the reasoning, the sharp-tongued humor, and perhaps that is why we might be inclined to accept Altan's reasoning, but what might we say to rebut it? Well, we might mention the Sicilian writer Leonardo Sciascia, who used murders of a similarly rural nature in his detective novels with great success. One could also point to the many Western murders that—though they were executed with the coarseness that "calls to mind a man bludgeoning a pumpkin with an axe"—went on to inspire, or indeed were inspired by—detective stories.

Not long after this particular column appeared, Çetin Altan wrote a collection of short detective stories, of a type that was very common in the early years of detective fiction. With these stories, in the style of G. K. Chesterton's Father Brown series, he gave up on the idea that society had not given the writer enough life experience to write detective fiction, discarding this view as excessively determinist.

But now let us dwell on his other assertion: "Everyone knows who was killed by whom, and why." If you bear in mind that many murders are committed in the hope that they will never be discovered, it is immediately evident that this statement cannot always be true. Four hundred years before Çetin Altan spoke of the dearth of murders by unknown assailants in our culture, the Ottoman state (then in the midst of what old-guard historians call the classical age) grew so concerned about murders by unknown assailants that it made an unprecedentedly serious effort to address it to the pertinent legalities. Today we know that Sheikh-ul-Islam

Ebussuud Efendi (who was the highest legal authority in the time of Süleyman the Magnificent, and whose decisions took on the aura of classical landmark precedents in the Western sense and influence rulings to this day) was often asked about who should pay the reparations for murders by unknown assailants.

QUESTION: When four villages are at war with one another and one man is killed by a club wielded by another man whose identity is unknown, who pays the blood money?

ANSWER: The people of the nearest village.

QUESTION: If someone gets killed close to a particular town and the murderer cannot be found, who pays the blood money? Is it the entire town, or is it just the people whose houses were close enough to hear the dying man's screams?

ANSWER: Those living close enough to hear the dying man's screams.

QUESTION: If a body is found in a religious establishment at a time when the nighttime tenants are not in the shop itself, but in their living quarters, and the murderer cannot be found, who is responsible for the blood money?

ANSWER: Those living close enough to the shop to hear the dying man's screams. If no one lives close by, then the Treasury—in other words, the state—is responsible.

We can see from these examples that the Ottoman penal code was greatly concerned with murders by unknown assailants, and that the state was aware that it had to take responsibility for such crimes—in other words, pay the blood money—if unable to lay it off on individual citizens. If one of these persons did not wish to take the blame, he was obliged to solve the murder himself. This was to introduce a possibility that we might have to take the blame for every murder that happened around us—the exact opposite of what we see today. To avoid the responsibility for a murder in those days, a person had to be open and alert to every sound and movement around him, to the point of paranoia. Because everyone knew he might be forced to take responsibility for every murder committed in his neighborhood, it is not hard to anticipate the ardor with which the common man would chase after criminals and murderers. In my personal observation, this understanding of responsibility and the anxiety it evokes is still the rule in Istanbul, even with its present population of ten million. Perhaps you could see this as a carry-over from the old anxieties about blood money, but the moral vision it suggests—a world in which everyone considers everyone else responsible for everything—is one that Dostoyevsky would have wholeheartedly approved.

But let us not seek to mislead anyone: Today's Istanbul—today's Turkey—is a world leader in state-sponsored murder by unknown assailants, not to mention systematic torture, trammels on freedom of expression, and the merciless abuse of human rights. In contrast to Nigeria, Korea, and China, however, Turkey also has a democracy strong enough to allow voters to force the state to refrain from such practices. It is therefore very easy to infer that most electors have shockingly little interest in human rights. What is difficult is to explain why, after four hundred years of responsibility by proximity, and fear of paying the price as their neighbors' keepers, they now take so little interest when the state is banning books and beating and torturing neighbors in the next building.

I mean only to alert you to this situation. I am not particularly interested in exploring or explaining it. This is probably because I don't wish to explain away one cultural shortcoming with another. There is in all such subjects something that kills the poet inside us. Sometimes the silence seems to suggest that, as Beckett once said, "There is nothing to be said," and at other times that "there is far too much to be said."

It is at times like this that I understand only too well why Turgenev wanted to forget everything to do with Russia, why he went to Baden-Baden and gave himself over to a life that was in every way divorced from her, why he would scold anyone who tried to discuss Russia's problems with him (as in that famous story), telling such people that he was not in the least interested in Russia and inclined rather to put the place out of his mind forever. This despite the fact that there have been many other times when I have thought that the best thing to do would be to stay in Turkey, lock myself up in a room, and travel into my imagination with the vague intention of writing a book. In fact, I did just that from 1975 to 1982, when murder and political violence, state oppression, torture, and prohibition were at their height. To lock myself up in a room to write a new history—a new story with allegories, obscurities, silences, and never-heard sounds—is, of course, better than to write another history of defects that seeks to explain our defects by means of other defects. To embark on such a journey there is no need to know exactly where you are going; it is enough to know where you do not wish to be.

Let us remain in that locked room I just mentioned, to look at the way in which I work with allegory and obscurity. There is a novel that was translated into Turkish as *The Secret of the Yellow Room* by the French author Gaston Leroux, best known in recent years for his *Phantom of the Opera*. *The Secret* is celebrated by devotees of detective fiction as the first and most brilliant example of the "murder in a locked room." The door of the room where the murder has taken place is locked, and inside is a body with a set number of suspects. After the murder, someone with a flair for solving puzzles examines the clues and, having established the facts, determines the reasons for the murder. Seventy years after Gaston Leroux wrote *The Secret of the Yellow Room,* the Spanish author Manuel Vázquez Montalbán wrote a book entitled *Murder in the Central Committee,* proving that the possibilities afforded by the murder-in-a-locked-room template are not easily exhausted; the locked room in this political detective novel is a conference room for a party resembling the Spanish Communist Party, and when the lights go out the general secretary is killed. Whatever form it takes, murder in a locked room offers a clear understanding of crime, law, and punishment. After the murder, an outside investigator, usually an agent of the state, arrives to question each suspect individually. These interrogations confirm that we are solely responsible to the central authority outside us for the crimes we have committed. The locked room is the best way to convey the idea that we are neither responsible nor guilty as a group, a neighborhood, or a society. We are either guilty as individuals or we are not guilty at all. This world in which we are only responsible to the state for our crimes is a long way from the moral universe that Dostoyevsky dreamed of.

I mentioned the locked room because I wanted to explain why, when we lack even the basic principles that might help us understand our history, we can only connect with it through allegory. What we need is a new variation on the murder-in-a-locked-room story, which I brought up only as an example. In the reworked version, the responsibility for the murder (this being an allegory, we might refer to it simply as the Crime) will attack the owner of the room in which it was committed, along with all those who live there and all those living close enough to hear the dying man's screams. From the moment we accept this—at an early point in the story—we will proceed as if we are playing chess by new rules, and it will be possible for us to foresee how the murderer or the criminal will work with the knowledge of our system. It is clear that, to keep from being found, to avoid becoming the sole person responsible, the murderer must act on the assumption that everyone in the vicinity is responsible.

This might bring us to Çetin Altan's theory, that responsibility for the crime lies inside the culture itself. But if we begin instead with allegories, obscurities, and faint new voices that we don't quite know how to use, we will at least be able to save ourselves from writing more histories of the defects and the differences that led us to defeat. In my youth, when I was curious to know and understand everything, and read columnists like Çetin Altan with a passion, I had the idea that I might one day become a writer. But I did not, like so many of those with similar dreams, think about what I might write; I thought instead about what stance I should take. My image of the writer drew less from the modernists, who used writing as a sort of vehicle of protection, than from the writers of the enlightenment, who wished to understand everything, show the reader everything. Now I know both approaches to be inadequate and overly derivative. In a society swarming with devils, the devil of modernism is not clever enough. To converse with the devils, the writers of the enlightenment too often accommodated state power and authority. Perhaps I am like most writers: Because I cannot deal in concepts, I look for allegories and tell stories. But I am not complaining, and I think myself lucky, because in my country allegories take the place of philosophy and people believe stories more than they do theories.

CHAPTER SIXTY-SIX

Entr'acte; or, Ah, Cleopatra!

Going to See a Film in Istanbul

*C*leopatra* went on general release throughout the world in 1964, but, as usual, those of us who lived in Istanbul did not get a chance to see Richard Burton and Elizabeth Taylor's star turn until two years later. In those days, films came to us several years after release, because Turkish distributors were not able to meet Hollywood's price for opening-run distribution, but this did not dampen Istanbul's appetite for the latest gems of Western culture. To the contrary, upon reading the latest gossip about the Burton-Taylor affair, and seeing the titillating news and photographs of *Cleopatra*'s most revealing scenes, İstanbullus would sigh with impatience and say, "Well, let's see when it finally gets here."

When I think back to that day when I first saw *Cleopatra,* what I remember best—and this is true for quite a few big American productions—is not the film itself but the thrill of watching it. I remember Liz Taylor—who recalled not Cleopatra but her own glittering film career as hundreds of slaves carried her throne with due ceremony; I remember the galleys sailing over a sea of Panavision, and not Mediterranean, blue, and Rex Harrison, who matched my own image of Julius Caesar, teaching his son Octavian how an emperor should walk and deport himself. But above all I remember sitting in my seat and seeing my dreams stretch out before me, from the curtains to the farthest corner, and, in that same space, my self coming into being.

How might I explain what was going on in that space? Like most of Turkey's Westernized middle class and like most of my generation, I went very seldom to see "domestic" films. When I went to a cinema, I wanted all the usual things—to lose myself in an illusion, to enter a story in darkness, and to be entranced by beautiful people in beautiful places—but also to come face-to-face with the West and to have fun while I was there. When I went home I would repeat in English the withering words that the handsome, cold-blooded hero had uttered in his most dramatic scene. Like so many others of my ilk, I paid careful attention to the way he folded a handkerchief before putting it in his pocket, the way he opened a whiskey bottle, and the way he leaned forward to light a woman's cigarette; I also kept an eye out for the latest Western inventions, like the transistor radio and the toaster. Not even when they conquered the whole of the Balkans and laid siege to Vienna, not even when they read all of Balzac in the Turkish translations sponsored by the Ministry of Education, had Turks ever come into such intimate contact with the private life of the West as they did at the cinema.

This is what makes going to the films as much fun as going on a trip or getting drunk: In films, we come face-to-face with the Other. Everything is on hand to make this encounter intense. Our eyes wish to see nothing else; our ears will not tolerate the crackling of wrappers or the chewing of nuts. We have come to this seat to forget our troubles, to forget the painful story that is our past and our future, and to forget the anxieties this story brings in its wake. To give ourselves over to the image of the other, and to his story, we are prepared to abandon our own selves, at least for a while. Just as a frame can turn an oil painting into a fetish, the darkness of the cinema excludes all else to frame us and our illusions.

Seven years before I saw *Cleopatra,* when I was five years old, someone we called the "film man" would come to the empty lot next to our summerhouse. He had a strange device: a portable projector that he set up on a table. If you paid the man five kuruş, you could peek through the eyehole and turn the crank and watch a film that lasted thirty seconds. I remember viewing many scenes from old films cobbled together in this way, but I have not a single memory of what I saw. What remains in my mind is my enchantment when, after waiting my turn, I would put my head under the black cloth draped over the machine to occlude the light and grope in the dark for the eyehole. It is not only that we come face-to-face with the Other in the cinema: What we see makes *everything* seem otherworldly in the space of an instant.

This is why—whatever the story—the cinema's teasing Other awakens our desires: for friendship, the pleasures of daily life, happiness, power, money, and sex, and of course for escape from all these things and their opposites. I remember my curiosity and amazement as I inspected the magazine pictures of Liz Taylor as Cleopatra soaking half naked in a magnificent milk bath. I was twelve years old, and her film-star body pulled me into a new world of guilt and desire. My confusion owed a lot to the fearful warnings of lycée teachers, friends who were anxious about tuberculosis, and the popular press: Films, like masturbation, weakened children's brains and ruined their eyes, and the make-believe world having got hold of them might never let go and so cut them off from reality.

It must have been to dilute the danger and excitement of their encounters with the Other that İstanbullus of the *Cleopatra* era were inclined to talk during films. Some would warn the pure-hearted hero of the enemy he could not see behind him; others would rain harsh words on the villains, but most would cry out in astonishment whenever the people on the screen displayed a habit or performed a ritual that was universally shocking: "Now look at that! The girl is eating an orange with a knife and fork!" This produced a degree of alienation that even Brecht could never have conceived, and it sometimes took on a nationalist tone. When Goldfinger, surrounded by all the latest technological gadgets and weaponry, offered James Bond Turkish tobacco, saying it was the best in the world, many filmgoers went so far as to applaud the villain. As for the scenes that the Turkish censors found too long and the love scenes from which they removed all indecent images, the silent tension in the audience would dissipate at those moments into loud jokes and laughter.

There were moments when desire seemed close enough to touch—as vivid as the beautiful dreams on the screen but real enough to defy them—and it was perhaps to remind us that we were not alone and helpless in the dark but sitting in a theater with our fellow citizens that they introduced the five-minute intermission that we in Istanbul call the Entr'acte. The custom is for mournful vendors to walk the aisles with ice-cream bars and popcorn while the nicotine addicts in the audience light up; though the West gave up on such intermissions long ago, I have something to say to effete snobs who complain that they are unnecessary and destroy the unity of the film, because personally I owe them a great deal—this essay included.

Fifty years ago, during the Entr'acte at what we know now as the Emek Sineması (the Labor Cinema) and then knew as Melek Sineması (or the Angel), my mother and father, each out with friends, went out to the lobby, and here they met for the first time. As I owe my existence to this chance encounter at the cinema, I have no choice but to side with those writers who have spoken so eloquently of their debt to this art.

CHAPTER SIXTY-SEVEN

Why Didn't I Become an Architect?

I would stand in awe before the ninety-five-year-old building: Like so many from that era, it was unpainted and had lost plaster here and there, and its dark and dirty surface had the air of some sort of frightening skin disease. The signs of age, neglect, and fatigue were what struck me first. But when I began to notice its little friezes, its witty leaves and trees, and its asymmetrical Art Deco designs, I forgot its sickly appearance, thinking instead of the happy, easy life this building had once enjoyed. I saw many cracks and holes in its rainspouts, its weatherboard, its friezes, and its eaves. Inspecting the several stories, including the shop on the ground floor, I could see that, like most buildings built a hundred years ago, it had originally been a four-story construction, the top two stories having been added twenty years ago. There were no friezes, no thick weatherboarding over the windows, and no fine handiwork on the facade. Sometimes these floors would not even be of the same height as those below, nor would their windows be aligned in the same way. Most of these floors had been added very hastily, profiting from home-improvement drives, loopholes in the law, and corrupt mayors turning a blind eye. Perhaps at first sight they had looked modern and clean next to the building's original century-old facade; twenty years later, their interiors seemed older and more dilapidated than those of the floors below.

When I would look up at the little bay windows—the traditional Istanbul architect's signature, hanging out over the street by three feet—my eye would settle on a flowerpot or a child peering out at me. My mind would automatically calculate that this building sat on a plot of about eight hundred and fifty square feet, work out how much usable space there was, and try to figure out whether or not it suited my needs. I was not looking for a building to turn into a home; I had begun to search

Istanbul's oldest neighborhoods—streets going back two thousand years: the back streets of Galata, Beyoğlu, and Cihangir, where Greeks and Armenians had once lived and, before them, the Genoese—for a stranger purpose. I needed this house for a book and a museum.

As I was gazing at the building from across the street, the grocer from the shop behind me came outside to tell me about the building—what condition it was in, how old it was, and who owned it—making it clear to me that the owner had engaged him to act on his behalf, if only as his eyes and ears.

"Would it be possible for me to go inside?" I asked, somewhat anxiously, not wishing to enter a strange house without the permission of those living in it.

"Go right in, brother, go right in and take a look, don't worry!" bellowed the worldly grocer.

Though it was a hot summer day, the entrance hall was spacious and extraordinarily cool (they don't make these beautiful high-ceilinged entrance halls anymore, not even in apartment buildings in the wealthiest areas), and I could no longer hear the cries of the children in the shabby streets outside or the noise from the plastics and machine shops opposite, only a few paces away, and all this reminded me that the houses in this area had been built with a very different sort of life in mind. I went up to the second floor, and then to the third, and with the encouragement of the curious grocer behind me, I entered whatever door, whatever apartment, I pleased. The people living here might not all be from the same family, but they came from the same Anatolian village and they kept their doors unlocked. As I wandered through these apartments, I greedily registered everything I saw, like a camera making a silent film.

Outside an apartment that led out to the entrance hall, I saw a woman dozing in an old bed pushed next to the wall. Before she could come out of her daze to look at me closely, I had gone into the adjoining room (there was no corridor), where I found four children between the ages of five and eight squeezed together on a little divan in front of a color television set. No one lifted a head to look at me; the little toes of their bare feet, which were dangling over the side of the high divan, were twitching to the rhythms of the adventure film they were watching.

When I wandered into the next room in this crowded house that was as quiet as the midday heat, I met with a woman who at once reminded me of the days when I'd had to supply my name, rank, and serial number: "Who are you?" asked this frowning mother, in her hand a huge teapot. As the grocer behind me explained the situation, I noticed that the room in which the woman was working was not a proper kitchen; the only access to this narrow space was through a room in which an elderly man was resting in his underpants, and of course I understood that the present configuration was not the original plan for this building. I tried to imagine what this floor had once looked like. I formed a sense of the underpants man's room in its entirety, staring at the walls, which, like all the others I had seen (except in the grocery) were flaking paint and plaster and a severe embarrassment.

With the help of neighborhood gossips and with eager guidance from the grocer, who had by now transformed from a helpful go-between into a real estate agent, as well as real agents working on commission, I spent the next month visiting hundreds of old apartments in that area—in a street where all the residents were Kurds from Tunceli, the Roma neighborhood in Galata, where all the women and children sat on the stoop to watch the passersby, or the alley where bored old ladies would shout down from their windows, "Why doesn't he come up and look at this place too?" I saw half-collapsed kitchens, old sitting rooms haphazardly divided in two, staircases whose steps had been worn away; rooms with broken wooden floorboards concealed under carpets; storerooms, machine shops, restaurants, and old luxury apartments with fine plaster work on their walls and ceilings, now being used as chandelier shops; empty buildings rotting away with no owners, or else owners who had emigrated or were locked in a property dispute; rooms with little children crammed in as tightly as objects in a cupboard; cool ground floors whose damp walls smelled of mold; basements in which someone had carefully stowed wood, gathered from underneath trees and from rubbish bins and the city's back streets, along with pieces of iron and all variety of rubbish; staircases in which no step was the same height as any other; leaky ceilings; buildings in which the lifts didn't work and the lights didn't work either; women in head scarves who watched through cracks in their doors as I walked past them on the stairs and past people sleeping in their beds; balconies where they'd hung their washing, walls that said NO LITTERING! and children playing in courtyards; and enormous wardrobes that all resembled one another and dwarfed everything else in the bedroom.

If I hadn't visited so many houses one after the other, I would never have seen so clearly the two essential things that people did in their homes: (1) stretch out in a chair or on a divan, a sofa, a cushioned bench, or a bed and doze, and (2) watch television all the hours of the day. Most of the time they did both at the same time, while also smoking and drinking tea. In areas of the city where property values were about the same, there was much too much space given over to stairs; I saw no houses that departed from this design. After seeing how much room was taken up by staircases in buildings with barely fifteen or twenty feet of frontage and no rooms in the back, I tried to forget the facades, buildings, and streets of the city and conjure up hundreds of thousands of staircases and stairwells; having done so, I came to see the divided properties of Istanbul as a forest of secret stairways.

At the end of my travels, what impressed me most was to see how these buildings, which despite their facades were small and humble dwellings made a hundred years ago for the city's Greek and Levantine populations by Armenian architects and contractors, were being used in ways so amazingly different from the ways that their builders could have hoped for or conceived. I had learned one thing from my years studying architecture: Buildings take the shape of their architects' and buyers' dreams. After the Greeks, Armenians, and Levantines who had dreamed up these buildings were forced to leave them in the early years of the last century, they came to reflect the imaginations of the succeeding occupants. I am not talking here about an active imagination shaping these buildings and streets to give the city a certain look. I am talking of the passive imagination of people who came from faraway places to streets and buildings already looking a certain way, who then changed their dreams to adapt to it.

I can liken this sort of imagination to that of a child who conjures up visions from the shadows on the walls before he goes to sleep in a dark room in the middle of the night. If he is sleeping in a strange and frightening room, he can make it bearable by imagining the familiar. If he is in a clean room he knows well, a room where he feels secure, he can build himself a dream world by likening the shadows to frightening creatures from legends. In both instances, his imagination is working with the fragmented and haphazard material at hand to create dreams that fit in with the place where the child happens to be. So the imagination in question is not in service to a person who is creating new worlds on a blank sheet of paper, it is in service to someone who is trying to fit in with a world already made. The waves of migration that Istanbul saw over the past century, the shifting of industries from one neighborhood to another, the emergence of a new Turkish bourgeoisie, the dreams of Westernization that had prompted some people to abandon these buildings and dilapidated rooms, to be replaced by others from elsewhere—everywhere you looked in Istanbul, you saw signs of that second, accommodating, imagination. The people who had built these partitions, who had turned stairwells and bay windows into kitchens and entrance halls into storerooms or waiting rooms, who had created living space by putting beds and wardrobes in the most unexpected places, who had bricked up walls and windows or put new windows and doors into walls or knocked holes through them, who had equipped all the stoves in these buildings with pipes that snaked across every wall and ceiling—who had taken all these measures to turn these places into home—these people were utterly foreign to the intentions of the architects who had conceived these houses a century earlier.

It is not by chance that I speak of blank sheets of paper. I studied architecture at Istanbul Technical University for about three years, but I did not graduate to become an architect. I now think that this had to do with the ostentatious modernist dreams I set down on those blank sheets. All I knew at the time was that I did not want to become an architect—or a painter, as I had dreamed for many years. I abandoned the great empty architectural drawing sheets that thrilled and frightened me, making my head spin, and instead sat down to stare at the blank writing paper that thrilled and frightened me just as much. That's where I've been sitting for twenty-five years now. As a book takes shape in my mind, I believe myself to be at the beginning of everything; I believe that the world will conform to my ideas—just as I did when I dreamed up buildings as an architectural student.

So let's ask the question that I heard quite a lot twenty-five years ago and that I still ask myself from time to time: Why didn't I become an architect? Answer: Because I thought the sheets of paper on which I was to pour my dreams were blank. But after twenty-five years of writing, I have come to understand that those pages are never blank. I know very well now that when I sit down at my table, I am sitting with tradition and with those who refuse absolutely to bow to rules or to history; I am sitting with things born of coincidence and disorder, darkness, fear, and dirt, with the past and its ghosts, and all the things that officialdom and our language wish to forget; I am sitting with fear and with the dreams to which fear gives rise. To bring all these things to the page, I had to write novels that drew from the past, and all the things that the Westernizers and the modern Republic wished to forget, but that embraced the future and the imagination at the same time. Had I thought, at the age of twenty, that I could do the same with architecture, I might well have become an architect. But in those days I was a resolute modernist who wished to escape from the burden, the filth, and the ghost-ridden twilight that was history—and what's more, I was an optimistic Westernizer, certain that all was going to plan. As for the peoples of the city in which I lived— who conformed to no rules with their complex communities and their histories—they did not figure in my dreams: I saw them instead as obstacles, there to keep my dreams from being realized. I understood at once that they would never let me make the sorts of buildings I wanted in those streets. But they would not object if I shut myself up in my own house and wrote about them.

It took me eight years to publish my first book. Throughout this time, and especially at the points when I had lost hope that anyone would ever publish me, I had a recurring dream: I am an architecture student, and I am in an architectural design class, planning a building, but there is very little time left before I have to hand my design in. I am sitting at a table, putting everything I have into my work, surrounded by half-finished sketches and rolls of paper, and, on all sides, inkstains are opening up like poison flowers. As I labor on, ideas come to me that are even more brilliant than the ones I had before, but despite my feverish efforts the fearsome deadline is fast approaching, and I know full well that I have no more chance of realizing this great new idea than I have of finishing the building on my sheet of paper. It is my fault that I cannot finish my project in the time I have left, my fault entirely. As I conjure up visions of ever greater intensity, I am so racked by guilt that the pain wakes me up.

The first thing to say about the fear that gave rise to this dream is that it is the fear of becoming a writer. Had I become an architect, I would at least have had a proper profession and would at least have been able to earn enough money to enjoy a middle-class life. But when I began to say, somewhat obscurely, that I was going to be a writer and write novels, my family told me I would suffer financial hardship in the years ahead. So in the face of all that guilt and that fearful running out of time, this was a dream that assuaged the pain of my longings. Because when I was studying to be an architect, I was still part of "normal" life. To work this hard, against the clock, and to dream intensely—this would only characterize my life later on, when I was writing novels against no deadlines whatsoever.

In those days, when people asked me why I had not become an architect, I would give the same answer in different words: "Because I didn't want to design apartments!" When I said *apartments,* I meant a way of life as well as a particular approach to architecture. It was during the 1930s that Istanbul's old historic neighborhoods emptied out, as the moneyed classes began to tear down their two- and three-story houses with their spacious gardens, using these and other empty lots for apartment buildings that within sixty years had utterly destroyed the city's old fabric. When I began school in the late 1950s, every child in my class lived in an apartment. In the beginning, the facades mixed a plain Bauhaus modernism with traditionally Turkish bay windows; later on they became poor, uninspired copies of the international style; and because the inheritance law ensured that many of the plots on which one built were very narrow, their interiors were all identical. Between them were stairwells and narrow ventilation shafts that some called "the darkness" and others "the light"; in the front was the sitting room and in the back, according to the size of the plot and the skill of the architect, were two or three bedrooms. There were long, narrow corridors connecting the single front room with the several rooms at the back; these, along the windows looking out onto "the light" and the windows in the stairwell, made all these apartments look terrifyingly alike; and they all smelled of mold, cooking oil, bird droppings, and want. What frightened me most during my years of studying architecture was the prospect of having to design cost-effective apartments on these narrow little plots in accordance with current housing regulations and the tastes of the half-Westernized middle class. In those days, many relatives and acquaintances who complained about dishonorable architects told me that, once I was an architect, they would make sure I could build my own apartments on the empty lots owned by their parents.

By not becoming an architect, I was able to escape this fate. I became a writer, and I have written a great deal about apartments. What I have learned from everything I have written is this: A building's hominess issues from the dreams of those who live in it. These dreams, like all dreams, are nourished by that building's old, dark, dirty, and disintegrating corners. Just as in some buildings we see facades become more beautiful with age, and interior walls take on a mysterious texture, so too can we see the traces of its journey from a building with no meaning into a home, a construction of dreams. This is how I understand the partitioned rooms, punctured walls, and broken staircases I described earlier. These are things for which an architect can find neither the traces nor the proof: the dreams with which the person who first occupies a new and ordinary building (conceived in a burst of modernizing, Westernizing enthusiasm and made as if it was starting from the beginning) turns it into a home.

When I was walking among the ruins of the earthquake that killed thirty thousand people, I felt the presence of this imagination again, and very powerfully—walking among all those fragments of walls, bricks,

and concrete, broken windows, slippers, lamp bases, curtains, and carpets: every building, every shelter, new or old, that a person entered, it
was his imagination that turned it into a home. Like Dostoyevsky's
heroes, who use their imaginations to cling to life even in the most hopeless circumstances, we too know how to turn our buildings into homes,
even when life is very hard.

But when these homes are destroyed by an earthquake, we are painfully reminded that they are also buildings. Just after that earthquake that
killed thirty thousand people, my father told me how he'd found his way
out of one apartment house and groped his way through the pitch-dark
street to take refuge in another apartment building two hundred yards
away. When I asked why he had done so, he said, "Because that building's safe. I made it myself." He meant the family apartment house where
I had spent my childhood, the building we once shared with my grandmother, my uncles, and my aunts, and that I have described so often—in
so many novels—and if my father took refuge there, I would say it was
not because it was a safe building but because it was a home.

CHAPTER SIXTY-EIGHT

Selimiye Mosque

A rchitecture was the preeminent Ottoman art, and it reached its apex
with the Selimiye Mosque in Edirne. In the seventies, when I was
studying architecture in Istanbul and much preoccupied with the principles underlying the great Ottoman monuments, especially those
designed by Sinan, I made a special trip to Edirne just to see it. The
mosque was just as I remembered it from my first visit with my father ten
years earlier, its great single-domed silhouette rising high above the vast
plain, dominating the landscape from many miles away. No other
Ottoman monument has imprinted its image on a city in quite this way.
Though Edirne is packed with picturesque historic buildings, they all
seem smaller next to this mosque and its great dome. Sinan built it for
Selim II between 1569 and 1575, when Ottoman military and cultural
power was at its height. In the sixteenth century, as Ottoman sultans
made their first incursions into Europe, this now-forgotten capital city
became central to—and emblematic of—the imperial project.

The more the empire grew, the more it needed to find its center. The
Selimiye expresses the Ottomans' centralizing impulse in its very
design, as did all of Sinan's work and indeed all great Ottoman religious
architecture: The dream was to construct a mosque that—whether
viewed from the inside or the outside—was a single mass, dominated by
a single dome. The great Ottoman mosques of earlier periods, like
Sinan's own earlier works, had a multitude of little domes and half
domes, and the beauty was in the harmonious interplay between the great
dome rising somewhat indistinctly from the center and the half domes,
weight towers, and buttresses crowded around it. With the Selimiye
Mosque, which Sinan called his crowning achievement, the overriding
ambition was to replace this busy confusion with one enormous dome.

When I was in my twenties, studying architecture, my classmates and I saw a link between the desire for a central dome and the mercilessly centralizing political and economic machinery of empire. But in a book written in his name by his friend the poet Sai, Sinan claimed to have taken his inspiration from Istanbul's Hagia Sophia.

Planted around the Selimiye's great dome are four minarets, the highest in the Islamic world; they too reflect the twinned intellectual concerns that shaped the mosque's design: the quest for a center, and the desire for symmetry. Inside two of these minarets are three separate and never-intersecting staircases leading to three separate balconies, a feat of consonance that echoes the building's timeless geometry. But after one is dazzled by the symmetrical extravagance of the exterior, the plain, pure symmetries of the interior come as a shock. This shock reveals the secret key to all Ottoman architectural thinking: that monumental exteriors proclaiming the wealth and power of the Ottoman Empire and the abiding greatness of its sultans should be allied with pure inner spaces that draw the faithful into direct communion with God. As with all great Ottoman mosques, Selimiye's interior derives its power not from paintings, ornaments, and embellishments but from its clean, spare lines. To enter it is to forget the power, determination, wealth, and technical mastery of the Ottoman Empire and its sultans and to succumb instead to the mysterious light seeping in through its multitude of tiny windows; it is to look at the interplay of light and dark and read in it man's insignificance. But this is not an architectural idiom that overwhelms the visitor with its soul-crushing perpendiculars; it is a circular architecture that affirms the oneness of humanity—the *umma*—and evokes the simplicity of life and death. As we stand inside Sinan's masterwork, it is his visible and invisible symmetries that call out to us; it is the mosque's sublime geometry that evokes God's perfection in the plain and powerful purity of the dome, the bare stone, and the eight slender pillars.

CHAPTER SIXTY-NINE

Bellini and the East

There are three artists we know as Bellini. The first, Jacopo Bellini, is remembered today not so much as a painter but as the man who brought the two more famous Bellinis into the world. His elder son, Gentile Bellini, was, during his lifetime (1429–1507), the most famous artist in Venice. Today he is remembered chiefly for his "voyage east" and the artworks it inspired, most particularly his portrait of Mehmet the Conqueror, while his brother, Giovanni, is celebrated by today's art historians as one of the great painters of his time. It is commonly acknowledged that his sense of color had an enormous impact on the Venetian Renaissance and therefore changed the course of Western art. When E. H. Gombrich speaks of that tradition in *Art and Scholarship,* remarking that "without Bellini and Giorgione, there would have been no Titian," it is Giovanni, the younger brother, to whom he refers. But it is to his elder brother, Gentile, that the exhibit "Bellini and the East" pays tribute.

After taking Istanbul in 1453, at the age of twenty-one, Mehmet II had as his first aim to centralize the Ottoman state, but he also continued his incursions into Europe, thus establishing himself in the world as a ruler of consequence. These wars, victories, and peace treaties, whose names every lycée student in Turkey must memorize and recite with nationalist fervor, led to large portions of Bosnia, Albania, and Greece coming under Ottoman rule. His power having been greatly enhanced by these conquests, Mehmet II was finally able to effect a peace treaty between the Ottomans and the Venetians in 1479, after almost twenty years of war, pillaging, and piracy in the Aegean islands and the fortified ports of the Mediterranean. When envoys began traveling between Venice and Istanbul to negotiate this treaty, Mehmet II expressed a wish for Venice to send him a "good artist," and the Venetian senate (very pleased with this peace treaty, though it meant giving up many of their forts and a great deal of land) decided to send Gentile Bellini, who was then busy adorning the walls of the great council hall of the Doge's Palace with his gigantic paintings.

So it is Gentile Bellini's "voyage east" and the eighteen months he spent in Istanbul as cultural ambassador that is the subject of the small but rich exhibition at the National Gallery in London. Though it includes many other paintings and drawings by Bellini and his workshop, as well as medals and various other objects that show the Eastern and Western influences of the day, the centerpiece of the exhibition is, of course, Gentile Bellini's oil portrait of Mehmet the Conqueror. The portrait has spawned so many copies, variations, and adaptations, and the reproductions made from these assorted images have gone on to adorn so many textbooks, book covers, newspapers, posters, banknotes, stamps, educational posters, and comic books, that there cannot be a literate Turk who has not seen it hundreds if not thousands of times. No other sultan from the Golden Age of the Ottoman Empire, not even Süleyman the Magnificent, has a portrait like this one. With its realism, its simple composition, and the perfectly shaded arch giving him such a victorious aura, it has come to be regarded as not only the portrait of Mehmet II but the icon of an Ottoman sultan, just as the famous poster of Che Guevara is the icon of a revolutionary. At the same time, the carefully worked details—the marked protrusion of the upper lip, the drooping eyelids, the fine feminine eyebrows, and, most important, the thin, long, hooked nose—evoke a singular individual who is nonetheless not so different from the citizens one sees in the crowded streets of Istanbul today. The most famous distinguishing feature is that Ottoman nose, the trademark of a dynasty in a culture without a blood aristocracy. In 2003, to celebrate the 550th anniversary of the Ottoman Conquest, the Yapi Kredi Bank had the painting brought from London to Istanbul and exhibited it in Beyoğlu, one of the busiest districts of the city; schoolchildren came in by the busload, and hundreds of thousands queued up to stare at the portrait with a fascination only a legend can inspire.

The Islamic prohibition against painting, the particular fears about portraits, and ignorance about what was happening in portraiture in Renaissance Europe meant that Ottoman artists did not and could not make portraits of sultans that were this true to life. And this cautiousness toward a human subject's distinguishing features were not confined to the world of art. Even Ottoman historians, who chronicled the military and political events of the age, were, despite the fact of there being no

corresponding religious prohibition against verbal description, disin-
clined to think or indeed write about their sultans' defining features, their
characters, or their spiritual complexities. After the founding of the modern Republic of Turkey in 1923, when the Westernizing drive was just
getting under way, the nationalist poet Yahya Kemal, who lived in Paris
for many years and was as well acquainted with French art and literature
as he was oppressed by doubts about his own literary and cultural heritage, once remarked ruefully, "If only we had painting and prose, we'd
be another nation!" In so saying, he may have been hoping to reclaim the
beauties of a lost age as documented in painting and literature. Even
when this was not, strictly speaking, the case—as when he stood before
Bellini's "realistic" portrait of Mehmet the Conqueror—what troubled
him was that the hand that drew the portrait lacked a nationalist motive.
One can sense a profound displeasure in these words, a Muslim writer's
dissatisfaction with his own culture. He is also succumbing to the common fantasy of effortless adaptation to the artistic products of an utterly
different culture and civilization, that this could somehow be accomplished without changing one's soul.

There are many examples of this childish fantasy in "Bellini and the
East" and its accompanying catalog. One is the watercolor from a Top-

kapı Palace album that is attributed to an Ottoman artist named Sinan Beg and is almost certainly inspired by Bellini's portrait, and to which the catalog gives the title "Mehmet II Smelling a Rose"; being neither a Venetian Renaissance portrait nor a classic Persian-Ottoman miniature, it leaves the viewer unsettled. In an article about Şeker Ahmet Pasha, another Turkish artist who drew from both Eastern (Ottoman-Persian miniature) and Western (European landscape painting, especially that of Courbet) traditions, John Berger spoke of this same unease, and though he felt it stemmed from the difficulties of harmonizing different techniques, like the use of perspective and the vanishing point, he also perceived that the underlying problem was the difficulty of harmonizing worldviews. In this Bellini-inspired Ottoman portrait, the one thing that makes up for the clumsiness of execution—and it seems to make the sultan uneasy as well—is the rose that Mehmet II is smelling. What realizes this rose and even its scent is not so much its color as Mehmet II's prominent Ottoman nose. Upon learning that the Ottoman artist who painted this watercolor was in fact a Frankish artist living among Ottomans and most probably an Italian, we are reminded yet again that cultural influences work in both directions with complexities difficult to fathom.

Another painting rightly attributed to Bellini defies scholarly disputes and concerns about political correctness to suggest, with extraordinary elegance, a more humane East–West story. This marvelously simple watercolor, no larger than a miniature, shows a youth sitting cross-legged. Because the paper that the ear-ringed youth is touching with his pen is blank, we cannot be sure if he is an artist or a scribe. But from the expression on his face, from his look of concentration and the shape of his lips, even from the confidence with which his left hand shields the paper in his lap, I can see at once that he is utterly devoted to his work. His dedication to a blank sheet of paper, and his heartfelt surrender of self, elicit my respect. I feel him to be someone who holds the beauty and perfection of his work (be it drawing or text) above all else; he is an artist who has achieved the happiness that can indeed only come from giving oneself over to one's work. My appreciation of the beauty of the beardless page's pale face magnifies with my appreciation of the artist's sympathy for his subject, which is so evident. It was first noted by the semiofficial historian Kritovoulos of Imbros and later by many Western-Christian chroniclers that Mehmet the Conqueror prized beautiful youths, took political risks for them, and commissioned their portraits. From this time onward, good looks were an important factor in the selection of pages in the Ottoman palace. The beauty of the young artist, and the way he gives himself over to the beauty of that which he is drawing, combined with the simplicity of the ground and the wall behind him— these give the painting an air of mystery that I sense every time I see it. Of course, the mystery has much to do with the fact that the paper into which the youth peers with such concentration is utterly blank. If this beautiful artist can think with such concentration of the thing he has yet to paint, it must mean that he can already see this image shimmering in his mind. We know from the way he has pressed his pen against the blank paper, from the way he is sitting, from his very expression, that this artist knows what he is about to do. But there is nothing in his surroundings— no object, text, sketch, mold, human figure, or view—to suggest what the subject in mind might be. We feel as if this moment frozen 525 years ago will soon cease to exist, that in the very next instant the artist scribe will begin to move the pen, and his beautiful face will light up with even greater happiness, as if he were watching someone else's pen race across the page.

A century ago, in 1905, this painting was still in Istanbul; today it belongs to the Isabella Stewart Gardner Museum in Boston. Years ago, after wandering among this museum's Titians and John Singer Sargents, I found my young painter on a display table in a corner, on one of the top

floors. To see him, I had to lift the thick cloth over the glass protecting the painting from light damage and bow my head. As I gazed down at the painting, the distance between me and it seemed to be the same as the distance between the painter and his blank sheet of paper. I was looking at Bellini's small painting in just the same way that a sultan might, in a private moment, look at a miniature illuminating the thick and heavy book in his hand. I too was gazing downward like the painter in the painting. What distinguishes Islamic painting from Western painting after the Renaissance no less than the religious prohibitions, and perhaps even more than those, is the secretive downward gaze that Bellini captures so knowingly in this portrait. Painting in Islamic culture was a restricted art, permissible only to decorate the insides of books and so confined to small spaces; never were these paintings meant to hang on walls, and they never did! As the cross-legged youth sits lost in thought, gazing down at the blank sheet that will become his painting, he assumes the same posture that the rich and powerful person—most likely a sultan or a prince—will be obliged to assume to look at this painting for his eyes only. Let us compare this pose—this downward gaze of the cross-legged artist bending over a blank sheet of paper—with the stance a Western artist might take to view his own painting—Velázquez, for example, viewing *Las Meninas,* likewise a painting within a painting, wherein an artist is caught in the act of creation. We see in both the things that define paintings as objects: the edges of the paper or canvas, the painter's pen or brush, and the pensive concentration on the artist's face. But Bellini's Eastern artist's gaze is not toward his world or his surroundings: It is fixed on the blank paper on his lap and we can tell from his expression that he is thinking of the world inside his head. It is the artistry of the Ottoman-Persian miniaturist to know and to recall all the great art that has preceded him and to remake it in a burst of poetic inspiration. But in his portrait of himself at work Velázquez is lifting his head to see the vanishing point, to the world reflected in the mirror on the wall behind him, to the world itself and the complexity of that which he is painting. We cannot see the painting within his painting either (though we guess that the scene before us is the one he is painting), but we can see from Velázquez's tired and self-interrogating look that his head is full of weighty questions arising from the painting's unbounded composition, whereas Bellini's young painter looks at his blank sheet with the happiness of a youth recalling—with almost metaphysical inspiration—a poem he has learned by heart.

In my corner of the world, the seated youth attributed to Bellini is well-known, even if it is not as famous as his portrait of Mehmet the Conqueror. The cross-legged figure is commonly thought to be Cem Sultan, who was treated so cruelly by his older brother and whose sorry fate is described in numerous exotic and melodramatic novels. In the textbooks of my childhood—penned by the passionately nationalist Westernizers of the early Republic—Cem Sultan was portrayed as being open to art and to the West, a broad-minded prince bursting with youthful vigor, while his older brother and his eventual poisoner, Bayezid II, was a fanatic who turned his back on the Western world. After the death of Mehmet the Conqueror, Bellini's portrait of the artist was sent first to the Aq Qoyunlu Palace in Tabriz and then to the Safavid Palace, in what is today Iran. Before it was returned to the Ottoman palace, either as war booty or a gift, this extraordinary painting was much copied, this time by Persian artists. One of these copies, now in the Freer Museum in Washington, D.C., is, at least according to those romantic souls who dream of Eastern and Western masters working on the same pictures, sometimes attributed to Behzad. To look at this adaptation from close up is to notice that where Bellini so elegantly chose to place a blank sheet of paper, the Safavid painter has placed a portrait; in so doing he reminds us how little Muslim artists knew about the Western art of portraiture, most particularly the concept of the self-portrait, and how they were beset by anxieties about their technical inadequacies in these areas. Harvard professor David Roxburgh discovered that, eighty years after its execution, Bellini's small portrait was placed in a Safavid album alongside other portraits, including some from the Ming dynasty. A sentence from its foreword shows that even the greatest Safavid artists found themselves lacking in this regard: "The custom of portraiture flourished so in the lands of Cathay [China] and the Franks [Europe]." But this is not to say that Persian artists were blind to the irresistible power of portraits. Consider the story of Hüsrev and Şirin, the classic Islamic tale that inspired more miniatures than any other, wherein the beautiful Şirin first falls in love with the handsome Hüsrev just by seeing his portrait. The irony of this topos is that the Persian artists charged with illustrating this scene were technically naïve by Venetian Renaissance standards of portraiture. In illuminated Persian manuscripts, this scene requires a painting within the painting, just as Bellini's and Behzad's retouched portraits do, but they almost always depict not a portrait but the idea of a portrait.

After the Renaissance, the West first knew its superiority over the East not on the battlefield but in art. A hundred years after Bellini's "voyage east," Vasari described how even Ottoman sultans obliged by their religion to take a dim view of painting were in awe of the skill Bellini showed in his Istanbul portraits and were inclined to praise them extravagantly. When writing of Filippo Lippi, Vasari relates how, after the painter was taken captive by Eastern pirates, his new master asked to have his portrait done; so taken was he by its shocking realism that he set Lippi free. In our own day, Western analysts, perhaps out of unease at the consequences of the West's military superiority, prefer not to talk of the indisputable power of the art of the Renaissance; instead, they point to Bellini's sensitive portraits to remind us with all good intentions that Easterners, too, have their humanity.

After the death of Mehmet the Conqueror, his son Bayezid II, who did not share his father's lifestyle or his passion for portraiture, had Bellini's portrait sold in the bazaar. In the Turkey of my childhood, our lycée textbooks lamented this rejection of Renaissance art as a mistake, a missed opportunity, and suggested that, had we gone on from where we'd started five hundred years ago, we might have produced a different kind of art and become "a different nation." Perhaps. Whenever I look at Bellini's cross-legged youth, I think this other path might have served miniaturists best. Because they could have painted so much better, once seated at tables—and also saved themselves from the aching joints and legs that make Beckett's heroes so miserable.

CHAPTER SEVENTY

Black Pen

We are troubled by the abundance of rumors about where we come from, who we are, where we're going, and who drew us. We are not, in essence, the sort to be easily deceived by gossip, and neither are we swayed by the stories, be they true or false, that people tell about us. Obviously, we don't give a damn about what academics say, and the same goes for the loose talk we hear when people subject our drawing to close examination. Like the donkey standing with us, we belong to this world; we step through it cautiously and know exactly where we are going. Our concern is that people have become so caught up in arguments about our origins and our likely destination that they've forgotten we are a drawing. We would have preferred you to take pleasure in us not because we come from the darkest corner of a story lost in a forgotten history but because we are a drawing. We ask that you try to see us in this way: to savor our full presence, our humble colors, and the way in which we have immersed ourselves in our conversation.

To find ourselves on this course, glueless, unfinished paper, to have been sketched so hastily and with such crude lines—this pleases us. Because the artist chose not to draw the horizon behind us or the earth, grass, and flowers on which we tread so heavily, he makes our raw virility all the more apparent. The eye is drawn to our gigantic fingers, to our rough clothing, to the strong and healthy gestures that bind us to the earth. Please note the alarm in the donkey's eyes and the demonic glint in ours; see the panic in our gaze, as if something has frightened us. At the same time it should be clear, from the winsome way the artist has drawn the donkey, the haphazard way he has sketched us, and the color he has given our cheeks, that the mood is light. The fear you see in our eyes, the panic, haste, and humorous alarm, the blank page that sur-

rounds us—all these things suggest that something important is happening. It is as if one day hundreds of years ago, we three and our donkey
were traveling along a road when we happened upon an artist—just as
one might in a story—and this artist, God be praised, this master artist
captured us on paper, as deftly as if—and please permit us to use an
expression from another age here—he'd taken our photograph. Our master artist got out his rough paper and his black pen and drew us so
quickly that he caught the chatterbox among us with his mouth open,
showing his ugly teeth in all their glory. We would like you to enjoy our
ugly teeth, our whiskers, our clumsy hands that look like bear paws, and
all the other dirty, tired, shabby, or even malevolent guises we've taken
in other drawings. Just remember: It's not us you're smiling at, it's our
drawing.

But we know it's the master artist that most concerns you. What a pity
it is that you belong to an age when people cannot learn to love a drawing without first knowing who the artist was. All right then: His name is
Muhammad Siyah Qalam, Muhammad of the Black Pen. It is probably
clear from his drawing's theme and style that our artist is the same as the
one who did so many other drawings of us nomads. But all scholars
agree that the signature on the edge of the drawing was only added much
later. We can confirm their hypothesis.

The person who drew us did not sign our drawings, because he belonged to an age when storytelling and artistry were more important than credits. To tell you the truth, we didn't mind this at all. We were, after all, drawn in a distant time when the point of a drawing was to illustrate a story, so for us it was enough to serve our stories well. We were humble. But long after these stories had been forgotten, in an age more inclined to accept us as drawings in our own right, a sharp-eyed retainer in the Topkapı Palace during the reign of Ahmed I (1603–17) took it upon himself to add this signature to a number of drawings. It was all rather haphazard, however, so "Black Pen" served more as an attribution than a signature.

The desire to link us with a master artist led to a further mistake, for this signature also appears in other drawings that were placed, for whatever reason, in the same album, although they bear no stylistic or thematic resemblance to our own. Just because we're in the same album, called the *Fatih* album, they give us all the same signature. However, the historians Dust Muhammad, Qadi Ahmad, and Mustafa Ali, who saw fit to write a few words about the great Persian and Ottoman artists, make no mention of Siyah Qalam. In other words, we know nothing about our deft and masterful artist except for his name.

But as a consolation for those who have been so anxious to conjure up for us a common style, a name, a signature, and a master, let us also say this: The name we've been awarded, Black Pen, refers to the thick-bordered black-and-white line drawings favored by Persian writers during the sixteenth century. So we can draw this conclusion: Black Pen is not the name of the artist who sketched us so hastily, as we three chatted and ambled along our road, but the name of the style he used. But if this is the case, what are we to make of the glorious reds and blues he has splashed all over us?

Almost everything people say about us contradicts everything else they've said, and we find it all very amusing. There have been scores of articles, theories, and learned conferences to establish where we come from—to prove that we are Uighurs, Turks, Mongols, or Persians, to establish that we lived at some point between the twelfth and fifteenth centuries—but after years of politely contradicting one another, scholars have come no closer to offering definitive or convincing evidence linking us with a particular time and place. All they do is arouse suspicion.

Turks gripped by romantic myths of nationalism are keen to establish that we come from Mongolia or Central Asia. And looking at the sweet djinns, devils, and demons that appear in the same albums, they like to link us with the shamans. Speaking for ourselves, we like the fact that these fearful but charming creatures wear the same crafty expressions and are drawn with the same crude, curling lines. Because other similarly drawn demons in the same albums appear to be of Chinese origin, some scholars claim we come from even farther afield, perhaps even from China; this speaks to our nomadic souls, awakening our love of the road, and so it too pleases us.

Scholars who claim that the demons in some drawings bear the influence of *The Shahname* (*The Book of Kings*), or that they are similar in style to those produced at the Whitesheep Palace in Tabriz, are inclined to place us within the borders of Iran. After all, most scholars tend to see us as belonging to the spoils of the war won by the great Ottoman sultan Selim I over the Safavids at Chaldiran in 1514. There are even those who have studied the bell-shaped headdress worn by our friend in red and decided that we must be Russian.

The doubt and admiration that all these guesses inspire have something in common with the admiration we hope to awaken in you by asking you to appreciate us as drawings. There is, first, the wonder, fear, and doubt stirred by the drawing itself. Then there is an air of mystery

aroused by the rumors and theories about our origins. We take pride in being the most enigmatic, discussed, disputed drawings from the remotest corner of the world. As for all those things they've written about us—yes, they do make us uneasy, because of this tendency to forget we're drawings. But all these theories they've spun about us in the timeless bastions of art history, all the suspicion, fear, and admiration that our many observers have heaped upon us—it all does give us a lovely air of enchantment.

What we really want to say is this: Stop trying to figure out whether we're from China, India, Central Asia, Iran, Transoxiana, or Turkistan. Stop trying to pinpoint where we are from and where we are going, and please pay attention instead to our humanity. See how caught up we are in what's going on. Our eyes are open wide and we are immersed in our work. We are trying to protect ourselves and, even as our panic grows, we are talking among ourselves. Our poverty is evident, as is our fear, our endless travels—we are huge barefooted men, we are horses, we are terrible creatures—feel our strength! A wind is blowing that ripples our clothes; we fear and tremble but we continue down the road. The bleak plain we are trying to cross has much in common with this colorless, featureless paper on which we are drawn. Neither mountains nor hills rise up from this level field; we are ageless, in a world beyond time.

Once you've begun to feel our humanity, it won't be long, we think, before you begin to sense the demons inside us. We are aware that—even as we fear those demons—we are made of the same stuff. Look at the horns of those creatures, and their hair, their curling eyebrows; our bodies curl the same way. Their hands and thick legs are just as crude as ours, but see how they pulse with life! Look first at the noses on the demons, and then look at ours; understand that we are brothers and fear us. But we see that you smile at the very thought that you should fear us.

There is, we know, a tragic reason why we cannot make you quake with fear. The stories we once belonged to have been lost. Just as you do not know who we are, where we came from, or where we are going, you don't even know which part of which story we fit into, and that is even worse. After passing through so many misadventures and catastrophes, after walking such great distances, it is almost as if we too have forgotten our stories, forgotten who we are.

We hear angry protests about our being Turks, Mongolians, men of Tabriz. Centuries after we were drawn, we've been linked with many peoples, nations, and stories. That razor-toothed, sharp-nailed, grinning demon over there—maybe he's taken one of us away, who knows where, perhaps even to the underworld. So yes, as, for example, many of the sages among you have already guessed, we could be from the great Persian epic, *The Book of Kings,* and we could depict the scene in which a giant demon named Akvan prepares to throw the sleeping hero Rüstem into the Caspian Sea. But what about the other drawings? What moments do they depict, and what stories do they belong to? As we three walk down the road with our donkey, what scene from what forgotten story are we bringing to life?

You don't know. So let us tell you a secret. We were traveling from some distant point in Asia, with our donkey, when we met an artist who drew our likeness—this much you already know. Well, look now at that friend you can see coming up behind the donkey: Our drawing is inside the portfolio he is holding in his arms. When evening falls, when we are all sitting together in a candlelit tent, this storyteller, perhaps someone not so different from the writer who is at this very moment using us as his mouthpieces, will tell us this tale. To add to our enjoyment, and to make sure his story stays in our minds, he will take out this drawing you are looking at right now and show it to us. We will not be the first drawing he shows, nor will we be the last. All the drawings he shows will illustrate our story.

But after centuries of wandering, defeat, and disaster, our stories are lost. The drawings that once illustrated these stories have been scattered across the world. Now even we have forgotten where we are from. We have been stripped of our stories and our identities. But it was still a lovely thing to have been drawn.

Once upon a time there was a storyteller who looked at us and—perhaps because he shared our unease—began his story like this:

"We are troubled by the abundance of rumors about where we come from, who we are, where we're going, and who drew us."

CHAPTER SEVENTY-ONE

Meaning

Hi! Thank you for reading me. I should be happy to be here, though I can't help feeling confused. I like the way your eyes are traveling over me. Because I'm here to serve you. Even though I'm not sure what that means. I don't even know what I am these days—isn't that a pity? I'm a concoction of signs; I long to be seen, but then I lose my nerve. Would I be better off hiding myself away in the shadows, far away, protected from all eyes? That's what I can't decide. I'm making such a big effort to be here, even with all these worries, strangely. Here's what I want you to understand: This kind of exposition is new to me. I've never existed in quite this way. In the old days, we were more to one side. I'd love to attract your attention, but without giving it too much thought, for that is when I feel most relaxed. So just keep me in the corner of your mind and forget I'm even there. I'd like to remind you—quietly, the way I did in the old days—how nice it was to exist for you without your even knowing it. I'm not really sure that this can ever really happen again, though. Because the real problem is this: I tend to think I'm a picture, when really all I am is words. Because when I'm letters, I think I'm a picture, and when I'm a picture I think I'm letters. But this is not out of ambivalence—this is my life. Let's see how long it takes for *you* to get used to it. If you ask me, the reason we can't understand each other is that the inside of your head is different. You see, the only reason I'm here is to mean something. But you look at me as if I'm just an object. Yes, I know—I do have a body. But my body is only here to help my meaning flap its wings and take flight. I know from the way you're looking at me that I have this body, that my left side and my right side are decorated with colors and figures. This pleases me and it confuses me. Once upon a time, when I was just a meaning, it never occurred to me that I was also

an object, and I didn't even have a mind; I was nothing more than a humble sign passing between two beautiful minds. I was not aware of my
own existence, and this was lovely. You could look at me and I would
think nothing of it. But now, as your eyes run across us letters, I feel as if
I have a body—as if all I am is a body—and a chill runs through me.
Okay, I'll admit it: I like it, just a little, and I go along with it, but I also
feel a little ashamed. But the moment it begins to please me, I want more
and that scares me. I end up asking myself, What's going to happen next?
I start worrying that my body is going to obscure my soul and that the
meaning—my meaning—will get pushed deep inside me. That's when I
start wanting to hide in the shadows. That's when you can no longer
understand me, and you start getting confused, and even you can't figure
out if you're reading me, or just staring at me. That's when even I get
scared of my body and wish I were just a meaning, but I also know I've
left it too late. There's no way I can go back to the good old days now, to
the days before you arrived; there's no going back to when I was just a
meaning. At a time like this I am neither fully here nor fully somewhere
else; instead, I hover between heaven and earth, undecided. This is
painful, and I try to console myself with bodily pleasures. I'd love to
attract your attention, but without your giving it too much thought, for
that is when I feel at my most relaxed. Should I be a meaning or an
object? A letter or a picture? Which reminds me, I—hang on, don't go
yet . . . I can't bear the thought of your turning the page yet . . . you still
don't understand me and already you're casting me away. . . .

OTHER CITIES,
OTHER CIVILIZATIONS

CHAPTER SEVENTY-TWO

My First Encounters with Americans

I n 1961 we moved to Ankara on account of my father's work, making our home in an expensive apartment house across from the city's most beautiful park, in which there was an artificial lake that was home to two weary swans. On the top floor lived an American family, whose blue Chevrolet we would sometimes hear rattling as they drove it into the garage. We kept a close eye on them.

Our interest was not in American culture but in the Americans themselves. When we sat with great crowds of other children at the reduced-price Sunday matinees in Ankara's film theaters, we had no idea whether the film we were watching was American or French. The subtitles told us all we needed to know: that what we were watching came to us from Western civilization.

Because there were many Americans living in this expensive new neighborhood at that time, we'd see them everywhere, and what interested us most were the things they consumed and discarded. The most fascinating objects were the Coca-Cola cans, which we collected—some of us retrieving them from rubbish bins—and later flattened by stamping on them furiously. (Maybe some of these were beer cans; maybe there were other brands.) In the beginning we used them for a game called Find the Can, and sometimes we'd cut and shape them into metal signs, use the tabs as money, but never in my life did we drink any cola or indeed anything else from cans like these.

In one of the new apartments in whose giant rubbish bins we found our cans there was a beautiful young American woman, to whom we paid great attention. Her husband was taking his car out of the garage one day, moving slowly past us, interrupting our football game, and as he watched her standing on the balcony in her nightdress, blowing him a kiss, we all fell silent for some time. No matter how much they loved each other, the grown-ups we knew would never have displayed their happiness in front of others in such a carefree way.

As for the things that Americans owned, and that passed into the hands of those who established relations with them, they came from the Post Exchange, or PX, known to us as the Piyeks, though I had never seen it, as the place was off limits except to American military and consular personnel and Turks were not allowed in. Blue jeans, chewing gum, Converse All-Star sneakers, the latest American record albums, chocolates that were salty and sweet and upset my stomach, barrettes of all colors, baby food, toys . . . some things found their way out of the Piyeks to be sold under the counter at certain stores in Ankara for exorbitant prices. My older brother was crazy about marbles, so he would save up his money and buy them from these stores, and laid next to his Turkish-made mica and glass marbles, these porcelain American marbles looked like jewels.

We found out about these marbles one day from the boy who lived with his family on the third floor and who went to school every morning in a big orange school bus of the type I would later see in films about American life. He was an only child, about our age, with no friends and an American-style crew cut. He probably saw us playing marbles in the garden with our friends, and he had hundreds of his own from the Piyeks. It seemed to us as if he had thousands of marbles when we had only a handful. Whenever he emptied them out of his bag, they made in their hundreds such a racket rolling across the floor that it really got on our nerves.

News of this abundance had soon spread to all our friends in the neighborhood. We'd go to the back garden in twos and threes, stand under the Americans' windows, and shout, "Hey, boy!" After a long silence, he would suddenly appear on the balcony and angrily toss down a handful of marbles, and having watched my friends scamper after the marbles and come to blows over them, he would suddenly disappear again. He stopped tossing out handfuls of marbles, throwing them instead one by one at regular intervals as my friends ran whispering about the garden.

One afternoon, this little king began to throw marbles onto our balcony too. They rained down intensely, some of the marbles bouncing off our balcony into the garden below. My brother and I couldn't hold ourselves back; we rushed out to the balcony to gather up the marbles. When the rain of marbles became even more intense, we began to whisper, "That one's mine, that one's yours!"

"What is going on here?" my mother cried. "Come inside, now."

Closing the door to the balcony, we watched the shower of marbles with shame from inside; the downpour had slackened somewhat. When he realized we weren't coming back onto the balcony, he went into his room to pour his hundreds of marbles onto the floor. When the coast was clear, my brother and I went back out to the balcony, where we shame-facedly and silently gathered up the remaining marbles, to joylessly divide them between us.

The next day, we followed our mother's instructions, and when he appeared on his balcony, we called from below, "Hey, boy, do you want to trade?"

Standing on our balcony, we showed him our own glass and mica marbles. Five minutes later, our doorbell rang. We gave him a few mica and glass marbles, and he offered us a handful of his expensive American marbles. We made the exchange in silence. Then he told us his name, and we told him ours.

What impressed us more than the value of the exchange was that his name was Bobby, that his squinting eyes were blue, and that his knees were dirty from playing outside, just like ours. In a panic, he raced back up to his own apartment.

CHAPTER SEVENTY-THREE

Views from the Capital of the World

New York, 1986

A friend came with his car to pick me up at Kennedy Airport. On our way to Brooklyn, we got lost on the expressway: poor neighborhoods, warehouses, brick buildings, decrepit gas stations, soulless apartments. . . . In fact I could see the Manhattan skyline rising behind them from time to time, but this wasn't the New York of my dreams. This is how I reached the easy conclusion that Brooklyn wasn't New York. I left my bags in my friend's Brooklyn brownstone, we drank some tea together, lit up cigarettes. As I walked around the apartment, I still kept thinking that this was not New York yet: The real thing, the place to go—the dream—was just over there, across the river.

An hour later, the sun that had made the day seem so long was about to set. We crossed the Brooklyn Bridge over to Manhattan. Cities have come to all look the same, but if any silhouette was still unmistakable, it was the New York I now saw. In Istanbul I'd just finished a new novel, and other matters had begun to pile up; I was tired; awake now for forty hours, but my eyes were wide open. It was as if I believed that, somewhere among the shadows of these giant silhouettes, I might find the key to not just everything on the face of the earth but to the originals of the dreams of all my years. Perhaps all great cities stir this sort of illusion.

As we began to drive along the avenues and streets of Manhattan, I tried to compare what I was seeing with the images in my mind. What drew my eye was something behind the crowded streets, behind the sidewalks along which people seem to move so slowly, as if in a peaceful dream, behind the lights of an ordinary evening. Just as my friend tired of driving up and down the city streets, I figured it out: My eyes couldn't stop searching, because they couldn't find the secret behind all these sights, the truth that all dreamers hope will one day be revealed to them. I decided to be humble: I would only be able to draw the secret out from this streetscape—the common pavements, the little neighborhood shops, the familiar glow of the streetlamps—through fortitude and resignation. If the great truth I had glimpsed in my dreams existed, I would not find it among the shadows of the skyscrapers but in the little observations I would now patiently gather.

I spent the next few hours taking in the sights around me in this way. I noticed the colors of the hoses and the numbers on the gas pumps; I looked at black boys rushing through the traffic with dirty rags to "clean" the windows of cars stopped in traffic; at men in shorts and running shoes and the metallic glow of bluish phone booths; at walls, bricks, sheets of glass, trees, dogs, yellow taxis, delicatessens. . . . It was as if I were seeing an elegant landscape set down on this earth fully formed, with its patiently repeating fire hydrants, garbage cans, brick walls, and beer cans. Every street, every neighborhood—even the places where we sat down to have a beer or coffee—seemed to serve the same happy dream.

I felt no differently about the people. The teenager in his leather jacket with the partly shaven head and a little purple ponytail at the top, the girl with an extraordinarily fat woman, that man in the suit who ran past me so quickly, the black men walking past me with huge transistor radios, the pale-faced, long-legged women with headphones running with dogs who had the same sense of purpose—all these people passed us on the sidewalk.

Late in the evening, after my friend's wife finished work and joined us, we went to sit among the crowded tables of a pastry shop that extended to a sidewalk café. They asked me a few things about Turkey and I mumbled a reply; they had more questions and I answered them. In this way I tried to convince myself that I had joined in the life of a city, now less a fiction made from ghostly echoes of the sounds and movements of a summer evening than a place apart, a real world filled end to end with real people. After that I watched the streets, whose images and lights I would come to know so well as they changed slowly from a dreamscape into real asphalt streets. Who can say which world was the real New York?

Still there are a few dreamlike images that I will never forget. The top of that table on the sidewalk was of white Formica. Sitting on it was a greenish beer bottle and our cream-colored coffee cups. The view of the crowds on the pavement was blocked by the wide back of a woman in a green pullover at the table in front of us. The pale orange light coming from the windows of the stone houses as their facades receded into the night, turning purple. Because the street was narrow, the streetlamp across the way was obscured by the leaves of a tree whose trunk stood on our side: Every once in a while I would see its white light playing on the huge silent cars parked along that curb.

Very late that night, after the tables on the sidewalk had emptied and the pastry shop was closing down, my friend yawned and asked if I had set my watch to New York time. I told him that the watch I had been wearing for fifteen years had broken during the flight; taking it from my wrist, I showed it to him, and I never wore that watch again.

The Police Watching Police TV

"Hey guys, look at my new watch," said one of the policemen.

He stretched out his arm. There were three of us in the backseat of the car. I was sitting next to the right-hand window, and next to me were two more policemen.

"Where did you get it?" asked the one sitting next to me.

"Some guy on the sidewalk. Eight bucks," said the policeman in the front.

"It'll break by tomorrow!" said the other.

"I've had it for two days already."

We were driving south along the Hudson on the West Side Highway, and our destination this morning was the courthouse. A month earlier, I'd been mugged. The black youths who'd mugged me had been clumsy enough to get caught and I had had to identify them, and now that they had confessed to all their crimes, I had been called to testify at their trial. When she had called me on the phone the day before, the prosecutor had realized that I wasn't keen to give evidence, and—perhaps suspecting I would try to get out of it—she told me a police car would bring me to court in the morning. These two blond policemen alongside me would also be testifying. They had caught my clumsy young muggers as they stood waiting for the next victim about two blocks away from where they'd mugged me.

As we entered the city traffic, the policemen began to discuss a television series. From what they said, I gathered that the characters were also in the NYPD, driving around in the same sort of blue-and-white cars as the one we were in now, warring with the same gangsters and drug dealers and suffering the same burnout. I was reminded of the provincial girls and unhappy daydreaming housewives of the nineteenth century who would put themselves in the place of the heroines of the novels they read, for these policemen had put themselves in the place of the heroes of this television series and were now discussing the series as if it presented their own lives. The language they used was different, though; most of their curse words I was hearing for the first time.

After passing through Chinatown, we arrived at the courthouse, where we embarked on yet another of those long journeys upward in a lift. Then they took me to the prosecutor's office. She did not fit my idea of a prosecutor; she looked more like a sweet, gentle ex-classmate. After telling me a few things very quickly, she said, "I'll be right back," and she rushed from the room.

Her desk was covered with papers, and to pass the time I thought I might take a look: These were the confessions of the boys who had mugged me. I knew already that the gun they had used was not a real one. I was still annoyed with them, though. They had referred to me as a "white guy." With my twenty dollars they'd bought crack. Realizing then that perhaps I should not have read these documents, I put them back on the table and, instead, leafed through a thick book I found sitting on the side: *The Prosecutor's Interrogation Handbook.* I read about why a prosecutor could not charge a defense lawyer who colluded with a murderer by refusing to disclose the whereabouts of a buried corpse. The prosecutor returned.

"You don't seem to want to be a witness," she said. We had left her office and were walking down the corridor.

"I feel sorry for the boys," I said.

"Which boys?"

"The ones who mugged me. How many years will they get?"

"But they took your twenty dollars," she said. "Do you know how they spent your money?"

We went down in the lift; the courtroom was in the skyscraper on the other side of the street. The prosecutor carried her papers pressed against her chest, the way a college student might do, greeting other prosecutors as we passed them and affably telling me a few things about herself: She was from Nevada and she had majored in marine biology in Arkansas, discovering only later the profession she was meant to follow.

"What profession?" I asked.

"Law," she said, making a circle with her lips.

We embarked on another journey in a lift. No one spoke, all eyes glued to the numbers flashing sequentially above the door. When we got out, the prosecutor stopped by a bench along the corridor.

"Wait here. When the judge calls you, just tell him the same thing you told me on your last visit," she said.

"This will be my last visit, I hope!" I said.

She left. I was not allowed inside the courtroom, so I sat down on the bench and waited. After a while, I was joined by the policemen who'd driven me in, but before long they got back up on their feet. Curious, I went over to ask them what was going on.

"The suspects have arrived, but the elevators are broken," one of the policemen told me.

"I'm wondering why they confessed to everything," I said.

"Because we treated them so well, that's why," said the other policeman with the thin mustache.

"But that doesn't explain why they confessed to all those other crimes," I said. "Doesn't this stand to increase their sentence? How many years are they going to get?"

"Four years per robbery count, so twenty-eight years."

"Can't a person defend himself?"

"Look, mister," said the one with the new watch, now beginning to look annoyed. "We didn't touch a hair on their heads. I had nothing to eat that night, but they did. You follow me?"

"I told them that if they confess to everything," said the other policeman, trying to explain, "I'd tell the judge they weren't bad guys and he'd give them a lighter sentence. They think I knew the judge in high school."

They both laughed.

The policeman with the new watch pointed down the corridor. "That's the guy who'll be testifying. He knows how to make a good impression."

"I'm their friend," said the policeman with the mustache.

They laughed again. I went back to my bench. The policemen were called into the courtroom. There was another long wait; the side of the bench was in direct sunlight, and I had begun to perspire. I stood up and began to walk up and down the long, empty corridor. Then I stopped to look at the New York skyline. It was as if everything—the skyscrapers and the billboards—were about to crumble before my eyes. More time passed, and finally the prosecutor appeared.

"So you're still with us, are you? The elevators are broken, and the suspects are coming up the stairs. We're still waiting for them."

After a while, the policemen returned. They were talking among themselves. I could not help but hear them. A friend of theirs had witnessed an incident in front of his house on his day off, and the fleeing

suspect had shot and wounded him. Because this fugitive suspect also
knew his address, the off-duty policeman had begun to receive threatening phone calls, and at that point he had moved to a different neighborhood. The policemen were laughing and talking about something else
when they passed me to go into the courtroom. No one came out for a
long time. As I sat in the silent corridor, I thought they had forgotten me.
The lights on the ceiling and the corridor's empty chairs and benches
were reflected on the polished marble floors. I perspired a little more.
After a while, the prosecutor came out again.

"They made it to the courthouse, but now we can't find them," she said.

"Aren't they coming up the stairs?"

"We're still waiting."

She left. I watched her high-heeled shoes cross the marble floor.
There was something about her gait that made me think of the way one
might with his fingers suggest a figure walking. She went through the
courtroom door and disappeared. By now I had lost the desire to check
my watch, and I have no idea how long I did nothing but sit there perspiring on that bench. I wondered if the policeman's new watch had broken yet; when I got up to take another look at the Manhattan skyline, it
seemed to be spewing out steam; I gazed into the clouds, trying to draw
some meaning from them. Much, much later, the prosecutor reappeared.

"The suspects are lost somewhere in the building. We can't find them
anywhere, so the judge has postponed the hearing. You can go now."

When I reached the street after another long journey in the lift, I
wanted to wash my face. I went into a restaurant, where a waiter said,
"The restroom is for customers only. You have to sit down."

"I'd like a hamburger," I said, without sitting down.

"Just a plain hamburger?"

"Yes."

I went into the restroom and washed my face.

Flavorless Sweet Rolls and Beautiful Vistas

When I told them that the cinnamon rolls we'd brought from the bakery
had lost their flavor, they laughed at me. It was a dark and rainy Saturday
afternoon, and we were drinking tea and discussing whether or not to go
to a Columbia University faculty party for students. They explained that
the heavenly cinnamon smell that made you long for the sweet rolls the
moment you walked into the bakery was actually an artificial fragrance
they pumped into the store. Conned by that aroma, customers longed to

touch these buns, when in fact there wasn't even an oven in the back. You might wish to call this a "lost illusion," as people used to say, or, more prosaically and descriptively, an absence of flavor. But you could also say it turned the store into a sham.

Until you get used to this city, you spend a good part of the day pondering these absent flavors; because we still know what a real brick wall looks like and how it is constructed, a concrete wall that's been made to look like a brick wall is a sham that causes most of us no pain. But how about when you see them beginning to put up huge buildings that are imitations of things they are not? The ostentatious postmodern structures that are now springing up all over New York City are the work of architects who do just this. These architects go out of their way to emphasize the fact that their buildings are imitations: With their enormous glass facades, their almost medieval twists and bends, they make me wonder whether they have no desire to be actually anything whatsoever. Do they wish only to deceive us, appearing to be something other than what they are? But then, can any deception so obvious be a deception at all?

Just as strange is how that the advertisements, radio slogans, billboards, and beautiful models on television will deceive you so openly. You know that the red chunks in the ice cream are artificially colored and are not strawberries, you know that not even the writers believe the blurbs on the backs of their books, you know that the famous actress who has been in the public eye for forty years is no longer so young as her face-lift suggests, and you know that someone else writes Ronald Reagan's speeches for him. But I don't get the impression that many people mind. The tired citizen walking down Fifth Avenue would explain it like this, perhaps: "Should I worry if this flower delighting my eyes is really plastic? It's a pleasure to look at, and it cheers my heart, and that's all that matters to me."

A person who has newly arrived in New York may read more into all this. What if the people here are like the cinnamon rolls; what if they are not sincere in their helpful smiles and friendly little questions; what if they're trying to fool me? During one of those long journeys in a lift, if one of the other passengers suddenly asks me how I am, does this man really want to *know*? After she has checked my reservation, is the girl in the travel agency genuinely interested in the details of my plans or does she simply feel she must act as if she is? Do they ask me these silly questions about Turkey just to make conversation, or because they are really curious? Why do they keep smiling at me, why are they always apologizing, why are they so solicitous?

After that rainy afternoon when we ate the flavorless cinnamon rolls, my friends had little patience for my theories on tastelessness. I must come from a country that put too great an emphasis on Right and Wrong, Good and Evil, Tasty and Flavorless. I was reading too much into things about which I knew little; I seemed to be expecting anonymous organizations, unfamiliar enterprises, television voiceovers, and the advertisements plastered all over every avenue to speak to me as sincerely as a neighbor or friend. Then, remembering a particular friend in common, we all burst into cruel laughter.

He had a doctorate, he was an expert in his field, he babbled, he devoured books. He'd lick his lips like a monkey and devour as well all the latest ideas coming out of sociology, psychology, and philosophy. We did acknowledge, albeit with a smile, that he was better than most of the lackluster boors who taught at neighboring universities, but he just couldn't find a job. Then we repeated what his wife had so mournfully told us: To those who now told him that to find work he would have to go from door to door, make himself known, and send out letters, he replied, "I'm not going to them; they should come to me." By now, most of his other friends had given up trying to change his mind. These friends soon gave up too, falling into a respectful silence that he appreciated.

This is when we returned to the question of the university party. We all knew that the moment we walked into that brightly lit room we would be overwhelmed again by the absence of flavor. At the entrance, someone trying to help us negotiate the crowd would write our names on big labels and stick them onto our lapels. The room would be bathed in a light as yellow as fried potatoes. I could already see the helpless searching faces of the other guests as they stood there clutching their drinks. Like products on a supermarket shelf we would let ourselves be introduced, and to this same end we would engage in short conversations; we would advertise ourselves by pointing out our distinguishing features, our areas of interest, our manner of speaking, our intellects, our sense of humor, our resilience, as well as generalizations and in-depth information about our culture. Just as an egg shampoo might be distinguished from an apple shampoo, we would then begin to take the places to which we had been assigned on New York's social shelf.

My two friends (who were husband and wife) screwed up their faces as if to agree with me. But earlier on we'd been laughing about how dazzling the supermarkets were here, with all their varied merchandise. Tens of thousands of different brands, colors, boxes, pictures, numbers, all sitting in these spacious, fragrant stores awaiting eyes to feast on them.

As your eyes travel over their colorful surfaces, you don't spend much time worrying that they might be about to deceive you; it is as if you've forgotten the old philosophical distinction between appearance and reality. You give yourself over to the beauties of this shopping heaven and you feast your eyes. With time, you learn that it doesn't matter if cinnamon rolls don't smell the same at home as they did in the bakery.

"I'm in the mood now," said my friend's wife. "At least we'll have gone out and seen people."

This is how we decided we should go.

People might leave stores and parties empty-handed, but in New York there is no reason not to feast your eyes.

An Encounter in the Subway; or, Missing, Presumed Dead

I rushed through the barrier and ran down the stairs, but I didn't make it. The doors had closed. The subway cars were speeding away. It was a time in the afternoon when trains passed less frequently, so I sat down on one of the benches on the platform to wait for the next one. Outdoors it was oppressively hot and bright, so I was happy to be sitting on this cool and empty bench. There was a warm and dusty shaft of light pouring through the grill from the Broadway sidewalk above. It was triangular in shape, like a ray of sunlight in a prehistoric cave; when people walked through it, they looked like ghosts. For a while I listened to a couple who sat down next to me.

"But they're still so little," the woman was saying.

"So be it," said the man, who was swinging his legs. "It's time we clamped down on them."

"They're such little babies, though," the woman said in a soft voice.

It was perhaps then that I first saw that face passing through the shaft of light, but I didn't take it in. It was only when I saw his tense silhouette pacing the full length of the platform that I recognized him. He was a classmate from my lycée days; he'd studied at a university in Istanbul for two years, got a bit involved with politics, and had suddenly gone missing. It was only later that we found out he'd gone to America; the word was that his wealthy parents had begun to worry about his political activities and sent him away, but I knew his parents were not that wealthy. Then—I don't remember who told me this—I heard he had died, in a car crash or a plane crash or something along those lines. As I watched him from the corner of my eye, and without feeling much excitement, I recalled that a New York acquaintance of mine had mentioned that he knew someone else from Istanbul; he'd given me the name, saying he worked for the power company. That had happened fairly recently. For some reason I had not remembered having previously heard of his death. Had I remembered, I don't think I would have been so surprised, I would simply have thought, as I was thinking now, that only one of these two rumors could be true.

When he went into a corner to lean against one of those giant steel pillars holding up the wide avenue above us, I stood and went over to him.

When I called to him by name, he looked surprised.

"Yes?"

He'd grown a Turkish-style mustache, but in New York it looked Mexican.

"So do you recognize me?" I asked in Turkish, but I could tell from the blank look on his face that he didn't. I had remained behind, in the life he had left fourteen years earlier.

When I told him my name, he remembered. In an instant he could see me as I'd been fourteen years before. Then we exchanged information, as if we had to explain to each other how we both came to be standing under 116th Street in a Manhattan subway station. He was married; he worked in telecommunications—not at the power company; he was an engineer; his wife was American; his home was far from here, in Brooklyn, but he owned it.

"Is it true what they say, that you're writing novels?" he asked me.

At that moment, the train came rattling into the station, a noise that still shocked me. When the doors opened up, there was a moment of silence, and he asked me something else.

"Have they really finished the Bosphorus Bridge?"

As we walked into the car, I smiled and answered his question. Inside it was hot and crowded: people of all races, youths in sneakers, coming down from the Bronx and Harlem. We stood there side by side like two brothers, holding on to the same pole, but as we were tossed this way and that, we looked into each other's faces like strangers. When I'd known him, there had been nothing strange about him, except that he didn't eat garlic and seldom cut his nails. He told me a few things that got lost in the noise of the train. It was when we stopped at 109th Street that I realized what he'd asked.

"Do the horse carts go over the Bosphorus Bridge too?"

I said a few more things, this time without smiling. What shocked me were not his questions but the attention he gave my answers; before long, the noise of the train made it impossible for him to hear me, but he still

looked at me with a face full of understanding, as if he'd heard everything I'd said. When the train stopped at 103rd Street, there was a tense
silence. Then, in a sudden burst of anger, he asked, "Do they still tap the
phones?" Then, with a wild laugh that sent chills down my spine, he
shouted, "Stupid idiots!"

He began excitedly to tell me a few more things, which I could not
hear above the roar of the train. When I looked at our hands side by side
on the pole, I was not at all happy to see how alike they looked. On his
wrist was a watch that showed the time in New York, London, Moscow,
Dubai, and Tokyo, just like mine.

At Ninety-sixth Street, there was some pushing and shoving. There
was an express train on the other side of the platform. He quickly took
my number, and then disappeared into the crowds jostling between the
two trains. Both trains left the station at the same time, and when I
looked into the windows of the express train as it slowly overtook us, I
could see him looking at me: curious, suspicious, and full of contempt.

I was glad that he didn't phone me, thinking he must have lost my
number, but a month later, in the middle of the night, he did call. He
bombarded me with annoying questions: Did I want to take up American
citizenship, why was I in New York, and had I heard why the Mafia had
committed its most recent murder, and did I know why the stock prices
for telephone and electric companies were falling on Wall Street? I
answered his torrent of questions, and he listened carefully to my
answers, accusing me of inconsistencies from time to time, like a policeman trying to catch out a suspect in a lie.

When he rang me again ten days later, it was even later at night and he
was drunker. He recited a long and detailed version of the story of Ana-
toli Zurlinsky, a KGB agent who had defected to America: Having discovered from newspaper accounts the building on Forty-second Street
where he'd met with CIA agents, my caller had gone to inspect it; to do
this, he'd gone into a barbershop to have a shave and caught the spy in a
few small lies. When I tried to point out the inconsistencies in his own
story, as he'd done with me, he got angry. He asked what I was doing in
New York and, with the same wild laugh he'd used to mock the Bosphorus Bridge, he put down the phone.

When he called me again, not long afterward, he spent half the time
talking to me and half the time arguing with his wife, who was telling
him how late it was. He talked about the telecommunications company at
which he worked, and about how he could listen in on any conversation
in the world, how his own phone was tapped too. Then, without warning,

he asked after a number of girls he'd known at university: Who was with whom, and how were they getting on, if they could at all? I told him a few colorless stories that ended in marriage, and after listening carefully, he laughed again with contempt.

"Nothing good can ever happen in that place," he said. "Nothing!" I must have been taken aback, because before I could say anything, he triumphantly announced, "Do you hear me, brother? Nothing good can happen there. Nothing ever will."

He repeated this sentence with relish during our next two telephone conversations, pressing his point. He talked about spies, Mafia tricks, tapped telephones, and the latest developments in electronics. From time to time I'd also hear his wife's faint voice. Once she tried to take either a drink or the telephone receiver from her husband's hand. I imagined one of those small apartments in a high-rise on the far side of Brooklyn; you paid in installments for thirty years and then it was yours. A friend of mine had told me that when you flushed the toilet, the pipes let out a mournful wail that could be heard not just in your own apartment but in all eight symmetrically arranged apartments sharing the same plumbing, and the sound of the cascading water caused all the cockroaches to come scuttling out of their hiding places. Later on, I was sorry I hadn't asked him about this. What he did ask me at about three in the morning was this.

"Do they have cornflakes in Turkey yet?"

"They tried to sell them as corn fritters, but they failed," I said. "The consumers poured hot milk over them."

He let out one of his wild laughs. "Right now it's eleven in the morning in Dubai!" he shouted. "In Dubai, in Istanbul . . ." He sounded happy when he hung up.

I thought he would call again. When he didn't call, for some reason I felt uneasy. After a month had passed, when I happened to see that ghostly triangular funnel of light coming through the grill onto the subway platform, I decided to look for him: partly because I wanted to shake him up, upset his peace of mind, and partly because I was curious. I found his name in the Brooklyn directory. A woman answered the phone, but she was not his wife. She asked me never to call that number again. The person who had had this number previously had died in a traffic accident.

The Fear of Cigarettes

I was probably lost in thought, dreaming up my novel; I must have been sitting in a room, chain smoking, so I didn't see him; they told me about

it later. Just before the great Yul Brynner died, his image appeared on the
TV screen. This bald actor, whom I'd never really liked and whose films
I didn't much like either, was lying in disarray on his hospital bed;
breathing painfully and looking straight into the viewers' eyes, he said
something like:

"By the time you see this, I will be dead. I am about to die from lung
cancer. It's all my fault. Now I'm dying a painful death. Though I was
rich and successful, I could have lived longer, I could have enjoyed life,
but I won't, and all because of cigarettes. Please don't do as I did; give up
smoking now. If you don't, you'll never enjoy life to the fullest, you'll
die an unnecessary death."

When my friend had finished telling me about this taped message that
had made such a deep impression on him, I smiled and offered him one
of my Marlboros and we both lit up. Then we looked into each other's
faces, but we couldn't manage to smile. I had always been able to smoke
in Turkey without giving it much thought, and though I had known it
would cause me some trouble in New York, I had not expected *this* much
trouble.

It wasn't what I heard on television and the radio or read in magazines and newspapers that caused me the most difficulty. I was already
used to such campaigns, had already seen plenty of terrifying images of
lungs clogged with tar, models of lungs so full of tar they looked like yellow sponges, nicotine plaques that obstructed veins to the point of causing heart attacks, and color illustrations of luckless hearts that were
failing because they had been inside smokers. I'd look blankly at magazine columns that railed against idiots who still smoked and pregnant
women who poisoned their unborn children with cigarettes, and as I
gazed at pictures of tombstones wreathed in cigarette smoke, I would
smoke my own cigarette in peaceful resignation. The promise of death
by cigarettes did not affect me any more than the promises of pleasure
offered by the advertisements for Marlboros and Pan Am that you used
to see on the sides of old apartment buildings, or by the images of Coca-
Cola and Hawaii that I'd see flashing on my TV screen. This death had
been thoroughly illuminated. I had seen all the images, but it still hadn't
registered in my mind. Cigarettes caused me another sort of problem in
New York: I'd be at one of those parties with beer, chips, and salsa, but
when I thoughtlessly lit up a cigarette I would see people racing away
from me as if I were about to infect them with AIDS.

They were not running away from the cancer that cigarette smoke
might cause, but from the smoker. I would only gradually come to under-

stand that my cigarette to them represented a lack of willpower and of culture, a disordered life, indifference, and (America's worst nightmare) failure. Later on, an acquaintance (who claimed to have changed from head to toe during his five years in America but who was still Turk enough that he could not resist the national habits of inventing unnecessary categories and propounding tactless theories) told me there were two classes of New Yorker: smokers and nonsmokers. Apart from the times when those belonging to the first class went out into the streets armed with knives, guns, and cigarette packs to rob those belonging to the second class as they walked anxiously through dark streets and sometimes even in broad daylight, you rarely saw the two groups involved in any sort of class conflict. Quite the contrary, newspapers and television companies were working very hard to unite these two distinct classes by means of cigarettes—which were a different price in every store and neighborhood—and in their advertisements. The models puffing on cigarettes in advertisements looked nothing like nicotine addicts and a lot like the class of people who worked hard, had plenty of willpower and culture, and didn't smoke. You'd hear inspiring and happy stories about people who'd made it from the smoking class into the nonsmoking class.

The acquaintance who'd changed from head to toe told me how he'd once got in touch with an organization that helped people give up smoking. When during the first days the nicotine withdrawal became almost impossible to bear, he'd called the help line. The sweet and compassionate voice on the phone told him how happy he'd be once he'd kicked the habit and how all he needed to do was grit his teeth a little longer, and when this acquaintance went on to tell me how this voice had informed him that there was meaning, perhaps even spiritual meaning, in the agony he was going through, he did not so much as smile. I lit up a cigarette, instantly sending him into a panic and lowering his opinion of me. By now I knew that the black man bumming cigarettes on Madison Avenue was an object of pity not because he did not have the money to buy cigarettes but because he smoked in the first place: This man had no willpower and no culture and expected little from life. If a man was of a smoking disposition, it shouldn't come as a surprise that he had become a beggar. Pity was slowly coming into fashion in New York.

In the Middle Ages, they believed God sent the plague down upon the earth to separate the guilty from the innocent. If you can guess that a fraction of those struck down by the plague might have rejected that idea, you can also understand why American smokers might be so eager to prove themselves good citizens. Whenever a group retreats to a corner to congregate around an ashtray at a meeting or a workplace, or convene in a smoking room (if one exists at all), these cursed addicts are quick to tell you that they're on the point of quitting. In fact they are good citizens, but because they have regrets about this habit that lack of culture, willpower, and success bequeathed them, they think of themselves as having succumbed to it only temporarily. They have in their minds a story that will offer them deliverance from the land of the thief and the sinner: After resolving their problems with their lovers, finishing their unfinishable dissertations, or finding jobs, they will give up this accursed habit and join the ranks of right-living Americans. Some may even grow uneasy about their sinful deportment around the ashtray and seek to prove to the rest that they aren't really guilty of the crime they are committing: They tell you that actually they don't smoke at all, they're just smoking *this* cigarette because of a particularly rough day, or the cigarette is extremely low in tar and nicotine, they smoke in fact only three cigarettes a day, and, as you have already seen, they carried no matches or lighters.

But there are always a few among the guilty who have so given themselves over to a life of sin that—in their own homes, at least—they embrace their habit with pride. I have met happy, cultivated, self-disciplined, and well-off people of the older generation who have been smoking for too long ever to give up and who have resigned themselves to the early death that cigarettes may bring them. Some of these same people were not at all resigned when they came into conflict with the young business types who were banning smoking at their places of work: This they saw as a curb on their freedom. I remember sitting with a writer much older than myself by the front window of a luncheonette, watching the cigarette ads on the tops of the yellow taxis going past us and talking at length about the taste of cigarettes. In the Italian sense of the expression, he also "smoked like a Turk." In the way that an idle aristocrat might discuss rare wines, he talked about the rough taste of long Camels and the nice, refined taste of short Kents, and it seemed to me that what he was fearlessly embracing was the taste of our sin: Every reference to cigarettes brought the love of life into conflict with the fear of death, leading me to wonder if New York's cigarette ideology isn't some sort of religion.

Forty-second Street

They'd met on the corner of Forty-second and, without pausing to speak, headed south to go into the first luncheonette they could find. When the rain began, the blacks who had been hawking cordless telephones and radios on Fifth Avenue withdrew from the street. Inside the diner it smelled of steam and cooking oil. Running parallel to the counter were a row of tables and red-upholstered booths. The man took off his old coat and carefully placed it next to him on the booth against the wall. The woman sat down, taking off her coat too. Sitting on one of the stools at the counter was an old man dozing over the sports pages.

"Don't hang your handbag there," said the man to the woman. "If someone snatches it, he'll be out the door before anyone can stop him."

The woman let her eyes wander over the menu. They were both close to thirty. As the man began groping nervously for his cigarettes, the woman moved the bag from where she had hung it and put it on top of the coat beside her.

"It's bad," she finally said. "They don't want any more buttons."

"Why not?"

"They haven't been able to sell the ones I already made for them yet."

"Have they paid you?"

"They've paid me half."

"How about the earrings?"

"They don't want buttons, and they don't want earrings."

The buttons were actually bracelets. She did designs on wooden beads and earrings and sold them to some hag of a vendor for two dollars a pair. She could no longer remember why she called the bracelets "buttons" but it was probably because these bracelets looked like buttons.

"Do you think I should get a job?" the woman asked.

"You know that wouldn't work," said the man. "If you did, you'd have no time left to paint."

"No one's ever bought one of my paintings."

"But they will," said the man. "Why don't we call Barış? He wanted to see your studio."

He and Barış had studied together at university in Istanbul. Now his old friend had come to New York for a meeting with a computer company.

"Do you think he'd buy something?" the woman asked.

"He did say he wanted to see your studio. Why else would he want to see your studio?"

"Because he's curious, maybe."

"If he sees something he likes, he'll buy it," said the man.

The waiter came to take their order.

"Two coffees," said the man. Then he turned to the woman and said, "You want coffee, right?"

"I want something to eat too," said the woman, but by now the waiter had left. For a time they were silent.

"What hotel is Barış staying at?" asked the man.

"He doesn't want to buy anything," said the woman. "He just wants to see it. I don't want to call him just because he might buy something."

"If he's not interested in buying anything, why would he want to see it?" said the man. "I can't imagine that he developed a taste for neo-expressionism while he was doing business in Istanbul."

"He's interested in knowing what I'm up to; it's as simple as that," said the woman. "He wants to see what sort of place I work in."

"By now, though, he'll have forgotten all about it."

"Forgotten what?"

"What he said, about wanting to see your paintings."

"He didn't say he wanted to see my paintings, he said he wanted to see my *studio*," said the woman. "He's a nice boy. Why should I trick him into buying paintings that no one in New York wants to buy either?"

"If you think you're cheating anyone who wants to buy your paintings, then you'll never sell a single one," said the man.

"If that's what I have to do to sell them, then I'd prefer not to sell them at all."

There was a silence.

"That's how everyone sells things," said the man. "Everyone always sells to their friends first."

"I am not living here in New York so I can sell paintings to my old friends from Turkey," said the woman. "This is not what I came to New York to do. Anyway, I don't think he'd buy anything."

"So tell me, why *did* you come to New York?" asked the man resentfully.

The waiter arrived with their two coffees. The woman gave no answer.

"So tell me, why *did* you come to New York?" the man asked again, this time with anger.

"Oh, please, don't start!" said the woman.

"I know why you came here. You didn't come for me. It's clear by now that you didn't come here to do paintings, either. You seem to have come here to paint little designs on rings and restrooms."

He knew this would offend her. The woman had done hundreds of designs for a company that produced Gentlemen and Ladies signs for restrooms: in the shape of umbrellas, cigars, high-heeled shoes, silhouettes of men and women, bowler hats, handbags, peeing children. When she had started working for them, she used to laugh about these things, but now she hated them.

"Okay. Barış is staying at the Plaza," said the woman.

"The Plaza is where good people stay," said the man.

"Aren't you going to call him?"

The man got up and walked to the far end of the luncheonette, and after he had found the hotel in the directory and dialed the number, the woman looked at him for some time. His face was pale, but he was powerfully built, with good posture, and in good health. Behind him were posters of the type one often saw in such places: Greece and the Aegean, FLY PAN AM TO THE SUNNY PARADISE OF RHODES. Room 712 did not answer. He returned to his seat.

"The good man is not there!"

"I didn't say he was a good man, I said he was a nice boy," the woman said carefully.

"If he's just a nice boy, why is he staying at the Plaza, why is he earning so much money?"

"He's a nice boy!" the woman insisted stubbornly.

"We don't have enough money to make it to Monday. He's nibbling on oysters and lobster at the Plaza, and he's a nice boy."

"Do you know what?" said the woman vengefully. "You're waiting around for nothing. I'm never going back to Turkey."

"I know—"

"You know why I'm not going back, don't you? Because I cannot abide Turkish men."

"And you're a Turkish girl," said the man angrily. "You're a Turkish girl who can't figure out how to sell her paintings. If you can even call them paintings."

They fell silent. Someone put a coin into the jukebox at the far end, and the restaurant filled with sweet and gentle music, and then a tired and troubled blues singer joined in. They listened. When the girl took her trembling hand off the table and nervously began to search through her coat pockets and her handbag, the man understood: She was looking for her lost handkerchief, to wipe away her tears.

"I'm leaving," said the man, standing up. He picked up his coat and went out.

The rain was falling harder now, and the street was darker. The patch of sky between the lights of the skyscrapers was as black as night. He walked to Forty-second Street and turned left. The men who had been hawking cordless telephones only a short while ago were now hawking umbrellas, which they'd hung on their arms and legs. When he reached Sixth Avenue, the street brightened. As people walked past them on the wet pavement, the blacks standing in the doorways and in front of shops ablaze with strip lights were chanting the same words, as if they'd all learned this song together: "Bad girls, amazing girls, bunny girls, girls-girls-girls. Come on in, come on in and check it out, sir; check it out, check it out: We have private booths, one-way mirrors, live shows, real nipples, girls-girls-girls; come in and check it out, look and see." Some men who had not yet decided were standing outside, looking at the posters: DREAMS OF A WILD CHILD, WET LIPS, INSATIABLE. Passing an empty lot near Seventh Avenue, he caught the smell of aloe. Gathered together in a dark corner, a group of Pakistanis dressed in long robes were selling the Koran in English, strings of huge prayer beads, bottles of aromatic oils, and religious pamphlets. After gazing blankly at the bus terminal for a very long time, he walked through the dark across Forty-first Street back to Fifth Avenue. The luncheonette was called Tom's Place. The woman was no longer at the table. He asked the waiter.

"Did the woman who was sitting here leave?"

"The lady who was sitting here?" asked the waiter. "The lady who was sitting here is gone."

THE *PARIS REVIEW*
INTERVIEW

Orhan Pamuk was born in 1952 in Istanbul, where he still lives. His family had made a fortune in railroad construction during the early days of the Turkish Republic and Pamuk attended Robert College, where the children of the city's privileged elite received a secular, Western-style education. Early in life he developed a passion for the visual arts, but after enrolling in college to study architecture he decided he wanted to write. He is now Turkey's most widely read author.

His first novel, Cevdet Bey and His Sons, was published in 1982 and was followed by The Silent House (1983), The White Castle (1985/1991 in English translation), The Black Book (1990/1994), and The New Life (1994/1997). In 2003 Pamuk received the International IMPAC Dublin Literary Award for My Name Is Red (1998/2001), a murder mystery set in sixteenth-century Istanbul and narrated by multiple voices. The novel explores themes central to his fiction: the intricacies of identity in a country that straddles East and West, sibling rivalry, the existence of doubles, the value of beauty and originality, and the anxiety of cultural influence. Snow (2002/2004), which focuses on religious and political radicalism, was the first of his novels to confront political extremism in contemporary Turkey and it confirmed his standing abroad even as it divided opinion at home. Pamuk's most recent book is Istanbul: Memories and the City (2003/2005), a double portrait of himself—in childhood and youth—and of the place he comes from.

This interview with Orhan Pamuk was conducted in two sustained sessions in London and by correspondence. The first conversation occurred in May 2004 at the time of the British publication of Snow. A special room had been booked for the meeting—a fluorescent-lit, noisily air-conditioned corporate space in the hotel basement. Pamuk arrived, wearing a black corduroy

*jacket over a light blue shirt and dark slacks, and observed, "We could die
here and nobody would ever find us." We retreated to a plush, quiet corner of
the hotel lobby where we spoke for three hours, pausing only for coffee and a
chicken sandwich.*

*In April 2005 Pamuk returned to London for the publication of Istanbul,
and we settled into the same corner of the hotel lobby to speak for two hours. At
first he seemed quite strained, and with reason. Two months earlier, in an
interview with the Swiss newspaper Der Tages-Anzeiger, he had said of
Turkey, "Thirty thousand Kurds and a million Armenians were killed in these
lands and nobody but me dares to talk about it." This remark set off a relentless campaign against Pamuk in the Turkish nationalist press. After all, the
Turkish government persists in denying the 1915 genocidal slaughter of Armenians in Turkey and has imposed laws severely restricting discussion of the
ongoing Kurdish conflict. Pamuk declined to discuss the controversy for the
public record in the hope that it would soon fade. In August, however,
Pamuk's remarks in the Swiss paper resulted in his being charged under Article 301/1 of the Turkish Penal Code with "public denigration" of Turkish identity—a crime punishable by up to three years in prison. Despite outraged
international press coverage of his case, as well as vigorous protest to the
Turkish government by members of the European Parliament and by International PEN, when this magazine went to press in mid-November Pamuk was
still slated to stand trial on December 16, 2005.*

—*Ángel Gurría-Quintana*

INTERVIEWER

How do you feel about giving interviews?

ORHAN PAMUK

I sometimes feel nervous because I give stupid answers to certain
pointless questions. It happens in Turkish as much as in English. I
speak bad Turkish and utter stupid sentences. I have been attacked
in Turkey more for my interviews than for my books. Political
polemicists and columnists do not read novels there.

INTERVIEWER

You've generally received a positive response to your books in
Europe and the United States. What is your critical reception in
Turkey?

PAMUK

The good years are over now. When I was publishing my first books, the previous generation of authors was fading away, so I was welcomed because I was a new author.

INTERVIEWER

When you say "the previous generation," whom do you have in mind?

PAMUK

The authors who felt a social responsibility, authors who felt that literature serves morality and politics. They were flat realists, not experimental. Like writers in so many poor countries, they wasted their talent on trying to serve their nation. I did not want to be like them, because even in my youth I had enjoyed Faulkner, Virginia Woolf, Proust—I had never aspired to the social-realist model of Steinbeck and Gorky. The literature produced in the sixties and seventies was becoming outmoded, so I was welcomed as an author of the new generation.

After the mid-nineties, when my books began to sell in amounts that no one in Turkey had ever dreamed of, my honeymoon years with the Turkish press and intellectuals were over. From then on, critical reception was mostly a reaction to the publicity and sales, rather than the content of my books. Now, unfortunately, I am notorious for my political comments—most of which are picked up from international interviews and shamelessly manipulated by some Turkish nationalist journalists to make me look more radical and politically foolish than I really am.

INTERVIEWER

So there is a hostile reaction to your popularity?

PAMUK

My strong opinion is that it's a sort of punishment for my sales figures and political comments. But I don't want to continue saying this, because I sound defensive. I may be misrepresenting the whole picture.

INTERVIEWER

Where do you write?

PAMUK

I have always thought that the place where you sleep or the place you share with your partner should be separate from the place where you write. The domestic rituals and details somehow kill the imagination. They kill the demon in me. The domestic, tame daily routine makes the longing for the other world, which the imagination needs to operate, fade away. So for years I always had an office or a little place outside the house to work in. I always had different flats.

But once I spent half a semester in the United States while my ex-wife was taking her Ph.D. at Columbia University. We were living in an apartment for married students and didn't have any space, so I had to sleep and write in the same place. Reminders of family life were all around. This upset me. In the mornings I used to say good-bye to my wife like someone going to work. I'd leave the house, walk around a few blocks, and come back like a person arriving at the office.

Ten years ago I found a flat overlooking the Bosphorus with a view of the old city. It has, perhaps, one of the best views of Istanbul. It is a twenty-five-minute walk from where I live. It is full of books and my desk looks out onto the view. Every day I spend, on average, some ten hours there.

INTERVIEWER

Ten hours a day?

PAMUK

Yes, I'm a hard worker. I enjoy it. People say I'm ambitious, and maybe there's truth in that too. But I'm in love with what I do. I enjoy sitting at my desk like a child playing with his toys. It's work, essentially, but it's fun and games also.

INTERVIEWER

Orhan, your namesake and the narrator of *Snow,* describes himself as a clerk who sits down at the same time every day. Do you have the same discipline for writing?

PAMUK

I was underlining the clerical nature of the novelist as opposed to that of the poet, who has an immensely prestigious tradition in

Turkey. To be a poet is a popular and respected thing. Most of the Ottoman sultans and statesmen were poets. But not in the way we understand poets now. For hundreds of years it was a way of establishing yourself as an intellectual. Most of these people used to collect their poems in manuscripts called divans. In fact, Ottoman court poetry is called divan poetry. Half of the Ottoman statesmen produced divans. It was a sophisticated and educated way of writing things, with many rules and rituals. Very conventional and very repetitive. After Western ideas came to Turkey, this legacy was combined with the romantic and modern idea of the poet as a person who burns for truth. It added extra weight to the prestige of the poet. On the other hand, a novelist is essentially a person who covers distance through his patience, slowly, like an ant. A novelist impresses us not by his demonic and romantic vision, but by his patience.

INTERVIEWER

Have you ever written poetry?

PAMUK

I am often asked that. I did when I was eighteen and I published some poems in Turkey, but then I quit. My explanation is that I realized that a poet is someone through whom God is speaking. You have to be possessed by poetry. I tried my hand at poetry, but I realized after some time that God was not speaking to me. I was sorry about this and then I tried to imagine—if God were speaking through me, what would he be saying? I began to write very meticulously, slowly, trying to figure this out. That is prose writing, fiction writing. So I worked like a clerk. Some other writers consider this expression to be a bit of an insult. But I accept it; I work like a clerk.

INTERVIEWER

Would you say that writing prose has become easier for you over time?

PAMUK

Unfortunately not. Sometimes I feel my character should enter a room and I still don't know how to make him enter. I may have more self-confidence, which sometimes can be unhelpful because then you're not experimenting, you just write what comes to the tip of your pen. I've been writing fiction for the last thirty years, so I should think that I've improved a bit. And yet I still sometimes come to a dead end where I thought there never would be one. A character cannot enter a room, and I don't know what to do. Still! After thirty years.

The division of a book into chapters is very important for my way of thinking. When writing a novel, if I know the whole story line in advance—and most of the time I do—I divide it into chapters and think up the details of what I'd like to happen in each. I don't necessarily start with the first chapter and write all the others in order. When I'm blocked, which is not a grave thing for me, I continue with whatever takes my fancy. I may write from the first to the fifth chapter, then if I'm not enjoying it I skip to number fifteen and continue from there.

INTERVIEWER

Do you mean that you map out the entire book in advance?

PAMUK

Everything. *My Name Is Red,* for instance, has many characters, and to each character I assigned a certain number of chapters. When I was writing, sometimes I wanted to continue "being" one of the characters. So when I finished writing one of Shekure's chapters, perhaps chapter seven, I skipped to chapter eleven, which is her again. I liked being Shekure. Skipping from one character or persona to another can be depressing.

But the final chapter I always write at the end. That is definite. I like to tease myself, ask myself what the ending should be. I can only execute the ending once. Toward the end, before finishing, I stop and rewrite most of the early chapters.

INTERVIEWER

Do you ever have a reader while you are working?

PAMUK

I always read my work to the person I share my life with. I'm always grateful if that person says, Show me more, or, Show me what you have done today. Not only does that provide a bit of necessary pressure, but it's like having a mother or father pat you on the back and say, Well done. Occasionally, the person will say, Sorry, I don't buy this. Which is good. I like that ritual.

I'm always reminded of Thomas Mann, one of my role models. He used to bring the whole family together, his six children and his wife. He used to read to all his gathered family. I like that. Daddy telling a story.

INTERVIEWER

When you were young you wanted to be a painter. When did your love of painting give way to your love of writing?

PAMUK

At the age of twenty-two. Since I was seven I had wanted to be a painter, and my family had accepted this. They all thought that I would be a famous painter. But then something happened in my head—I realized that a screw was loose—and I stopped painting and immediately began writing my first novel.

INTERVIEWER

A screw was loose?

PAMUK

I can't say what my reasons were for doing this. I recently published a book called *Istanbul*. Half of it is my autobiography until that moment and the other half is an essay about Istanbul, or more precisely, a child's vision of Istanbul. It's a combination of thinking about images and landscapes and the chemistry of a city, and a child's perception of that city, and that child's autobiography. The last sentence of the book reads, " 'I don't want to be an artist,' I said. 'I'm going to be a writer.' " And it's not explained. Although reading the whole book may explain something.

INTERVIEWER

Was your family happy about this decision?

PAMUK

My mother was upset. My father was somewhat more understanding because in his youth he wanted to be a poet and translated Valéry into Turkish, but gave up when he was mocked by the upper-class circle to which he belonged.

INTERVIEWER

Your family accepted you being a painter, but not a novelist?

PAMUK

Yes, because they didn't think I would be a full-time painter. The family tradition was in civil engineering. My grandfather was a civil engineer who made lots of money building railroads. My uncles and my father lost the money, but they all went to the same engineering school, Istanbul Technical University. I was expected to go there and I said, All right, I will go there. But since I was the artist in the family, the notion was that I should become an architect. It seemed to be a satisfying solution for everyone. So I went to that university, but in the middle of architectural school I suddenly quit painting and began writing novels.

INTERVIEWER

Did you already have your first novel in mind when you decided to quit? Is that why you did it?

PAMUK

As far as I remember, I wanted to be a novelist before I knew what to write. In fact, when I did start writing I had two or three false starts. I still have the notebooks. But after about six months I started a major novel project that ultimately got published as *Cevdet Bey and His Sons*.

INTERVIEWER

That hasn't been translated into English.

PAMUK

It is essentially a family saga, like the *Forsyte Saga* or Thomas Mann's *Buddenbrooks*. Not long after I finished it I began to regret having written something so outmoded, a very nineteenth-century novel. I regretted writing it because, around the age of twenty-five or twenty-six, I began to impose on myself the idea that I should be a modern author. By the time the novel was finally published, when I was thirty, my writing had become much more experimental.

INTERVIEWER

When you say you wanted to be more modern, experimental, did you have a model in mind?

PAMUK

At that time, the great writers for me were no longer Tolstoy, Dostoyevsky, Stendhal, or Thomas Mann. My heroes were Virginia Woolf and Faulkner. Now I would add Proust and Nabokov to that list.

INTERVIEWER

The opening line of *The New Life* is, "I read a book one day and my whole life was changed." Has any book had that effect on you?

PAMUK

The Sound and the Fury was very important to me when I was twenty-one or twenty-two. I bought a copy of the Penguin edition. It was hard to understand, especially with my poor English. But there was a wonderful translation of the book into Turkish, so I would put the Turkish and the English together on the table and read half a paragraph from one and then go back to the other. That book left a mark on me. The residue was the voice that I developed. I soon began to write in the first person singular. Most of the time I feel better when I'm impersonating someone else rather than writing in the third person.

INTERVIEWER

You say it took years to get your first novel published?

PAMUK

In my twenties I did not have any literary friendships; I didn't belong to any literary group in Istanbul. The only way to get my first book published was to submit it to a literary competition for unpublished manuscripts in Turkey. I did that and won the prize, which was to be published by a big, good publisher. At the time, Turkey's economy was in a bad state. They said, Yes, we'll give you a contract, but they delayed the novel's publication.

INTERVIEWER

Did your second novel go more easily—more quickly?

PAMUK

The second book was a political book. Not propaganda. I was already writing it while I waited for the first book to appear. I had given that book some two and a half years. Suddenly, one night there was a military coup. This was in 1980. The next day the would-be publisher of the first book, the *Cevdet Bey* book, said he wasn't going to publish it, even though we had a contract. I realized that even if I finished my second book—the political book—that day, I would not be able to publish it for five or six years because the military would not allow it. So my thoughts ran as follows: At the age of twenty-two I said I was going to be a novelist and wrote for seven years hoping to get something published in Turkey . . . and nothing. Now I'm almost thirty and there's no possibility of publishing anything. I still have the two hundred and fifty pages of that unfinished political novel in one of my drawers.

Immediately after the military coup, because I didn't want to get depressed, I started a third book—the book to which you referred, *The Silent House*. That's what I was working on in 1982 when the first book was finally published. *Cevdet* was well received, which meant that I could publish the book I was then writing. So the third book I wrote was the second to be published.

INTERVIEWER

What made your novel unpublishable under the military regime?

PAMUK

The characters were young upper-class Marxists. Their fathers and mothers would go to summer resorts, and they had big spacious rich houses and enjoyed being Marxists. They would fight and be jealous of one another and plot to blow up the prime minister.

INTERVIEWER

Gilded revolutionary circles?

PAMUK

Upper-class youngsters with rich people's habits, pretending to be ultraradical. But I was not making a moral judgment about that. Rather, I was romanticizing my youth, in a way. The idea of throwing a bomb at the prime minister would have been enough to get the book banned.

So I didn't finish it. And you change as you write books. You cannot assume the same persona again. You cannot continue as before. Each book an author writes represents a period in his development. One's novels can be seen as the milestones in the development of one's spirit. So you cannot go back. Once the elasticity of fiction is dead, you cannot move it again.

When you're experimenting with ideas, how do you choose the form of your novels? Do you start with an image, with a first sentence?

There is no constant formula. But I make it my business not to write two novels in the same mode. I try to change everything. This is why so many of my readers tell me, I liked this novel of yours, it's a shame you didn't write other novels like that, or, I never enjoyed one of your novels until you wrote that one—I've heard that especially about *The Black Book.* In fact I hate to hear this. It's fun, and a challenge, to experiment with form and style, and language and mood and persona, and to think about each book differently.

The subject matter of a book may come to me from various sources. With *My Name Is Red,* I wanted to write about my ambition to become a painter. I had a false start; I began to write a monographic book focused on one painter. Then I turned the painter into various painters working together in an atelier. The point of view changed, because now there were other painters talking. At first I was thinking of writing about a contemporary painter, but then I thought this Turkish painter might be too derivative, too influenced by the West, so I went back in time to write about miniaturists. That was how I found my subject.

Some subjects also necessitate certain formal innovations or storytelling strategies. Sometimes, for example, you've just seen something, or read something, or been to a movie, or read a newspaper article, and then you think, I'll make a potato speak, or a dog, or a tree. Once you get the idea you start thinking about symmetry and continuity in the novel. And you feel, Wonderful, no one's done this before.

Finally, I think of things for years. I may have ideas and then I tell them to my close friends. I keep lots of notebooks for possible novels I may write. Sometimes I don't write them, but if I open a notebook and begin taking notes for it, it is likely that I will write that novel. So when I'm finishing one novel my heart may be set on one of these projects, and two months after finishing one I start writing the other.

Many novelists will never discuss a work in progress. Do you also keep that a secret?

I never discuss the story. On formal occasions, when people ask what I'm writing, I have a one-sentence stock reply: A novel that takes place in contemporary Turkey. I open up to very few people and only when I know they won't hurt me. What I do is talk about the gimmicks—I'm going to make a cloud speak, for instance. I like to see how people react to them. It is a childish thing. I did this a lot when writing *Istanbul*. My mind is like that of a little playful child, trying to show his daddy how clever he is.

The word *gimmick* has a negative connotation.

You begin with a gimmick, but if you believe in its literary and moral seriousness, in the end it turns into serious literary invention. It becomes a literary statement.

Critics often characterize your novels as postmodern. It seems to me, however, that you draw your narrative tricks primarily from traditional sources. You quote, for instance, from the Thousand and One Nights and other classic texts in the Eastern tradition.

That began with *The Black Book,* though I had read Borges and Calvino earlier. I went with my wife to the United States in 1985, and there I first encountered the prominence and the immense richness of American culture. As a Turk coming from the Middle East, trying to establish himself as an author, I felt intimidated. So I regressed, went back to my "roots." I realized that my generation had to invent a modern national literature.

Borges and Calvino liberated me. The connotation of traditional Islamic literature was so reactionary, so political, and used
by conservatives in such old-fashioned and foolish ways, that I
never thought I could do anything with that material. But once I
was in the United States, I realized I could go back to that material
with a Calvinoesque or Borgesian mind frame. I had to begin by
making a strong distinction between the religious and literary connotations of Islamic literature, so that I could easily appropriate its
wealth of games, gimmicks, and parables. Turkey had a sophisticated tradition of highly refined ornamental literature. But then the
socially committed writers emptied our literature of its innovative
content.

There are lots of allegories that repeat themselves in the various
oral storytelling traditions—of China, India, Persia. I decided to use
them and set them in contemporary Istanbul. It's an experiment—
put everything together, like a Dadaist collage; *The Black Book* has
this quality. Sometimes all these sources are fused together and
something new emerges. So I set all these rewritten stories in Istanbul, added a detective plot, and out came *The Black Book.* But at its
source was the full strength of American culture and my desire to be
a serious experimental writer. I could not write a social commentary
about Turkey's problems—I was intimidated by them. So I had to
try something else.

INTERVIEWER

Were you ever interested in doing social commentary through literature?

PAMUK

No. I was reacting to the older generation of novelists, especially in
the eighties. I say this with all due respect, but their subject matter
was very narrow and parochial.

INTERVIEWER

Let's go back to before *The Black Book.* What inspired you to write
The White Castle? It's the first book where you employ a theme that
recurs throughout the rest of your novels—impersonation. Why do
you think this idea of becoming somebody else crops up so often in
your fiction?

It's a very personal thing. I have a very competitive brother who is only eighteen months older than me. In a way, he was my father— my Freudian father, so to speak. It was he who became my alter ego, the representation of authority. On the other hand, we also had a competitive and brotherly comradeship. A very complicated relationship. I wrote extensively about this in *Istanbul.* I was a typical Turkish boy, good at football and enthusiastic about all sorts of games and competitions. He was very successful in school, better than me. I felt jealousy toward him, and he was jealous of me, too. He was the reasonable and responsible person, the one our superiors addressed. While I was paying attention to games, he paid attention to rules. We were competing all the time. And I fancied being him, that kind of thing. It set a model. Envy, jealousy— these are heartfelt themes for me. I always worry about how much my brother's strength or his success might have influenced me. This is an essential part of my spirit. I am aware of that, so I put some distance between me and those feelings. I know they are bad, so I have a civilized person's determination to fight them. I'm not saying I'm a victim of jealousy. But this is the galaxy of nerve points that I try to deal with all the time. And of course, in the end, it becomes the subject matter of all my stories. In *The White Castle,* for instance, the almost sadomasochistic relationship between the two main characters is based on my relationship with my brother.

On the other hand, this theme of impersonation is reflected in the fragility Turkey feels when faced with Western culture. After writing *The White Castle,* I realized that this jealousy—the anxiety about being influenced by someone else—resembles Turkey's position when it looks west. You know, aspiring to become Westernized and then being accused of not being authentic enough. Trying to grab the spirit of Europe and then feeling guilty about the imitative drive. The ups and downs of this mood are reminiscent of the relationship between competitive brothers.

Do you believe the constant confrontation between Turkey's Eastern and Western impulses will ever be peacefully resolved?

I'm an optimist. Turkey should not worry about having two spirits, belonging to two different cultures, having two souls. Schizophrenia makes you intelligent. You may lose your relation with reality— I'm a fiction writer, so I don't think that's such a bad thing—but you shouldn't worry about your schizophrenia. If you worry too much about one part of you killing the other, you'll be left with a single spirit. That is worse than having the sickness. This is my theory. I try to propagate it in Turkish politics, among Turkish politicians who demand that the country should have one consistent soul—that it should belong to either the East or the West or be nationalistic. I'm critical of that monistic outlook.

INTERVIEWER

How does that go down in Turkey?

PAMUK

The more the idea of a democratic, liberal Turkey is established, the more my thinking is accepted. Turkey can join the European Union only with this vision. It's a way of fighting against nationalism, of fighting the rhetoric of Us against Them.

INTERVIEWER

And yet in *Istanbul,* in the way you romanticize the city, you seem to mourn the loss of the Ottoman Empire.

PAMUK

I'm not mourning the Ottoman Empire. I'm a Westernizer. I'm pleased that the Westernization process took place. I'm just criticizing the limited way in which the ruling elite—meaning both the bureaucracy and the new rich—had conceived of Westernization. They lacked the confidence necessary to create a national culture rich in its own symbols and rituals. They did not strive to create an Istanbul culture that would be an organic combination of East and West; they just put Western and Eastern things together. There was, of course, a strong local Ottoman culture, but that was fading away little by little. What they had to do, and could not possibly do enough, was invent a strong local culture, which would be a combination—not an imitation—of the Eastern past and the Western present. I try to do the same kind of thing in my books. Probably new generations will do it, and entering the European Union will not destroy Turkish identity but make it flourish and give us more freedom and self-confidence to invent a new Turkish culture. Slavishly imitating the West or slavishly imitating the old dead Ottoman culture is not the solution. You have to do something with these things and shouldn't have anxiety about belonging to one of them too much.

INTERVIEWER

In *Istanbul,* however, you do seem to identify with the foreign, Western gaze over your own city.

PAMUK

But I also explain why a Westernized Turkish intellectual can identify with the Western gaze—the making of Istanbul is a process of identification with the West. There is always this dichotomy, and you can easily identify with the Eastern anger too. Everyone is sometimes a Westerner and sometimes an Easterner—in fact a constant combination of the two. I like Edward Said's idea of Orientalism, but since Turkey was never a colony, the romanticizing of Turkey was never a problem for Turks. Western man did not humiliate the Turk in the same way he humiliated the Arab or Indian. Istanbul was invaded only for two years and the enemy boats left as they came, so this did not leave a deep scar in the spirit of the nation. What left a deep scar was the loss of the Ottoman Empire, so I don't have that anxiety, that feeling that Westerners look down on me. Though after the founding of the Republic, there was a sort of intimidation because Turks wanted to Westernize but couldn't go far enough, which left a feeling of cultural inferiority that we have to address and that I occasionally may have.

On the other hand, the scars are not as deep as other nations that were occupied for two hundred years, colonized. Turks were never suppressed by Western powers. The suppression that Turks suffered was self-inflicted; we erased our own history because it was practical. In that suppression there is a sense of fragility. But that self-imposed Westernization also brought isolation. Indians saw their oppressors face-to-face. Turks were strangely isolated from the

Western world they emulated. In the 1950s and even 1960s, when a foreigner came to stay at the Istanbul Hilton it would be noted in all the newspapers.

INTERVIEWER

Do you believe that there is a canon or that one should even exist? We have heard of a Western canon, but what about a non-Western canon?

PAMUK

Yes, there is another canon. It should be explored, developed, shared, criticized, and then accepted. Right now the so-called Eastern canon is in ruins. The glorious texts are all around but there is no will to put them together. From the Persian classics, through to all the Indian, Chinese, and Japanese texts, these things should be assessed critically. As it is now, the canon is in the hands of Western scholars. That is the center of distribution and communication.

INTERVIEWER

The novel is a very Western cultural form. Does it have any place in the Eastern tradition?

PAMUK

The modern novel, dissociated from the epic form, is essentially a non-Oriental thing. Because the novelist is a person who does not belong to a community, who does not share the basic instincts of community, and who is thinking and judging with a different culture than the one he is experiencing. Once his consciousness is different from that of the community he belongs to, he is an outsider, a loner. And the richness of his text comes from that outsider's voyeuristic vision.

Once you develop the habit of looking at the world like that and writing about it in this fashion, you have the desire to disassociate from the community. This is the model I was thinking about in *Snow.*

INTERVIEWER

Snow is your most political book yet published. How did you conceive of it?

PAMUK

When I started becoming famous in Turkey in the mid-1990s, at a
time when the war against Kurdish guerrillas was strong, the old
leftist authors and the new modern liberals wanted me to help them,
to sign petitions—they began to ask me to do political things unrelated to my books.

Soon the establishment counterattacked with a campaign of
character assassination. They began calling me names. I was very
angry. After a while I wondered, What if I wrote a political novel in
which I explored my own spiritual dilemmas—coming from an
upper-middle-class family and feeling responsible for those who
had no political representation? I believed in the art of the novel. It
is a strange thing how that makes you an outsider. I told myself
then, I will write a political novel. I started to write it as soon as I
finished *My Name Is Red.*

INTERVIEWER

Why did you set it in the small town of Kars?

PAMUK

It is notoriously one of the coldest towns in Turkey. And one of the
poorest. In the early eighties, the whole front page of one of the
major newspapers was about the poverty of Kars. Someone had cal-
culated that you could buy the entire town for around a million dollars. The political climate was difficult when I wanted to go there.
The vicinity of the town is mostly populated by Kurds, but the center is a combination of Kurds, people from Azerbaijan, Turks, and
all other sorts. There used to be Russians and Germans too. There
are religious differences as well, Shia and Sunni. The war the Turkish government was waging against the Kurdish guerrillas was so
fierce that it was impossible to go as a tourist. I knew I could not
simply go there as a novelist, so I asked a newspaper editor with
whom I'd been in touch for a press pass to visit the area. He is influential and he personally called the mayor and the police chief to let
them know I was coming.

As soon as I had arrived I visited the mayor and shook hands
with the police chief so that they wouldn't pick me up on the street.
Actually, some of the police who didn't know I was there did pick
me up and carried me off, probably with the intention of torturing
me. Immediately I gave names—I know the mayor, I know the

chief. . . . I was a suspicious character. Because even though Turkey is theoretically a free country, any foreigner used to be suspect until about 1999. Hopefully things are much easier today.

Most of the people and places in the book are based on a real counterpart. For instance, the local newspaper that sells 252 copies is real. I went to Kars with a camera and a video recorder. I was filming everything and then going back to Istanbul and showing it to my friends. Everyone thought I was a bit crazy. There were other things that actually occurred. Like the conversation I describe with the editor of the little newspaper who tells Ka what he did the previous day, and Ka asks how he knew, and he reveals he's been listening to the police's walkie-talkies and the police were following Ka all the time. That is real. And they were following me too.

The local anchorman put me on TV and said, Our famous author is writing an article for the national newspaper—that was a very important thing. Municipal elections were coming up, so the people of Kars opened their doors to me. They all wanted to say something to the national newspaper, to let the government know how poor they were. They did not know I was going to put them in a novel. They thought I was going to put them in an article. I must confess, this was cynical and cruel of me. Though I was actually thinking of writing an article about it too.

Four years passed. I went back and forth. There was a little coffee shop where I occasionally used to write and take notes. A photographer friend of mine, whom I had invited to come along because Kars is a beautiful place when it snows, overheard a conversation in the little coffee shop. People were talking among themselves while I wrote some notes, saying, What kind of an article is he writing? It's been three years, enough time to write a novel. They'd caught on to me.

INTERVIEWER

What was the reaction to the book?

PAMUK

In Turkey, both conservatives—or political Islamists—and secularists were upset. Not to the point of banning the book or hurting me. But they were upset and wrote about it in the daily national newspapers. The secularists were upset because I wrote that the cost of being a secular radical in Turkey is that you forget that you also

have to be a democrat. The power of the secularists in Turkey comes
from the army. This destroys Turkey's democracy and culture of tolerance. Once you have so much army involvement in political culture, people lose their self-confidence and rely on the army to solve
all their problems. People usually say, The country and the economy
are a mess, let's call in the army to clean it up. But just as they
cleaned, so did they destroy the culture of tolerance. Lots of suspects were tortured; a hundred thousand people were jailed. This
paves the way for new military coups. There was a new one about
every ten years. So I was critical of the secularists for this. They also
didn't like that I portrayed Islamists as human beings.

The political Islamists were upset because I wrote about an
Islamist who had enjoyed sex before marriage. It was that kind of
simplistic thing. Islamists are always suspicious of me because I
don't come from their culture, and because I have the language, attitude, and even gestures of a more Westernized and privileged person. They have their own problems of representation and ask, How
can he write about us anyway? He doesn't understand. This I also
included in parts of the novel.

But I don't want to exaggerate. I survived. They all read the
book. They may have become angry, but it is a sign of growing liberal attitudes that they accepted me and my book as they are. The
reaction of the people of Kars was also divided. Some said, Yes, that
is how it is. Others, usually Turkish nationalists, were nervous about
my mentions of Armenians. That TV anchorman, for instance, put
my book in a symbolic black bag and mailed it to me and said in
a press conference that I was doing Armenian propaganda—which
is, of course, preposterous. We have such a parochial, nationalistic
culture.

INTERVIEWER

Did the book ever become a cause célèbre in the Rushdie sense?

PAMUK

No, not at all.

INTERVIEWER

It's a terribly bleak, pessimistic book. The only person in the whole
novel who is able to listen to all sides—Ka—is, in the end, despised
by everyone.

I may have been dramatizing my position as a novelist in Turkey. Although he knows he is despised, he enjoys being able to maintain a dialogue with everyone. He also has a very strong survival instinct. Ka is despised because they see him as a Western spy, which is something that has been said about me many times.

About the bleakness, I agree. But humor is a way out. When people say it's bleak, I ask them, Isn't it funny? I think there is a lot of humor in it. At least that was my intention.

INTERVIEWER

Your commitment to fiction has gotten you into trouble. It is likely to get you into further trouble. It has meant severing of emotional links. It's a high price to pay.

PAMUK

Yes, but it's a wonderful thing. When I'm traveling, and not alone at my desk, after a while I get depressed. I'm happy when I'm alone in a room and inventing. More than a commitment to the art or to the craft, which I am devoted to, it is a commitment to being alone in a room. I continue to have this ritual, believing that what I am doing now will one day be published, legitimizing my daydreams. I need solitary hours at a desk with good paper and a fountain pen like some people need a pill for their health. I am committed to these rituals.

INTERVIEWER

For whom, then, are you writing?

PAMUK

As life gets shorter, you ask yourself that question more often. I've written seven novels. I would love to write another seven novels before I die. But then, life is short. What about enjoying it more? Sometimes I have to really force myself. Why am I doing it? What is the meaning of all of it? First, as I said, it's an instinct to be alone in a room. Second, there's an almost boyish competitive side in me that wants to attempt to write a nice book again. I believe less and less in eternity for authors. We are reading very few of the books written two hundred years ago. Things are changing so fast that today's books will probably be forgotten in a hundred years. Very few will be read. In two hundred years, perhaps five books written today will be alive. Am I sure I'm writing one of those five? But is that the meaning of writing? Why should I be worrying about being read two hundred years later? Shouldn't I be worried about living more? Do I need the consolation that I will be read in the future? I think of all these things and I continue to write. I don't know why. But I never give up. This belief that your books will have an effect in the future is the only consolation you have to get pleasure in this life.

You are a best-selling author in Turkey, but the books you sell at home are outnumbered by your sales abroad. You have been translated into forty languages. Do you now think about a wider global readership when writing? Are you now writing for a different audience?

PAMUK

I am aware that my audience is no longer an exclusively national audience. But even when I began writing, I may have been reaching for a wider group of readers. My father used to say behind the backs of some of his Turkish author friends that they were "only addressing the national audience."

There is a problem of being aware of one's readership, whether it is national or international. I cannot avoid this problem now. My last two books averaged more than half a million readers all over the world. I cannot deny that I am aware of their existence. On the other hand, I never feel that I do things to satisfy them. I also believe that my readers would sense it if I did. I've made it my business, from the very beginning, that whenever I sense a reader's expectations I run away. Even the composition of my sentences—I prepare the reader for something and then I surprise him. Perhaps that's why I love long sentences.

INTERVIEWER

To most non-Turkish readers, the originality of your writing has much to do with its Turkish setting. But how would you distinguish your work in a Turkish context?

PAMUK

There is the problem of what Harold Bloom called "the anxiety of influence." Like all authors, I had it when I was young. In my early thirties I kept thinking that I might have been too much influenced by Tolstoy or Thomas Mann—I aimed for that kind of gentle, aristocratic prose in my first novel. But it ultimately occurred to me that although I may have been derivative in my techniques, the fact that I was operating in this part of the world, so far away from Europe— or at least it seemed so at the time—and trying to attract such a different audience in such a different cultural and historical climate, it would grant me originality, even if it was cheaply earned. But it is also a tough job, since such techniques do not translate or travel so easily.

The formula for originality is very simple—put together two things that were not together before. Look at *Istanbul,* an essay about the city and about how certain foreign authors—Flaubert, Nerval, Gautier—viewed the city, and how their views influenced a certain group of Turkish writers. Combined with this essay on the invention of Istanbul's romantic landscape is an autobiography. No one had done this before. Take risks and you will come up with something new. I tried with *Istanbul* to make an original book. I don't know if it succeeds. *The Black Book* was like that too—combine a nostalgic Proustian world with Islamic allegories, stories, and tricks, then set them all in Istanbul and see what happens.

INTERVIEWER

Istanbul conveys the sense that you have always been a very lonely figure. You are certainly alone as a writer in modern Turkey today. You grew up and continue to live in a world from which you are detached.

PAMUK

Although I was raised in a crowded family and taught to cherish the community, I later acquired an impulse to break away. There is a self-destructive side to me, and in bouts of fury and moments of anger I do things that cut me off from the pleasant company of the community. Early in life I realized that the community kills my imagination. I need the pain of loneliness to make my imagination work. And then I'm happy. But being a Turk, after a while I need the consoling tenderness of the community, which I may have destroyed. *Istanbul* destroyed my relationship with my mother—we don't see each other anymore. And of course I hardly ever see my brother. My relationship with the Turkish public, because of my recent comments, is also difficult.

INTERVIEWER

How Turkish do you feel yourself to be, then?

PAMUK

First, I'm a born Turk. I'm happy with that. Internationally, I am perceived to be more Turkish than I actually see myself. I am known as a Turkish author. When Proust writes about love, he is seen as someone talking about universal love. Especially at the beginning, when I wrote about love, people would say that I was writing about Turkish love. When my work began to be translated, Turks were proud of it. They claimed me as their own. I was more of a Turk for them. Once you get to be internationally known, your Turkishness is underlined internationally, then your Turkishness is underlined by Turks themselves, who reclaim you. Your sense of national identity becomes something that others manipulate. It is imposed by other people. Now they are more worried about the international representation of Turkey than about my art. This causes more and more problems in my country. Through what they read in the popular press, a lot of people who don't know my books are beginning to worry about what I say to the outside world about Turkey. Literature is made of good and bad, demons and angels, and more and more they are only worried about my demons.

TO LOOK OUT THE WINDOW

A Story

I.

If there's nothing to watch and no stories to listen to, life can get tedious. When I was a child, boredom was something we fought off by listening to the radio or looking out the window into neighboring apartments or at people passing in the street below. In those days, in 1958, there was still no television in Turkey. But we didn't like to admit it: We talked about television optimistically, just as we did the Hollywood adventure films that took four or five years to reach Istanbul's film theaters, saying it "had yet to arrive."

Looking out the window was such an important pastime that when television did finally come to Turkey, people acted the same way in front of their sets as they had in front of their windows. When my father, my uncles, and my grandmother watched television, they would argue without looking at one another, pausing now and again to report on what they'd just seen, just as they did while gazing out the window.

"If if keeps snowing like this, it's going to stick," my aunt would say, looking at the snowflakes swirling past.

"That man who sells *helva* is back on the Nişantaşı corner!" I would say, peering from the other window, which looked out over the avenue with the streetcar lines.

On Sundays, we'd go upstairs with my uncles and aunts and everyone else who lived in the downstairs apartments to have lunch with my grandmother. As I stood at the window, waiting for the food to arrive, I'd be so happy to be there with my mother, my father, my aunts, and my uncles that everything before me seemed to glow with the pale light of the crystal chandelier hanging over the long dining table. My grandmother's sitting room was dark, as were the downstairs sitting rooms, but to me it always seemed darker. Maybe this was because of the tulle curtains and the heavy drapes that hung at either side of the never-opened balcony doors, casting fearsome shadows. Or maybe it was the screens inlaid with mother-of-pearl, the massive tables, the chests, and the baby grand piano, with all those framed photographs on top, or the general clutter of this airless room that always smelled of dust.

The meal was over, and my uncle was smoking in one of the dark adjoining rooms. "I have a ticket to a football match, but I'm not going," he'd say. "Your father is going to take you instead."

"Daddy, take us to the football match!" my older brother would cry from the other room.

"The children could use some fresh air," my mother would call from the sitting room.

"Then you take them out," my father said to my mother.

"I'm going to my mother's," my mother replied.

"We don't want to go to Granny's," said my brother.

"You can have the car," said my uncle.

"Please, Daddy!" said my brother.

There was a long, strange silence. It was as if everyone in the room was thinking certain thoughts about my mother, and as if my father could tell what those thoughts were.

"So you're giving me your car, are you?" my father asked my uncle.

Later, when we had gone downstairs, while my mother was helping us put on our pullovers and our thick checked woolen socks, my father paced up and down the corridor, smoking a cigarette. My uncle had parked his "elegant, cream colored" '52 Dodge in front of the Teşvikiye Mosque. My father allowed both of us to sit in the front seat and managed to get the motor started with one turn of the key.

There was no line at the stadium. "This ticket for the two of them," said my father to the man at the turnstile. "One is eight, and the other is ten." As we went through, we were afraid to look into the man's eyes. There were lots of empty seats in the stands, and we sat down at once.

The two teams had already come out to the muddy field, and I enjoyed watching the players run up and down in their dazzling white shorts to warm up. "Look, that's Little Mehmet," said my brother, pointing to one of them. "He's just come from the junior team."

"We know."

The match began, and for a long time we didn't speak. A while later my thoughts wandered from the match to other things. Why did footballers all wear the same strip when their names were all different? I imagined that there were no longer players running up and down the field, just names. Their shorts were getting dirtier and dirtier. A while later, I watched a ship with an interesting smokestack passing slowly down the Bosphorus, just behind the bleachers. No one had scored by halftime, and my father bought us each a cone of chickpeas and a cheese pita.

"Daddy, I can't finish this," I said, showing him what was left in my hand.

"Put it over there," he said. "No one will see you."

We got up and moved around to warm up, just like everyone else. Like our father, we had shoved our hands into the pockets of our woolen trousers and turned away from the field to look at the people sitting behind us, when someone in the crowd called out to my father. My father brought his hand to his ear, to indicate that he couldn't hear a thing with all the noise.

"I can't come," he said, as he pointed in our direction. "I have my children with me."

The man in the crowd was wearing a purple scarf. He fought his way to our row, pushing the seatbacks and shoving quite a few people to reach us.

"Are these your boys?" he asked, after he had embraced my father. "They're so big. I can hardly believe it."

My father said nothing.

"So when did these children appear?" said the man, looking at us admiringly. "Did you get married as soon as you finished school?"

"Yes," said my father, without looking him in his face. They spoke for a while longer. The man with the purple scarf turned to my brother and me and put an unshelled American peanut into each of our palms. When he left, my father sat down in his seat and for a long time said nothing.

Not long after the two teams had returned to the field in fresh shorts, my father said, "Come on, let's go home. You're getting cold."

"I'm not getting cold," said my brother.

"Yes, you are," said my father. "And Ali's cold. Come on, let's get going."

As we were making our way past the others in our row, jostling against knees and sometimes stepping on feet, we stepped on the cheese

pita I'd left on the ground. As we walked down the stairs, we heard the
referee blowing his whistle to signal the start of the second half.

"Were you getting cold?" my brother asked. "Why didn't you say you
weren't cold?" I stayed quiet. "Idiot," said my brother.

"You can listen to the second half on the radio at home," said my
father.

"This match is not on the radio," my brother said.

"Quiet, now," said my father. "I'm taking you through Taksim on our
way back."

We stayed quiet. Driving across the square, my father stopped the car
just before we got to the off-track betting shop—just as we'd guessed.
"Don't open the door for anyone," he said. "I'll be back in a moment."

He got out of the car. Before he had a chance to lock the car from the
outside, we'd pressed down on the buttons and locked it from the inside.
But my father didn't go into the betting shop; he ran over to the other
side of the cobblestone street. There was a shop over there that was decorated with posters of ships, big plastic airplanes, and sunny landscapes,
and it was even open on Sundays, and that's where he went.

"Where did Daddy go?"

"Are we going to play upstairs or downstairs when we get home?" my
brother asked.

When my father got back, my brother was playing with the accelera-
tor. We drove back to Nişantaşı and parked again in front of the mosque.
"Why don't I buy you something!" said my father. "But please, don't ask
for that Famous People series again."

"Oh, please, Daddy!" we pleaded.

When we got to Alaaddin's shop, my father bought us each ten packs
of chewing gum from the Famous People series. We went into our building; I was so excited by the time we got into the lift that I thought I might
wet my pants. It was warm inside and my mother wasn't back yet. We
ripped open the chewing gum, throwing the wrappers on the floor. The
result:

I got two Field Marshal Fevzi Çakmaks; one each of Charlie Chaplin, the wrestler Hamit Kaplan, Gandhi, Mozart, and De Gaulle; two
Atatürks, and one Greta Garbo—number 21—which my brother didn't
have yet. With these I now had 173 pictures of Famous People, but I still
needed another 27 to complete the series. My brother got four Field Marshal Fevzi Çakmaks, five Atatürks, and one Edison. We tossed the chewing gum into our mouths and began to read the writing on the backs of
the cards.

Field Marshal Fevzi Çakmak
General in the War of Independence
(1876–1950)

MAMBO SWEETS CHEWING GUM, INC
*A leather soccer ball will be awarded to the lucky person
who collects all 100 famous people.*

My brother was holding his stack of 165 cards. "Do you want to play
Tops or Bottoms?"

"No."

"Would you give me your Greta Garbo for my twelve Fevzi Çakmaks?" he asked. "Then you'll have one hundred and eighty-four cards."

"No."

"But now you have two Greta Garbos."

I said nothing.

"When they do our inoculations at school tomorrow, it's really going
to hurt," he said. "Don't expect me to take care of you, okay?"

"I wouldn't anyway."

We ate supper in silence. When *World of Sports* came on the radio, we
found out that the match had been a draw, 2–2, and then our mother came
into our room to put us to bed. My brother started getting his bag ready
for school, and I ran into the sitting room. My father was at the window,
staring down at the street.

"Daddy, I don't want to go to school tomorrow."

"Now how can you say that?"

"They're giving us those inoculations tomorrow. I come down with a
fever, and then I can hardly breathe. Ask Mummy."

He looked at me, saying nothing. I raced over to the drawer and got
out a pen and a piece of paper.

"Does your mother know about this?" he asked, putting the paper
down on the volume of Kierkegaard that he was always reading but
never managed to finish. "You're going to school, but you won't have
that injection," he said. "That's what I'll write."

He signed his name. I blew on the ink and then folded up the paper
and put it in my pocket. Running back to the bedroom, I slipped it
into my bag, and then I climbed up onto my bed and began to bounce
on it.

"Calm down," said my mother. "It's time to go to sleep."

2.

I was at school, and it was just after lunch. The whole class was lined up two by two, and we were going back to that stinking cafeteria to have our inoculations. Some children were crying; others were waiting in nervous anticipation. When a whiff of iodine floated up the stairs, my heart began to race. I stepped out of line and went over to the teacher standing at the head of the stairs. The whole class passed us noisily.

"Yes?" said the teacher. "What is it?"

I took out the piece of paper my father had signed and gave it to the teacher. She read it with a frown. "Your father's not a doctor, you know," she said. She paused to think. "Go upstairs. Wait in Room Two-A."

There were six or seven children in 2-A who like me had been excused. One was staring in terror out the window. Cries of panic came floating down the corridor; a fat boy with glasses was munching on pumpkin seeds and reading a Kinova comic book. The door opened and in came thin, gaunt Deputy Headmaster Seyfi Bey.

"Probably some of you are genuinely ill, and if you are, we won't take you downstairs," he said. "But I have this to say to those of you who've lied to get excused. One day you will grow up, serve our country, and maybe even die for it. Today it's just an injection you're running away from—but if you try something like this when you grow up, and if you don't have a genuine excuse, you'll be guilty of treason. Shame on you!"

There was a long silence. I looked at Atatürk's picture, and tears came to my eyes.

Later, we slipped unnoticed back to our classrooms. The children who'd had their inoculations started coming back: Some had their sleeves rolled up, some had tears in their eyes, some scuffled in with very long faces.

"Children living close by can go home," said the teacher. "Children with no one to pick them up must wait until the last bell. Don't punch one another on the arm! Tomorrow there's no school."

Everyone started shouting. Some were holding their arms as they left the building; others stopped to show the janitor, Hilmi Efendi, the iodine tracks on their arms.

When I got out to the street, I slung my bag over my shoulder and began to run. A horse cart had blocked traffic in front of Karabet's butcher shop, so I weaved between the cars to get to our building on the other side. I ran past Hayri's fabric shop and Salih's florist shop. Our janitor, Hazim Efendi, let me in.

"What are you doing here all alone at this hour?" he asked.

"They gave us our inoculations today. They let us out early."

"Where's your brother? Did you come back alone?"

"I crossed the streetcar lines by myself. Tomorrow we have the day off."

"Your mother's out," he said. "Go up to your grandmother's."

"I'm ill," I said. "I want to go to our house. Open the door for me."

He took a key off the wall and we got into the lift. By the time we had reached our floor, his cigarette had filled the whole cage with smoke that burned my eyes. He opened our door. "Don't play with the electrical sockets," he said, as he pulled the door closed.

There was no one at home, but I still shouted out, "Is anyone here, anyone home? Isn't there anyone home?" I threw down my bag, opened up my brother's drawer, and began to look at the film ticket collection he'd never shown me. Then I had a good long look at the pictures of football matches that he'd cut out of newspapers and glued into a book. I could tell from the footsteps that it wasn't my mother coming in now, it was my father. I put my brother's tickets and his scrapbook back where they belonged, carefully, so he wouldn't know I'd been looking at them.

My father was in his bedroom; he'd opened up his wardrobe and was looking inside.

"You're home already, are you?"

"No, I'm in Paris," I said, the way they did at school.

"Didn't you go to school today?"

"Today they gave us our inoculations."

"Isn't your brother here?" he asked. "All right then, go to your room and show me how quiet you can be."

I did as he asked. I pressed my forehead against the window and looked outside. From the sounds coming from the hallway I could tell that my father had taken one of the suitcases out of the cupboard there. He went back into his room and began to take his jackets and his trousers out of the wardrobe; I could tell from the rattling of the hangers. He began to open and close the drawers where he kept his shirts, his socks, and his underpants. I listened to him put them all into the suitcase. He went into the bathroom and came out again. He snapped the suitcase latches shut and turned the lock. He came to join me in my room.

"So what have you been up to in here?"

"I've been looking out the window."

"Come here, let's look out the window together."

He took me on his lap, and for a long time we looked out the window together. The tips of the tall cypress tree that stood between us and the apartment building opposite began to sway in the wind. I liked the way my father smelled.

"I'm going far away," he said. He kissed me. "Don't tell your mother. I'll tell her myself later."

"Are you going by plane?"

"Yes," he said, "to Paris. Don't tell this to anyone either." He took a huge two-and-a-half-lira coin from his pocket and gave it to me, and then he kissed me again. "And don't say you saw me here."

I put the money right into my pocket. When my father had lifted me from his lap and picked up his suitcase, I said, "Don't go, Daddy." He kissed me one more time, and then he left.

I watched him from the window. He walked straight to Alaaddin's store, and then he stopped a passing taxi. Before he got in, he looked up at our apartment one more time and waved. I waved back, and he took off.

I looked at the empty avenue for a long, long time. A streetcar passed, and then the water seller's horse cart. I rang the bell and called Hazim Efendi.

"Did you ring the bell?" he said, when he got to the door. "Don't play with the bell."

"Take this two-and-a-half-lira coin," I said, "go to Alaaddin's shop, and buy me ten chewing gums from the Famous People series. Don't forget to bring back the fifty kuruş change."

"Did your father give you this money?" he asked. "Let's hope your mother doesn't get angry."

I said nothing, and he left. I stood at the window and watched him go into Alaaddin's shop. He came out a little later. On his way back, he ran into the janitor from the Marmara Apartments across the way, and they stopped to chat.

When he came back, he gave me the change. I immediately ripped open the chewing gum: three more Fevzi Çakmaks, one Atatürk, and one each of Leonardo da Vinci and Süleyman the Magnificent, Churchill, General Franco, and one more number 21, the Greta Garbo that my brother still didn't have. So now I had 183 pictures in all. But to complete the full set of 100, I still needed 26 more.

I was admiring my first 91, which showed the plane in which Lindbergh had crossed the Atlantic, when I heard a key in the door. My mother! I quickly gathered up the gum wrappers that I had thrown on the floor and put them in the bin.

"We had our inoculations today, so I came home early," I said. "Typhoid, typhus, tetanus."

"Where's your brother?"

"His class hadn't had their inoculations yet," I said. "They sent us home. I crossed the avenue all by myself."

"Does your arm hurt?"

I said nothing. A little later, my brother came home. His arm was hurting. He lay down on his bed, resting on his other arm, and looked miserable as he fell asleep. It was very dark out by the time he woke up. "Mummy, it hurts a lot," he said.

"You might have a fever later on," my mother said, as she was ironing in the other room. "Ali, is your arm hurting too? Lie down, keep still."

We went to bed and kept still. After sleeping for a little my brother woke up and began to read the sports page, and then he told me it was because of me that we'd left the match early yesterday, and because we'd left early our team had missed four goals.

"Even if we hadn't left, we might not have made those goals," I said.

"What?"

After dozing a little longer, my brother offered me six Fevzi Çakmaks, four Atatürks, and three other cards I already had in exchange for one Greta Garbo, and I turned him down.

"Shall we play Tops or Bottoms?" he asked me.

"Okay, let's play."

You press the whole stack between the palms of your hands. You ask, "Tops or Bottoms?" If he says Bottoms, you look at the bottom picture, let's say number 68, Rita Hayworth. Now let's say it's number 18, Dante the Poet, on top. If it is, then Bottoms wins and you give him the picture you like the least, the one you already have the most of. Field Marshal Fevzi Çakmak pictures passed back and forth between us until it was evening and time for supper.

"One of you go upstairs and take a look," said my mother. "Maybe your father's come back."

We both went upstairs. My uncle was sitting, smoking, with my grandmother; my father wasn't there. We listened to the news on the radio, we read the sports page. When my grandmother sat down to eat, we went downstairs.

"What kept you?" said my mother. "You didn't eat anything up there, did you? Why don't I give you your lentil soup now. You can eat it very slowly until your father gets home."

"Isn't there any toasted bread?" my brother asked.

While we were silently eating our soup, our mother watched us. From the way she held her head and the way her eyes darted away from us, I knew she was listening for the lift. When we finished our soup, she asked, "Would you like some more?" She glanced into the pot. "Why don't I have mine before it gets cold," she said. But instead she went to the window and looked down at Nişantaşı Square; she stood there looking for some time. Then she turned around, came back to the table, and began to eat her soup. My brother and I were discussing yesterday's match.

"Be quiet! Isn't that the lift?"

We fell quiet and listened carefully. It wasn't the lift. A streetcar broke the silence, shaking the table, the glasses, the pitcher, and the water inside it. When we were eating our oranges, we all definitely heard the lift. It came closer and closer, but it didn't stop at our floor; it went right up to my grandmother's. "It went all the way up," said my mother.

After we had finished eating, my mother said, "Take your plates to the kitchen. Leave your father's plate where it is." We cleared the table. My father's clean plate sat alone on the empty table for a long time.

My mother went over to the window that looked down at the police station; she stood there looking for a long time. Then suddenly she made up her mind. Gathering up my father's knife and fork and empty plate, she took them into the kitchen. "I'm going upstairs to your grand-mother's," she said. "Please don't get into a fight while I'm gone."

My brother and I went back to our game of Tops or Bottoms.

"Tops," I said, for the first time.

He revealed the top card: number 34, Koca Yusuf, the world-famous wrestler. He pulled out the card from the bottom of the stack: number 50, Atatürk. "You lose. Give me a card."

We played for a long time and he kept on winning. Soon he had taken nineteen of my twenty Fevzi Çakmaks and two of my Atatürks.

"I'm not playing anymore," I said, getting angry. "I'm going upstairs. To Mummy."

"Mummy will get angry."

"Coward! Are you afraid of being home all alone?"

My grandmother's door was open as usual. Supper was over. Bekir, the cook, was washing the dishes; my uncle and my grandmother were sitting across from each other. My mother was at the window looking down on Nişantaşı Square.

"Come," she said, still looking out the window. I moved straight into the empty space that seemed to be reserved just for me. Leaning against her, I too looked down at Nişantaşı Square. My mother put her hand on my head and gently stroked my hair.

"Your father came home early this afternoon, I hear. You saw him."

"Yes."

"He took his suitcase and left. Hazim Efendi saw him."

"Yes."

"Did he tell you where he was going, darling?"

"No," I said. "He gave me two and a half lira."

Down in the street, everything—the dark stores along the avenue, the car lights, the little empty space in the middle where the traffic policemen stood, the wet cobblestones, the letters on the advertising boards that hung from the trees—everything was lonely and sad. It began to rain, and my mother passed her fingers slowly through my hair.

That was when I noticed that the radio that sat between my grandmother's chair and my uncle's—the radio that was always on—was silent. A chill passed through me.

"Don't stand there like that, my girl," my grandmother said then.

My brother had come upstairs.

"Go to the kitchen, you two," said my uncle. "Bekir!" he called. "Make these boys a ball; they can play football in the hallway."

In the kitchen, Bekir had finished the dishes. "Sit down over there," he said. He went out to the glass-enclosed balcony that my grandmother had turned into a greenhouse and brought back a pile of newspapers that he began to crumple into a ball. When it was as big as a fist, he asked, "Is this good enough?"

"Wrap a few more sheets around it," said my brother.

While Bekir was wrapping a few more sheets of newsprint around the ball, I looked through the doorway to watch my mother, my grandmother, and my uncle on the other side. With a rope he took from a drawer, Bekir bound the paper ball until it was as round as it could be. To soften its sharp edges, he wiped it lightly with a damp rag and then he compressed it again. My brother couldn't resist touching it.

"Wow. It's hard as a rock."

"Put your finger down there for me." My brother carefully placed his finger on the spot where the last knot was to be tied. Bekir tied the knot and the ball was done. He tossed it into the air and we began to kick it around.

"Play in the hallway," said Bekir. "If you play in here, you'll break something."

For a long time we gave our game everything we had. I was pretending to be Lefter from Fenerbahçe, and I twisted and turned like he did. Whenever I did a wall pass, I ran into my brother's bad arm. He hit me, too, but it didn't hurt. We were both perspiring, the ball was falling to pieces, and I was winning five to three when I hit his bad arm very hard. He threw himself down on the floor and began to cry.

"When my arm gets better I'm going to kill you!" he said, as he lay there.

He was angry because he'd lost. I left the hallway for the sitting room; my grandmother, my mother, and my uncle had all gone into the study. My grandmother was dialing the phone.

"Hello, my girl," she said then, in the same voice she used when she called my mother the same thing. "Is that Yeşilköy Airport? Listen, my girl, we want to make an inquiry about a passenger who flew out to Europe earlier today." She gave my father's name and twisted the phone cord around her finger while she waited. "Bring me my cigarettes," she said then to my uncle. When my uncle had left the room, she took the receiver away from her ear.

"Please, my girl, tell us," my grandmother said to my mother. "You would know. Is there another woman?"

I couldn't hear my mother's answer. My grandmother was looking at her as if she hadn't said a thing. Then the person at the other end of the line said something and she got angry. "They're not going to tell us," she said, when my uncle returned with a cigarette and an ashtray.

My mother saw my uncle looking at me, and that was when she noticed I was there. Taking me by the arm, she pulled me back into the hallway. When she'd felt my back and the nape of my neck, she saw how much I'd perspired, but she didn't get angry at me.

"Mummy, my arm hurts," said my brother.

"You two go downstairs now, I'll put you both to bed."

Downstairs on our floor, the three of us were silent for a long time. Before I went to bed I padded into the kitchen in my pajamas for a glass of water, and then I went into the sitting room. My mother was smoking in front of the window, and at first she didn't hear me.

"You'll catch cold in those bare feet," she said. "Is your brother in bed?"

"He's asleep. Mummy, I'm going to tell you something." I waited for my mother to make room for me at the window. When she had opened up that sweet space for me, I sidled into it. "Daddy went to Paris," I said. "And you know what suitcase he took?"

She said nothing. In the silence of the night, we watched the rainy street for a very long time.

3.

My other grandmother's house was next to Şişli Mosque and the end of the streetcar line. Now the square is full of minibus and municipal bus stops, and high ugly buildings and department stores plastered with signs, and offices whose workers spill out onto the pavements at lunchtime and look like ants, but in those days it was at the edge of the European city. It took us fifteen minutes to walk from our house to the wide cobblestone square, and as we walked hand in hand with my mother under the linden and mulberry trees, we felt as if we had come to the countryside.

My other grandmother lived in a four-story stone and concrete house that looked like a matchbox turned on its side; it faced Istanbul to the west and in the back the mulberry groves in the hills. After her husband died and her three daughters were married, my grandmother had taken to living in a single room of this house, which was crammed with wardrobes, tables, trays, pianos, and other furniture. My aunt would cook her food and bring it over or pack it in a metal container and have her driver deliver it for her. It wasn't just that my grandmother would not leave her room to go two flights down to the kitchen to cook; she didn't even go into the other rooms of the house, which were covered with a thick blanket of dust and silky cobwebs. Like her own mother, who had spent her last years alone in a great wooden mansion, my grandmother had succumbed to a mysterious solitary disease and would not even permit a caretaker or a daily cleaner.

When we went to visit her, my mother would press down on the bell for a very long time and pound on the iron door, until my grandmother would at last open the rusty iron shutters on the second-floor window overlooking the mosque and peer down on us, and because she didn't trust her eyes—she could no longer see very far—she would ask us to wave at her.

"Come out of the doorway so your grandmother can see you, children," said my mother. Coming out into the middle of the pavement with us, she waved and cried, "Mother dear, it's me and the children; it's us, can you hear us?"

We understood from her sweet smile that she had recognized us. At once she drew back from the window, went into her room, took out the large key she kept under her pillow, and, after wrapping it in newsprint, threw it down. My brother and I pushed and shoved each other, struggling to catch it.

My brother's arm was still hurting, and that slowed him down, so I got to the key first, and I gave it to my mother. With some effort, my mother managed to unlock the great iron door. The door slowly yielded as the three of us pushed against it, and out from the darkness came that smell I would never come across again: decay, mold, dust, age, and stagnant air. On the coat rack right next to the door—to make the frequent robbers think there was a man in the house—my grandmother had left my grandfather's felt hat and his fur-collared coat, and in the corner were the boots that always scared me so.

A little later, at the end of two straight flights of wooden stairs, far, far away, standing in a white light, we saw our grandmother. She looked like a ghost, standing perfectly still in the shadows with her cane, lit only by the light filtering through the frosted Art Deco doors.

As she walked up the creaking stairs, my mother said nothing to my grandmother. (Sometimes she would say, "How are you, darling Mother?" or "Mother dear, I've missed you; it's very cold out, dear Mother!") When I reached the top of the stairs, I kissed my grandmother's hand, trying not to look at her face, or the huge mole on her wrist. But still we were frightened by the lone tooth in her mouth, her long chin, and the whiskers on her face, so once we were in the room we huddled next to our mother. My grandmother went back to the bed, where she spent most of the day in her long nightgown and her woolen vest, and she smiled at us, giving us a look that said, All right, now entertain me.

"Your stove isn't working so well, Mother," said my mother. She took the poker and stirred the coals.

My grandmother waited for a while, and then she said, "Leave the stove alone now. Give me some news. What's going on in the world?"

"Nothing at all," said my mother, sitting at our side.

"You have nothing to tell me at all?"

"Nothing at all, Mother dear."

After a short silence, my grandmother asked, "Haven't you seen anyone?"

"You know that already, Mother dear."

"For God's sake, have you no news?"

There was a silence.

"Grandmother, we had our inoculations at school," I said.

"Is that so?" said my grandmother, opening up her large blue eyes as if she were surprised. "Did it hurt?"

"My arm still hurts," said my brother.

"Oh, dear," said my grandmother with a smile.

There was another long silence. My brother and I got up and looked out the window at the hills in the distance, the mulberry trees, and the empty old chicken coop in the back garden.

"Don't you have any stories for me at all?" pleaded my grandmother. "You go up to see the mother-in-law. Doesn't anyone else?"

"Dilruba Hanım came yesterday afternoon," said my mother. "They played bezique with the children's grandmother."

In a rejoicing voice, our grandmother then said what we'd expected: "That's the palace lady!"

We knew she was talking not about one of the cream-colored palaces we read so much about in fairy tales and newspapers in those years but about Dolmabahçe Palace; it was only much later I realized that my grandmother looked down on Dilruba Hanım—who had come from the last sultan's harem—because she had been a concubine before marrying a businessman, and that she also looked down on my grandmother for having befriended this woman. Then they moved to another subject that they discussed every time my mother visited: Once a week, my grandmother would go to Beyoğlu to lunch alone at a famous and expensive restaurant called Aptullah Efendi, and afterward she would complain at great length about everything she'd eaten. She opened the third ready-made topic by asking us this question: "Children, does your other grandmother make you eat parsley?"

We answered with one voice, saying what our mother told us to say. "No, Grandmother, she doesn't."

As always, our grandmother told us how she'd seen a cat peeing on parsley in a garden, and how it was highly likely that the same parsley had ended up barely washed in some idiot's food, and how she was still arguing about this with the greengrocers of Şişli and Nişantaşı.

"Mother dear," said my mother, "the children are getting bored; they want to take a look at the other rooms. I'm going to open up the room next door."

My grandmother locked all the rooms in the house from the outside, to keep any thief who might enter through a window from reaching any other room in the house. My mother opened up the large cold room that looked out on the avenue with the streetcar line, and for a moment she stood there with us, looking at the armchairs and the divans under their dust covers, the rusty, dusty lamps, trays, and chairs, the bundles of old newspaper; at the worn saddle and the drooping handlebars of the creaky girl's bicycle listing in the corner. But she did not take anything out of the trunk to show us, as she had done on happier days. ("Your mother used to wear these sandals when she was little, children; look at your aunt's school uniform, children; would you like to see your mother's childhood piggy bank, children?")

"If you get cold, come and tell me," she said, and then she left.

My brother and I ran to the window to look at the mosque and the streetcar in the square. Then we read about old football matches in the newspapers. "I'm bored," I said. "Do you want to play Tops or Bottoms?"

"The defeated wrestler still wants to fight," said my brother, without looking up from his newspaper. "I'm reading the paper."

We'd played again that morning, and my brother had won again.

"Please."

"I have one condition: If I win, you have to give me two pictures, and if you win, I only give you one."

"No, one."

"Then I'm not playing," said my brother. "As you can see, I'm reading the paper."

He held the paper just like the English detective in a black-and-white film we'd seen recently at the Angel Theater. After looking out the window a little longer, I agreed to my brother's conditions. We took our Famous People cards from our pockets and began to play. First I won, but then I lost seventeen more cards.

"When we play this way, I always lose," I said. "I'm not playing anymore unless we go back to the old rules."

"Okay," said my brother, still imitating that detective. "I wanted to read those newspapers anyway."

For a while I looked out the window. I carefully counted my pictures: I had 121 left. When my father left the day before, I'd had 183! But I didn't want to think about it. I had agreed to my brother's conditions.

In the beginning, I'd been winning, but then he started winning again. Hiding his joy, he didn't smile when he took my cards and added them to his pack.

"If you want, we can play by some other rules," he said, a while later. "Whoever wins takes one card. If I win, I can choose which card I take from you. Because I don't have any of some of them, and you never give me those."

Thinking I would win, I agreed. I don't know how it happened. Three times in a row I lost my high card to his, and before I knew it I had lost both my Greta Garbos (21) and my only King Faruk (78). I wanted to take them all back at once, so the game got bigger: This was how a great many other cards I had and he didn't—Einstein (63), Rumi (3), Sarkis Nazaryan, the founder of Mambo Chewing Gum–Candied Fruit Company (100), and Cleopatra (51)—passed over to him in only two rounds.

I couldn't even swallow. Because I was afraid I might cry, I ran to the window and looked outside: How beautiful everything had seemed only five minutes earlier—the streetcar approaching the terminus, the apartment buildings visible in the distance through the branches that were losing their leaves, the dog lying on the cobblestones, scratching himself so lazily! If only time had stopped. If only we could go back five squares as we did when we played Horse Race Dice. I was never playing Tops or Bottoms with my brother again.

"Shall we play again?" I said, without taking my forehead off the windowpane.

"I'm not playing," said my brother. "You'll only cry."

"Cevat, I promise. I won't cry," I insisted, as I went to his side. "But we have to play the way we did at the beginning, by the old rules."

"I'm going to read my paper."

"Okay," I said. I shuffled my thinner-than-ever stack. "With the old rules. Tops or Bottoms?"

"No crying," he said. "Okay, high."

I won and he gave me one of his Field Marshal Fevzi Çakmaks. I wouldn't take it. "Can you please give me seventy-eight, King Faruk?"

"No," he said. "That isn't what we agreed."

We played two more rounds, and I lost. If only I hadn't played that third round: When I gave him my 49, Napoleon, my hand was shaking.

"I'm not playing anymore," said my brother.

I pleaded. We played two more rounds, and instead of giving him the pictures he asked for, I threw all the cards I had left at his head and into the air: the cards I had been collecting for two and a half months, thinking about each and every one of them every single day, hiding them and nervously accumulating them with care—number 28, Mae West, and 82, Jules Verne; 7, Mehmet the Conqueror, and 70, Queen Elizabeth; 41,

Celal Salik the columnist, and 42, Voltaire—they went flying through the air to scatter all over the floor.

If only I was in a completely different place, in a completely different life. Before I went back into my grandmother's room, I crept quietly down the creaky stairs, thinking about a distant relative who had worked in insurance and committed suicide. My father's mother had told me that suicides stayed in a dark place underground and never went to Heaven. When I'd gone a long way down the stairs, I stopped to stand in the darkness. I turned around and went upstairs and sat on the last step, next to my grandmother's room.

"I'm not well off like your mother-in-law," I heard my grandmother say. "You are going to look after your children and wait."

"But please, Mother dear, I beg you. I want to come back here with the children," my mother said.

"You can't live here with two children, not with all this dust and ghosts and thieves," said my grandmother.

"Mother dear," said my mother, "don't you remember how happily we lived here, just the two of us, after my sisters got married and my father passed away?"

"My lovely Mebrure, all you did all day was to leaf through old issues of your father's *Illustrations*."

"If I lit the big stove downstairs, this house would be cosy and warm in the space of two days."

"I told you not to marry him, didn't I?" said my grandmother.

"If I bring in a maid, it will only take us two days to get rid of all this dust," said my mother.

"I'm not letting any of those thieving maids into this house," said my grandmother. "Anyway, it would take six months to sweep out all this dust and cobwebs. By then your errant husband will be back home again."

"Is that your last word, Mother dear?" my mother asked.

"Mebrure, my lovely girl, if you came here with your two children what would we live on, the four of us?"

"Mother dear, how many times have I asked you—pleaded with you—to sell the lots in Bebek before they're expropriated?"

"I'm not going to the deeds office to give those dirty men my signature and my picture."

"Mother dear, please don't say this: My older sister and I brought a notary right to your door," said my mother, raising her voice.

"I've never trusted that notary," said my grandmother. "You can see from his face that he's a swindler. Maybe he isn't even a notary. And don't shout at me like that."

"All right, then, Mother dear, I won't!" said my mother. She called into the room for us. "Children, children, come on now, gather up your things; we're leaving."

"Slow down!" said my grandmother. "We haven't even said two words."

"You don't want us, Mother dear," my mother whispered.

"Take this, let the children have some Turkish delight."

"They shouldn't eat it before lunch," said my mother, and as she left the room she passed behind me to enter the room opposite. "Who threw these pictures all over the floor? Pick them up at once. And you help him," she said to my brother.

As we silently gathered the pictures, my mother lifted the lids of the old trunks and looked at the dresses from her childhood, her ballet costumes, the boxes. The dust underneath the black skeleton of the pedal sewing machine filled my nostrils, making my eyes water, filling my nose.

As we washed our hands in the little lavatory, my grandmother pleaded in a soft voice. "Mebrure dear, you take this teapot; you love it so much, you have a right to," she said. "My grandfather brought it for my dear mother when he was the governor of Damascus. It came all the way from China. Please take it."

"Mother dear, from now on I don't want anything from you," my mother said. "And put that into your cupboard or you'll break it. Come, children, kiss your grandmother's hand."

"My little Mebrure, my lovely daughter, please don't be angry at your poor mother," said my grandmother, as she let us kiss her hand. "Please don't leave me here without any visitors, without anyone."

We raced down the stairs, and when the three of us had pushed open the heavy metal door, we were greeted by brilliant sunlight as we breathed in the clean air.

"Shut the door firmly behind you!" cried my grandmother. "Mebrure, you'll come to see me again this week, won't you?"

As we walked hand in hand with my mother, no one spoke. We listened in silence as the other passengers coughed and waited for the streetcar to leave. When finally we began to move, my brother and I moved to the next row, saying we wanted to watch the conductor, and began to play Tops or Bottoms. First I lost some cards, then I won a few back. When I upped the ante, he happily agreed, and I quickly began to lose again. When we had reached the Osmanbey stop, my brother said, "In exchange for all the pictures you have left, here is this Fifteen you want so much."

I played and lost. Without letting him see, I removed two cards from the stack before handing it to my brother. I went to the back row to sit with my mother. I wasn't crying. I looked sadly out the window as the streetcar moaned and slowly gathered speed, and I watched them pass us by, all those people and places that are gone forever: the little sewing shops, the bakeries, the pudding shops with their awnings, the Tan cinema where we saw those films about ancient Rome, the children standing along the wall next to the front selling used comics, the barber with the sharp scissors who scared me so, and the half-naked neighborhood madman, always standing in the barbershop door.

We got off at Harbiye. As we walked toward home, my brother's satisfied silence was driving me mad. I took out the Lindbergh, which I'd hidden in my pocket.

This was his first sight of it. "Ninety-one: Lindbergh!" he read in admiration. "With the plane he flew across the Atlantic! Where did you find this?"

"I didn't have my injection yesterday," I said. "I went home early, and I saw Daddy before he left. Daddy bought it for me."

"Then half is mine," he said. "In fact, when we played that last game, the deal was you'd give me all the pictures you had left." He tried to grab the picture from my hand, but he couldn't manage it. He caught my wrist, and he twisted it so badly that I kicked his leg. We laid into each other.

"Stop!" said my mother. "Stop! We're in the middle of the street!"

We stopped. A man in a suit and a woman wearing a hat passed us. I felt ashamed for having fought in the street. My brother took two steps and fell to the ground. "It hurts so much," he said, holding his leg.

"Stand up," whispered my mother. "Come on now, stand up. Everyone's watching."

My brother stood up and began to hop down the road like a wounded soldier in a film. I was afraid he was really hurt, but I was still glad to see him that way. After we had walked for some time in silence, he said, "Just you see what happens when we get home. Mummy, Ali didn't have his injection yesterday."

"I did too, Mummy!"

"Be quiet!" my mother shouted.

We were now just across from our house. We waited for the streetcar coming up from Maçka to pass before we crossed the street. After it came a truck, a clattering Beşiktaş bus spewing great clouds of exhaust, and, in the opposite direction, a light violet De Soto. That was when I saw my uncle looking down at the street from the window. He didn't see me; he was staring at the passing cars. For a long time, I watched him.

The road had long since cleared. I turned to my mother, wondering why she had not yet taken our hands and crossed us over to the other side, and saw that she was silently crying.

My Father's Suitcase

The Nobel Lecture

Two years before his death, my father gave me a small suitcase filled with his writings, manuscripts, and notebooks. Assuming his usual joking, mocking air, he told me he wanted me to read them after he was gone, by which he meant after he died.

"Just take a look," he said, slightly embarrassed. "See if there's anything inside that you can use. Maybe after I'm gone you can make a selection and publish it."

We were in my study, surrounded by books. My father was searching for a place to set down the suitcase, wandering back and forth like a man who wished to rid himself of a painful burden. In the end, he deposited it quietly in an unobtrusive corner. It was a shaming moment that neither of us ever forgot, but once it had passed and we had gone back into our usual roles, taking life lightly, our joking, mocking personas took over and we relaxed. We talked as we always did, about the trivial things of everyday life, and Turkey's never-ending political troubles, and my father's mostly failed business ventures, without feeling too much sorrow.

I remember that after my father left, I spent several days pacing to and fro past the suitcase without once touching it. I was already familiar with this small black leather suitcase, and its lock, and its rounded corners. My father would take it with him on short trips and sometimes use it to carry documents to work. I remembered that when I was a child, and my father came home from a trip, I would open this little suitcase and rummage through his things, savoring the scent of cologne and foreign countries. This suitcase was a familiar friend, a powerful reminder of my childhood, my past, but now I couldn't even touch it. Why? No doubt it was because of the mysterious weight of its contents.

I am now going to speak of this weight's meaning. It is what a person creates when he shuts himself up in a room, sits down at a table, and retires to a corner to express his thoughts—that is, the meaning of literature.

When I did touch my father's suitcase, I still could not bring myself to open it. I did know what was inside some of those notebooks. I had seen my father writing things in a few of them. This was not the first time I had heard of the heavy load inside the suitcase. My father had a large library; in his youth, in the late 1940s, he had wanted to be an Istanbul poet, and had translated Valéry into Turkish, but he had not wanted to live the sort of life that came with writing poetry in a poor country with few readers. My grandfather—my father's father—had been a wealthy businessman; my father had led a comfortable life as a child and a young man, and he had no wish to endure hardship for the sake of literature, for writing. He loved life with all its beauties—this I understood.

The first thing that kept me distant from the contents of my father's suitcase was, of course, the fear that I might not like what I read. Because my father knew this, he had taken the precaution of acting as if he did not take its contents seriously. After working as a writer for twenty-five years, it pained me to see this. But I did not even want to be angry at my father for failing to take literature seriously enough. . . . My real fear, the crucial thing that I did not wish to know or discover, was the possibility that my father might be a good writer. I couldn't open my father's suitcase because I feared this. Even worse, I couldn't even openly admit this myself. If true and great literature emerged from my father's suitcase, I would have to acknowledge that inside my father there existed an entirely different man. This was a frightening possibility. Because even at my advanced age I wanted my father to be only my father—not a writer.

A writer is someone who spends years patiently trying to discover the second being inside him, and the world that makes him who he is. When I speak of writing, what comes first to my mind is not a novel, a poem, or literary tradition, it is a person who shuts himself up in a room, sits down at a table, and alone, turns inward; amid the shadows, he builds a new world with words. This man—or this woman—may use a typewriter, profit from the ease of a computer, or write with a pen on paper, as I have done for thirty years. As he writes, he can drink tea or coffee, or smoke cigarettes. From time to time he may rise from his table to look out through the window at the children playing in the street, and, if he is lucky, at trees and a view, or he can gaze out at a blank wall. He can write

poems, plays, or novels, as I do. All these differences come after the crucial task of sitting down at the table and patiently turning inward. To
write is to turn this inward gaze into words, to study the world into which
that person passes when he retires into himself, and to do so with
patience, obstinacy, and joy. As I sit at my table, for days, months, years,
slowly adding new words to the empty page, I feel as if I am creating a
new world, as if I am bringing into being that other person inside me, in
the same way someone might build a bridge or a dome, stone by stone.
The stones we writers use are words. As we hold them in our hands,
sensing the ways in which each of them is connected to the others, looking at them sometimes from afar, sometimes almost caressing them with
our fingers and the tips of our pens, weighing them, moving them
around, year in and year out, patiently and hopefully, we create new
worlds.

The writer's secret is not inspiration—for it is never clear where that
comes from—it is his stubbornness, his patience. That lovely Turkish
saying "to dig a well with a needle" seems to me to have been framed
with writers in mind. In the old stories, I love the patience of Ferhat, who
digs through mountains for his love—and I understand it too. In my
novel *My Name Is Red,* when I wrote about the old Persian miniaturists
who had drawn the same horse with the same passion, memorizing each
stroke, for so many years that they could re-create that beautiful horse
even with their eyes closed, I knew I was talking about the writing profession, and my own life. If a writer is to tell his own story—tell it
slowly, and as if it were a story about other people—if he is to feel the
power of the story rise up inside him, if he is to sit down at a table and
patiently give himself over to this art—this craft—he must first have
been given some hope. The angel of inspiration (who pays regular visits
to some and rarely calls on others) loves those who put their faith in him,
and it is when a writer feels most lonely, when he feels most doubtful
about his efforts, his dreams, and the value of his writing, when he thinks
his story is only his story—it is at such moments that the angel chooses
to reveal to him stories, images, and dreams that will draw out the world
he wishes to build. If I think back on the books to which I have devoted
my entire life, I am most surprised by those moments when I have felt as
if the sentences, dreams, and pages that have made me so ecstatically
happy have not come from my own imagination—that another power
has found them and generously presented them to me.

I was afraid of opening my father's suitcase and reading his notebooks because I knew that he would not tolerate the difficulties I had

endured, that it was not solitude he loved but crowds, salons, jokes, company, mixing with friends. But later my thoughts took a different turn. These thoughts, these dreams of renunciation and patience, were prejudices I had derived from my own life and my own experience as a writer. There were plenty of brilliant writers who wrote surrounded by crowds and family life, in the glow of company and happy chatter. In addition, my father had, when we were young, tired of the monotony of family life, and left us to go to Paris, where—like so many writers—he'd sat in his hotel room filling notebooks. I knew, too, that some of those very notebooks were in this suitcase, because during the years before he brought it to me, my father had finally begun to talk to me about that period in his life. He had spoken about those years even when I was a child, but he would not mention his vulnerabilities, his dreams of becoming a writer, or the questions of identity that had plagued him in his hotel room. He would tell me instead about all the times he'd seen Sartre on the pavements of Paris, about the books he'd read and the films he'd seen, all with the elated sincerity of someone imparting very important news. When I became a writer, I never forgot that it was partly thanks to the fact that I had a father who would talk of world writers so much more than he spoke of pashas or great religious leaders. So perhaps I had to read my father's notebooks with this in mind, and remembering how indebted I was to his large library. I had to bear in mind that when he was living with us, my father, like me, enjoyed being alone with his books and his thoughts—and not pay too much attention to the literary quality of his writing.

But as I gazed so anxiously at the suitcase my father had bequeathed me, I also felt that this was the very thing I would not be able to do. My father would sometimes stretch out on the divan in front of his books, abandon the book in his hand, or the magazine, and drift off into a dream, lose himself for the longest time in his thoughts. When I saw on his face an expression so very different from the one he wore amid the joking, teasing, and bickering of family life—when I saw the first signs of an inward gaze—I would, especially during my childhood and my early youth, understand, with trepidation, that he was discontented. Now, so many years later, I know that this discontent is the basic trait that turns a person into a writer. To become a writer, patience and toil are not enough: We must first feel compelled to escape crowds, company, the stuff of ordinary, everyday life, and shut ourselves up in a room. We wish for patience and hope so that we can create a deep world in our writing. But the desire to shut oneself up in a room is what pushes us into action.

The precursor of this sort of independent writer—who reads his books to his heart's content and who, by listening only to the voice of his own conscience, disputes with others' words; who, by entering into conversation with his books, develops his own thoughts, and his own world—was most certainly Montaigne, in the earliest days of modern literature. Montaigne was a writer to whom my father returned often, a writer he recommended to me. I would like to see myself as belonging to the tradition of writers who, wherever they are in the world, in the East or in the West, cut themselves off from society and shut themselves up with their books in their room. The starting point of true literature is the man who shuts himself up in his room with his books.

But once we shut ourselves away, we soon discover that we are not as alone as we thought. We are in the company of the words of those who came before us, of other people's stories, other people's books, other people's words, the thing we call tradition. I believe literature to be the most valuable hoard that humanity has gathered in its quest to understand itself. Societies, tribes, and peoples grow more intelligent, richer, and more advanced as they pay attention to the troubled words of their authors, and, as we all know, the burning of books and the denigration of writers are both signals that dark and improvident times are upon us. But literature is never just a national concern. The writer who shuts himself up in a room and first goes on a journey inside himself will, over the years, discover literature's eternal rule: He must have the artistry to tell his own stories as if they were other people's stories, and to tell other people's stories as if they were his own, for this is what literature is. But we must first travel through other people's stories and books.

My father had a good library—fifteen hundred volumes in all, more than enough for a writer. By the age of twenty-two, I had perhaps not read them all, but I was familiar with each book—I knew which were important, which were light but easy to read, which were classics, which an essential part of any education, which were forgettable but amusing accounts of local history, and which French authors my father rated very highly. Sometimes I would look at this library from a distance and imagine that one day, in a different house, I would build my own library, an even better library—build myself a world. When I looked at my father's library from afar, it seemed to me to be a small picture of the real world. But this was a world seen from our own corner, from Istanbul. The library was evidence of this. My father had built his library from his trips abroad, mostly with books from Paris and America, but also with books bought from the shops that sold books in foreign languages in the 1940s and 1950s and Istanbul's old and new booksellers, whom I also knew. My world is a mixture of the local—the national—and the West. In the 1970s, I too began, somewhat ambitiously, to build my own library. I had not quite decided to become a writer—as I related in *Istanbul,* I had come to feel that I would not, after all, become a painter, but I was not sure what path my life would take. There was inside me a relentless curiosity, a hope-driven desire to read and learn, but at the same time I felt that my life was in some way lacking, that I would not be able to live like others. When I gazed at my father's library I could not help thinking that I was living far from the center of things, in the provinces, an impression shared by all of us who lived in Istanbul in those days. There was another reason for my anxiety, and my fear of being somehow lacking, for I knew only too well that I lived in a country that showed little interest in its artists, be they painters or writers, and that gave them no hope. In the seventies, when I would take the money my father gave me and greedily buy faded, dusty, dog-eared books from Istanbul's old booksellers, I would be as affected by the pitiable state of these second-hand bookstores—and by the despairing dishevelment of the poor, bedraggled booksellers who laid out their wares on roadsides, in mosque courtyards, and in the niches of crumbling walls—as I was by their books.

As for my place in the world—in life, as in literature, my basic feeling was that I was not in the center. In the center of the world there was a life richer and more exciting than our own, and with all of Istanbul, all of Turkey, I was outside it. Today I think that I share this feeling with most people in the world. In the same way, there was a world literature, and its center, too, was very far away from me. Actually what I had in mind was Western, not world, literature, and we Turks were outside it. My father's library was evidence of this. At one end, there were Istanbul's books— our literature, our local world, in all its beloved detail—and at the other end were the books from this other, Western, world, to which our own bore no resemblance, to which our lack of resemblance gave us both pain and hope. To write, to read, was like leaving one world to find consolation in the other world's otherness, the strange and the wondrous. I felt that my father had read novels to escape his life and flee to the West— just as I would do later. Or it seemed to me that books in those days were things we picked up to escape our own culture, which we found so lacking. It wasn't just by reading that we left our Istanbul lives to travel west—it was by writing too. To fill those notebooks of his, my father had gone to Paris, shut himself up in his room, and then brought his writings back to Turkey. As I gazed at my father's suitcase, it seemed to me that this was what was causing me disquiet. After working in a room for twenty-five years to survive as a writer in Turkey, it galled me to see my father hide his deep thoughts inside this suitcase, to act as if writing was work that had to be done in secret, far from the eyes of society, the state, the people. Perhaps this was the main reason why I felt angry at my father for not taking literature as seriously as I did.

Actually I was angry at my father because he had not led a life like mine, because he had never quarreled with his life, and had spent his life happily laughing with his friends and his loved ones. But part of me knew that I could also say that I was not so much angry as jealous, that the second word was more accurate, and this, too, made me uneasy. That would be when I would ask myself in my usual scornful, angry voice: What is happiness? Was happiness thinking that I lived a deep life in that lonely room? Or was happiness leading a comfortable life in society, believing in the same things as everyone else, or acting as if you did? Was it happiness, or unhappiness, to go through life writing in secret, while seeming to be in harmony with all around you? But these were overly ill-tempered questions. Wherever had I got this idea that the measure of a good life was happiness? People, papers, everyone acted as if the most important measure of a life was happiness. Did this alone not suggest that it might be worth trying to find out if the exact opposite was true? After all, my father had run away from his family so many times— how well did I know him, and how well could I say I understood his disquiet?

So this was what was driving me when I first opened my father's suitcase. Did my father have a secret, an unhappiness in his life about which I knew nothing, something he could only endure by pouring it into his writing? As soon as I opened the suitcase, I recalled its scent of travel, recognized several notebooks, and noted that my father had shown them to me years earlier but without dwelling on them very long. Most of the notebooks I now took into my hands he had filled when he had left us and gone to Paris as a young man. Whereas I, as with so many writers I admired—writers whose biographies I had read—wished to know what my father had written, and what he had thought, when he was the age I was now. It did not take me long to realize that I would find nothing like that here. What caused me most disquiet was when, here and there in my father's notebooks, I came upon a writerly voice. This was not my father's voice, I told myself; it wasn't authentic, or at least it did not belong to the man I'd known as my father. Underneath my fear that my father might not have been my father when he wrote was a deeper fear: the fear that deep inside I was not authentic, that I would find nothing good in my father's writing. This increased my fear of finding my father to have been overly influenced by other writers and plunged me into the despair that had afflicted me so badly when I was young, casting my life, my very being, my desire to write, and my work into question. During my first ten years as a writer, I felt these anxieties more deeply, and even as I fought them off, I would sometimes fear that one day, I would have to admit to defeat—just as I had done with painting—and, succumbing to disquiet, give up novel writing, too.

I have already mentioned the two essential feelings that rose up in me as I closed my father's suitcase and put it away: the sense of being marooned in the provinces, and the fear that I lacked authenticity. This was certainly not the first time they had made themselves felt. For years I had, in my reading and my writing, been studying, discovering, deepening these emotions, in all their variety and unintended consequences, their nerve endings, their triggers, and their many colors. Certainly my spirits had been jarred by the confusions, the sensitivities, and the fleeting pains that life and books had sprung on me, most often as a young man. But it was only by writing books that I came to a fuller understanding of the problems of authenticity (as in *My Name Is Red* and *The Black Book*) and the problems of life on the periphery (as in *Snow* and *Istanbul*). For me, to be a writer is to acknowledge the secret wounds that we carry inside us, the wounds so secret that we ourselves are barely aware of them, and to patiently explore them, know them, illuminate them, to own these pains and wounds, and to make them a conscious part of our spirits and our writing.

A writer talks of things that everyone knows but does not know they know. To explore this knowledge, and to watch it grow, is a pleasurable thing; the reader is visiting a world at once familiar and miraculous. When a writer shuts himself up in a room for years on end to hone his craft—to create a world—if he uses his secret wounds as his starting point, he is, whether he knows it or not, putting a great faith in humanity. My confidence comes from the belief that all human beings resemble one another, that others carry wounds like mine—that they will therefore understand. All true literature rises from this childish, hopeful certainty that all people resemble one another. When a writer shuts himself up in a room for years on end, with this gesture he suggests a single humanity, a world without a center.

But as can be seen from my father's suitcase and the pale colors of our lives in Istanbul, the world did have a center, and it was far away from us. In my books I have described in some detail how this basic fact evoked a Chekhovian sense of provinciality, and how, by another route, it led to my questioning my authenticity. I know from experience that the great majority of people on this earth live with these same feelings, and that many suffer from an even deeper sense of insufficiency, lack of security, and sense of degradation than I do. Yes, the greatest dilemmas facing humanity are still landlessness, homelessness, and hunger . . . but today our televisions and newspapers tell us about these fundamental problems more quickly and more simply than literature can ever do. What literature needs most to tell and investigate today are humanity's basic fears: the fear of being left outside, and the fear of counting for nothing, and the feelings of worthlessness that come with such fears; the collective humiliations, vulnerabilities, slights, grievances, sensitivities, and imagined insults, and the nationalist boasts and inflations that are their next of kin. . . . Whenever I am confronted by such sentiments, and by the irrational, overstated language in which they are usually expressed, I know they touch on a darkness inside me. We have often witnessed peoples, societies, and nations outside the Western world—and I can identify with them easily—succumbing to fears that sometimes lead them to commit stupidities, all because of their fears of humiliation and their sensitivities. I also know that in the West—a world with which I can identify with the same ease—nations and peoples taking an excessive pride in their wealth and in their having brought us the Renaissance, the Enlightenment, and Modernism, have, from time to time, succumbed to a self-satisfaction that is almost as stupid.

This means that my father was not the only one, that we all give too much importance to the idea of a world with a center. Whereas the thing that compels us to shut ourselves up to write in our rooms for years on end is a faith in the opposite: the belief that one day our writings will be read and understood, because people all the world over resemble one another. But this, as I know from my own and my father's writing, is a troubled optimism, scarred by the anger of being consigned to the margins, of being left outside. The love and hate that Dostoyevsky felt toward the West all his life—I have felt this, too, on many occasions. But if I have grasped an essential truth, if I have cause for optimism, it is because I have traveled with this great writer through his love-hate relationship with the West, to behold the other world he has built on the other side.

All writers who have devoted their lives to this task know this reality:

Whatever our original purpose, the world that we create after years and years of hopeful writing will, in the end, move to other very different places. It will take us far away from the table at which we have worked with sadness or anger, take us to the other side of that sadness and anger, into another world. Could my father have not reached such a world himself? Like the land that slowly begins to take shape, slowly rising from the mist in all its colors like an island after a long sea journey, this other world enchants us. We are as beguiled as the Western travelers who voyaged from the south to behold Istanbul rising from the mist. At the end of a journey begun in hope and curiosity, there lies before them a city of mosques and minarets, a medley of houses, streets, hills, bridges, and slopes, an entire world. Seeing it, we wish to enter into this world and lose ourselves inside it, just as we might a book. After sitting down at a table because we felt provincial, excluded, on the margins, angry, or deeply melancholic, we have found an entire world beyond these sentiments.

What I feel now is the opposite of what I felt as a child and a young man: For me the center of the world is Istanbul. This is not just because I have lived there all my life, but because for the last thirty-three years I have been narrating its streets, its bridges, its people, its dogs, its houses, its mosques, its fountains, its strange heroes, its shops, its famous characters, its dark spots, its days, and its nights, making them part of me, embracing them all. A point arrived when this world I had made with my own hands, this world that existed only in my head, was more real to me than the city in which I actually lived. That was when all these people and streets, objects and buildings would seem to begin to talk among themselves, and begin to interact in ways I had not anticipated, as if they lived not only in my imagination or my books, but for themselves. This world that I had created like a man digging a well with a needle would then seem truer than all else.

My father might also have discovered this kind of happiness during the years he spent writing, I thought as I gazed at my father's suitcase: I should not prejudge him. I was so grateful to him, after all: He'd never been a commanding, forbidding, overpowering, punishing, ordinary father, but a father who always left me free, always showed me the utmost respect. I had often thought that if I had, from time to time, been able to draw from my imagination, be it in freedom or childishness, it was because, unlike so many of my friends from childhood and youth, I had no fear of my father, and I had sometimes believed very deeply that I had been able to become a writer because my father had, in his youth,

wished to be one too. I had to read him with tolerance—seek to understand what he had written in those hotel rooms.

It was with these hopeful thoughts that I walked over to the suitcase,
which was still sitting where my father had left it; using all my
willpower, I read through a few manuscripts and notebooks. What had
my father written about? I recall a few views from the windows of
Parisian hotels, a few poems, paradoxes, analyses. . . . As I write I feel
like someone who has just been in a traffic accident and is struggling to
remember how it happened, while at the same time dreading the prospect
of remembering too much. When I was a child, and my father and
mother were on the brink of a quarrel—when they fell into one of those
deadly silences—my father would at once turn on the radio, to change
the mood, and the music would help us forget it all faster.

Let me change the mood with a few sweet words that will, I hope,
serve as well as that music. As you know, the question we writers are
asked most often, the favorite question, is: Why do you write? I write
because I have an innate need to write! I write because I can't do normal
work like other people. I write because I want to read books like the ones
I write. I write because I am angry at all of you, angry at everyone. I
write because I love sitting in a room all day writing. I write because I
can only partake in real life by changing it. I write because I want others,
all of us, the whole world, to know what sort of life we lived, and continue to live, in Istanbul, in Turkey. I write because I love the smell of
paper, pen, and ink. I write because I believe in literature, in the art of the
novel, more than I believe in anything else. I write because it is a habit, a
passion. I write because I am afraid of being forgotten. I write because I
like the glory and interest that writing brings. I write to be alone. Perhaps
I write because I hope to understand why I am so very, very angry at all
of you, so very, very angry at everyone. I write because I like to be read.
I write because once I have begun a novel, an essay, a page, I want to finish it. I write because everyone expects me to write. I write because I
have a childish belief in the immortality of libraries, and in the way my
books sit on the shelf. I write because it is exciting to turn all of life's
beauties and riches into words. I write not to tell a story, but to compose
a story. I write because I wish to escape from the foreboding that there is
a place I must go but—just as in a dream—I can't quite get there. I write
because I have never managed to be happy. I write to be happy.

A week after he came to my office and left me his suitcase, my father
came to pay me another visit. As always, he brought me a bar of chocolate (he had forgotten I was forty-eight years old); as always, we chatted

and laughed about life, politics, and family gossip. A moment arrived when my father's eyes went to the corner where he had left his suitcase and saw that I had moved it. We looked each other in the eye. There followed a pressing silence. I did not tell him that I had opened the suitcase and tried to read its contents; instead I looked away. But he understood. Just as I understood that he had understood. Just as he understood that I had understood that he had understood. But all this understanding only went so far as it can go in a few seconds. Because my father was a happy, easygoing man who had faith in himself: He smiled at me the way he always did. And as he left the house, he repeated all the lovely and encouraging things that he always said to me, like a father.

As always, I watched him leave, envying his happiness, his carefree and unflappable temperament. But I remember that on that day there was also a flash of joy inside me that made me ashamed. It was prompted by the thought that maybe I wasn't as comfortable in life as he was, maybe I had not led as happy or footloose a life as he had, but that I had devoted it to writing—you've understood. . . . I was ashamed to be thinking such things at my father's expense. Of all people, my father, who had never been the source of my pain—who had left me free. All this should remind us that writing and literature are intimately linked to a lack at the center of our lives, and to our feelings of happiness and guilt.

But my story has a symmetry that immediately reminded me of something else that day, and that brought me an even deeper sense of guilt. Twenty-three years before my father left me his suitcase, and four years after I had decided, aged twenty-two, to become a novelist, and, abandoning all else, shut myself up in a room, I finished my first novel, *Cevdet Bey and Sons;* with trembling hands I had given my father a typescript of the still unpublished novel, so that he could read it and tell me what he thought. This was not simply because I had confidence in his taste and his intellect: His opinion was very important to me because he, unlike my mother, had not opposed my wish to become a writer. At that point, my father was not with us, but far away. I waited impatiently for his return. When he arrived two weeks later, I ran to open the door. My father said nothing, but he at once threw his arms around me in a way that told me he had liked it very much. For a while, we were plunged into the sort of awkward silence that so often accompanies moments of great emotion. Then, when we had calmed down and begun to talk, my father resorted to highly charged and exaggerated language to express his confidence in me or my first novel: He told me that one day I would win the prize that I am here to receive with such great happiness.

He said this not because he was trying to convince me of his good opinion, or to set this prize as a goal; he said it like a Turkish father, giving support to his son, encouraging him by saying, "One day you'll become a pasha!" For years, whenever he saw me, he would encourage me with the same words.

My father died in December 2002.

Today, as I stand before the Swedish Academy and the distinguished members who have awarded me this great prize—this great honor—and their distinguished guests, I dearly wish he could be among us.

INDEX